D0742792

1255 Park Avenue
P.O. Box 668
Park City, Utah 84060
Phone: (435) 649-5600

A HISTORY OF
Sanpete County

A HISTORY OF

Sanpete County

Albert C.T. Antrei
Allen D. Roberts

1999
Utah State Historical Society
Sanpete County Commission

ISBN 0-913738-42-5
Library of Congress Catalog Card Number 98-61326
Map by Automated Geographic Reference Center—State of Utah
Printed in the United States of America

Utah State Historical Society
300 Rio Grande
Salt Lake City, Utah 84101-1182

Contents

Preface

The colonization of the Sanpete Valley, beginning in 1849, was a milestone in the settlement of the American West. Coming a little more than two years after the arrival of the first vanguard of Mormon pioneers in the Salt Lake Valley in July 1847, the settlement at Manti, 120 miles south of Salt Lake City, put Mormons in the heart of Ute Indian territory. The Sanpete Valley became the springboard for the settlement of other areas to the south and east. The first attempt in 1855, the Elk Mountain Meadows Mission at the crossing of the Colorado River near present-day Moab, failed when Indian hostilities forced the abandonment of the mission. More successful were the settlements of Sevier Valley to the south in the 1860s and of Castle Valley across the Wasatch Plateau to the east in the 1870s. In both cases the expanding population in Sanpete Valley and the limited water and land resources necessitated the development of these more remote locations.

An important reason for the increase in Sanpete County's population was the arrival of a large number of converts to the Mormon faith from the Scandinavian countries—Denmark, Sweden, and

Norway. Beginning with the arrival of the first Scandinavians in the mid-1850s, by 1870 Sanpete County's population was 80 percent first- or second-generation Scandinavian, while the town of Ephraim was 94 percent Scandinavian. The Scandinavians brought a distinctive culture to Sanpete Valley that has continued through the twentieth century.

The first two decades of settlement were marked by difficulties with the Ute Indians that led to the Walker War from 1853–54 and the Black Hawk War from 1865–72. Sanpete Valley was a key location during both conflicts, and at the culmination of the Black Hawk War the Sanpete Valley Utes left for new homes on the Uintah Reservation in eastern Utah's Uinta Basin.

The 1870s brought two important religious developments to Sanpete Valley. First was the arrival of a young Presbyterian minister, Duncan James McMillan, in 1875. McMillan undertook a vigorous missionary effort among Sanpete Valley residents that led to the establishment of small Presbyterian churches in many towns in the valley where dedicated missionaries and teachers taught Sanpete youngsters. The legacy of these efforts is Wasatch Academy in Mount Pleasant the oldest private boarding school in Utah. Second was the construction of the Manti temple which began in 1877 and was completed in 1889. The third LDS temple completed in Utah, the Manti temple with its sentinel-like location above Manti is considered by many to be the symbolic heart of Sanpete Valley. Faithful Mormons visit the temple to perform sacred ordinances, and each summer the south side of the temple and temple hill are used as the outdoor stage for the Mormon Miracle Pageant which over 100,000 visitors attend.

Agriculture has played an important role in the economic development of the Sanpete Valley. The valley fields and high mountain pastures led to the expansion of a pioneer cattle industry that was followed by a boom in sheep and wool at the turn of the twentieth century. Today the county is best known for the high quality turkeys that are produced and processed in the valley.

Sanpete County has not developed in isolation, and like the rest of the state and nation, the county's sons and daughters served in the armed forces during the world wars and other conflicts. County residents experienced the difficulties of the Great Depression of the

1930s and benefited from government public relief programs. Mount Pleasant, Ephraim, and Manti took advantage of the philanthropy of Andrew Carnegie to build Carnegie public libraries in their communities which helped strengthen a commitment to education that had been manifest with the founding of Snow College in 1888.

On the eve of the twenty-first century, Sanpete County residents are preparing for the changes and opportunities that the future have in store while maintaining firm ties to the past through a strong commitment to educational and religious institutions and the preservation of a rich historical and architectural heritage.

Unlike other volumes in the Centennial County History Series, which mark the first attempt to provide a summary history of events of both the nineteenth and twentieth centuries, this volume is based on a substantial body of historical literature which begins with one of Utah's first county histories, W. H. Lever's *History of Sanpete and Emery Counties* published in 1898, and concludes with one of the most recent county histories prior to this series, *The Other Forty-Niners: A topical history of Sanpete County, Utah, 1849–1983* edited by Albert C. T. Antrei and Ruth D. Scow. In addition to these works, Gary B. Peterson and Lowell C. Bennion's *Sanpete Scenes: A Guide to Utah's Heart* published in 1987 has become a favorite of many residents and visitors to the county and won an award from the American Association for State and Local History. An earlier county history, *These Our Fathers,* was compiled by Sanpete County Camps of the Daughters of Utah Pioneers in 1947. Other community histories and personal histories are a rich source of information about Sanpete County, as is the popular, locally-published annual *Saga of the Sanpitch.*

To provide an overview history of Sanpete County that meets the length requirements for the centennial county history series and fits within the guidelines outlined by the Utah State Legislature, this volume has been crafted from several parts—excerpts from *The Other 49ers;* material from a draft history of Sanpete County prepared by Allen D. Roberts; a chapter on contemporary Sanpete County written by Maxine Hanks; sections written by the staff of the Utah State Historical Society; and histories of Sanpete County communities compiled from several sources or written by local contributors.

As this explanation suggests, many people have contributed to this volume. Special thanks are extended to Eleanor P. Madsen, Joanne Mortensen, Melvin T. Smith, and LaMond Tullis—members of the Sanpete Centennial County History Committee who read drafts of chapters and offered constructive comments and provided helpful direction for the project.

Members of the original Sanpete County History Committee which was organized in 1977 for *The Other 49ers* book include Chairwoman Ruth D. Scow, Albert Antrei, Gertrude Beck, Scott and Euleda Cook, Ida Donaldson, Elva Jensen, Leo C. Larsen, Rose McIff, Ted Mower, Diana Majors Spencer, Jane Thomas, and Hazel White.

Others who have rendered invaluable assistance include Monte Bona, Joe Blain, Martha Sonntag Bradley, and Mary Louise Seamons.

Present and former staff members of the Utah State Historical Society whose work has contributed to this volume include Thomas Carter, Craig Fuller, Ken Hansen, Kent Powell, John S. H. Smith, and Gary Topping.

Finally, this book would not have been possible without the commitment of Sanpete County officials. Kristine Frischknecht, Sanpete County Clerk, has coordinated the project and provided the necessary direction and support to bring the book to completion. Present and former county commissioners who have provided support and assisted the project include Robert D. Bessey, Leonard Blackham, J. Keller Christenson and Eddie L. Cox.

General Introduction

W hen Utah was granted statehood on 4 January 1896, twenty-seven counties comprised the nation's new forty-fifth state. Subsequently two counties, Duchesne in 1914 and Daggett in 1917, were created. These twenty-nine counties have been the stage on which much of the history of Utah has been played.

Recognizing the importance of Utah's counties, the Utah State Legislature established in 1991 a Centennial History Project to write and publish county histories as part of Utah's statehood centennial commemoration. The Division of State History was given the assignment to administer the project. The county commissioners, or their designees, were responsible for selecting the author or authors for their individual histories, and funds were provided by the state legislature to cover most research and writing costs as well as to provide each public school and library with a copy of each history. Writers worked under general guidelines provided by the Division of State History and in cooperation with county history committees. The counties also established a Utah Centennial County History Council to help develop policies for distribution of state-appropriated funds and plans for publication.

Each volume in the series reflects the scholarship and interpretation of the individual author. The general guidelines provided by the Utah State Legislature included coverage of five broad themes encompassing the economic, religious, educational, social, and political history of the county. Authors were encouraged to cover a vast period of time stretching from geologic and prehistoric times to the present. Since Utah's statehood centennial celebration falls just four years before the arrival of the twenty-first century, authors were encouraged to give particular attention to the history of their respective counties during the twentieth century.

Still, each history is at best a brief synopsis of what has transpired within the political boundaries of each county. No history can do justice to every theme or event or individual that is part of an area's past. Readers are asked to consider these volumes as an introduction to the history of the county, for it is expected that other researchers and writers will extend beyond the limits of time, space, and detail imposed on this volume to add to the wealth of knowledge about the county and its people. In understanding the history of our counties, we come to understand better the history of our state, our nation, our world, and ourselves.

In addition to the authors, local history committee members, and county commissioners, who deserve praise for their outstanding efforts and important contributions, special recognition is given to Joseph Francis, chairman of the Morgan County Historical Society, for his role in conceiving the idea of the centennial county history project and for his energetic efforts in working with the Utah State Legislature and State of Utah officials to make the project a reality. Mr. Francis is proof that one person does make a difference.

ALLAN KENT POWELL
CRAIG FULLER
GENERAL EDITORS

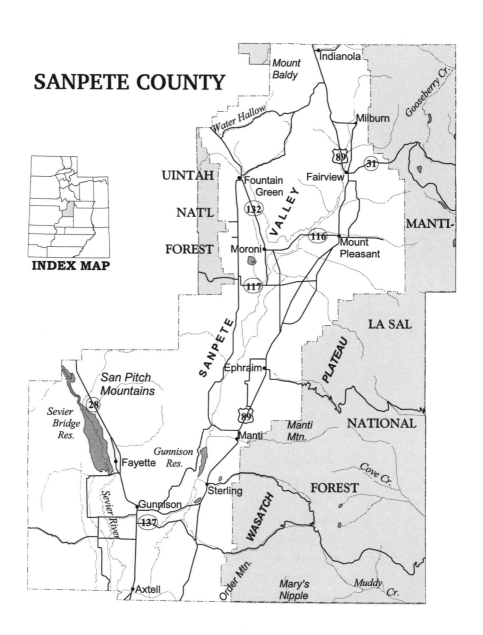

SANPETE COUNTY

INDEX MAP

UINTAH

NAT'L

FOREST

SANPETE

San Pitch
Mountains

Sevier
Bridge
Res.

Sevier River

Gunnison
Res.

Mount
Baldy

Indianola

Gooseberry Cr.

Water Hallow

Milburn

89

31

Fountain
Green

Fairview

VALLEY

132

116

Moroni

Mount
Pleasant

117

MANTI-

LA SAL

PLATEAU

Ephraim

89

NATIONAL

28

Fayette

Manti
Mtn.

Cove Cr.

Gunnison

Sterling

FOREST

137

Axtell

WASATCH

Order Mtn.

Mary's
Nipple

Muddy
Cr.

Manti

CHAPTER 1

THE LAND
AND EARLY PEOPLE

While religious motivations brought the first pioneers to Sanpete Valley in 1849, they were able to stay and build successful communities because of the generally favorable characteristics of the land. Before the Mormons, the local Ute groups learned to subsist off the land, mostly by hunting, gathering edible native plants, and sometimes by planting a few crops. Using more advanced agricultural techniques, Mormon settlers were able to live off the land almost immediately, rather than relying on wild plants, fish, and game. Though they were thwarted at times by terrible floods, hail storms, frosts that came too early and late, drought, grasshopper "wars," and infestations of other crop-destroying insects and diseases, it is doubtful that anyone starved or suffered too severely from malnutrition. Perhaps the greatest limitation of the land was the unavailability of water. Although water is plentiful in the Wastach Plateau to the east, and to a lesser extent in the lower mountains to the west, securing a reliable, safe, and flood-resistant supply of water for every colony took enormous work. Even with modern equipment, the struggle to deliver a regular supply of water for all farming, industrial, and culinary needs continues today.

Upon bringing water to the valley's virgin earth and raising life-sustaining crops, and using the nearby ranges for foraging their animals, the early settlers took to the hills and mountains to discover and develop the county's other natural resources. In the foothills they found usable coal, lime, clay, building stone, gravel, and other products of the earth. In the mountains they harvested timber, herbs, fish, and game. From 1849 until after 1890, when outside goods were imported via the railroad, the county's residents relied almost entirely on what the land would give them. The county's growth was limited more by what the land could yield than by any human factor.

The Land

The county today is roughly sixty miles long and thirty miles wide, encompassing a total of 1,820 square miles in the exact geographical center of Utah. Of that area, only some 220 square miles of valley floor are considered arable. The eastern and western borders follow approximately the summits of the Wasatch Plateau and the Gunnison Plateau, respectively, and much of the surface area is mountainous. A nine-mile-wide tract of hilly desert known as the Moroni Upland divides the northern third of the valley into a "Y" shape and robs the valley of even more cultivable area.

The Sanpete Valley is like a bowl, tilted in a southwesterly direction. At its lowest point, the junction of the Sanpitch and Sevier rivers near Gunnison, the elevation of the valley is about 5,000 feet. The arable area occurs between that level and about 6,000 feet, with the average elevation of the valley falling roughly midway between those two figures. Manti, at approximately the center of the valley, is at 5,575 feet. The mountains on the east and west sides of the valley tower above the valley floor another 2,000 to 5,000 feet. South Tent Peak, in the Wasatch Plateau northeast of Ephraim, is the highest point in the county at 11,283 feet.

The Wasatch Plateau has historically been more important to the economy of Sanpete County than the Gunnison Plateau (known locally as "the West Mountains"). It is much higher, trapping much more snow in the winter months which can be utilized for irrigation

Horseshoe Mountain rises above Sanpete Valley to the east. (Utah State Historical Society)

water. Also, because of its greater moisture, it has supported larger quantities of vegetation and wildlife. Passing through various life zones, the Wasatch Plateau demonstrates a greater variety of plant and animal types, ranging from spring- fall- and winter-use ranges at lower elevations to summer-use range above 9,000 feet. The Gunnison Plateau is much more severely eroded and thus supports less vegetation and wildlife, although it has a great potential for water development. It has been used extensively for livestock grazing in the spring, fall, and winter months, particularly in the last two decades of the nineteenth century. Both plateaus are scored by mountain canyons that provide easily accessible relief from the heat and barrenness of the valley floor.

Sanpete Valley is the gift of the mountains. The valley basin, presumably of the same sedimentary material as the mountains, is of unknown but vast depth. Only once in the history of Sanpete County have well-drillers struck bedrock in the main part of the valley floor, and that was at 650 feet; other wells have been sunk to much greater depths without meeting such rock.

Lying along the eastern rim of the Great Basin, the Sanpete Valley exhibits all of the basin's features: basin alternating with range, interior drainage, saltflats, and bunchgrass-sagebrush-greasewood vegetative types broken by higher types of "pygmy forest" (juniper, pinyon pine). The Sanpete Valley floor is composed of many hundreds of feet of alluvial material eroded from the mountains over eons of time. The agents of that erosion are the streams that seasonally pick up silt from run-off on the mountain sides and carry it into the valley. The most casual observer driving through Sanpete Valley cannot fail to notice evidence of the continuation of that process in the multitudes of alluvial fans of all sizes issuing from the mouths of the canyons. The process has greatly accelerated since the advent of livestock raisers, who, late in the nineteenth century, overgrazed the Wasatch Plateau, destroying the plant cover that had kept erosional processes at a normal rate. The floods that began in the late 1880s and continued into the early twentieth century carried vast quantities of material into the valley, from microscopic particles to boulders, and caused dramatic buildup of soil on the valley floor.

The velocity of the streams varies in inverse proportion to their distance form the mountains, which accounts for the nature of the distribution of eroded materials. As streams slow down, their ability to carry heavier particles gradually decreases, so that the coarser material is deposited higher in the watercourse, and only the finer material finds its way to the valley floor. That selective process has left fine sand, clay, and loam on the valley floor ideal for agricultural purposes.

Early Descriptions of the County

The pioneers used the language of their times to describe the land they were settling. They had differing views of its quality and potential, and, as one historian put it, "To the Mormon pioneer, this Sanpete became both wilderness of Sinai and Promised Land."[1] Seth Taft, a member of the 1850 vanguard pioneer group, was skeptical about the virtues of the future Manti area. He saw " . . . only a long narrow canyon, and not even a jack rabbit could survive its desert soil." Another member of the group, Mrs. Adelia Cox Sidwell, was more poetic but also lacked enthusiasm as she wrote of "Journeying . . . through an unbroken wilderness, with the stupendous Wasatch

Mountains frowning down on every side, edging and walling in the leaden green of lifeless sage flats and the naked limbs of trees and brush. . . ." [2]

Early explorer Jim Bridger reportedly told Mormon president Brigham Young that the area was "nice grazing country and much superior for agricultural purposes to the Great Salt Lake Valley." [3] After visiting the county to form his own opinion, Young gave a positive assessment of the area during a September 1850 general conference in Salt Lake City, in an effort to attract more colonists to Sanpete. He described the valley " . . . as good a valley as you ever saw; the goodness of the soil cannot be beaten." [4] Another pioneer, Albert Smith, held a similarly optimist view, saying "Altho these valleys lays a good many thousand feet above the level of the sea yet they will produce most all kinds of frute & all kinds of grain pares & all kinds of plums, &c." [5]

In 1880 Mormon apostle Orson Pratt interviewed some of Sanpete's earliest settlers regarding their first impressions of the valley. C. W. Madsen responded that "The appearance of the site of the settlement . . . was dry, barren and forbidding; but a canal 3–1/2 miles long would water the site, from the Sanpitch River; and it was made in 1863. [6] Madsen added, "Sage and rabbit brush, the Redman and the Kiote, a species of wolf were the most prominent features of the landscape and presented a most uninviting appearance to the new settlers, most of who went to other parts of the Territory, on account of the forbidding aspects of things generally and the severity of the first winter." [7] It should be remembered that those describing the county were comparing it to their homelands which, whether in Illinois, New England, or somewhere in Europe, may have been considerably more lush in forests, verdant in fields, and plentiful in wildlife.

The lamentations of the pioneers upon initial inspection of their proposed new homeland are partly justified. They found the valley soil either arid and covered with sagebrush and greasewood, or "Bare, hard-packed alkali mud." On plowing, planting, and watering the virgin soil, however, it proved sufficiently fertile to produce a variety of crops which sustained the county's twenty or so agricultural villages. The new colonists were not particularly fond of the valley vegetation they encountered. The rabbit brush and greasewood were "very difficult to dig out and too green to burn since the wood of the plants is hard and gnarly, and their roots, because of the scarcity of water, extend deep and far."[8] On the positive side was the wild hay which grew in meadows near Chester after the area was flooded with spring runoff. This natural occurrence initially blessed the county's northern towns with enough hay to feed livestock with no cost or expense of time in cultivation. The settlers also expressed their appreciation for the beauty and shade proffered by the trees and shrubs in the foothills and along stream banks. Eli A. Day remembered " . . . willows, squaw bushes, birches, kinniknik, wild rose bushes, hawthorn, Bullberry, Cottonwoods, a very few cedar (and) pines . . ."[9]

Many of the foothills and mountains surrounding the valleys held vast areas of lush grass so tall it would conceal the grazing sheep. Women and children went into the hills in the summer and collected edible fruits, including service berries, choke cherries, bull berries, wild currants, strawberries, ground cherries, and elder berries. Some of these gifts of nature were dried or put in cold storage for eating in the winter. Although the pioneers were disappointed at the lack of trees in the valley floor (a condition they remedied by quickly planting a large number of trees), they found a great variety of species of large, useful trees in the hills and mountain forests. In the foothills were pinyon pine, juniper, cottonwood, scrub oak, alder, birch, and maple. In the mountains were expansive stands of Douglas and Alpine fir and Colorado blue and Englemann spruce, among others. Sawmills were set up almost immediately upon the founding of each settlement, supplying wood products for construction, furniture, and a host of other uses.

The newcomers also found an abundance of animal life. The pioneer group fought off hundreds of rattlesnakes during their first spring in 1850. But the valley floor also contained numerous rabbits and hares, plus beavers, squirrels, gophers, deer, waterfowls, and ubiquitous mice. Their predators were there too: eagles, hawks and owls, skunks, weasels and mink, and competing at the top of the food chain, coyotes, bobcats, mountain lions, and bears. The presence of wolves in Sanpete is apparently debatable, but black and grizzly bears were common and hunted aggressively. Trappers captured silver and red foxes, bobcats, and pine martens in the canyons. When settlers tired of rabbit meat, they found mule deer plentiful, until they were driven out by sheep and cattle. Before it was reduced to a trickle by the removal of irrigation water, the Sanpitch River maintained populations of trout and less desirable suckers and chubs. In the early days, the tributary streams were so full of trout that they were caught by the bushel.[10]

In fact, the natural environment of Sanpete County proved to be much more diverse than its early occupants realized. They soon proved they could live there and add their own overlay to the existing landscape. Sanpete's total landscape now is a mostly compatible mixture of both the natural and the human-built and planted environment. It speaks volumes about how its settlers and developers struck compromises with the land and exploited it, usually to their benefit, but sometimes at the expense of the land itself. Not environmentalists in today's sense, nor even aware of the long-range consequences of many of their actions, the early generations destroyed much of the wild plant and animal life that sustained them. In their effort to subdue their harsh and sometimes hostile environment, they also altered the land itself in ways that later haunted them. The adverse effects of erosion, its resultant flooding, and the loss of fish, fowl, and mammals have been in part remedied by increased private awareness and public management of the remaining resources. But the clock cannot be turned back, and no restoration effort can return Sanpete's land to its more pristine, pre-settlement condition.

Still, most people then and now are generally pleased with the result of bringing civilization to the county. Town locations and layouts, building types, styles, and materials, and planting and irrigations patterns all speak to the delicate relationship between the people and the land, and provide a tangible reminder that "This is the Place" for those who lived and still live here.

Geology

Sanpete's surface geology is diverse and complex. Within the county are three major geologic areas, plus many other smaller, more anomalous features. Along the entire eastern edge of Sanpete is the cretaceous-born Wasatch Plateau. It is unique among Utah's eight high plateaus as the only one capped entirely by sedimentary rocks.

Geologist William L. Stokes has described it as "an erosional remnant undergoing geologically rapid removal along a ragged eastern margin and a summit area protected in place by the thin, resistant Flagstaff Limestone (Paleocene)." He adds that the "western edge coincides with an abrupt decent of beds along the Wasatch Monocline."[11]

On the western side of the county are the Gunnison Plateau and the Valley Mountains, including the San Pitch Mountains, considered "two distinctly transitional features." They show both "resemblances to the Colorado Plateau in the age of formations, and to the Great Basin in their trends, dimensions, and relations to faults." The Valley Mountains are made mostly of Tertiary formations, while the Gunnison Plateau contains both Cretaceous and Jurassic deposits. Its east face is "abrupt and cut by several deep and scenic canyons that reveal a complicated history of deposition and deformation." The plateau's summit is relatively flat, with peaks ranging from 8,000 to 9,500 feet in elevation.[12] Geologist Haika Chronic adds that the "Mesozoic sedimentary rocks in the San Pitch Mountains are mostly ancient lake deposits. The character of the mountains changes with these flat-lying, poorly consolidated strata."[13]

In between the two major north-to-south-running mountain ranges is the Sanpete-Sevier Valley Section, a long, narrow depression named for the two rivers (and counties) that traverse it. The depression is of primarily structural origin rather than being significantly river-cut. The average width of the lowlands along the rivers is ten to fifteen miles. The erosion-caused depression fill is of "unknown but vast" depths. A geologist observes that "The structure of the valley bottom appears deceptively simple; the surficial deposits of soil and alluvial fans mask a complex areas of subsidence caused by faulting, folding, and the removal of salt from buried Jurassic formations."[14] Sedimentary rocks from the Tertiary and Octaceous periods also are apparent in the surface geology. In the northwest corner of Sanpete Valley is a large area of extrusive igneous rock left by volcanic activity in the Tertiary period. Most of the rest of the county's tectonic ("architecture of the rocks in the upper part of the earth's crust") nature is considered "Platform deposits of Paleozoic, Mesozoic and Cenozoic age overlying basement rocks of Precambrian age."[15]

Geologic studies and seismic records show that Sanpete County lies within the Intermountain Seismic Belt, a major zone of earthquake activity. Quakes of 4.3 to 5.0 on the Richter magnitude scale have been felt in the Manti-Ephraim area and near Moroni and Wales. No serious damage or loss of life has occurred during Sanpete's historic period. However, geological evidence indicates that dangerous earthquakes of 7.5 have occurred in Utah within the last 300 years. Quakes of equal or greater magnitude may be expected in the future, portending problems for the county's many non-reinforced historic buildings and their inhabitants.[16]

Soils and Mineral Resources

Reflecting the county's varied topography and climate, three predominant soils exist, called Entisols, Aridisols, and Mollisols. Least plentiful but of greatest use to Sanpete's farmers are the younger Entisols on stream flood plains, valley bottoms and on alluvial terraces and fans, all generally along the Sanpitch and Sevier rivers. Surrounding the areas of Entisols are larger, higher areas of Aridisols, occurring in high valleys, terraces, and fan slopes where precipitation is less than twelve to fourteen inches per year. Shadscale, pinyon pine, and juniper grow here, and its bare rock outcroppings have been exploited with stone quarries. The highest, thickest, and darkest soils are the Mollisols found in the mountains. These relatively fertile soils have been formed under grassland or forested vegetation and are rich in humus. They exist well above the 5,000 foot level in upper foothills, mountain slopes and high plateaus which enjoy greater precipitation. Sanpete's stockmen have long fed their animals on these rangelands. Many of Sanpete's wildlife populations and recreational areas are found in the highlands, as are timber-rich forests which have provided wood products for the county's towns for 150 years.[17]

Although apparently not rich in rare minerals, minor amounts of silver, copper, lead, and zinc have been located and mined in Sanpete County. Other local minerals with commercial value include gypsum and anhydrite, fuller's earth, aragonite and calcite, clay, beryllium, limestone and dolomite, and salt.

In the county's Flagstaff Limestone and Green River Formation are found widely distributed carbonate rocks, including limestone, dolomite and dolomite limestone which have been quarried for a variety of purposes, including dimensioned building stone, road-building material, lime, and, until the last sugar plant closed in 1961, for sugar refining in Centerfield. Some of the carbonate stone has been used as an ingredient in local cement which is prepared from a mix of limestone, shale, sand, and some other minor constituents. Most of the dimensioned stone used historically has been limestone (calcitic dolomite) taken from the Green River Formation and, to a lesser extent, sandstone removed from the Crazy Hollow Formation. As early as 1852, a block of Sanpete oolite was carved with Mormon and Utah symbols and hauled to the nation's capitol where it still remains as part of the famous Washington Monument. The monumental LDS temple in Manti was made of oolite limestone called Sanpete White or Manti Stone. This easily worked, light cream-colored stone was also used in the Sanpete County Courthouse, the Park Building at the University of the Utah, and for the portions of the interiors of the Utah and California state capitols. Local sandstone was used mostly in buildings in Fairview and Mount Pleasant, including the LDS North Ward church in Fairview and the storefronts of several of the commercial buildings in Mount Pleasant's historic business district.[18]

From the earliest days of settlement, pioneers at the south end of the county quarried salt from the Redmond Hills, a low ridge in the middle of the Sevier valley. About 10,000 tons per year are removed from this source and sold in rough blocks for cattle. Crushed salt is used by sheep men, as well as for melting snow on winter roads. Among the local salt businesses are the Albert Poulson Salt Company and the Redmond Clay and Salt Company.[19]

Welded tuff has been quarried by the Azome Utah Mining Company in the Goldens Ranch Formation near the Juab County line. Marketed as Azomite, the product is crushed at the quarry, trucked to the company's plant in Sterling, and further crushed for use as feed additive for domestic animals, poultry grit and soil conditioner. In the Dipping Vat Formation along the Redmond Hills, several bentonite pits are quarried intermittently for local use as linings for stock ponds, reservoirs, and irrigation ditches. The unusual material swells to more than three times its original volume after being ground and made wet. The "waterproof" product is also used for patching leaks, protecting roofs, and as a filler in soap. Another local stone, aragonite, a form of calcium carbonate, is available in the Green River Formation. Colorful, translucent, and attractive, it is useful as decorative stone and also has utility as a white crystalline material, filling thin fractures and lining cavities.

Coal was discovered in 1854 near Wales and mined from the Cretaceous and Paleocene formations on the east side of the Gunnison Plateau. Some of the coal was exported to markets in Salt Lake City. Later another coal deposit was discovered and mined in the Morrison area east of Sterling. The coal is all of the bituminous type. Coal mining had ceased by the early 1940s, partly because the coal is so deeply buried that it is too expensive to extract. Lignite exists in the Dry Canyon area east of Milburn. After it is mined, it is mixed with turkey feathers to produce soil conditioner.[20]

Largely untapped in its potential is a great reserve of petroleum and natural gas that lies in sedimentary rock underlying the entire county. Commercial-sized natural gas fields have been found in Carbon and Emery counties, including one north of Joe's Valley at the eastern margin of Sanpete County. Well drilling in Sanpete has been limited, however, despite the identification of several promising subterranean formations. Tests made in Moroni area have been favorable and may result in future gas mining activity. The Green River Formation, which contains enormous amounts of oil shale in the Uinta Basin, is also exposed in the Sanpete and Sevier valleys and probably underlies the Cedar Hills area in the Moroni Upland. Most of the area with oil production potential, however, is in the public domain and is not available for mining.[21]

Climate and Weather

Sanpete's semi-arid climate is affected by the distant Sierra-Nevada Mountain Range. Pacific storms on their way east must cross this range, but, heavy with moisture, they often lose their precipitation before reaching the intermountain region. The clouds reaching the Sanpete and Gunnison valleys are thus often dry, giving the area an average of only twelve to fifteen inches of precipitation annually. Prolonged periods of extremely low temperatures are usually prevented by the Rocky Mountains which act as a barrier to continental arctic air masses approaching the area.

Sanpete is covered by two climatic zones, the temperate Undifferentiated Highlands in the east and north, and the warmer Steppe in the central, south and west parts of the county. Annual normal precipitation varies widely across the county from eight to ten inches in the lower, north central and west areas, to forty to fifty inches on the Wasatch Plateau, and more than fifty inches on the highest peaks. Much of the latter comes in the form of snow, which averages 150–200 inches in the northeast mountains, to only twenty to forty inches in the southern part of the county. The inhabited valleys receive an annual snowfall of forty to seventy inches. Depending on whether the snow is "dry" or "wet," an inch of water equals fifteen to twenty inches of snow.[22]

The climatic information for Manti is fairly typical for other towns on the valley floor. Due to its elevation of 5,575, summers are pleasantly cool. The daily temperature range during the summer is fairly high, averaging thirty-three degrees. In July and August most highs are in 80s with lows in the 50s. Winters are moderately cold but usually not severe. Highs are typically in the 30s with lows of about 15 degrees, although sub-zero conditions occur roughly every third year.

Weather observations in Manti date back to 1893. Since then the mean annual precipitation has been 12.28 inches, while the mean snowfall has been 50.4 inches a year, although winters of twice that snow depth have been experienced. The greatest daily amount of rain was the 1.75 inches that fell one June day in 1943. The heaviest snow falls in December through March, while there is none between June and September. Precipitation is uniformly distributed between October and May, averaging about an inch in each of these three months. June through August are drier, but heavy storms during the summer have caused significant flooding and damage.

Manti's mean annual temperature is 61.3 degrees Fahrenheit, with a record high day of 103 in 1960 and a record low of -27 degrees in 1927. Of importance to farmers is the fact that the average date of the last frost is 24 May, while the average first frost is 28 September. This means that typically there are 128 consecutive days without frost. This moderate-length growing season is suitable for wheat, hay, and sugar beets, crops which have flourished locally.[23]

Sanpete has had its share of weather extremes and disasters. The first officially recorded tornado in Utah was reported in 1941, and they are very rare, but on 16 June 1955 two funnel clouds touched down in the county, damaging sheds, breaking branches, and uprooting trees. Fortunately no injuries were reported. The thirty-foot-wide spout of a tornado in Gunnison damaged several buildings in 1964. Late and early frosts have frequently ruined crops, as on 14–15 June 1976 when an unusually late frost destroyed thousands of acres of wheat and barley.

Flooding has been a frequent a severe problem in Sanpete from the earliest days of settlement. As early as 30 July 1852, Manti was flooded with ten inches of water. In August 1878 the citizens of Wales recorded an eerie event. The town was enveloped by a cloud "that was suddenly divided by a light," followed by a "terrific roar" and a cloudburst that greatly damaged fields and crops. On 16 August 1889, a thunderstorm swelled Manti Creek to over eight feet, bringing full size trees, logs, and brush into town, causing extensive damage. A flood on 6 August 1901 north of Fairview washed out bridges and culverts, buried wagons and hay rakes in mud, and carried away haystacks and animals. Many residents were forced to live in temporary housing until their own houses were repaired. The 15 August 1915 flood in Ephraim broke previous records for damage as twenty-five-cubic-foot boulders and mud swept through town. Mount Pleasant was hit often and hard. Typical was the flood of 19 June 1918, caused by a cloudburst east of town. Its raging water swept away houses, outbuildings, automobiles, and machinery. It flooded cellars, covered streets with a thick layer of mud, and ruined crop-laden fields and gardens. One farmer could not escape the torrent and drowned. On 1 June 1943, two inches of rain fell quickly on Ephraim, flooding ditches and the Sanpitch River.

Heavy rains on Pioneer Day—24 July 1946—propelled boulders and mud out of Pleasant Creek, engulfing Mount Pleasant in the city's worst-ever flood. One could traverse Main Street, inundated in three to four feet of water, only by boat. Buildings and houses in and around the business district were badly damaged by water, rocks, and

Flood debris in Manti about 1900. (Utah State Historical Society)

debris. Some cars were carried five blocks away by the torrent. Livestock and poultry were killed. Crops were ruined and the city cemetery was severely damaged.[24] Disaster-stricken Palisades Park was victimized by the 11 June 1965 flash flooding of Sheep Creek Canyon. The flood killed seven campers—a mother, father, three children and two nephews. It also did more than $1 million in damage, completely destroying three recreation areas and seven bridges, and five miles of newly paved highway. The flooding of 1982, described later, also brought damage and destruction.

On 1 June 1963 a series of deadly thunderstorms and lightning bolts killed seven people in northern Utah, including a fifteen-year-old boy who was struck dead while herding sheep near Indianola. Lightning strikes in June 1977 were especially destructive in Mount Pleasant where they hit and burned out the city water pump, hydroelectric generator, and television transmitting station, leaving the area without water or TV for several days.

Water

The valleys of the county have relied on the higher elevations not only for wood products but for the water so necessary to the farms and ranches scattered throughout the region. Agricultural uses have always accounted for most of the water demand in Sanpete. Poultry require 0.6 gallons per day per bird, and large livestock need about thirty-five gallons each day. During much of the year, sheep and cattle feed on ranges, but in other months they are concentrated in valley pastures and feed lots where water must be delivered to them. It is estimated that each farm family uses an average of 650 gallons per day, plus an amount needed to sustain animals and crops. Crops require from thirteen inches of water per year for small truck crops to twenty-six inches annually for alfalfa, small grain, and corn. Given the low annual precipitation—the valley floors receive only twelve inches or less—irrigation is needed to support the more water-consumptive crops. Each year about 57,000 acres of land are irrigated in Sanpete County.

Fortunately, ample supplies of water exist in the county and are covered by water rights. Numerous permanent and intermittent streams descend from the mountains into the Sanpete and Upper Sevier valleys and the entire drainage from the Sanpitch River and a portion of the Sevier River drainage are found within the county. The Wasatch Plateau annually receives as much as forty inches of precipitation, much of which is stored as snow. On the Gunnison Plateau, the average is twenty-five inches annually. The storage of spring runoff water from mountain watersheds is thus essential to sustaining the livestock—and agriculture-based economy.

The county's water resources derive from both surface water and groundwater, the former consisting of rivers, streams, and reservoirs, and the latter of underground sources such as springs, drilled and artesian wells, and the basins they fill. The Sevier River near Gunnison provides an average flow of 157,800 acre-feet annually, while below the Sevier Bridge Reservoir the flow increases to 173,000 acre feet. Water from the Sanpitch drainage is diverted for irrigation purposes by the Moroni and Mount Pleasant Canal and water is stored in the Wales Reservoir, the Gunnison Reservoir, the Gunnison

Highland Reservoir, and Funks Lake. Downstream and north of the mouth of the Sanpitch River near Gunnison, the Sevier River flows about seven miles northwest into the Sevier Bridge Reservoir. When filled to capacity, it is 80 feet deep and contains 235,962 acre-feet of water, making it the largest reservoir in the county, although most it lies in Juab County behind Yuba Dam.

The part of Sevier Valley situated in Sanpete County contains two groundwater basins, the Redmond-Gunnison and the Gunnison-Sevier Bridge Reservoir. Unlike these, the Sanpete Valley is a single, enclosed groundwater basin. Groundwater under artesian conditions occurs throughout the Redmond-Gunnison Basin and about 150,000 acre-feet of groundwater are stored in its sand and gravel deposits. This resource is not readily accessible, however. The distance to the water table varies from ten to 160 feet, and it is estimated that less than 1,000 acre-feet per year could be developed annually. The Gunnison-Sevier Bridge Reservoir Basin has a water table of 30–90 feet and contains about 300,000 acre-feet of stored water, of which roughly 15,000 acre-feet could be removed annually without adversely affecting the flow of the Sevier River. In Sanpete Valley, 1,500 wells had an average discharge of two gallons per minute in 1964, producing about 16,000 acre-feet of water. Of this amount, 11,600 acre-feet went to irrigation, 500 to public supplies, 400 to industrial uses, and 3,500 to water domestic stock. Due to variations in precipitation, the annual discharge of wells varies considerably.

A small amount of usable water comes from about a third of the county's 88 springs. The Redmond-Gunnison Basin receives about 4,000 acre-feet annually from spring water while the Sevier Bridge Reservoir Bridge Basin receives about 12,000 acre-feet. In addition, there are at least twelve thermal or "hot" springs in the county which have not yet been put to practical use. The usability of water, of course, depends on its location, the consistency of its availability and its mineral content. In Sanpete County, overall water quality is good and becomes better with depth in the alluvial fill.

The quality of the county's rivers, streams, ponds, and reservoirs is also measured, albeit with different criteria, by recreationists. Several bodies of water are popular for fishing, swimming, boating, and water skiing. Several natural ponds of a few acres in size exist in the Wasatch Plateau mountain range. Small reservoirs include Gooseberry Lake, Ferron, and Huntington. Lowland reservoirs also serve recreational purposes but are subject to wide fluctuations in water level and area. The principal reservoirs are Funks Lake in Palisades State Park, Nine Mile Reservoir, Wales and Gunnison reservoirs, plus a small portion of the Sevier Bridge Reservoir.

Early Peoples

The Sanpitch-Sevier drainage offered a perfect location for inhabitants like Paleo-hunters, Archaic hunters, Fremont horticulturalists, and the later Paiute/Shoshoni gatherers.

To date, archaeologists and interested scholars actually know little about the specifics of life along the Sanpitch River and the surrounding mountain areas. They want to know more, but necessary background work has not been done. However, what is known is fascinating, and the little work that has been carried out by professional archeologists over the years has given at least a skeleton to the prehistory.[25]

As early as 1852, army surveyor John W. Gunnison published drawings of petroglyphs—figurative drawings pecked in stone—by Sanpete's early inhabitants. Gunnison's book, *Mormons or Latter-Day Saints,* which depicts unusual figures found near Manti, was the first publication to refer to Indian "rock art" in Utah.[26] In two sites near Gunnison and in Mellor Canyon near Fayette are ancient, heavily patinated petroglyphs of human and animal figures, geometric patterns, and other, rather mysterious depictions. Based on the style of art, they appear to have been made by the Fremont people, but the large hands and feet at one of the Gunnison sites suggests Anasazi artists as well. A fourth site on a sandstone cliff on the north side of the Sevier Bridge Reservoir features three anthropomorphic figures with headdresses drawn in Fremont Style.[27]

During the beginning periods of professional archeological research in Utah in the 1930s, Sanpete County received some attention from scientifically conducted archeological studies. In 1935, Elmer R. Smith conducted excavations at the Fremont culture site near Ephraim. A manuscript describing these excavations was prepared, but it was never published in any journals available to the public (copies are available at the University of Utah). Excavations at the same sites were continued in 1937 by John Gillin and a joint expedition of the University of Utah and the Peabody Museum of Harvard University. This expedition excavated one large site and tested two others. The site that was excavated by Smith and Gillin is called Witch's Knoll (42SP1). This is a large Fremont site approximately three miles southeast of Ephraim, and consists of fourteen mounds on a knoll about sixty feet in height. More about this site will be discussed when the Fremont Indians are described, since it is the key to understanding the Fremont culture in the area.

The next archeological work that was done in the county was the excavation by Jack Rudy in 1953 of a possible Paiute/Shoshoni burial. Because items such as powder horns were found, the burial was judged to be proto-historic.

No other professional work was carried out in the country until 1975, although local amateur archeologists and historians kept interest alive. The lack of activity in Sanpete Valley by the professional is explained by the commitment of the University of Utah to projects in other parts of the state, notably the Glen Canyon area of southern Utah and the West Desert. In 1975 work began again in Sanpete County because projects of the Utah Power and Light Company in the county required archeological clearance work under environmental laws. This brought a number of archeologists into the county, and the work of looking for sites was started again. From 1975 until 1978, 80 additional sites were recorded.

There is a total of only 91 recorded archeological sites in Sanpete County. When one considers that Sevier County to the south has recorded 1,400 sites, and other surrounding counties have listed hundreds of sites, the obvious conclusion is that there is great potential for more archeological work to be done in Sanpete County by supervised amateurs and professional archeologists.

The first occupants of Utah and Sanpete County were hunters of such Late Pleistocene fauna as mammoths, sloths, camels, and bison. The artifacts that identify this culture are the fluted spear points characteristic of these hunters. Clovis and Folsom points, for example, are well-made with long flutes, which helped with the hafting of the point to a sturdy spear that allowed the killing of large animals.

Surface finds of these fluted points have been made throughout Utah, but none has been made in well-dated sites anywhere in the state. Although there are no reported Paleo-Indian points from the Sanpete County proper, there are reports of points in Salina Canyon and in Millard County (the Tripp site in Sevier County and the 43MD300 site in Millard), and one point in Emery County. By correlation with dated sites in other areas of North America, the evidence is that the Sanpete area was occupied by big-game hunters 8,500 to 12,000 years ago. However, a number of archeologists believe that these hunters were probably here much earlier, probably around 30,000 B.C. The occupation by man of Sanpete County could be that early.

Comparatively less is known of these early people in Sanpete County than prehistoric cultures elsewhere. However, research in the valley is important not only to gain knowledge of early man in Utah, but to gain information of wider significance, since the area is part of a cultural transition zone between the Great Plains and the Colorado Plateau.

The earliest dwellers of the Sanpete Valley are assumed to have been big game hunters because all that is known about them derives from information gathered at butchering sites. It is probable, however, that the Sanpitch (Sanpete) drainage afforded these early men a wider variety of food than just large game animals.

In summary, Sanpete County may have been inhabited as early as 30,000 B.C. by small bands, each the size of a large family of ten to fifteen people, subsisting on abundant game in the mountains and gathering wild edible plants in the valley areas. These people may have maintained this lifestyle until approximately 8,500 B.C. (a total of about 20,000 years), at which time changes were probably forced on the inhabitants by extinction of some of the larger game animals. This event closed the longest occupation period of the site and brought new developments to the area.

About 8,500 years ago, a group of people in Utah (including the Sanpete area), characterized by the use of an atlatl (a type of spear launcher), some milling stones, and a variety of textiles, appeared on the scene. These were apparently nomadic or semi-nomadic peoples who occupied the caves, rock shelters, and perhaps open area. There is no evidence that these people built shelters of any type in the open, but that lack may have been the result of the deterioration of such shelters over thousands of years. What we know about these hunters and gatherers is limited to knowledge gained from the excavation of caves and rock shelters only. Since no excavations of this type are known in Sanpete County, knowledge of these people in this area is limited to logical deductions in general terms.

In Utah there were probably two types of Archaic people. One group lived in the Great Basin and used food sources around valley-floor marshes. The other group lived in the high plateau areas and probably utilized a wider variety of food. Sanpete County is between these two areas, and the Archaic people who lived in this area probably had adapted to both ways of life, representing a blend of the two methods of survival.

Two sites in Sanpete County provide evidence of the Archaic people who used the general area. These two Archaic sites are on opposite sides of the county, supporting the theory that the Archaic hunter ranged over all of what is now Sanpete County. One site is located in the mountains between Swasey Creek and Fuller Creek on the Emery County border; the second site is near the south end of the Sevier Bridge Reservoir, near the Juab County line. Both of these sites yielded a type of point known as "the Elko Series." This point does not help reveal whether the sites were used in early Archaic times or in later times, but they do suggest the presence of those people in Sanpete County for some time during the period. Thus the first firm evidence of man in the Sanpete Valley comes from the Archaic period, possibly 8,500 years ago.

About 2,500 years ago the people for some unknown reasons suddenly left this area as well as all Utah in general. The only available clue is that some changes in lake levels and climates possibly necessitated emigration in search of better localities for survival. For whatever reason, some archeologists believe that the Sanpete area was empty of people for perhaps 1,500 years. At the end of that time, the Sanpete Valley saw the arrival of a different type of people when the first Sanpete farmers arrived—those referred to as the Fremont people, or the Fremont culture. Where they came from, we do not know, but they were the first farmers to domesticate crops and settle in relatively large villages in Utah.

In Sanpete the best-known Fremont site is called Witch's Knoll, three miles southeast of Ephraim. The site originally consisted of fourteen mounds on a round swell sixty feet high, at the base of the foothills of the Wasatch Plateau. This site was not one of the largest of the Fremont villages, but it contained varied forms of architecture, such as turtle-back adobe granaries, bin granaries, and clay-lined living structures. One of the dwellings, for example, was a clay-lined, twenty-two-foot-square structure, with a clay-rimmed central fire basin.

Artifacts at Witch's Knoll are typical of the Fremont, consisting of a wide variety of left-over items: Pottery, gaming pieces, pendants, figurines, metates, and manos. Also located at the site were the bones of deer, antelope, and bison, as well as corn fragments. Neither antelope nor bison was in the area when white settlers arrived in 1849. Beyond this one excavated village site, archeological knowledge of how the Fremont people lived in Sanpete County is limited to eight other sites containing a few identifying artifacts. The hope is that many more village sites exist in the area and that future work will provide more information about the earliest farmers of the Sanpete Valley. The conjecture is that the Fremont culture lived year-round in the Sanpitch drainage itself, farming the bottom lands or the alluvial slopes out of canyon mouths, not too different in principle from modern farmers. The mountain ranges that surround the valley were used to hunt deer, to gather wood, and to search for edible wild plants.

For unknown reasons, around 1300 A.D. the Fremont farmer also left Sanpete County. This same thing happened all around the state, involving even the more specialized Anasazi farmers in this mysterious hegira. The outward migration left the valley open for the eventual arrival of the modern Native Americans who became familiar to the European settlers of Sanpete County in 1849.

Approximately 600 years ago, a group of nomadic hunters moved into Utah and into the Sanpete Valley area. These people lived much as did the neolithic archaic hunters centuries before them. Some investigators think this newer group of hunters drove out the Fremont farmers. In the Sanpete area, a change to a drier climate may have caused the Fremont farmer's crops to fail at a regular rate, and the new people moving into the area did a better job of adapting. The new residents have been called by various names: Ute, Paiute, Goshute, Shoshoni. All these groups spoke a common language known as "Numic." Some evidence indicates that the latest nomadic residents of the county were probably Paiute or Shoshoni, and not Utes, as commonly thought. A number of limited sites in the Sanpete County are very likely Paiute/Shoshoni. These sites are identified by their forms of pottery. Perhaps the biggest find that relates to this period is a burial site excavated by Jack Rudy near Indianola in 1953. This site, however, indicated only one of the latest periods of the nomadic Indian in the valley; with the burial were such trade goods as powder horns, obtained from European traders.

In summary, there is evidence in Sanpete of a wide range of use by different people through long periods of time. Possibly as early as 30,000 years ago, early Pleistocene hunters and gatherers moved into the Sanpete Valley, following bands of large game animals. With the extinction of some of these fauna, hunters for the most part were replaced by gatherers, who exploited different types of resources and did not rely heavily on one type of food. Such primitive agriculturists lived in Sanpete for probably 10,000 years. However, some scholars think the Sanpete area was void of humans for 1,500 years.

As in many similar cycles, these farmers were replaced by a group of people who reacted to their food sources much as did the archaic hunters. These newcomers survived until a new group of wanderers came to push them out, just as these latter hunters may have done to the earlier farmers.

When Mormon settlers arrived in 1849, they began a new cycle for utilization of the Sanpete Valley area.

ENDNOTES

1. Gary B. Peterson and Lowell C. Bennion, *Sanpete Scenes, A Guide to Utah's Heart.* (Eureka, UT: Basin/Plateau Press, 1987), 8.

2. Adelia B. Cox Sidwell, "Reminiscences of Early Manti," 1–2.

3. Andrew Jenson, quoted in the *Deseret News,* 14 August 1897.

4. Ibid.

5. Albert Smith, "Autobiography." 55.

6. Orson Pratt, interview with C. A. Madsen, Gunnison, 3 July 1880.

7. Ibid.

8. Wilhelmina Madsen, "Autobiography," 9–10, copy at the Utah State Historical Society.

9. Eli A. Day, "Biography of Abraham Day." 15, copy at the Utah State Historical Society.

10. Ernest Munk, "Pioneer Personal History," 2

11. William Lee Stokes, *Geology of Utah* (Salt Lake City: Utah Museum of Natural History, 1986), 247.

12. Ibid., 248.

13. Haika Chronic, *Roadside Geology of Utah* (Missoula, MT: Mountain Press Publishing, 1990), 228.

14. Stokes, *Geology of Utah,* 248.

15. Dean C. Greer et al, *Atlas of Utah* (Provo: Brigham Young University Press, 1981), 21–23.

16. Ibid., 26–27.

17. Ibid., 28–29.

18. Ibid., 38, 40.

19. Ibid., 49–50.

20. Ibid., 57–58.

21. Ibid., 59–62.

22. Ibid., 70.

23. Mark Eubank, *Utah Weather* (Bountiful, UT: Horizon Publishers, 1979), 187–89.

24. Ibid., 74–113.

25. The background research archaeology in the Sanpete County area was drawn from research material provided by Dr. David Madsen. See also John Gillin, *Archaeological Investigations in Central Utah*, Papers of the Peabody Museum of American Archaeology and Ethnology, 17: 2.

26. Kenneth B. Castleton, *Petroglyphs and Pictographs of Utah*, Vol. 2 (Salt Lake City: University of Utah Museum of Natural History, 1987), 9.

27. Ibid., 85–88.

CHAPTER 2

EXPLORATION
AND SETTLEMENT

On 14 June 1849, twenty-three months after the initial party of Mormon pioneers arrived in Utah, Brigham Young received a visit from Ute chiefs Wakara (anglicized to Walker) and Sowiette and a band of Ute Indians. They came to Salt Lake City to ask the leader of the white newcomers to permanently locate Mormon people in the central Utah valley named after Walker's brother, Chief Sanpitch. The valley was described as good land with much water.

Seeking both to gain the Indians' favor as well as find a suitable living environment for the burgeoning population of Saints—and envisioning the center of the Mormon kingdom being even farther south—Brigham Young sent an exploring party to determine the viability of honoring Walker's request. Led by Chief Walker, the party of investigators, consisting of Joseph Horne, W. W. Phelps, Ira Willes, and D. B. Huntington, camped on the present site of Manti on 20 August 1849. They explored the area for a few days and were entertained there by the local Indians. Upon returning to Salt Lake City, they reported favorably on the possibilities of settlement.[1]

Following the advice of the scouts, Young called Isaac Morley to organize about fifty families and individuals to form a pioneering group to head for "San Pete."

The Vanguard Party Of Mormon Pioneers

Before massive colonization began, Young directed further exploration of inviting areas. After the harvest of 1849, he called fifty men to organize the Southern Exploring Company led by Apostle Parley P. Pratt and his counselors William W. Phelps and David Fullmer. Their direction was to explore the valleys south of the Wastach Front, and identify resources and sites for future settlements in the "mountains of Israel." This small company carefully recorded their findings—soil conditions, vegetation, streams, timber, pasturage, lime and stone deposits, and other pertinent information. After first visiting Fort Utah (later Provo), they crossed the Utah and Juab valleys as far as Salt Creek (the future site of Nephi) where they traversed up Salt Creek Canyon and down into upper northwest Sanpete Valley. They arrived at the site of eventual Manti only twelve days after Isaac Morley and the vanguard party reached the place.[2]

The vanguard settlers had left Salt Lake City by 28 October 1849, and arrived in Sanpete Valley twenty-three days later on 19 November 1849. Along the way they found it necessary to clear roads and build bridges over creeks and ravines that impeded their progress. Isaac Morley was assisted in his leadership duties by Charles Shumway and Seth Taft. A few of the colonists wanted to build the first settlement at Shumway Springs, while others desired to move south and settle in the Gunnison area. Among the latter was Seth Taft, who spoke at the first council meeting held at the Manti site on the evening of their arrival, 19 November 1849. He opined that the Manti area was "only a long narrow canyon and not even a jack rabbit could exist on its desert soil."[3] He was outvoted, however, and the Manti site became home.

The vanguard group of 224 men, women, and children settlers was nearly twice as large as the "charter" group of Mormons that first entered the Great Basin in late July 1847. Two years later the Sanpete entourage consisted of 240 cattle, horses, wagons, tools, supplies, food, and several farm and domestic animals. They planned to bring enough provisions to last them throughout the winter. At the advice of Isaac

Morley, the people moved to the south side of Temple Hill, where they hoped to be sheltered from the wind and snow coming in from the northwest. Some of the people lived in their tents or wagon boxes, while others built crude dugouts in the hillside or began log cabins.

Little did they know that the winter of 1849–50 would be one of the earliest and most severe ever recorded. Thirty-two inches of snow fell in the valley soon after the pioneers arrived. The snow was so deep that the livestock could not reach the underlying grass, so men and boys spent their days maintaining fires, shoveling away the snow, and creating windrows to provide a small measure of protection against the blasts of winter and to form an enclosure to keep out wolves and coyotes. Despite this work, Morley reported that by March they had already lost forty-one oxen, thirty-eight cows, three horses, and fourteen head of young stock. By June more half of all the cattle had perished.[4] Yet the dead cattle kept the pioneers alive through the winter and provided enough additional meat to feed the local Indians, who were thus befriended by the generosity of their new white neighbors.

In December, after making their camp ready to survive the winter, twelve men under the leadership of Jerome Bradley were sent back to Salt Lake City to obtain enough supplies to sustain the settlers until spring. The returning relief train was detained at Provo because of reports of Indian hostilities. Ammon and Tabbinaw, two brothers of Chief Walker, volunteered to serve as guides, and led the party to the forks of Salt Creek where, in January 1850, they became snowbound. (This situation caused Isaac Morley and other settlers to found Nephi at the mouth of Salt Creek Canyon in 1851.) Tabbinaw rode into the Manti settlement and reported the startling news that he had seen a naked white man lying across the Sanpitch River. A rescue party was formed and raced to the river to find that the man was a messenger from the supply train, which had been snowed in. Walking across the crusted snow, he had continuously broken through, and the rough edges of the snow crust had torn his clothes to shreds. Exhausted and blinded by the snow, he was taken back to the Manti encampment and nursed back to health. The relief party was brought safely into the settlement in March by "sleds drawn by hand over the icy crust covering snow 8 to 20 feet deep."[5]

By this time the pioneers had managed to erect a log schoolhouse and twenty primitive cabins, although most people were still living in tents, caves, and dugouts. Despite the severity of the winter and the food shortage caused by the delay of the supply train, the initial band of settlers managed to stay in good health. It was only through great resourcefulness that the fifty families of colonists survived that first, fierce winter in temporary shelters without meeting the same dreadful fate as the Donner-Reed party of 1846.

As the snows melted under the spring sun, the settlers began to plant crops in the never-tilled earth. By May they had put in 250 acres of potatoes, wheat, barley, and oats. Another relief party from Salt Lake City arrived with ten loads of grain to tide the colonists over until their crops matured. Brigham Young made his first visit to Sanpete on 4 August 1850, and the next day helped the settlers choose a permanent site for their city. During the October LDS general conference, Morley was allowed to choose another 100 men and their families to strengthen the Sanpete colony. They arrived in late fall, and by the end of 1850, Manti was an established center of about 365 people. The General Assembly of Deseret granted Manti a city charter on 7 April 1851.

In May 1850 with the first sustained warm weather, however, the new settlement was thrown into a panic by the appearance of numerous rattlesnakes emerging from hibernation, and Adelia Cox Sidwell, a child of ten at the time, recalled in her later years:

> They had come from caves situated above us in the ledge of rock that had been our shelter and shield, from the piercing northern blast of winter, they invaded our homes with as little compunction as the plague of Egypt did the Palace of the Pharaoh. They arrogated to themselves the privilege of occupying our beds and cupboards (pantries we had none). The male portion of the community turned out en masse with torches to enable them with more safety to prosecute the war of extermination, and the slaughter continued until the "wee small" hours . . . The number killed that first night (was estimated) as near three hundred.[6]

Remarkably, no one was bitten by the reptiles, and the events in time became the origin of some folklore tales of horror in which the

The Nathanial Beach log cabin was erected in the Little Fort in Manti in 1853. (Albert Antrei)

settlers were spared harm and death itself through miraculous God-given deliverance.

Four Waves of Settlement

The exploration and settlement of Sanpete County paralleled on a smaller scale the radiating pattern of settling the entire Mormon Corridor, with Manti rather than Salt Lake City at the center. Even as the initial settlement was being established, explorers were venturing out into all corners of the valley and surrounding mountain environs, identifying natural resources and other areas suitable for farming and building towns. Parley P. Pratt's party had explored Sanpete's two major valleys in November 1849 while also investigating Juab and Sevier counties on its way to southern Utah. Small parties scouted in the county during lulls between work and skirmishes with the Indians. The first wave of new settlement ventures looked to the north starting in late 1851 and continuing through 1854.

During this period the Allred Settlement (now Spring City), the Hambleton Settlement (now Mount Pleasant), Cottonwood Creek or Fort Ephraim (now Ephraim), and Coalbed (Wales) were founded.

Five years later, following the Walker War, a second wave of colonization occurred, resulting in the exploration and creation of the six villages of Fairview, Fountain Green, Moroni, Gunnison, Chester, and Centerfield, as well as the resettlement of the four earlier colonies abandoned in 1853. A decade later, after the Black Hawk War, a third and last Mormon settlement period spread colonists to the more remote, smaller but still habitable regions of the county. Among the twelve new settlements, Thistle Valley (later Indianola) was settled in 1871, Arropine (now Mayfield) by two separate groups in 1873, Pettyville in 1873, Axtell in 1874, and now-defunct Dover in 1875.

Even after the arrival of the railroad, new colonies were established, although they were smaller and had more difficulty surviving. Between 1894–1912, only four new towns were attempted and all of them—Morrison, Clarion, New Jerusalem, and Oak Creek—are either very small or non-existent today.[7]

Land Distribution and Use

While land was generally given at no cost to newcoming immigrants, methods of distribution varied from drawing lots to being disbursed on a first-come-first-served basis at the discretion of the local bishop. In a theocracy the bishop wore many hats: ecclesiastical leader, controller of land, water and the economy, judge, and final authority on every subject. Depending on the circumstances, some would get a lot of land or none, good land or poor, near the center of town or far away in the outskirts. Once land was received, community rules dictated the terms of keeping the land, usually requiring fencing, watering, improving, and using the land. Even when these dictates were met, people sometimes had difficulty holding on to the land they have been given and improved. James Van Nostrand Williams, for example, developed four parcels of land, all of which he lost to other settlers who took them from him.

No matter what resources were discovered in the Sanpete Valley or nearby, the people themselves were found in settlement patterns peculiar to them and different from all other settlements in the American Far West. The "Mormon pattern" is well known, and responsibility for it must be attributed to the general authorities of the Mormon church. Polices of settlement and land ownership in early Sanpete followed generally the plan of that church, that all participants in a settlement would receive "an inheritance" of land based on need. The typical method of establishing land holdings in any given "colony" was to have the land surveyed and plotted into four-to-ten acre pieces, which were then distributed to the settlers according to the size of a family and ability to use the acreage. Accordingly, Jesse W. Fox surveyed the first town site in Manti in the summer of 1850 into 110 blocks of four acres each and parcels along the edges, big and small. A man with five wives and families received five times more land than a bachelor, and often the bachelor received less desirable acreage because he had no family to support.

In addition to a town lot, or lots, a family also received agricultural land outside of town (but close to the fort area) and possessed the right to graze stock or cut wild hay on a commonly held town meadow. However, this area also happened to be used by Indians. This fact required daily guard duties around grazing herds to prevent them from being run off.

Egalitarianism was thought to be the ideal in land distribution procedures, although as we shall see, the ideal was sometimes subverted. After the land was surveyed each family drew lots to see which ground was to be to its specific "inheritance." The surveyor was careful to see that each farm lot included, so far as possible, an equal share of all kinds of terrain so that no family received an unfair advantage or disadvantage.[8]

When Williams, a single man, was called to move from Payson to Moroni in 1857, he initially received from Bishop Bradley twenty acres of land. When a new group of immigrants arrived, he "willingly . . . gave up one-half to accommodate others." He started grubbing the sage brush off the remaining acres when it was decided that young single men would take another cut of one-half to help other newcomers. This he did but "not with the best of feelings." Another proposed cut would have reduced his holdings to only 2.5 acres, even though he had already cleared and sown 8.5 which were "growing nicely." Williams protested to the bishop but was told, "You can either obey or you can leave." Not content, he explained his situation to President Orson Hyde who had called him there. Hyde told him, "Well, we have to put up with many unpleasant things, which does seem too bad. But then you are young and have no family to provide for which many have."[9]

Feeling more sympathetic, nearby Bishop William Seeley told him if he would let go of his Moroni land and move to Mount Pleasant, he would give him the land he needed, already cleared, and it would never be taken away. Williams took the offer. He sold his planted acres for what the new owner could give him in the fall. His new land was a forty-acre parcel two miles north of town situated between two creeks. He would have plowed, sown, and watered his ground, but no men were allowed to work their land until after the rock fort was completed. The latter project was done on time for the 4th of July. After planting, he began erecting a log house in the southeast corner of the fort.

In 1863 a new policy required that farm land must be fenced by a certain time or be forfeited. As he had been called to go to the eastern states as a teamster to help the immigration, Williams did not know of the new rule and was not there to do the fencing. Upon returning and learning of the requirement, he was assured by the bishop that he would be exempt from the rule and that the bishop would take care of the fencing for him. When Williams returned a second time, he found his land now fenced, had been taken by the bishop and added to his own holdings. The distraught man's protests were for naught. Discouraged, he moved to another community where, despite his contribution as a school teacher, the same story played out a fourth time as a he had yet another improved parcel of land taken from him unjustly. Pioneer justice was as harsh as the times they lived in.[10]

New immigrants were typically given a temporary home upon arriving in Sanpete. They would move often and live in several makeshift residences before obtaining a permanent dwelling on land of their own. The experience of the Danish family of Paul Christian and Christina Nelson Madsen is fairly typical. After arriving in Gunnison with their five sons on 22 July 1874, they were given a small log home with a dirt floor and dirt roof. They then moved 1.5 blocks east along Main Street into a dugout cellar where the seven lived until the next spring when they relocated into another small log cabin, two blocks farther east. In the fall of 1875, they obtained their own first home, a

The first post office in Wales was located in the Midgley home. (Courtesy Jane Thomas)

14-by-16-foot dugout. Here they lived for eleven years until finally trading for another small house to which they added two rooms. Here they stayed until the death of the parents. Throughout these years the family survived in "humble circumstances," counting themselves among the town's "mostly poor" population.[11]

The Mormons brought a unique village form of settlement with them to the Great Basin. It originated in Joseph Smith's "Plat for the City of Zion," intended for Independence, Missouri in 1833 and revised thereafter for uses elsewhere. The plat or idealized city plan was history made visible—the values and precepts of the Mormon people in physical form. The townsite plan was repeated several hundred times throughout the Great Basin, including Sanpete County, with its gridded plans, wide, poplar-lined streets, irrigation ditches, and large blocks divided into building lots where houses, garden plots, barns, and outbuildings served domestic needs. The "big field," located adjacent to town, was surveyed and distributed in five-, ten-, or twenty-acre plots for farming or stock raising.[12] One British observer traveling through the area described the ubiquitous formula:

> Take half as much ground as you can irrigate, and plant it thickly with fruit trees. Then cut it up into blocks by cutting roads

through at right angles; sprinkle cottages among the blocks, and plant shade-trees along both sides of the roads, Then take the other half of your ground and spread it out in fields around your settlement, sowing to taste.[13]

Settlement in Mormon villages became ritualized with each arriving group of immigrants from the East. In a letter President Young established his preference for village life:

In all cases in making new settlements the Saints should be advised to gather together in villages, as has been our custom from the time of our earliest settlement in these mountain valleys. The advantages of this plan, instead of carelessly scattering out over a wide extent of country are, many and obvious to all those who have a desire to serve the Lord. By this means the people can retain their ecclesiastical organizations, have regular meetings of the quorums of the Priesthood and establish and maintain day and Sunday schools . . . they can also co-operate for the good of all in financial and secular matters, in making ditches, fencing fields, building bridges and other necessary improvements. Further than this they are a mutual protection and sources of strength against horse and cattle thieves, land jumpers, etc., and against hostile Indians, should there be any.[14]

The settlement of Sanpete County as a network of such villages reflected the intent to space resources and way stations, extending the sphere of Mormon influence through systematic expansion and growth. The line of travel of the transportation routes through the area also played a key role in determining the locations of towns. But perhaps the most important was the proximity to water, lumber, grazing, and agricultural land. Variations on the basic grid plan were caused by geographical anomalies plus irrigation canals traversing roads and fields.

In spite of difficult times, colonization moved ahead rapidly and efficiently during the first decade. From the initial base in Manti, groups moved out to found other communities, either directly or in cooperation with groups from elsewhere. Conditions in the early months and years of these new villages were always a challenge, both to the spirit and to the body. For example, the pioneers of Duck

Springs (Moroni) spent the fall and winter of 1859 in dugouts scooped out of the banks of the Sanpitch River. Washed out of their primitive home by the high water of the spring runoff, they made sure that the next winter found them in more secure habitations on higher ground, away from the river.[15]

The location of each community in Sanpete was determined first by the availability of water, timber, and soil. Towns on the eastern side of the valley were established on alluvial flood plains which provided fertile areas for cultivation and adequate supplies of water. With much less water available in the West Mountains (the Gunnison Plateau), communities established there relied mainly on the availability of springs. Regularly, in the spring of each year a large flow of water gushed out of Maple Canyon, but it lasted for only a short time. There was also a sizeable flow of water out of Uinta Springs, which is located west of Fountain Green for which the community was initially named.

Nearly all communities in Sanpete found reliable sources of surface water. For convenience, Wales was located in proximity to coal mines and drew its water coincidentally out of Wales Canyon. Chester was founded in the area where springs surface in such great numbers that many of them were incorporated into individual houses. Gunnison's water was initially derived from Twelve-Mile Creek, which is a tributary of the Sanpitch near its confluence with the Sevier. Mayfield's water came from the same source.

Flowing water from the mountain snowpack for irrigation initially regulated the movement of people in the valley, for the average rainfall did not provide enough moisture for the growing season. For about twenty years after the first settlement, no farm or ranch was possible unless it had some kind of access to a surface spring, creek, or lake.

Each family, upon receiving a town lot, would, in the classic fashion of the plot of the "City of Zion," place on it not only a house, garden, and orchard, but a stable, corral, chicken coop, pigsty, and granary as well. The tax assessment rolls of past years indicate that the original plan in Sanpete County was for four town lots to the block, which provided ample space for the multiple use to which they were put. They also indicate a considerable amount of subdivision even in the earliest records, which date from the 1870s. That subdi-

The Orson Hyde Home in Spring City. (Utah State Historical Society)

vision reflects the need for more lots, an effect caused by large families and increasing immigration.

With the rapid population increases in Sanpete County during the nineteenth century, it was only natural that some settlers experienced conflicts over land distribution and that the Mormon church's land policies should fall under criticism.

Mention has already been made of James Van Nostrand Williams's experience. A somewhat similar conflict between individual and community occurred in 1860 at Fairview, then known as North Bend. According to the ward minutes, LDS church authorities had decided to maintain strict separation between grazing and farming lands:

> Isaac Y. Vance and Eliza Jones called the people together to consider the propriety of farming south of the town, and keeping cattle north, to preserve the crops according to the Bishops wishes. The people were in favor of farming south. After Vance and Jones had shown the impropriety of the people undertaking to fence so many fields, and dig so many water ditches with all the rest of the necessary work upon their hands, and assured the people that there was more land surveyed south than would be farmed this season.[16]

But Lewis C. Zabriskie and his son, William, rejected that plan, and their decision to stake off as much acreage as they needed north of town caused considerable disunity in the struggling community. Their assertion of squatter's rights over community-planned settlement stirred no little eddy of individualism in the pool of cooperative effort.[17]

Occasionally it happened that someone would increase his holdings beyond his standard "inheritance." This was possible because "inheritances" could be sold, traded, or returned to the church.

Andrew Peter Olsen of Ephraim grasped opportunity when he saw it. Many Sanpete farmers felt they could support only a limited number of cattle on their lands and therefore were destroying all new calves over the number they could feed. A former livestock man in Denmark, Olsen bought up many of the "surplus" calves. This meant that he had to buy additional land for hay and pasture. He looked immediately towards those people with "inheritances" they were not using, namely those who lived and worked in town as storekeepers and craftsmen. These people were more than willing to sell their excess land to Andrew, and in this manner he accumulated nearly 400 acres around Ephraim and Chester.[18]

Until 1872 land ownership in Sanpete County was by law no

more than a "squatter's right"—land based upon church surveys and recorded in ecclesiastical records. Following a United States government survey after 1872, however, such rights were transformed through mayor's deeds into real title under the established law of the United States. Henceforth, land distribution was the privilege of the federal government through the land agent system, i.e., through the General Land Office of the U.S. Department of the Interior. After 1872 all land claims had to be made in accordance with existing homestead laws on federal statute books.

As early as 1860, it had become apparent in some settlements that the land brought under cultivation far exceeded the amount of available water. Peter O. Hansen records a meeting that year at Spring City in which Orson Hyde "exhorted the farmers to reduce their farming to about half, and the mechanics to let farming alone." Subdivisions of water rights so that newcomers could bring more land under cultivation was the problem, as Hansen noted later in the year when he harvested his wheat. "The reason why my wheat turned out so slim was that we were overcrowded with new settlers and thus robbed of our water when we needed it the most. I sat down one evening and counted the cost of my wheat and found it to be $2½ pr. bsh. What a fine way to get rich!"[19]

It was not long before Mount Pleasant found that it had overextended its cultivated area, and Orson Hyde visited them with the same message he had preached in Spring City. "Pres. O. Hyde," the ward clerk records, "spoke about the necessity for the inhabitants of this Settlement to make a new fence around the field and cast out a part of the field as it is too large in relation to the amount of water than can be used for irrigation to it."[20]

Ephraim learned the lesson more slowly; in fact, when Oluf C. Larsen returned there in October 1866, after the Black Hawk War drove him out of Circle Valley, he found that a land boom was under way, with each new settler getting ten acres. A reaction resulted in 1867, when Canute Peterson arrived in Ephraim from Lehi to become bishop. Larsen reported that Brother Canute wanted land for himself and ordered "against the wishes of the old settlers" that yet another new field be opened up and every settler in Ephraim be given another five acres.[21]

This house was built during the 1860s in Manti for Frederick Walter Cox and his four wives. (Albert Antrei)

The ill-advised generosity which prompted settlers to subdivide their previous water rights again and again, according to Oluf Larsen, was primarily a result of the Black Hawk War. As is common in times of hardship, a spirit of cooperation began to prevail which had been conspicuously absent in some communities. Before the war, water hoarding had been fairly common, with so much over-irrigation that drainage had sometimes been necessary. It was Larsen's opinion that "if such spirits (as the water hoarders) had ruled in Utah it never would have been settled, but by war and other adversities among the communities the irrigable land areas were trebled and yet there was room for more."[22]

Insects and Predators

After the scarcity of water, grasshoppers were the first threat to agriculture. Although they appeared in 1855 in large enough quantities to worry farmers, it was not until late in the 1860s that enough land had been cultivated to create really alarming numbers. At Gunnison in July the grasshoppers stayed for four days "in such numbers that their weight on the growing grain laid it on the ground," resulting in a loss of about half of the crops.[23]

In 1870 grasshoppers returned. The *Deseret News* reported in June that "so great is the destruction wrought that if the people of [Sanpete] county raise enough wheat for bread for themselves, they will do very well," and went on to sound the death knell for crops in each community: Fairview, "the crops almost entirely devoured; the people all resowing"; Mount Pleasant, "all the small grain gone; may raise potatoes and peas"; Ephraim, "three thousand acres of small grain gone; five thousand acres left; potatoes and peas look well."[24]

But the farmers, whose resourcefulness in cultivating and irrigating the desert had created the grasshopper problem, were also resourceful in devising ways to combat the grasshopper. Although none of the extermination methods proved totally effective, the simultaneous and persistent application of all the methods did produce a gradual decline in the problem.

Of the early methods of extermination, planting alternative crops was perhaps the most effective. Instead of planting grains, which were ideal grasshopper fodder, maturing at the very time when grasshoppers hatch, farmers planted peas, which mature early, or potatoes, which mature underground.[25] The great advantage of the alternative crop method is that it is natural. It was in essence a return to pre-settlement conditions, since there was very little food for the grasshoppers when they hatched. Unfortunately, the settlers were determined to feed not only themselves, but the rest of Utah as well, which meant that they were committed to the cultivation of grains. Bound by priorities to grain cultivation, they could not make the complete shift to alternative crops that alone could have ended the grasshopper plague quickly.

Among direct methods of extermination, the most effective was egg destruction. Rather than wait for the live grasshoppers to appear, farmers raked the grasshopper eggs out into the sunlight, which killed them, or else plowed them so deeply underground that they were smothered. The grasshoppers that did hatch required a variety of means of extermination. Farmers drove the insects into rows of straw, then burned the straw; they also drove them into large pits and burned them; they flooded the irrigation canals and drove the grasshoppers into the water; they tied parachute-like pieces of canvas between two horses and pulled them across the fields. During especially bad sieges, all able-bodied people were called into the fields to kill grasshoppers. As Sanpete grew more prosperous, the county commissioners paid a bounty of one dollar per bushel for grasshoppers. At last, the farmers tried chemical warfare, putting out bran poisoned with arsenic.[26]

The grasshopper plague produced a heavy strain on all residents of the county, whether farmers or not, and came close to undoing the entire settlement. In 1901, an especially bad grasshopper year, the county commission voted to reject all petitions submitted by merchants for reductions in assessed valuation or taxation. To justify that policy, they pointed out that business prosperity in Sanpete County was so closely linked to agricultural prosperity that merchants had a vested interest in a bad year for farmers in assuming a somewhat greater tax burden.[27] The 1901 grasshopper plague, in other words, so upset the agricultural sector of the economy that special aid had to be appropriated from another sector.

Rabbits, ground squirrels, gophers, and the alien English sparrow joined the grasshoppers in plundering Sanpete County. Early in the twentieth century, rabbit drives became popular social and sporting events, with teams from one community challenging other communities to try to outdo them in rabbit- slaying proficiency. The losing team agreed to provide dinner for the community effort. All participants were asked to form a long line to drive the rabbits into a large enclosure, where they could be clubbed to death. As many as 5,000 rabbits were killed by that method. During an especially bad month, as many as 20,000 rabbits might be killed.[28]

Neither the ground squirrels nor the sparrows could be driven effectively, so the county commission established bounties at first, then abandoned bounties in favor of free poison distribution. The squirrel bounty, created in 1896, was two cents. The sparrow bounty was one cent, and five cents per dozen for sparrow eggs. In 1899 the rates went up to five cents for squirrels and three cents per sparrow. In 1912 the commissioners ordered free poison distributed to farmers requesting it, and, illustrating the indiscriminate effects of poison, ordered that alfalfa leaves be used as the vehicle rather than grain.

The sparrows, so they claimed, would eat the poisoned alfalfa leaves, but other song and game birds, which had been killed by the poisoned grain, would not.[29]

Carnivorous as well as herbivorous animals benefitted from the settlement of Sanpete County. The livestock, which the settlers grazed on the mountainsides and foothills, proved to be provender for the bears, wolves, coyotes, and mountain lions as the farmers' grain was for the grasshoppers. Consequently, the livestock men began a program of extermination of predatory animals from the very outset of their grazing enterprises.

The original idea came from Brigham Young. Just before Christmas 1850, he wrote to Isaac Morley to instruct him that "you will do well to destroy all the wolves, foxes and bears that you reasonably can, this winter, as we find by experience, that they increase yearly in the neighborhood of this valley, and are a sad nuisance to us."[30] Their yearly increase, of course, was a direct result of the presence of the settlers' livestock, which upset the ecological balance by providing predators with a plentiful source of relatively defenseless prey. Brigham's orders soon became policy. In 1855 the county court offered a bounty on wolf pelts of fifty cents or one dollar, according to size. The response was enthusiastic. In 1857 the county paid twenty-one dollars in wolf bounties. By 1860 it paid forty-eight dollars.[31]

Coyotes were slaughtered in even greater numbers. During the winter months, when farmers had little else to do and the coyote threat to livestock was greatest, coyotes became special targets for extermination efforts. Upwards of one hundred coyotes per month was not an uncommon toll, and the figures reached as high as 192 in March 1898, and 174 in December 1914. There were bounties on the rare predators as well: bears, mountain lions, and wildcats.

Beyond the issues of land, water, insects, and wild predators, Sanpete settlers faced other challenges, including the influx of a large Scandinavian population and relations with the valley's native inhabitants.

ENDNOTES

1. Andrew Jenson, "History of Sanpete Stake," Manuscript in L.D.S. Historian's Office, Salt Lake City.

2. For an account of the Pratt expedition see Donna T. Smart, "Over the Rim to the Red Rock Country: The Parley P. Pratt Exploring Company of 1849," *Utah Historical Quarterly* 62 (Spring 1994).

3. Belinda Cox Sidwell, "Reminiscences of Early Days in Manti," *Manti Sentinel,* published serially beginning 1 August 1889, copy in Western Americana, University of Utah, Salt Lake City.

4. Eugene Campbell, *Establishing Zion: The Mormon Church in the American West, 1847- 1869* (Salt Lake City: Signature Books, 1988), 66.

5. "Inventory of the County Archives of Utah, No. 20, Sanpete County (Manti)," Utah Historical Records Survey, Division of Community Service Programs, Work Projects Administration, Salt Lake City, 1941, 4–5.

6. Sidwell, "Early Days in Manti."

7. For brief histories of all the communities in Sanpete County see chapter 15.

8. "Autobiography of James Van Nostrand Williams," Utah State Historical Society Archives.

9. Ibid.

10. "History of Martin Madsen," 4 November 1948, Utah State Historical Society Archives.

11. Mormon settlement practice are studied in many works including Richard H. Jackson ed., *The Mormon Role in the Settlement of the West,* (Provo, UT: Brigham Young University Press, 1978); G. Lowry Nelson, *The Mormon Village,* (Salt Lake City: University of Utah Press, 1952); Milton R. Hunter, *Brigham Young the Colonizer,* (Salt Lake City: Deseret News Press, 1940); Nels Anderson, *Deseret Saints: The Mormon Frontier in Utah,* (Chicago: University of Chicago Press, 1942); and Leonard J. Arrington, *Great Basin Kingdom: Economic History of the Latter-Day Saints of Utah, 1847–69,* (Boston: Harvard University Press, 1958).

12. Philip S, Robinson, *Sinners and Saints,* (Boston: Roberts Brothers, 1883), 146.

13. James R. Clark, comp., *Messages of the First Presidency,* 5 vols. (Salt Lake City: Bookcraft, 1965) 2:350–51.

14. N.P. Peterson, *Pioneer Sketches,* 1864, 15.

15. John S. H. Smith, interview with Reese Thomson, 15. The classic account of Mormon settlement, with particular focus on Ephraim, is Lowry Nelson, *The Mormon Village* (Salt Lake City: University of Utah Press, 1952), but more research needs to be done on this topic in Sanpete Valley in light of Wayne Wahlquist's suspicions of the uniformity Nelson portrays. See Wayne L. Wahlquist, "A Review of Mormon Settlement Literature," *Utah Historical Quarterly* 45 (Winter 1977): 4–21.

16. Fairview Ward Minutes, 1 April 1860.

17. Ibid.

18. John K. Olsen, Ephraim, Interview by Ken C. Hansen, 19 December 1977.

19. Peter O. Hansen, "Reminiscences, 141–43.

20. Mount Pleaant ward minutes, 20 September 1862.

21. Oluf C. Larsen, "Autobiography," 37, 49.

22. Ibid., 51

23. Ibid., Journal History of the Church, 14 July 1869.

24. Journal History of the Church, 14 July 1869, 23 June 1870.

25. Albert Smith Autobiography, 63; Journal History of the Church, 23 June 1870.

26. Oluf C. Larsen "Autobiography," 51; Journal History of the Church, 18 July 1869, 19 June 1880; Ernest Munk Pioneer Personal History, 1–2; Niels P. Peterson Pioneer Sketches, 19; J. Hatten Carpenter Diary, 3 May 1901; *Gunnison Valley News,* 7 February 1924.

27. Sanpete County Commissioners' Minutes, Book E 29–30 (20 July 1901).

28. Ken C. Hansen, interview with Barney Hyde, 27 March 1978; *Mt. Pleasant Pyramid,* 10 January 1913, and 7 February 1913; J Hatten Carpenter Diary, 8 February 1913.

29. Sanpete County Commissioners' Minutes, Book C,288 (10 July 1896), 454 (8 February 1899); Book F, 7–8 February 1916, 6–7 May 1912. The Sanpete County *Bounty Record* shows that the bounty laws were at times very effective. Although the number and species taken varied drastically by seasons, as many as 7,684 sparrows were killed in one month (March 1898) and as many as 8,147 ground squirrels (June 1918).

30. Journal History of the Church, 23 December 1850.

31. Sanpete County Court Minutes, Book A, 27 (5 March 1855); 45 (4 March 1858); 71 (3 June 1861).

CHAPTER 3

THE SCANDINAVIAN
HERITAGE

When Mormon apostle Erastus Snow and his companions checked into a cheap hotel in Copenhagen on 14 June 1850, they had little inkling of the success they were eventually to enjoy, for the fact that they were able to offer both economic opportunity through emigration to America and the possibility that any man of good character could become a priest was to make the Scandinavian mission, particularly in Jutland, one of the most productive fields in the history of the Mormon church.[1] During the following half century, 45,524 Scandinavians converted to Mormonism, and over 30,000 of them emigrated to the United States. Mormondom's total gain was somewhat less than those figures, for 13,417 fell away from the church for one reason or another and were excommunicated, but even with those losses, some 68 percent of emigrants remained faithful and joined their brethren and sisters in Utah. The province of Jutland, where the lot of the Danish peasant was most lacking in present happiness and hope of improvement, yielded no fewer than 53 percent of all Danish converts and 27 percent of all converts from Scandinavia.[2]

The relative success of the Mormon missionaries in Denmark, in comparison with the other Scandinavian countries, largely resulted from the favorable reception given them at first by officials in the Danish capital. Though that welcome later dimmed somewhat under prodding by United States consular officials and the Lutheran church, the missionaries always had a relatively free hand in Denmark, and the immense appeal of their message worked upon the Danes with powerful results. The social and cultural conditions that accounted for the Mormon success in Denmark were endemic to the whole of Scandinavia, but the other Scandinavian states outlawed and actively persecuted the missionaries and drastically reduced their harvest of converts. Fifty-seven percent of Mormon converts from Scandinavia who emigrated to the United States were Danes, while only 32 percent were from Sweden, 10 percent were from Norway, and less than 1 percent was from Iceland.[3]

Nineteenth-century America may have been the land of opportunity for Europe's impoverished classes, but only if they could stand the cost of emigration and cope with the linguistic and cultural shock of a new land. The great advantage of the Mormon call to Zion was that it was, in William Mulder's phrase, "a shepherded migration"; although many of the wealthier converts made their way to Utah individually, a great many more, particularly the poor, came in companies, often under the leadership of a returning missionary. Careful organization made great economies possible. For the ocean passage, the Mormon church would charter entire ships like the *Amazon*, which Charles Dickens visited while it was docked in the Thames in 1863.[4] The overland journey to Utah could be financed through loans from the Perpetual Emigrating Fund, a revolving fund created by the LDS church and supposedly sustained by repayments from grateful recipients. Though many defaulted on their loans, the PEF did accomplish its purpose of providing cheap transportation. Emigration in tightly organized companies also helped cushion the Mormon converts against the harmful effects of sudden immersion in an alien culture. The converts began English classes even before leaving their home countries, but unlike those who came alone and immediately had to arrange for transportation, housing and jobs, the Mormon emigrants had the opportunity to develop facility in

This house was built in Manti in the 1850s by Danish immigrant Christian Ipsen Munk. (Courtesy Ruth D. Scow)

English more slowly. In fact, the leaders of the emigrant parties actively discouraged contacts between their people and non-Mormons, even to the point of developing their own trail across the plains on the opposite side of the Platte River from the main overland emigration.[5]

The principal task that all Scandinavian converts faced was outlined by the church in a general epistle from the First Presidency, which stated, "All Saints of foreign birth who come here . . . should learn to speak English as soon as possible, and adopt the manners and customs of the American people."[6]

Although the first Danish converts may have arrived in Sanpete County as early as the fall of 1852, the main influx of Danes began with the company led by the Swede John Erik Forsgren, which arrived in Salt Lake City on 30 September 1853. Some of the 199 adults and 95 children followed Forsgren to Box Elder County, but most of the company settled that fall in Manti, Spring Town, and Ephraim. The arrival of the Forsgren company was an event of the highest significance in the history of Utah and especially Sanpete County. William Mulder calls the *Forest Monarch*, the ship in which the Forsgren company crossed the Atlantic, "the *Mayflower* of the Mormon migration from Scandinavia," and adds that "the Forsgren company left a golden track in Utah history" both in terms of propaganda value for the Scandinavian mission and in determining the settlement pattern for subsequent Scandinavian emigrants.[7]

Although important concentrations of Scandinavians developed in Brigham City, Salt Lake City, and Cache Valley, nowhere in Utah did the Scandinavians concentrate more significantly than in Sanpete and Sevier counties. By 1870 the Scandinavians comprised approximately 94 percent of the population of Ephraim and 80 percent of the population of the county as a whole.[8] The national origin of the Sanpete County Scandinavians accurately reflected the uneven success of the Scandinavian mission: in 1890 Sanpete County had 2,101 Danes, 587 Swedes, and 209 Norwegians.[9]

The "shepherded migration" may have eased cultural transitions, but life for the newly arrived Sanpete County Danes was still hard. Though the soil of Jutland was poor, it had been cultivated for centuries and there was plenty of rainfall to water it. The land taken up by the Danes in Sanpete County had never felt a plough and was covered with deep-rooted desert vegetation. Water was at a premium, and elaborate irrigation schemes were required. Finally, there was the constant Indian menace, for the first large influx of Danes arrived in the midst of the Walker War. Peter Madsen of Ephraim described his new life vividly:

> Now I was cometh in a new School. Here was many thing to learn, now to be a foreigner in a new land, every thing was different from the land I came from, here we have to cut the brush of first, and then try to plowe with Oxen, and a simple plough to, and prepare for to watered the grain, and make water ditches from the Creek, there was so much to do I had to work hard all the time, and then I had to stand guard sometime to watch for the Indians, we had plenty grass for our Stock, I had 2 yoke of Oxen and 1 Cow, we could get all the hay we want, but we had to cut it by armpower.[10]

The Scandinavian response to the challenge and opportunity presented by Sanpete County did not go unnoticed or unpraised by their non-Scandinavian brethren. An assessment made by an English pioneer, reminiscing at the close of the settlement period, lauded their efforts:

> I have seen many Scandinavian families come into Manti in pio-
> neer days with no means of support. Most of them had small
> trunks that contained all their earthly wealth, a few clothes and
> some bedding. Some walked from Salt Lake City to Sanpete
> County. Former countrymen would take them into their homes
> for a few weeks. Then the new immigrant would acquire a lot,
> build himself a small adobe home, surround it with a willow
> woven fence. Soon a few acres of ground were added to his accu-
> mulations, every foot of which was utilized. Mother and father and
> every child in the Scandinavian home worked. None of the wheat
> they raised was wasted and after it was thrashed with the flail, the
> Scandinavians cleaned their wheat with hand-turned mills. They
> chopped their animal feed with a hand chopper so that it would go
> farther, and provide better animal food. There was no waste. I am
> an Englishman, but I have always said that the Scandinavian was
> thrifty, honest and God fearing, and set us a worthy example.[11]

Cultural adjustment had an occasional tragic note as well. The Ole Sitterud family was among the early settlers of Fountain Green, and as the only Norwegians in that community, they had great diffi-culty in communicating with their neighbors. When a baby of theirs died in 1878, Sitterud could enlist no help in arranging a proper bur-ial, so he made the casket and buried the infant himself. The orphaned brothers and sister of Annie Catherine Olsen were so poor when they arrived in Utah that they had to split up in order to sur-vive. Annie herself moved in with a family who had a crippled son from whom she learned to speak English, but the loneliness, as she later recalled, was an ordeal:

> Just imagine, if you can, a child of 14 years of age losing my
> mother, my father, brothers and sister going away, where I did not
> know, or if I would ever see them again, being left with perfect
> strangers who couldn't speak a word of Danish, [nor] was I able to
> speak an English word. I used to go out and hide and cry till my
> heart would almost break. As soon as they would miss me they
> would come and hunt me up. The cripple boy would teach me

The Spring City Danish LDS Church. (Sanpete County)

what to call different things and it wasn't long until I could talk enough to make them understand what I meant.[12]

Dress, diet, physical appearance, poverty, folkways and other cultural attributes of the Scandinavian Mormons were significant barriers to the cultural assimilation encouraged, indeed demanded, by the Mormon church, but the greatest obstacle was learning a new language. They were, to be sure, several other motives and aids available to the converts. The English classes and emigration *en masse* helped delay and ease the necessity of coping with a largely alien culture. Of equal importance, perhaps, was the realization that the revelations claimed by the prophet of their newly espoused religion were all recorded in English.

Nevertheless, the problem was immense. For the Danes in Sanpete County, the presence of large numbers of Indians complicated the language problem even further, as Christian Nielsen of Manti explained in a letter to a relative back home:

We have to learn the English language now, which is a bit difficult for the elders; the children learn it quickly. Most of the Danish children and young folk talk fairly good English and Indian,

The Peter Monson House was constructed in Spring City between 1871 and 1883. (Utah State Historical Society)

> because we come into conversation with them more often than we
> have opportunity to talk with Americans. We can begin to talk a
> little in both tongues; our children constantly talk English or
> Indian.[13]

Nielsen's letter hints that the exigencies of frontier settlement may
have left the earliest parties of Danish immigrants up to their own
devices linguistically. Systematic study of English seems not to have
begun among the Danes of Sanpete County until 1857, when Peter
O. Hansen established special schools for that purpose in both
Ephraim and Manti.[14]

In contrast to the Lutheran Scandinavians who settled in large
numbers in the Mississippi Valley, the Mormon Scandinavians
adopted Anglo-American culture rapidly. While the Lutheran church
acted as a conservative force, keeping the old languages and folkways
alive, the Mormon church pressed its adherents to abandon the old
ways and conform to the mainstream of Utah cultural life as rapidly
as possible. Realizing, though, that a complete and immediate break

with the past was impossible, the Mormon church allowed special Scandinavian church services and social gatherings as temporary expedients until acculturation was complete. Special Scandinavian meetings were a prominent feature of Sanpete County life from the very beginning of the Scandinavian influx. Hans Dinesen, who arrived in Manti in 1853, reported meeting that winter with Erastus Snow, who "had instructions from Prest. Young to 'organize the Scandinavian meetings,' and he said 'this should last as long as the Scandinavian emigration should continue.'"[15] They lasted, in fact, much longer than that; as late as the 1920s there were enough first-generation Scandinavian immigrants in Sanpete County to justify church services and occasional social gatherings in the native tongues.[16] The custom on Sundays was to hold English services in the morning and Danish services in the afternoon. The Danish services were extremely popular, and even sometimes attracted visitors like Azariah Smith and J. Hatten Carpenter, who spoke only English, though Carpenter attended infrequently and admitted that lack of comprehension made the services "not very interesting to us."[17]

Carpenter was a close observer and faithful recorder of Manti social life, and his diary affords a unique opportunity to view the gradual decline of Scandinavian gatherings during the twentieth century. In July 1904, for example, he recorded a huge influx of Scandinavians (not, apparently, all from Sanpete County) for a reunion held in the "very crowded" Manti Tabernacle. Unfortunately, the affair was very poorly organized and many of the visitors were displeased:

> People disgusted with the way Scandinavian Reunion turned out. Cut off short last night & people coming in from N&S to attend walking the streets & none to look after them[.] Showing bad management. They had some sort of a meeting in Peacock's orchard in aft[ernoon] but a faint attempt. Much indignation felt. It is too bad after some 2000 people coming down to have a good time.[18]

By 1914 such affairs were mainly entertainment for the elderly, though a dance held that year showed better organization than the 1904 event: "A violinist who had been in this country only a couple of years, was secured from Centerfield. He played music familiar to the Scandinavians and they certainly enjoyed the dance as strongly as if they were in the Fatherland."[19] Another decade, though, saw a great loss of vitality in the Scandinavian culture of Sanpete County, evidently a result of the rapid disappearance of the original generation of immigrants for whom their Old World culture was a factor of some importance. The *Manti Messenger* reported that year that the Scandinavian organization in Manti had fallen apart, and though it notes that a reorganization session had been scheduled, it was apparent that little interest remained.[20]

In the process of cultural assimilation, the Scandinavian Mormons shed some of their folkways more readily than others. One that was particularly hard to abandon was their love of coffee. Over their cups, Utah Danes had a gentle rejoinder to those unfortunate orthodox who sniffed unappreciative noses: "Brother Joseph never meant that Word of Wisdom for the Danes!"[21]

Although the Mormon church never officially condoned such violations, it enforced the Word of Wisdom less stringently among the Danes than elsewhere, evidently regarding minor infractions as a small price to pay for their otherwise faithful participation. "I remember that having a coffee pot on the stove was not a particularly serious matter," says Halbert S. Greaves, "even in families where the father might be in the bishopric."[22]

One would expect that the common religious enthusiasm of the Mormon pioneers would help mitigate the social frictions that grow naturally out of contacts between large groups with vastly different ethnic backgrounds. Instances of such brotherly cooperation are common, perhaps even typical, in Sanpete County history, but that history is not, on the other hand, a story of uninterrupted tranquility. As early as 1855, the Manti Ward minutes suggest social friction: in the afternoon meeting on 15 April, "Titus Billings spoke on the necessity for interpreting important items to the Danish," indicating that the Danes had been left out of important decisions. Later in the year, "Bishop Snow spoke as Bishop of the Stake and against nationality one good man was as good as another no matter where he came from." At the meeting organizing the Fairview Ward in 1860, Mormon apostle Orson Hyde said that "he had been informed of young men in our midst there did not do right, that they had insulted some of the danish brethren at Thistle Valley said he wanted them to come forward, and make an acknowledgment, or he should ask for a vote of disfellowship."[23]

One of the most serious outbursts of ethnic antagonism occurred, ironically, at Christmas in 1875. J. C. A. Weibye's journal records the affair in some detail:

> Sunday 26th we had no Circle prayer on account of we 6 Danish brethren did not feel to dress, on account of some partiality and Nationality shown to us Danish; in the evening we invited Bishop J. B. Maiben to meet with Brother Hans Jensen, Jens Hansen and me in Bro. Hans Jensen's house and we had a long talk with him, and he promised to hear us out and to do right to our Country People as well as English and Americans (he is from London, England) good feelings prevailed in our conversation, it was old friendly.[24]

Although there are many more reports of discrimination and ethnic antagonism directed against the Scandinavians as a group, it is important to remember that the Scandinavians consisted of three distinct national groups, and that they brought with them ancient prejudices against one another. Christian Jensen reports a folk legend at Mount Pleasant that claims that the Danes always have the prettiest wives, while the Swedes have the homeliest ones. The reason for the uneven distribution of beauty is that the Swedes are much harder workers, while the Danes, who are always loafing, have more of an opportunity to court the best girls. Another popular story has it that a Swede, engaged in a furious argument with a Dane, exclaimed, "What could be dirtier than a dirty Dane?" to which the Dane replied, "A clean Swede."[25]

There is fairly clear evidence that ethnic antagonism went considerably deeper than occasional outbursts. Reminiscences from several Sanpete County towns indicate that Scandinavians tended to settle together in clearly identifiable districts of town. In Mount Pleasant, for example, the Second Ward district in the southwest quarter of town is alleged to have had a much higher percentage of Danes than elsewhere, and was known locally as the "Copenhagen" district. The district was so clearly identifiable, according to Eli A. Day, that gangs of boys from each district would often engage in fights reminiscent of the ethnic gang wars among big city neighborhoods.[26]

The lines of demarcation between the Danish North Ward and the non-Danish South Ward in Spring City were equally clear. Danish segregation became severe enough that the Danes built their own chapel and held Mormon services in it well into the twentieth century. Segregation in education and social activities seems to have existed too, though perhaps in a less severe form. For example, the treatment a schoolboy could expect to receive from his teacher depended somewhat upon where he lived in relation to the teacher: a teacher from the other ward would probably be much less cordial than one from the student's own ward. One resident recalls that a dance pavilion erected in the Danish ward was attended by others, but was regarded as mainly a Danish rendezvous.[27]

The phenomenon of demographic concentration of Scandinavians is difficult to explain, for a number of plausible hypotheses are available, but interpretive principles for choosing among them are elusive. One might easily conjecture that the need for cultural support in a largely alien environment led the Scandinavians to settle near one another. One of the Spring City residents interviewed by Cindy Rice thought that such cultural factors were important:

> Their customs were somewhat different than the rest of the community. In fact, due to their customs and traditions, they were inclined to become clannish, possibly because of a language barrier, dress, and so forth. . . .
>
> With regard to the manner of dress, the only difference I know of between the Scandinavian and the English were that the Scandinavians wore clothes made of Linsey, a hand-woven material, wooden shoes or wooden bottom shoes, stockings were hand-knit, knee-length for all.[28]

The relatively late arrival of the Scandinavian settlers in most communities may have influenced their settlement pattern as well. After the original settlers had surveyed the town site and fields and distributed town lots and farms, latecomers had to settle wherever they could find room, which probably meant outside the non-Scandinavian nucleus of settlement. Finally, there are various cynical explanations which hold that such demographic concentrations were a result of deliberate discrimination by wealthy, non-Scandinavian church leaders. None of these hypotheses is mutually exclusive, and one might reasonably expect, given the observable complexity in most other human relations even on frontiers, that all contain elements of validity.

Although the Scandinavian settlers made a wide variety of distinctive cultural contributions to life in Sanpete County, by far the most famous is their tradition of humor. The humor seems to be almost exclusively the contribution of the Danes, and at its lowest level it consists of the elaborate network of nicknames devised to cope with the relatively small fund of names employed by the Scandinavians. In order to distinguish one Jens Jensen from several others who might live in the same town, each became known by a nickname identifying him by profession, prominent physical attribute, or perhaps a colorful incident in his past. "Panter" Hansen, Jacob "Jake-butcher" Jensen, and "Grin Billy" are typical examples of nicknames with obvious origins, but others, like "Brazilian Blacksmith" Jensen, "Scottie Water-eye" Christensen, and "Absolutely" Mortensen, are more obscure.[29]

Often these names supplanted a given name so completely that it would come as a surprise to be called anything else. A stranger, stopping at the Wise Bench on Ephraim's Main Street, inquired after a Jacob Jensen. No one could help him, but the stranger persisted; "I have his address. He lives in the South Ward, four blocks east of Main Street. Are you sure you don't know Jacob Jensen?" Jake-butcher, one of the old-timers idling on the Wise Bench, suddenly straightened up, scratched his head, and said, "Hell, that's me."

Most students of the Danish nicknames seem content to explain them as merely a common-sense response to the proliferation of identical names. But one cannot thereby account for the lack of such nicknames in Denmark, nor for a similar lack of them in other Sanpete County towns than Ephraim. Perhaps a certain amount of cultural disorientation occurred in the metamorphosis of the Ephraimites from Danes to Americans, but the lack of similar mani-

festations of disorientation elsewhere leads one to dismiss the phenomenon of nicknames as a peculiar local amusement.

The humorous anecdotes told by the Ephraim Danes are as prolific as the nicknames. All of them reveal a tradition of low peasant
humor that is far older than their American experience. Some of
them, furthermore, can tell the folklorist and social historian something about their social attitudes. Most of them show in various ways
a democratic skepticism regarding authority, which in Ephraim is
primarily LDS church authority.

One story concerns a church leader who was not immune to economic temptation. It is especially interesting because it is not simply
the story of exposure of corruption, it reveals a shrewd pragmatism
which the folk culture believes should temper all morality:

> "Brother Olsen, they say you are a high priest." "I am a high coun-
> cil." "I notice when you sack wool, you put the very best fleece in
> the top of the sack where the wool-buyer will see it. Do you think
> that is honorable?" "They know after dealing with the rest of you
> that if I ain't got a good fleece there, I ain't got one at all."[30]

Another story, which a Mormon bishop tells on himself, shows
that church leaders, in the tradition of their church, were first among
equals in their congregations and did not always yield to the temptation to take themselves too seriously:

> One time I had been in the hotel telling stories to the Lion's Club.
> I met Sister Swenson. She says, "Brother Peterson, have you been
> in there?" I sayed "Yes, Sister Swenson." She said, "Are you a Lion,
> Bishop?" I said, "There ain't any other kind."[31]

Finally, there is a genre of anecdotes about a Dane who gets away
with saying something profane or obscene in church. Sometimes he
escapes reprimand by presenting his expression as a malapropism
associated with his lack of fluency in the English language. At other
times, as in the anecdote quoted below, he simply makes a frontal
assault on the pretensions of the church leaders:

> Jens Jenson was a good fellow, you know, and they all liked
> him as an honest fellow, but his only fault was that he swore so
> much. The bishop came to him and said, "Jens, you should come

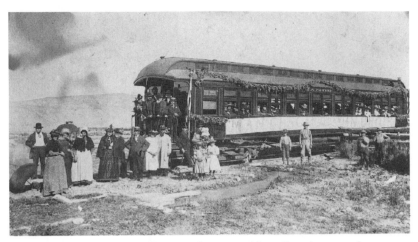

The Manti Scandinavian Choir ready to travel by railroad to a performance. (Utah State Historical Society)

to church. Come up to church." And Jens finally came up. It happened to be testimony meeting and all of his old friends were popping up giving their testimony, and Jens finally got nerve enough.

He stood up, got started and said, "Oh good hell. I can't do it." And he sat down; so right after church the bishop came up and pats him on the shoulder. "You are doing all right, Jens. Now the only thing the matter with you is you swear a little too much. Especially you should not swear in church." "Well," he says, "Bishop, you do a hell of a lot of preaching and I do a hell of a lot of swearing, but neither one of us means a damn thing by it."[32]

Stories with a church setting are particularly numerous. A Danish musician, appearing on the program at a church social with his singer wife, just could not match his music to his wife's singing. "Eloise, I have played on both the black and white keys, and by gosh, you are singing right in the cracks."

The tale is told of an Ephraim testimony meeting in which one sister exploded before the congregation, "There is Brodder Yensen. He takes my water turn. He turns his cows into my pasture. He swipes my milk can. And there he is singing in the choir."

Another testimony called forth this doleful picture of the last days. "In the last days, ven the moon iss turned into blood—." The speaker paused and then pointed questioningly at his cowed listeners, "Vare vill you be? I tell vare I vill be!" After another pause he concluded triumphantly, "I vill be vit the ten virgins!"[33]

Residents of Sanpete County rightly regard their Danish cultural traditions as a precious local heritage. Cultural resources of that kind provide a color and a diversity too often lacking in rural American society. Without impugning the loyalty of the Danish Mormons to either their adopted church or their adopted country, the remarkable persistence of their ancient folkways reminds us that they were Danes long before they were Mormons or Americans, and the Old World perspectives they retained continue to enrich the cultural life of Sanpete County.

ENDNOTES

1. The basic work on the Mormon Scandinavian experience is William Mulder, *Homeward to Zion: The Mormon Migration from Scandinavia* (Minneapolis: University of Minnesota Press, 1957).

2. Ibid. Chapter 5, "Ugly Ducklings," describes the social composition of the Mormon converts from Denmark; see especially 102–104.

3. William Mulder, "Mormons From Scandinavia, 1850–1900: A Shepherded Migration," *Pacific Historical Review* 23 (1954): 227; George M. Stephenson, "The Background of the Beginnings of Swedish Immigration, 1850–1875," *American Historical Review* 31 (July 1925): 708–23. Helge Seljaas, "Norwegians in 'Zion' Teach Themselves English," *Norwegian-American Studies* 26 (1974): 220–28. Seljaas cites figures that illustrate the severe attenuation of Mormon proselytizing caused by the opposition of the Norwegian government. Nearly a million Norwegians emigrated to America during the nineteenth century, which shows that the lure of opportunity was powerful there, but only about 4,500 of them were converted to Mormonism.

4. See William Mulder and A. Russell Mortensen, eds., *Among the Mormons: Historic Accounts By Contemporary Observers* (New York: Alfred A. Knopf, 1958; paperback reprint ed., Lincoln: University of Nebraska Press, 1973), 334–44.

5. See the map in Wallace Stegner, *The Gathering of Zion: The Story of the Mormon Trail* (New York: McGraw-Hill, 1964), frontispiece.

6. Quoted in Mulder, *Homeward to Zion*, 252.

7. William Mulder, "Scandinavian Sage," in Helen Z. Papanikolas, ed., *The Peoples of Utah* (Salt Lake City: Utah State Historical Society, 1976), 167–70.

8. U.S. Census, 1870, Volume I, Population.

9. Ibid., 1890. Seljaas, "Norwegians in 'Zion,'" 220–21 accounts for the relative scarcity of Norwegians in rural Utah communities by pointing out that most of the Norwegian Mormons were city-dwellers with little interest or ability in farming.

10. Peter Madsen Autobiography, 25; J. H. Hougaard Autobiography, 28–29.

11. Daughters of Utah Pioneers, *Scandinavia's Contribution to Utah* (Salt Lake City, 1939), 25–26.

12. Ole Sitterud Biography, 3; Annie Catherine Olsen Autobiography, 5.

13. Quoted in William Mulder, "Mother Tongue, 'Skandinavieme' and 'The Swedish Insurrection' in Utah," *Swedish Pioneer Historical Quarterly* 7 (January 1956): 4.

14. Peter O. Hansen Reminiscences, 135–36.

15. "Hans Dinesen's Narrative," 13, Manti Ward Manuscript History.

16. John S. H. Smith, interview with Christian Jensen, 9 December 1971, 19.

17. Martin P. Kuhre Diary, 48, 51; Azariah Smith Diary, *passim;* J. Hatten Carpenter Diary, 12 June 1921.

18. J. Hatten Carpenter Diary, 17, 18, and 19 July 1904.

19. Ibid., 16 January 1914.

20. *Manti Messenger,* 8 August 1924.

21. Virginia Sorensen, *Where Nothing Is Long Ago: Memories of a Mormon Childhood* (New York: Harcourt, Brace & World, 1963), 162.

22. John S. H. Smith, Interview with Halbert S. Greaves, 13 January 1972, 8–9. Virginia Sorensen also deals effectively with this theme in her novel, *On This Star* (New York: Reynal & Hitchcock, 1946), where the Jensen brothers, who are narrowly orthodox Mormons otherwise, regard coffee as an essential accompaniment to their yearly deer hunt.

23. Manti Ward Minutes, 15 April, 16 September 1855; Fairview Ward Minutes, 25 June 1860.

24. J.C.A. Welbye Journal, 26 December 1875.

25. John S. H. Smith, interview with Christian Jensen, 19–20; *Gunnison Valley News,* 3 March 1949.

26. Hilda Madsen Longsdorf, *Mountain Pleasant* (Mount Pleasant, Utah: Mount Pleasant Historical Society, 1939) 157; Eli A. Day Reminiscences, 35; see also Alonzo Morley's allegation of official discrimination against the Scandinavians at Moroni, *Community psychology of Moroni, Utah* (n.p.: n.p., 1924), 10–11.

27. Cynthia Rice, "A Geographic Appraisal of the Acculturation Process of Scandinavians in the Sanpete Valley, Utah, 1850–1900," (M.A. thesis, University of Utah, 1973), 262–63, 267–68; Rice, Interview with George Crisp, 23 April 1974, 12; Interview with Floyd and Lavee Draper, 23 April 1974, 11, 13.

28. Cindy Rice, Interview with Henry S. and Rose R. Schofield, 11 April 1974, 4–5.

29. Bruce Jennings, "An Essay in Nicknames"' Hector Lee, Bruce Jennings, Royal Madsen, and P.C. Petersen, "Nicknames of the Ephraimites"; Lucille Johnson Butyler, "Ephraim's Humor" (M.A. thesis, University of Utah, 1950.

30. Butler, "Ephraim's Humor," 78.

31. Ibid., 88. Presentation of this story has been slightly abridged.

32. Ibid., 127.

33. This and other Sanpete Scandinavian stories are taken from Lucille J. Butler, "Ephraim's Humor." Slight changes in presentation have been made.

CHAPTER 4

INDIAN RELATIONS

Mormons were not the first white people to encounter the Indians of Sanpete Valley. The Spanish Franciscans, Dominguez and Escalante, and the American-Flemish Jesuit, Pierre De Smet, had earlier described in their journals and letters Indians that probably included the groups established in Sanpete Valley.

On 30 September 1776, Escalante recorded a meeting, in present-day Juab County, with a party of twenty Indians identified by Utah Indian authority William R. Palmer as "Sanpitch" Indians from Sanpete and Sevier valleys:

> Very early there came to the camp twenty Indians. . . . all wrapped in blankets made of rabbit and hare skins. They conversed with us very pleasantly until nine o'clock in the morning. . . . These had a much shorter beard than the Lagunas, and their noses were pierced; through the hole in the nose was carried a small polished bone of the deer, hen or other animal. In features they resembled the Spaniards more than all the other Indians now known in America. . . . They use the language of the Timpanogotzis.[1]

While Escalante portrayed the Sanpitch Indians sympathetically, with their fur robes and bones in their noses, sixty-five years later, in 1841, De Smet recorded a less attractive portrait, which agreed with descriptions by Mormons in the next decade:

> There is not, perhaps, in the whole world, a people in deeper state of wretchedness and corruption; the French commonly designated them "the people deserving of pity," and this appellation is most appropriate. Their lands are uncultivated heaths; their habitations are holes in the rocks, or the natural crevices of the ground, and their only arms, arrows and sharp-pointed sticks. Two, three, or at the most four of them may be seen in company, roving over their sterile plains in quest of ants and grasshoppers, on which they feed. When some insipid root, or a few nauseous seeds, they made, as they imagine, a delicious repast. They are so timid, that it is difficult to get near them; the appearance of a stranger alarms them. Every one, thereupon, hides himself in a hole; and in an instant this miserable people disappear and vanish like a shadow. Sometimes, however, they venture out of their hiding places, and offer their newly born infants to the whites in exchange for some trifling articles.[2]

De Smet hoped to return to work with the Utes but that did not happen and the task of evangelizing and bringing the white culture to the Indians of Sanpete Valley fell to the Mormons.

Sanpete Valley and its surrounding mountains harbored several bands of Indians during the summer months, all of Ute stock led by chief with names like Wakara (Anglicized to Walker), Arapeen (or Arropine), and Sanpitch. Each of these brothers had his own followers, his own habits and skills, and his own yearly itinerary. Walker, for example, the most powerful of the Utes, led his mounted band of warriors on horse-stealing and slave-trading excursions throughout the entire Great Basin and into California, while the more peaceful and sedentary people of Arapeen developed techniques for jerking meat, tanning hides, and cultivating the soil.[3]

Of Great Basin ethnic stock, all of the Utes had traditionally survived as semi-nomadic food-gatherers and hunters of small game. In small groups, they followed the seasons and growing conditions over a wide territory. Early in the nineteenth century, however, the bands associated with Walker and Arapeen—to which the tribal name "Ute" is applied in Sanpete County—acquired horses and guns, elements of the more war-like buffalo-hunting Plains Indians.[4]

In contrast, the band known as "the Sanpitch" presented as dismal a scene to the Mormons as it had to the Catholic De Smet. Azariah Smith's diary notes that "there are a good many natives camped at this place, in their low-degraded state, with scarcely any clothing, and not much to eat except what they beg around through camp." Albert Smith, his father, added that they "had not guns & not a pony & no clothing nor beding save rabits skins soad together & no houses save what they made out of sage & grease wood brush. There living was on fish wich Sanpete [River] was full of & rabits buries & grass sead."[5] They differed from the Utes, according to contemporary observers, primarily in economic state: "The Saampitches were the veriest slaves to this more power tribe of Utes who treated them very cruelly; but could a Saampitch by fair means or foul, become the happy possessor of a horse, a gun and a blanket, he was admitted as a member of the Ute tribe."[6]

Walker's Utes elicited widely varied responses from the Mormon settlers. At one extreme is the typically Victorian reaction of terror, contempt, and moral outrage exemplified by two of the best local contemporary sources. A hunting scene from the F.W. Cox *Family History* reveals the Indian's techniques:

> We watched the Indians sometimes hunting rabbits on the hill. They would first form a large circle. Then would ride round and round drawing nearer and nearer together until the poor bunnies were completely surrounded. Then they began shooting them with their bows and arrows. . . . They would take them to their "wickieups" where the rabbits were thrown on the fire hide and all. When the meat was done what was left of the hide was stripped off and dinner was ready.[7]

A curious mixture of compassion, outrage and inquisitiveness characterizes Adelia Cox Sidwell's description of the Utes celebrating a victory over the Shoshones in 1850:

> For two weeks they held their feasts and war-dances, in honor of their victory; the prisoners all having their heads closely shaven were easily designated by the settlers who frequently went out to

A brush dwelling used by Ute Indians in the Sanpete Valley. (Courtesy Fairview Museum)

> observe and admire the savage pageantry, which was exhibited by a barbarous refinement of cruelty. . . . These savages compelled the poor captive squaws to sing, dance and bear aloft a pole from which depended the painted scalps of perhaps their nearest male relative; and oft times in excess of grief, the monotony of their song and dances were broken with tears and sobs as they bent beneath their ghastly burden, shouts of derision and mirth met these human weaknesses.[8]

At the other extreme those who lived closer to the Indians, primarily sheep and cattle herders, developed a higher estimation of their character. H. J. Gottfredson, for example, recalled:

> [The Utes] were hospitable if a person came to their camp hungry, and they expected the same from the whites. If they were trusted with anything, they could as a rule be depended upon, and were generally truthful; they dispised a falsifier. There were many small bands of Indians in the country at that time, and we could run onto an Indian camp in many places.[9]

John Lowry, Jr., a famous interpreter during the Indian wars in Sanpete County, corroborates Gottfredson in his appraisal of the

Indian character. His attitude toward the Utes, according to his biographer,

> was clear and uncomplicated. He was anxious to be friendly when friendship was possible and to that end he learned the Ute and Shoshone languages, he made trading trips among the Navajos, he ground Indian grain in his mill, and he provided food to his hungry Indian neighbors. But as much as he believed in peace he was no less persuaded that the settlers could survive and prosper only if they were quick to punish the loss of their cattle and to revenge the death of their friends.[10]

From his arrival in 1849 with the Morley party until the spring of 1865, Lowry exemplified this firm but friendly policy in his Indian associations. Ironically, in 1865 this same John Lowry angrily pulled from his horse the young and most recent Ute chief, known as Jake Arapeen, an act which is commonly believed to have started the Black Hawk War. However, Lowry always denied that such difficulties were ever considered significant enough by the Indians themselves to provoke a general uprising.[11]

The motivations of Chief Walker, who met with Brigham Young in 1849 to offer his summer hunting ground for white settlement, can only be conjectured—a likely reason however was to obtain cattle to feed his people.[12] Feast and famine occurred in seasonal cycles among these wanderers after food. After the extinction of Utah's buffalo herds, Walker had to travel as far as the Great Plains for big game.[13] A permanent settlement of whites, he knew, would surely include herds of cattle, which would feed his people without the need for extensive hunting excursions.

On Brigham Young's part, the appeal of a friendly invitation reinforced his determination to establish Zion in the wilderness at an early date. The further possibility of winning converts among the Indians increased the incentive. Chief Walker himself was baptized in 1850; but even granting the best of intentions the cultural gap proved too great to breach.

Much of the trouble that later arose between the Mormons and the Utes resulted from the Indian's lack of understanding of the white man's sense of individual property and the white man's refusal or inability to accept the Indian culture on its own terms—a conflict repeated countless times throughout the West. Coexistence, with each culture intact, was impossible; compromise seemed unattainable, for the cherished ideals of one culture were the unpardonable sins of the other. Thus the battle was engaged.

Mormons cut off a lucrative source of income for the Utes—the slave trade. For many years the Utes had enslaved tribes they defeated in battle. They then either kept captured children as their own servants or sold them to Mexican slave traders, who periodically passed through the area. As slaves, and as the offspring of contemptible enemies, the children were naturally objects of abuse by the Utes. Outraged by this cycle of enslavement, abuse, and slave trading, the Mormons put an end to it as quickly as possible.

To do so, they broke the cycle at two points. First, they took the abused slave children from the Indians and cared for them in their own homes. "At one time," the *Cox Family History* tells us, "they brought so many youngsters that nearly all the older residents in Manti had an Indian boy or girl. A great many of them grew to manhood and womanhood among our people."[14] Further, they eliminated the market for slaves by excluding the slave traders. After the Mexican Cession of 1848, and especially after Utah's admission to the territorial status in 1850, the Mormons had a legal basis for exclusion of the traders. In April 1853 a band of Mexican slave traders licensed to deal in New Mexico Territory (which included present-day Arizona) appeared in Sanpete Valley to trade with the Utes. The Indians, in Brigham Young's words, "became considerably excited, because the inhabitants would not allow them to trade Indian children for guns and ammunition." The Mormon leader subsequently took "the necessary legal steps to prevent their trading within the bounds of this Territory." Upon arriving in Manti, where the situation was on the verge of violence, he agreed to a compromise: "I found the Indians much bent on trading children to the Mexicans, though they told me that if we would pay them as high a price as the Mexicans offered, and pay in horses, guns and ammunition, they would trade with us."[15] The trade was completed and a conflict with the Utes thus temporarily avoided; but the loss of an important means of livelihood without a ready substitute increased the Utes' dependence upon the settlers.

The winter of 1849–50 witnessed the beginning of this growing dependency, which became increasingly onerous to the settlers. Even along the settlers' route to Sanpete Valley, the Indians "from time to time . . . exacted food or other valuables as a 'ticket' to travel toward their destination."[16] The Utes under Walker were accustomed to hunting in Sanpete Valley during the summer, then wintering farther south in Sevier Valley, where the weather was often less harsh. This year, however, knowing that a train of settlers would soon arrive, they were still in the valley when winter struck.

The winter of 1849–50 in Sanpete Valley was to become legendary for its length and severity, and the settlers, who arrived in late November, were ill-prepared.[17] Fortunately for the Indians, the livestock the settlers brought with them had to be left outside in snowdrifts several feet deep in sub-zero weather. The settlers suffered considerable loss, but the Indians enjoyed a steady supply of frozen beef. It was hardly what Brigham Young meant in his oft-quoted injunction to feed, rather than fight, the Indians, but the advantages to the Indians were the same.

Dependence became a way of life for the Indians, and, from the Mormon point of view, the corollaries to dependence—indolence, greed, theft, and other vices—accompanied what they saw as Indian capriciousness. Brigham Young, in a letter to the commissioner of Indian Affairs, described the cycle of dependence:

> Wherever small settlements are made the Indians gather round them in greater or less numbers, and are constantly importuning for clothing, provisions, arms and ammunition, even when their few articles of exchange are exhausted, which is soon the case, and when their demands, usually exorbitant from contrasting their known poverty and wants with the fancied wealth and comforts of the whites, are not complied with, they indulge angry feelings and often practice stealing horses, cattle, clothing &c, casing much loss of property and requiring great forbearance.

The Indians were victims of poverty, he continued; since "this territory is poorly supplied with fish and game . . . the Indian is raised to a roaming and indolent life, and to consider thieving as an honorable and praiseworthy avocation."[18] Actually, Sanpete Valley was a productive hunting ground for the Utes. Brigham Young and western settlers generally failed to recognize that Indians regarded begging and stealing as neither immoral nor ignoble. As their culture was accustomed merely to taking what the land provided, any available surplus seemed as freely offered as nature's bounty. They viewed the extra effort expended by whites to accumulate food and possessions as merely an eccentric imperative of white culture that worked to the Indians' advantage; thus they violated the settlers' property.

As elsewhere in the West, an Anglo-European group had introduced utterly different priorities for the use of the land and its resources—priorities that were destined to destroy the Indian way of life.[19] Agricultural and pastoral people, the Mormons conceived land use in terms of inalienable ownership of precisely defined parcels and the chattels thereon. Furthermore, rather than utilizing just what nature provided unaided, the settlers altered the normal yield by plowing, planting, redirecting water, and generally changing the face of the earth with which their predecessors, the Utes, had been so familiar. Consequently, as more and more settlers plowed more and more acres, the modifications to the natural condition of the valley, already incompatible with the Indian way of life, became irreversible.

According to H. R. Day, Indian agent for the district that included Sanpete County, the Utes began to sense their doom about a year after the whites arrived. In a letter dated 2 January 1851, he wrote of a growing Indian feeling that the Mormon settlers were encroaching upon their hunting grounds and bringing their way of life to a close:

> The Chiefs said they claimed all the lands upon which were settled the Mormons, and that they were driving them further every year, making use of their soil and what little timber there was and expressed a wish If their Great Father was so powerful, that he would not permit the Mormons to drive them out of the Vallies into the Mountains, where they must starve.[20]

Mormon leaders encouraged treating the Indians according to the Golden Rule as not only the most compassionate policy, but the most diplomatic as well. Azariah Smith reported that "we are taught to be kind to [the Indian], in their low and degraded state. And it is a good thing to learn them Peace by Seting a good example before them."[21]

Realizing that their arrival meant doom for the Indians, the Mormons attempted to prepare the Indians to adapt to white culture. They tried, in the matter of slavery, to compensate the Indians for having the white man's morality forced upon them by purchasing and assuming responsibility for raising children previously destined for a life of slavery. Besides being given adequate food and clothing, such children were to be educated alongside white children, and county selectmen were ordered to make sure that their guardians made good on that commitment.[22]

The ultimate object of feeding, clothing, educating and treating the Indians humanely was to make them over as completely as possible in the image of the white man, including clothes, social standards, cultural values, and agrarian economy.

In pursuit of that end, Mormon church and federal government were perfectly agreed. Isaac Morley, the Mormon leader in Sanpete Valley, told his people "that he hoped eventually to see [the Indians] clothed as we clothe following the same customs and arts that we do."[23] S.K. Gifford, who preached to the Indians during the Mormon Reformation in 1856, regarded it as essential that they should "wash up and learn to work, etc."[24]

Likewise, secular Indian policy urged upon the Indians their rapid adoption of the culture and economy of the white man. Garland Hurt, Indian agent for the district that included Sanpete County, reported to Brigham Young (as superintendent for Indian Affairs in Utah Territory) a conference he held with the Indians at Manti in 1855:

> We made a short speech to them on the importance of learning to farm. We told them that the deer and antelope were getting scarcer every day and the time would soon come when the Indians would be obliged to starve if they did not learn how to work and raise wheat and potatoes and have cattle and sheep to kill when they were hungry. I told them that it was the desire of their Great Father that they should settle on the land and work it as his people did,

and if they would do so, there were a great many things for them to learn that they could not learn if they continued to roam about from place to place as they had done. I dwelt more particularly upon the prospect of having schools among them to teach their children how to read and write as many of them had seen our people do.[25]

Agriculture, stock raising, stationary residence, and education—these were the characteristics basic to the white man's economy and culture that Hurt expected the Indians to embrace. The Mormons concurred. The government's motives in getting the Indians settled and engaged in farming were simple. It wanted dispossession and pacification as quickly and as simply as possible to end the continuing conflicts and to make the continent safe for expansion. The Mormons wanted those things too, but their reasons for wanting them were more complicated than those of the government. They identified the Indians as Lamanites, a people of ancient lineage who, according to the Book of Mormon had once enjoyed a special status with God. The Mormons believed it to be their responsibility in modern times to minister to the Lamanites, settling, clothing, educating, and civilizing that ancient people in order to restore them to their former glory and thus to assume once again their place in God's favor and in His plan for humankind. "We feed and clothe [the Indians]," said James Farmer of Ephraim, "for they will yet be the battle-ax of the Lord, and will fight for the Kingdom of God."[26] Similarly, Isaac Morley admonished the Saints to establish an Indian policy "that will win their favor and that they may see that we intend to do them good and be the instruments in the hands of the Lord in enlightening their minds both for temporal & spiritual good."[27]

Occasional open conflict was nonetheless unavoidable. The Indians eventually saw that they had invited their own destruction when they asked Brigham Young to send settlers to Sanpete Valley. Walker himself, realizing the significance of his invitation, adopted a fierce disposition, hoping to frighten the settlers away. Mrs. Sidwell recalled that he "was in the habit of reminding the settlers in forcible language of what he was capable of doing, and judging from subsequent events, the temptation was doubtless frequently very strong upon him, to make a 'breakfast spell,' of the white population."[28]

During the Mormons' first winter in Manti, perhaps as many as 700 Indians were encamped at the base of the semi-circular ring of foothills extending to the east and south of Temple Hill, surrounding and outnumbering the white settlers so that the latter felt like "a mouse in a lion's paw."[29]

The Indians' greater numbers and Walker's variable personality may have encouraged his belligerence; but other Indians were equally harsh in their denunciations of the whites and in their demands for fair treatment. "I am neither a dog [nor] a bull," said Walker's successor, Arapeen, when told that he must live on the Sanpete Reservation. "I come to this earth like any other man and I will go where I please." On another occasion Arapeen accused the Mormons of killing his brother; in a fiery speech in the Mormon church at Manti, to punctuate his message, "he struck the stand twice with his tomahawk."[30]

Although only a few years between 1850 and 1870 were completely free of clashes between whites and Indians in Sanpete County, on two occasions the murders, ambushes, and skirmishes reached sufficient frequency and generality to be called "war." The first, known as "Walker's War," lasted from July 1853 to May 1854, though serious hostilities ended earlier.

Walker's War was both started and settled outside of Sanpete County, and brought more inconvenience to the Sanpete settlers than bloodshed.[31] From the standpoint of the Mormons, the Utes were not especially formidable opponents in any conventional military sense. Disliking the risks of pitched battles and lacking both the knowledge of and determination for siege, the Utes chose rather to wear the Mormons down by begging, stealing, and attacking isolated individuals, families, and settlements where the numerical superiority of the Indians—their only advantage—made victory certain and safe.[32] Moreover, the settlers had already constructed several forts at Manti and had another under construction at Ephraim. Upon news of Indian menace, a large bass drum was beaten to call those working outside back to the forts, where they were quite secure.[33]

Nevertheless, unprotected small settlements, outlying mills (evacuated after Brigham Young's proclamation of 25 July 1853), settlers isolated by guard duty, and travelers fared less well. The destruction by fire of Allred's Settlement, now Spring City, on 6 January

1854, was but one of innumerable burnings. During the first week of October 1853, four unarmed men hauling wheat from Manti's harvest to Salt Lake City were brutally mutilated at Uintah Springs, now Fountain Green, and two others were killed at a grist mill near Manti. Later the same month, the party of Captain John Gunnison, for whom Gunnison City was named, was massacred near Fillmore.[34]

"This [war] occurring in the midst of our wheat Harvest," wrote Brigham Young to the commissioner of Indian Affairs, "is causing us much inconvenience and loss, and we do not yet know, what amount of loss of life and destruction of property will be included In the final result."[35] Economic losses, especially in livestock, were heavy. One hundred seventy head, presumably of cattle, were driven to Salt Lake City to escape Indian rustlers, but the Indians continually threatened those that were left.[36] The entire herd, except for one cow, was stolen at Allred's Settlement one night, and the last important event of the war was the burning of the buildings there. The site was not resettled until 1859.[37]

Peace negotiations staggered through the early months of 1854, culminating in a final agreement on 12 May between the two leaders, Walker and Brigham Young, in Juab County. Meanwhile, construction of defensive forts continued throughout the territory. Later that year Walker returned to Manti ostensibly to seek a Mormon wife. After two documented refusals—possibly others as well—he left Sanpete for good.[38] More information remains of the ritual carnage of his burial than on the cause of his death near Fillmore. The official cause is given as a ruptured blood vessel in his neck; but local legend mentions a broken heart.[39]

Walker was succeeded as chief by his brother Arapeen, who presided during the next few years over an armed and uneasy truce. In the hope of permanent peace, he had deeded the land of his fathers to Brigham Young as a trustee for the church on 23 December 1855 in Ephraim.

The Indians had tried alternative means of dealing with the multiplying white men—coexistence in the same territory, intimidation, and finally war—all to no avail. By the mid-1850s, they had become desperate for some plan that would guarantee them even a part of their ancestral hunting ground on which to live. Thus, when Indian agent Garland Hurt approached them in 1855 with a new proposal, they were ready to listen.

On the last day of 1855, Hurt reported to Brigham Young that he had met with Arapeen and had persuaded him to settle on a reservation. Arapeen chose the site himself, and Hurt surveyed it, agreeing that it was an excellent choice:

> We found sufficient water to irrigate two thousand acres or more, and more land than there is water to irrigate, which lies in a cove in the mountains, with timber convenient and an abundance of nutritious grass. We laid out four townships on 144 square miles.[40]

The Twelve Mile Creek Reservation represented a compromise. The Indians would be guaranteed a certain area immune to white encroachment, but the area was small enough that it could not accommodate the traditional Indian way of life. Cultural extinction was to be the price of survival.

It was a compromise, but a compromise imposed by victors who, in retrospect, may seem insensitively culture-bound, but were, in fact, acting on the belief of their time that white Americans were divinely ordained to spread the American ideal into the western territories. Nor were Mormons alone in that belief. The secular phrase "Manifest Destiny," coined in 1845, expresses both the political philosophy of expansionism and a chauvinistic confidence in white America's moral and cultural superiority. Periodically revived in political debate, the phrase crystallizes the attitudes of Brigham Young, Garland Hurt, and the typical settler—all of whom, like the phrase itself, were children of the nineteenth century.

Consequently, Brigham Young, in his 1856 report as superintendent of Indian Affairs for Utah Territory, expressed hope for the reservation purely in terms of benefits to the whites and of the benefits to the Indians in becoming like whites. Pleased that the reservation placed the whites in Sanpete County firmly in control at last, he hoped that the red men would be successfully induced to materially contribute to their own support, and thereby not only relieve the whites, with whom they came in contact, of a constant harassing, and great expense, but steadily advance themselves in the habits, means, and appliances of civilized life.[41]

The reservation apparently had a fairly promising beginning. In November 1857, almost two years after its inception, Hurt submitted a list of property which indicated that the reservation was becoming productive. One hundred ninety-five acres were under cultivation, and reservation buildings included a two-room adobe house forty feet long, a log house, a corral, and a blacksmith shop. With twelve work animals, one cow, and a variety of farm implements and cooking equipment, he estimated the total property to be worth about $5,000.[42]

Ultimately, however, the Utes were not accustomed to farming, had little taste for it, and finally refused altogether. In 1858 Hurt reported that "the practice of redeeming these wretched creatures from savage indolence to habits of industry and morality, has been greatly interrupted during the past season, and it is now very difficult to induce some of the Indians who labored well on the farms last year to resume again these useful exercises." Since the Indians would not work, total loss was avoided only by paying white farmers to travel twelve miles from Manti to cultivate the crops. But that, of course, only encouraged Indian apathy, as Jacob Forney, Hurt's superior, pointed out: "Heretofore no pains have been taken to make the Indians labor. They were permitted to roam about the Country, Stealing, begging &c and only camped around the farms, when the crops were ripening, to carry it away and destroy it."[43]

Within a few years, Congress had passed the Homestead Act, limited church-owned properties, and confiscated the lands of the Sanpitch Indians; and the Indian agents ceased their efforts to maintain Twelve Mile. When the Uintah Reservation in northeastern Utah opened in the 1860s, most of the Sanpete Valley Utes, for whom the Twelve Mile Creek Reservation had been intended, moved there. Late in 1863, acting governor Amos Reed asked the territorial legislature to request permission from Congress to liquidate the reservation and allow white settlers to acquire its lands:

> It has been lying idle for several years past and there is little possi-
> bility of its ever again being required for Indian purposes. The land
> is capable of producing good crops and, in justice to the people,
> ready and willing to reduce it to profitable cultivation, should be

vacated as an Indian reservation, to which it is not adapted and for which it is evidently not required.[44]

Congress granted Reed's appeal, and in 1864 the Twelve Mile Creek Reservation in Mayfield passed out of existence.

The Utes who remained in Sanpete Valley were understandably angered by the 1864 act of Congress which required them to give up all land and title rights and to remove to the Uintah Reservation within a year. Before the end of the grace period, a series of events had occurred which triggered the Black Hawk War, the longer and more serious of the two Indian wars in Sanpete County.[45] During the winter of 1864–65, an epidemic of smallpox—a "white man's" disease—swept through the Gunnison area, exposing a small band of dispossessed Utes who were camped nearby. Among the casualties was Chief Arapeen.

The incident involving John Lowry, Jr., in which he scuffled with Arapeen's son, the new Chief Yene-wood (also known as Jake Arapeen), took place in April 1865, by a little adobe house once set on a lot on First West, just north of First South, in Manti. On Sunday, 1 April 1865, Jake Arapeen appeared at a council meeting in Manti, not, as the whites expected, to attempt a settlement of differences, but to demand redress for his father's death. The Utes believed that the settlers had formed a league with evil spirits and were using supernatural means to dispose of them; they could stop the sickness and death, they thought, by destroying the agents of evil—the white leaders.[46] Lowry, who claimed to be protecting first an unarmed family and then himself, pulled the chief from his horse as he was reaching for an arrow and beat him up rather badly.[47] The Utes had by then endured fifteen years of white encroachment and ten years of distasteful reservation life, both on Twelve Mile Creek and in the Uinta Basin, and some writers, as well as common opinion, held that the Utes seized upon the Lowry incident as a focal point for their frustrations, a point (as already explained) that Lowry later firmly denied. However, on the next day, twenty-year-old Peter Ludvigson, with a small group of riders from Manti, was ambushed at Nine Mile. All escaped but Ludvigson, who was killed. A strip of his back along the spine had been cut off from neckbone to tailbone.[48]

The Ute leader Black Hawk. (Utah State Historical Society)

The subsequent uprising known as the Black Hawk War took its name from a young Ute warrior who attracted a small but growing band determined to avenge the indignities to their people. F. H. Head, superintendent of Indian Affairs for Utah Territory, said in 1865 that Black Hawk's band "consisted at first of but 44 men, who were mostly outlaws and desperate characters from his own and other tribes," yet during that year they killed thirty-two whites in Sanpete and Sevier counties and stole over 2,000 cattle and horses.[49]

Black Hawk's success against what should have been overwhelming disadvantages produced considerable anxiety among government officials responsible for Indian affairs. In the first place, he seemed to draw strength from adversity:

> Forty of his warriors were killed by the settlers in repelling his different attacks. His success in stealing, however, enabled him to feed abundantly, & mount all Indians who joined him, & the prestige acquired by his raids was such that his numbers were constantly on the increase, despite his occasional losses of men.

Even more serious, a general Indian uprising in the Great Basin threatened to coalesce around the Black Hawk rebellion:

> His band, from what I consider entirely reliable information, now numbers 100 warriors, nearly one half of whom are Navajoes . . . I am very apprehensive that unless Black Hawk is severely chastised, an Indian war of considerable magnitude may be inaugurated. He has never met with a serious reverse, having always attacked small settlements or unprotected families. He has thus acquired a considerable reputation among the various Indian tribes & I fear many of the more adventurous will join him from the band now friendly.[50]

The next year, 1866, LDS church leaders consolidated the embryonic Sevier County settlements and outlying Sanpete communities into the forts at Manti, Ephraim, Mount Pleasant, Moroni, and Gunnison. Livestock were also "forted up" with the settlers. At Fort Ephraim, "all the cows, horses and oxen were corralled within the fort wall at night, and carefully herded in the day. . . . The arrangement . . . was that the cattle were corralled in the center and the houses, camps and wagons closer to the walls."[51] Inevitably, confinement produced its own problems: "After a few weeks living within the walls," wrote Emma Capson Metcalf of Fort Gunnison, "a letter was sent to President Wells asking permission to have the Kraals, Pig Stys and Sheep pens outside the fort to keep it from becoming disagreeably unsanitary."[52]

Although the danger was serious, local settlers and the territorial militia proved strong enough to put down the rebels; an armistice was signed in Strawberry Valley on 19 August 1868, and peace returned by summer of 1869.[53]

The history of conflict between settlers and Indians largely excludes the Sanpitch band, fearful and unassuming from the beginning. Immediately upon the arrival of the white settlers in Sanpete Valley, the Sanpitch Indians transferred their dependence from the Utes to the whites and became permanent fixtures about the settlements, primarily begging, but doing a little menial labor for their bread, also. Because of this customary timorousness, Sanpete County residents in the summer of 1858 were shocked and baffled by the news that the Sanpitches were responsible for the massacre of four Danish travelers in Salt Creek Canyon. Indian agent Garland Hurt, attempting to explain this departure from their normally meek character, wrote to his superiors that they

> are an inferior band of the Utahs, very destitute and not infrequently adopted by the whites as domestics, and upon whom they are almost entirely dependent for subsistence and for protection from encroachments of the more powerful bands. What induced them to commit this deed is not fully known to me, but information derived from the other bands would seem to indicate that they did it in compliance with a time honored custom which prevails among them of killing someone on the occasion of the death of a chief.[54]

The next year, Jacob Forney, Hurt's successor, found "a small band, 22 men, 16 women, & 10 children, the remains of a once considerable Tribe, called *San-Pitch*," hanging around Ephraim, presumably begging and looking for odd jobs.[55] Many Sanpitches later joined the Utes on the Uintah Reservation, where, during the winter of 1865–66, they starved as a result of government neglect and became so disgusted with the whites that they joined Black Hawk's rebels in the spring.[56]

Even by 1865 there was no effort to come to the Sanpete Valley

Moroni residents in front of a bastion erected in 1866 as a defense against Indians. The bastion was razed in 1890. (Courtesy Ida Donaldson)

by way of Thistle. The penetration of Indianola's flats came from the south, from the Sanpete settlements. What happened to the family of John Given when they extended themselves across the flats to the present Utah County-Sanpete boundary is sadly attested to by the monument in their memory at that spot. On 27 May 1865, this family of six was attacked at daybreak by Utes and killed. Two young men living with the family escaped the attack somehow and survived to carry news of the tragedy to Fairview. A party of armed men found the Given homestead burned, their livestock killed or run off, and the bodies of the Givens among the embers. The six bodies were taken to Fairview for burial. This was an incident among many experienced during the 1860s in Utah generally, typical of the hit-and-run guerrilla warfare conducted by Black Hawk and his followers.

After the Black Hawk War, the Sanpitches generally did not return to the Uintah Reservation, although thirty-six were there in 1873.[57] Instead, they tried farming unclaimed land on the old Twelve Mile Creek Reservation in Mayfield. They gave the project more earnest effort than the Utes, but had even less success:

They are migratory in their habits and remain on the land they claim as their own but a small part of the year. They attempted the cultivation of a few acres of land this year [1870], but their crops were destroyed by grasshoppers. They subsist by means of hunting and of such supplies as they receive from [the government]. They have some horses, but no cows nor oxen.[58]

With the notice in 1873 that there were only thirty-six Sanpitch Indians at the Uintah reservation, the Sanpitches received no more notice as a separate tribal entity by the administrators of Indian Affairs; that date thus serves as a terminal point in their history.

With the last treaty directing the Indians to Uintah Basin in August of 1872, and the last white casualty at the hands of the Utes the following month, the Indian wars were over. From that time forward, the area belonged exclusively to the white farmers and livestock men. Most of the Indians, following the orders of the government, moved to the Uintah Reservation in northeastern Utah, although a few isolated families remained among the whites, and a small number who had converted to the Mormon church adopted an agrarian life at Indianola, the church's Indian colony at the extreme northern end of Sanpete County.

The Black Hawk War became a legendary episode in Sanpete County history, one that old pioneers recalled vividly and bequeathed to their children in stories and journals. Until the 1920s, descendants of Black Hawk War veterans gathered occasionally for encampments held in central Utah communities where the battles were fought. They sang songs, told the stories of their fathers, and relived this most violent and romantic chapter in Sanpete County's past. All that has now ended, significantly with the passing of the generations involved.

ENDNOTES

1. Escalante Journal, 30 September 1776, quoted in W. R. Harris, *The Catholic Church in Utah* (Salt Lake City: Intermountain Catholic Press, 1909), 185–86. Commenting on this passage, Palmer says the Indians were "Sampitches," who lived "farther eastward in the Sanpete and Sevier Valleys, but their men made frequent pilgrimages out over the western desert." "Utah Indians Past and Present," *Utah Historical Quarterly* 1 (April 1928): 40.

2. Pierre De Smet, "Reminiscences of Indian Habits and Character," *Utah Historical Quarterly 5* (January 1932): 26–27, reprints a letter of 17 February 1841. Another description of the Sanpitch Indians is found in Thomas J. Farnham's "Travels in the Great Western Prairies, May 21— October 16, 1839," quoted in William J. Snow, "Utah Indians and the Spanish Slave Trade," *Utah Historical Quarterly 2* (July 1929): 69.

3. *Memory Book to Commemorate Gunnison Valley's Centennial, 1859–1959* (Gunnison, UT: 1959), 23.

4. 1865 *Report of the Commissioner of Indian Affairs,* 142–48.

5. Azariah Smith *Journal,* 5 January 1851; Albert Smith Autobiography, 56. The spelling is Albert Smith's.

6. Adelia Cox Sidwell, *Reminiscences,* 5.

7. *F. W. Cox Family History,* Pt. 2, 9.

8. Sidwell, Reminiscences, 6.

9. Peter Gottfredson, *Indian Depredations in Utah,* 2nd ed. (Salt Lake City: Merlin G. Christensen,, 1969), 322.

10. Walker Lowry, *Wallace Lowry* (n.p.: Stinehour Press, 1974), 51. In spite of the title, this book amounts to a history of the Lowry family.

11. Gottfredson *Indian Depredations in Utah,* 335–38.

12. John K. Olsen, "What Did Walker Want?" *Saga of the Sanpitch,* 11, 17.

13. *Gunnison Valley Centennial Book,* 23.

14. *F. W. Cox Family History,* Pt. 2, 8.

15. Brigham Young to Commissioner of Indian Affairs, 28 June 1853, 1–2, microfilm collection of "Letters Received by the Office of Indian Affairs." Letters from this collection will hereafter be cited only by correspondents and dates. *Utah Historical Quarterly* for July 1929 contains several articles bearing directly on Indian slavery in Sanpete County. See especially Snow, "Utah Indians and Spanish Slave Trade," 67–73; and the compilation of "Utah Laws Against Indian Slavery," 84–86.

16. *Isaac Morley on the Frontier,* 38.

17. Sidwell, Reminiscences.

18. Brigham Young to Commissioner of Indian Affairs, 28 June 1853, 3–4.

19. The ecological dislocations that spelled the end for Indian life in Sanpete County followed the same pattern as elsewhere in Utah. See Beverly P. Smaby, "The Mormons and the Indians: Conflicting Ecological Systems in the Great Basin," *American Studies 16* (Spring 1975): 35–47.

20. H. R. Day to Luke Lea, Commissioner of Indian Affairs, 2 January 1851, 5. Day was strongly anti-Mormon and no doubt exaggerates the anti-

Mormonism of the Indians, but there seems to be no reason to doubt the substantial accuracy of his report as evidence of Indian fears of disposses-sion. See Gottfredson, *Indian Depredations in Utah*, 323–24, and Orson Hyde's report, Journal History of the Church, 26 December 1870, for cor-roboration.

21. Azariah Smith, *Journal*, 27 August 1855.

22. Sanpete County Court Minutes (Book A), 7 December 1857.

23. Manti Ward Minutes, 6 October 1850.

24. S. K. Gifford Diary, 13.

25. Garland Hurt to Brigham Young, 31 December 1855, 4–5.

26. Journal History of the Church, 10 January 1855. Farmer's letter to some English friends was designed to show how good conditions in Utah were, and thus to encourage immigration. Statements like the one quoted here, coupled with the generally good relations between Mormons and Indians, helped fan persistent fears among non-Mormons of a large-scale Mormon-Indian alliance.

27. Manti Ward Minutes, 7 July 1850.

28. Sidwell, *Reminiscences*, 7

29. Ibid. The estimates of the number of Indians at Manti in 1849–50 range from 250 (Manti Ward Minutes, 14 July 1850) to 700 (Sidwell, Reminiscences). Both figures were probably close to correct at various times, since the Indians were constantly on the move.

30. Livy Olsen, "The Life Story of a Western Sheriff," 7; Manti Ward Minutes, 21 November 1858. The Mormons claimed that U.S. troops, not they, were responsible for the death of Arapeen's brother.

31. It began in Springville, Utah, on 17 July 1853, in a squabble over some biscuits, and was brought to an end by an agreement at Chicken Creek in the following May. More concise accounts of the Sanpete Indian wars than Gottfredson's may be found in the *Inventory of the Sanpete County Archives* (Salt Lake City; Historical Records Survey, 1941), 15–26; and Sonne, *World of Wakara, 161–205.*

32. The standard account of that warfare is Gottfredson, *Indian Depredations in Utah,* which contains detailed, first-hand accounts of prac-tically every little skirmish and ambush in Sanpete County during this period. See Also John Alton Peterson, *Utah's Black Hawk War,*(Salt Lake City: University of Utah Press, 1998), for a more current and analytical dis-cussion of the battle accounts.

33. F.W. Cox *Family History*, Pt. 1, 13; Niels P. Peterson, *Reminiscences,* 4.

34. Conway Ballantyne Sonne, *World of Wakara* (San Antonio: Naylor Co., 1962), 161- 205.

35. Brigham Young to Commissioner of Indian Affairs, 23 July 1853, 2.

36. Azariah Smith Journal, 26 July 1853.

37. S.K. Gifford Diary, 9–10.

38. *Song of a Century*, 35; Gottfredson, *Indian Depredations*, 77–78.

39. Christian Jensen, "My Tom Sawyer Town," *Ford Times*, March 1953.

40. Garland Hurt to Brigham Young, 31 December 1855, 3–4.

41. 1856 *Report of the Commissioner of Indian Affairs*, 225.

42. Hurt, "List of Agency Property, at the Sanpete Settlement," 30 November 1857, in "Letters Received by the Office of Indian Affairs."

43. Garland Hurt to Jacob Forney, Superintendent of Indian Affairs for Utah Territory, 14 September 1858, 4–5; Forney to Commissioner of Indian Affairs, 15 February 1859, 3.

44. Journal of the Church, 15 December 1863; James Duane Doty to Commissioner of Indian Affairs, 28 January 1864, 2.

45. For a detailed study of the Black Hawk War see Peterson, *Utah's Black Hawk War*.

46. During 1867 Orson Hyde estimated the Black Hawk depredations cost Sanpete County residence over $100,000 in lost agricultural produce, since only one third to one half of available men could farm, the rest having to fight Indians. Journal History of the Church, 25 November 1867. Utah Territory asked for $1.5 million from the U.S. government to defray the costs of four Sanpete County settlements, that had to be "broken up and removed at much expense and loss." Journal History of the Church, 22 February 1868.

47. This is Lowry's own account as given by Gottfredson, *Indian Depredations*, 335. See also James V.N. Williams, *Autobiography*, 101.

48. *Saga of the Sanpitch*, II, 22.

49. F. H. Head, to Commissioner of Indian Affairs, 30 April 1866, 1.

50. Head, 30 April 1866, 2–3.

51. *These Our Fathers*, 73.

52. *Gunnison Valley Centennial Memory Book*, 45.

53. *Ibid.*

54. Garland Hurt to Jacob Forney, 14 September 1858, 3–4.

55. Jacob Forney to Commissioner of Indian Affairs, 21 June 1866, 3.

56. F. H. Head to Commissioner of Indian Affairs, 21 June 1866, 3.

57. 1873 *Report to the Commissioner of Indian Affairs*, 51.

58. 1870 *Report to the Commissioner of Indian Affairs*, 142.

CHAPTER 5

EARLY GOVERNMENT AND POLITICS

T he first Sanpete settlers brought with them a tradition of local government shared by most nineteenth century Americans. While the boundaries between religious and political realms were often blurred in the early decades, by the beginning of the twentieth century, Sanpete county government was expanding beyond the basic services of roads and law enforcement to provide some welfare services for the county's indigent. At the same time, in the political arena, county residents were beginning to identify themselves with the two major national political parties—Democrats and Republicans—as the earlier political parties—the Mormon dominated Peoples Party and the non-Mormon Liberal Party—no longer seemed relevant or desired after Utah was finally granted statehood on 4 January 1896.

Creation of Sanpete County and Early County Government

The legislature of the provisional government of the State of Deseret created Sanpete County on 31 January 1850. One year later the territorial legislature enlarged the borders on 3 March 1851 to include "all that portion of the Territory bounded on the north by

Utah County, east by the Territorial line, south by latitude 38 degrees 30 and west by Juab Millard counties."[1] Sanpete included land today embraced by several other counties including Sevier, Carbon, Emery, Grand, Piute, Wayne, Uintah, Utah, Juab, and San Juan. The county's boundaries underwent considerable change during the nineteenth century. In fact, since Utah was first settled and its original six counties designated, there have been as many as 90 county boundary changes.

Originally, the political situation in Sanpete County represented a balancing act between the militia, the Mormon church and the local city councils although, during the first three decades the Mormon church virtually dominated all decision-making processes. Writing in his diary during 1850, Samuel K. Gifford described one occasion with the potential for heated confrontation.

> The Military, whose right it was to take charge of building forts, proposed to make a good stone wall all around nine blocks, taking in the outside streets. The City Council thought they ought to have the say of where and how the forts should be constructed. Then comes the Church Authorities and said the Priesthood must rule. And soon the debate became quite warm. But as none wished to go against the Priesthood, Father Morley succeeded in getting in a row of houses built on the east side of the nine blocks, leaving the street outside the doors opening to the west.[2]

After Sanpete County was established, its first administrative body was the Sanpete County Court which consisted of a probate judge, George Peacock of Manti, and three selectmen. Each of these men was elected at large. Their first meeting was 30 March 1852. After 1896 the county court was replaced by a board of commissioners with three members, one serving as chair. The group first met in the Manti schoolhouse. In 1864 the county's first courthouse was built for $850. This eighteen-by-twenty-foot building was constructed with locally produced adobe and plastered on the inside and outside both. In 1873 a stone addition to this building increased the available space and in 1885 a stone vault was constructed next to the building for the preservation of county records. An appropriation of $2,000 in 1894 provided the funds necessary to remodel the court-

The Manti City Council House was built in 1855–56 and used as a church, school, theater, and for other social activities. (Utah State Historical Society)

house and build a court room and assessor's office on the second floor.

Leadership Struggles

Sanpete's political history was a rocky road for the first couple of decades. Much of the turmoil during that time consisted of power struggles within the LDS church hierarchy, but there are also instances of populistic dissatisfaction with distasteful or incompetent leaders who the rank and file were expected to sustain automatically.

The earliest of hierarchal struggles concerned the personality and competence of Isaac Morley, under whose leadership Sanpete was settled on Brigham Young's orders. Almost from the beginning, there had been significant disagreements between Morley and others on the exact place of settlement. The "others" included Seth Taft and Jake Butterfield. After a winter of near-silence, and after losing every one of his cattle in that first winter, Taft bundled up his wife and two daughters in the spring of 1850 and returned to the Salt Lake Valley,

where in time he became the bishop of the Ninth Ward and a patri-
arch in the LDS church. Butterfield, a Mormon Battalion veteran, was
neither as prudent nor as fortunate. His words became ever more bitter during the winter of 1849–50, and at the instigation of Isaac
Morley he was excommunicated and banished by a bishop's court in
February 1850.

Dissatisfaction flared up even more significantly between Morley
and Bishop John Lowry, Sr., who was supported by Titus Billings and
Elijah Averett. In 1853 there was serious trouble over the construction of a council house at Manti. It is not at all clear why this was an
issue, but it seems that Morley attempted to back out of a commitment to finish the building which had been agreed upon by all the
church leaders, and thereby he aroused the ire of Lowry's faction.
Concluding that Morley had become intolerable, Averett and Billings
went to Salt Lake City to confer with Brigham Young and Heber C.
Kimball to try to effect Morley's replacement. Upon their return, a
special ward meeting was convened on Wednesday, 23 November
1853, and a tense showdown between the two factions resulted in
Morley's resignation.

It was awkward for Young and Kimball, but they handled it with
diplomacy and humaneness. Morley, at the age of sixty-seven, was
one of the great old workhorses of the Mormon church. He had sheltered Joseph Smith in his home at Kirtland, Ohio, and had endured
most of the persecutions of the earliest days of the church's history.
He had also been one of the central leaders in the westward trek and
a member of the Council of Fifty: thus, his position as leader of one
of the first and most crucial of the colonies in the Great Basin was the
crown to a long, distinguished career. Dismissal of such a venerable
figure was not to be taken lightly. Averett reported that upon being
told of the situation at Manti, "President Young turned away, saying
that he knew all about it and did not wish to hear any more." Heber
C. Kimball had commented further, that

> President Morley was a good a man as there was on earth but he
> was getting old and childish and that he was a man of poor tem-
> poral economy and that was the cause of things not going better
> here; that his mind did not run into temporal affairs but was taken

up in spiritual affairs therefore was not calculated to be President of a Branch.[3]

The First Presidency sent Averett and Billings back to Manti to report the conference, hoping that Morley would realize that it was time for him to step down. Morley did understand what was expected, and the account in the ward minutes of Morley's moment of truth is touching. He began by protesting that he had tried to support Bishop Lowry, but confessed that he knew he had "crossed him" at times, and added, "If this has offended him I do think it ought not to of had that effect on him." Having spoken, he faced the hard reality of the situation.

> President Morley said brethren I wish you to choose you a new President, yet I wish a place among you. I would say further for your benefit; had the brethren who has recently visited Great Salt Lake City - I say had they of laid the case before the President in its true light I think it would of appeared in a different light from what is now does - Pres. Morley appeared very humble and burst into tears and sat down.[4]

Isaac Morley spent his last days in Mount Pleasant, but after his death in 1865, at the age of seventy-nine, his remains were returned to Manti for burial, the town which he had worked so hard to help found.

Political turmoil within the church leadership did not end with the Morley affair. In 1859 H.J. Hals wrote that "there came many sorrows among the people in Manti, because of the conditions there between the Bishop and his counselors."[5] Nor did Morley's resignation resolve the Council house business. In 1870 Albert Smith noted that Bishop Andrew J. Moffitt had fallen between two stools in trying to finish both the meetinghouse and the council house, with the result that neither of the buildings was completed at that time. Moreover, the materials which had been transported to the council house site had lain there so long that people had stolen them for their own houses, and they were entirely gone.[6]

Manti was not the only town with internal problems. The Fairview Ward minutes record a bitter conflict on 27 May 1860 between the bishops of that town and Mount Pleasant concerning a certain plot of land to which each community laid claim.

> Some three weeks ago Bishop William Seeley of Mount Pleasant sent a herd of cattle within three miles of our settlement on land that we have surveyed, as we needed more land. Bishop James N. Jones requested him to move them away, which he refused to do, he then sent him a letter with request to move them, but he still refused, then President Chapman wrote him a letter requesting him to move them away, and restore good feelings but still to no purpose.[7]

For the most part, bickerings between church leaders affected the rank-and-file membership very little. H.J. Hals, referring to the problem within the Manti bishopric in 1859, points out that "I and many others had sense enough not to get mixed up in it, took no part in it and minded our own business."[8]

Occasionally, there were popular protests, primarily where church leaders asked their people to sustain unpopular nominees for church or town offices. In 1865, when Bishop Andrew J. Moffitt presented, after Sunday evening services, a list of particularly unpalatable nominees for city offices to be elected the following day, he was met with instant rebellion, notwithstanding the fact that there were a couple of general authorities from Salt Lake City present, "Considerable opposition was made manifest," wrote one witness, "which caused some sharp reproves from Elder George A. Smith and Franklin D. Richards."[9]

During the Black Hawk War in the 1860s, when the people of Fairview moved for a time to Mount Pleasant for protection, Apostle Orson Hyde found that he had to arbitrate a dispute between the people of Fairview and their bishop, whom they accused of taking advantage of his office to make money. Although Hyde expressed approval of the bishop in his judgment of the facts as they were presented to him, he found it expedient to nominate another bishop for Fairview, a man whom the people immediately sustained.[10]

The sense of cultural unity and mission that the early settlers brought with them into the Sanpete Valley led them to expect the same unanimity in secular elections that they usually showed in vot-

The original Sanpete County Courthouse. (Utah State Historical Society)

ing to sustain their church leaders. Occasionally they did achieve such secular unanimity, but the breathless enthusiasm with which the *Deseret News* reported a unanimous vote at a political convention in Mount Pleasant in 1874 suggests that such events were not common. "Not a dissentient!" the paper exulted.[11]

Not surprisingly, then, the organization of formal political parties in the county in the late 1870s bewildered some residents and impressed others as a sign of cultural decline. Referring to the election of city officers in Fayette in 1879, John Bartholomew said, "We experienced that which never before happened in this precinct, namely, voting for more than one candidate for one office, and there were three for the office of Magistrate. This caused considerable confusion, and quite a bad feeling among the people."[12]

Political Parties

The emergence of the Liberal and People's parties (non-Mormon and Mormon, respectively) at Manti in the 1880s alarmed J.C.A. Weibye, especially when "The Liberal gained the Victory over the Peoples party, so the Priesthood got defited." Weibye could not help but ascribe such a development to the influx of "gentiles" (some Presbyterians) and to a spiritual decline among Mormons.

It is a very sorry full thing that we as Latter Day Saints are split in two Parties, in a good many instances are Fathers against Sons, and Brother (in the flesh) against Brothers, a good many of the Citizens (Liberal) Party do not pay Tithing, nor come to Meetings, but still have a standing in the Church, and some few of the Peoples Party, as just the same, but they all seems to be much taken up in Politic, more than in their Religion, and I am sorry to say that infidelity is growing in our midst, especially among the young men, more than among the female, Tobacco and Whiskey-drinking is more prevalent in our city, and we now have two Whiskey-saloons and Drugstore.[13]

Confusion reigned again in the 1890s when Utah abandoned the Mormon vs. non-Mormon party division in favor of the national Republican and Democratic party organizations. "Here there were lots of rallies and stump speeches and half of the lies told in those meetings were not true," H.J. Hals wrote of Manti in 1892, "and it brought a good deal of confusion and disunion."[14]

Roads

The main roads now traversing Sanpete County were generally built along the same routes taken by its first settlers. These roads, in turn, often followed those used by the earlier Native Americans to travel within and between the habitable valleys. For both Indians and pioneers, as well as millennia of wildlife on the move, the traffic ways often developed along water courses where feed, water, and fuel were available. Insofar as possible, the routes were also the most efficient or shortest distances between places, literally the paths of least resistance. Later, telegraph, telephone, and railroad lines also followed the initial routes.

Although the State of Deseret, Utah's first civil government, was short-lived (March 1849 through September 1851), among its lasting legislative enactments was the creation of eight counties(including "San Pete," and four major cities, among them Manti) and the establishment of road policies. One of the first officers to serve the State of Deseret was Joseph L. Heywood, surveyor of highways. During the provisional state's first legislative session in late 1849, the new governing body passed "An Ordinance Providing for State and County

The old Gunnison waterwagon about 1915 was used to settle the dust on Sanpete streets before they were paved. (Courtesy LaMar Larsen)

Road Commissions." Approved 15 January 1849, the document consisted of eight sections giving the General Assembly the authority to "open, alter, widen, extend, establish, grade, pave, or otherwise improve, and keep in repair, streets, avenues, lanes, and alleys; and to establish,, erect and keep in repair aqueducts and bridges."[15]

The offices of county road commissioner and precinct supervisor were created in 1850. The county court appointed one or more county road commissioners to two-year terms. Precinct road supervisors were to be elected annually by voters within the precincts. In 1862 the office of district road supervisor was created, apparently consolidating the earlier positions of county and precinct road supervisors. They were to be appointed by the court, receive pay for their work, and serve one-year and later, two-year terms. In 1896, following statehood, district road commissioners were to be appointed by the board of county commissioners. The office of district road supervisor was abolished in 1909 when the board of county commissioners was required to appoint a county road commissioner biennially. This new position was also abolished in 1921 when the duties of this office were given to the board of county commissioners.[16]

Authorizing the building of roads and paying for them were two different matters. With many competing needs for funds, territorial and county support was generally inconsistent and inadequate, often relying upon "probably the two most unsatisfactory methods known for highway financing . . . the poll tax, or statute labor, and upon toll road and toll bridge financing . . ."[17] In 1855, for example, the county road from Manti to Nephi had to be paid for with delinquent territorial taxes from the years 1852–54.[18]

Roads were also built through the efforts of municipal public works agencies which relied on Mormons tithing 10 percent of their increase in goods and, infrequently, cash, as well as every tenth day of their labor. With these donated resources, roads, bridges, canals, and public buildings were constructed throughout the county. In 1850 Brigham Young instructed the settlers in Sanpete Valley to devote their labor and tithing to making "a good state road north across the swamp, ditching it well on each side, and building a bridge across the river."[19] On 23 August 1864 Orson Hyde reported to the *Deseret News* that a good road had been laid between Fairview and Spanish Fork Creek and that a road from Sanpete Valley to Utah Valley was being planned.[20]

Some of the early road design was done by the federal government. As part of the federal effort to explore the West and the Great Basin in particular, Albert Sidney Johnston, the brevet general who established Camp Floyd, instructed Captain James H. Simpson of the topographical engineers to conduct reconnaissance work to identify potential traffic routes through the territory. A Colonel Loring reported a "trail through San Pete Valley," which was thought capable of "making a short and feasible road . . ." to southern locations.[21]

Road-building expenditures seem to have been spent in a four-tiered priority. Of greatest importance were major routes from the county to the north and Salt Lake City. Second were roads connecting the settlements within the county. Next were roads leading out of the county to adjoining counties, especially to the east and south. Finally, roads were opened to the natural resources in the mountains, water courses, mines, quarries, agricultural areas, and recreation areas.

Care and Assistance

During the 1850s, Sanpete county was a raw frontier with only the most rudimentary city and county government bureaucracies.

The economy of the county was unstable because of Indian difficulties and grasshopper problems. Thus the cities and county were
unable, from lack of manpower, governmental machinery, and funds,
to support a program for the care of helpless citizens, such as the
mentally ill or the blind. It was customary for the occasional person
who was unable to support or care for himself to be sheltered by relatives or looked after by neighbors. Such effects were unorganized,
but there was a definite consciousness of those in need.

Unfortunately, Sanpete County had such cases very early. The
first one was Azariah Smith, a member of the first colonists in 1849.
Smith had been a member of the Mormon Battalion, and shortly
after enlisting, he was thrown from his horse and injured his head
badly. About the time of his arrival at Manti, he began having frequent seizures that rendered him sometimes dangerous to others.
According to Albert Smith, his father,

> [Azariah] would have spells of hollowing & would strike anyone
> that went near him & my woman folks became afraid of him. . . . I
> mite mention many things such as his smashing three of my
> dors—striking Sophia [Albert's wife] in her face cosing the blood
> to flow striking the children & they being afraid of him &c.[22]

No doubt partly because of his condition, Azariah's wife divorced
him. Alone and unable to care for himself, Smith moved in with his
father.[23]

The burden on Albert Smith must have been almost unbearable.
Azariah was not only helpless, but dangerous, which meant that not
only did Albert have to clear land and grow food for an extra mouth,
but he had also to keep constant guard over his son. Consequently, as
Albert put it, "I was obliedge to take him with me wareever I went."
The need for constant vigilance produced some complicated family
shufflings whenever Albert had to be away from home, as when he
took a load of oats to sell at Camp Floyd in 1861. A trip to Camp
Floyd was a shopping holiday for rural Utahns, but Albert had to
leave one of his wives at home so he could take Azariah along and
thus guard him.[24]

The care Albert Smith provided for his son was more than
restraint. During Azariah's lucid moments (which became more and

more frequent until he was eventually quite himself again), Albert provided a means of rehabilitation:

> these hollowing spells gradually wore of & when he was the welest he was able to do a little. I bought him some shomakers tools & he in the fall would fix up our shoes not for the proffit but to occupy his mind & keap him from studying all the time which I found to be vary injurious.[25]

Although care of the socially unfortunate was primarily the responsibility of relatives in the pioneer period, county and city governments were aware of the existence of those citizens, and, beginning quite early, attempted to contribute to their care. From 1875, for example, Manti consistently remitted Azariah Smith's taxes ($1.30 in 1875). In 1862, the Sanpete County Court provided for the care and support of one insane man by appointing a guardian and appropriating an allowance of $1.50 per week plus clothing.[26]

As the economy matured and government became stronger, the county and larger towns maintained regular accounts in their budgets for dependent people. By 1889 Ephraim had an "indigent expense account" that provided (no doubt among other things) for the burial of the dead baby of an indigent mother and for dispensing medicine to the indigent sick.[27] Manti, in 1898, even provided meals for tramps at fifteen cents apiece, to be spent by the marshal.

In 1862 the county had attempted to provide a permanent shelter, as well as support, for an unstable man named Harvey Marble. The county court appropriated $43.30 for the construction of a "snug little home" for Marble and his large family. In 1865 Marble was moved to Sevier County, but Sanpete County had established a precedent in providing housing for indigents, and others would later lead to the construction of the County Infirmary at Fairview.[28]

Sanpete County's rapidly increasing population, along with the general economic depression of 1893–97, created an alarming increase in the county indigent roll. From 1880 to 1890, the number of indigents supported by the county jumped from five to twenty-four, and the amount paid from $18.95 to $1,067.30. In 1894 there were forty people on the roll, and they received $1,787.81.[29] Faced with those staggering increases, the county commissioners in 1895 began looking for a way to keep the indigent budget within bounds. The idea they settled upon was to purchase a farm where able-bodied indigents could work, supporting themselves and at least some of the more helpless.

On 16 April 1895 the Sanpete County Court appointed a committee to investigate the desirability of establishing an infirmary. Upon its favorable report, the court ordered correspondence with the officials of all Sanpete County communities regarding possible sites for the institution. Fairview, Gunnison, Moroni, Mount Pleasant, and Spring City all submitted proposals. But, in spite of the fact that it inspected and considered all sites, the court never seemed to have had any doubt that the Fairview site, an already established and functioning farm, was an excellent choice.[30]

On 3 September 1895, the court awarded contracts for the construction of a large, two-story brick institution at the site for housing and caring for the residents.

At first, the infirmary seemed to be a success. The forty people on the county indigents roll dropped to thirty-one in 1895, but after the county reduced existing indigent accounts in 1895, preparatory to moving as many recipients as possible to the infirmary, the number dropped to fourteen. In 1897 the first full year of operation of the infirmary only two people were on the roll.[31] When the infirmary closed in 1931, the county indigent roll had dropped to fifty-nine, but the infirmary had only seven residents.[32]

The county did attempt to make the infirmary financially sound. In the first place, infirmary residents who had funds of their own, or had relatives who had funds, were expected to contribute to their support, and the county was aggressive in seeing that they did so. The adjoining counties, Emery and Sevier, were also allowed to send residents to the infirmary. Those counties had to make regular payments for their support, but the amounts charged were only estimated actual costs of caring for the residents. Sanpete County, in other words, did not profit through such transactions. Inmates from other counties were an advantage if they were healthy enough to augment the infirmary labor force, but they made insignificant financial contributions.[33]

When the infirmary closed in 1931, the county commissioners

The Sanpete County Courthouse under construction. (Utah State Historical Society)

explained that they did so "on account of the high cost of its maintainance [sic]." They placed the seven remaining inmates in private homes (all but two in Mount Pleasant) with stipends of $25 per month, and auctioned off most of the moveable goods. The property itself was leased to a private party.[34]

Although the infirmary was ultimately not successful, it gave Sanpete County valuable experience in the administration of welfare agencies and during the latter years of its existence, the county did indeed begin providing separate tax levies for welfare and creating permanent institutions like the Poor Fund, the Widowed Mothers Fund and the Old Age Pension Fund. County revenues were sometimes too scanty to support such programs adequately but county officials took their welfare commitments seriously. Service clubs and the Mormon Church's Relief Society began to fill the vacuum left by closing the infirmary.[35] Finally, the infirmary died on the eve of the New Deal, which provided funds and agencies that in many ways supplanted or injected new financial life into the county programs.

Law Enforcement and Fire Protection

Such basic social services as police and fire protection became desirable very early in the history of Sanpete County, but it was not until the late decades of the nineteenth century that city councils and the county court finally institutionalized those services. During the early years in each settlement, the police, for example, were haphazardly recruited, paid, and poorly supplied with jails and other necessary equipment. The two men who made up the police force of Spring City in the 1870s were paid only by remission of their city taxes. With no more inducements than that, it became difficult to recruit for the job, and the lack of adequate facilities further hindered the effort. In 1879 the mayor of Spring City began a recruitment attempt, and one man who was asked to serve said that he would do so only if the city provided a jail for him to use.[36]

Beginning in the 1880s, most communities showed an inclination to support their police force more solidly and consistently. In 1883 Ephraim ordered that the police force be furnished with "some weapons of deffence in the shape of 2 derringers and 4 clubs and also some marks of distinguishing the officers in the shape of stars or buttons also two jail locks." Later that year the Manti City Council hired six policemen (three in each ward) to serve under the supervision of the city marshall.[37]

Jail construction remained a problem throughout the county until at least the end of the nineteenth century. The county built a jail in 1861, but various communities lagged behind. Manti's jail was somewhat older, but had been so poorly maintained that by 1890 the city had to rent three cells from the county. Spring City found a suitable site in 1875, but Gunnison had no jail until 1894. Ephraim began looking for a site in 1871, but the search was fruitless for over a decade.[38]

Fire protection was somewhat slower in coming, even though it was just as urgent a need as police protection. Although the wide streets and predominately stone or adobe buildings in Sanpete County seemed more fire resistant, the danger of fire was nevertheless great. One of the disadvantages of the Mormon village design was the close proximity of barns and stables to the residences. The dry wood and straw in the barns and stables were highly flammable, and fires spread easily to the wooden roofs of nearby houses.[39]

Wisely, the earliest fire-prevention efforts of the city governments were attempts to minimize the inherent fire hazards. Manti, in 1879, passed "An Ordinance for the Prevention of Fires in Manti City" which required that chimneys and stove pipes extend at least three feet above the roof. The law prohibited open fires, unattended candles and smoking in barns and stables, and also authorized the city marshall to inspect all buildings where fire was a potential danger and to enforce compliance with the ordinance.[40]

Sanpete Valley's limited supply of water was as great a hindrance to effective fire fighting as it was to agriculture. In 1886, Manti did for fire-fighting what it had done for agriculture: it provided marshaling of its resources, meager though they were, in such a way as to make water available at critical times. The city council ordered the water master, upon hearing the fire alarm, to open the headgate of the ditch nearest to the fire, that that water would be immediately available at the site.[41]

Shortly after the turn of the century, the various communities began organizing fire departments and purchasing equipment, but really effective fire-fighting efforts were slow to develop. Although Manti organized a ten-man fire department in 1900 and arranged for the purchase of hoses, buckets, and ladders, their effectiveness was minimal as late as the 1920s. Mount Pleasant organized a fire department in 1914, but Gunnison did not seriously propose one until 1925. As late as 1928, the water supply and equipment available at Gunnison were inadequate to stop a big fire.[42]

Endnotes

1. *Laws of Utah,* 1852, 163.

2. Samuel K. Gifford diary, 10. It is interesting that Morley was not a member of the city council, but regularly attended and frequently exerted his influence over decisions.

3. Manti Ward minutes, 23 November 1853.

4. Ibid. See also Cordelia Morley Cox Biographical sketch, which gives as the reason for Morley's departure Brigham Young's opinion that the job was "too much for so old a man as Father Morley was."

5. H. J. Hals Autobiography, 7.

6. Albert Smith Autobiography, 70.

7. Fairview Ward Minutes, 27 May 1860.

8. H.J. Hals Autobiography, 7: George Peacock diary, 12 February 1865; Milford B. Shipp diary, 12 February 1865; Mount Pleasant ward minutes, 5 August 1866. Hyde was himself an unpopular leader; David Candland called him "an easy influenced man and an unfaithful friend . . . his treachery and abuse is remembered and the history of it engraven on my heart." David Candland diary, 1 July 1861. George Peacock, a political opponent, alleged that Hyde and Ephraim's Bishop Canute Peterson conspired to defeat him for re-election as probate judge, using their church influence. Peacock diary, 2 August 1869; 6 February 1870.

9. H.J. Hals Autobiography, 7

10. Ibid.

11. Journal History of the Church, 23 July 1874.

12. John Bartholomew diary, 4 August 1879.

13. J.C.A. Weibye, journals, 1880s.

14. H.J. Hals Autobiography, 110.

15. *Laws and Ordinances of the State of Deseret,* Salt Lake City: Compiled 1851, published 1919; quoted in Ezra C. Knowlton, *History of Highway Development in Utah,* (Salt Lake City: State Road Commission, Utah Department of Highways, 1967), 16.

16. *Laws of Utah,* chapter 118, section 1, 1909, and chapter 60, 1921.

17. Knowlton, *Highway Development in Utah,* 19.

18. Ibid., 735.

19. Brigham Young to Isaac Morley, Journal History, 23 December 1850.

20. Howard H. Barron, *Orson Hyde, Missionary, Apostle, Colonizer,* (Bountiful: Horizon Publishers, 1977), 228.

21. James H. Simpson. *Report of Explorations Across the Great Basin of the Territory of Utah,* (Washington, D.C., 1876), 41.

22. Albert Smith Autobiography, 33.

23. Azariah Smith Journal, 12 April, 27 April, 24 July 1853, 17 October, 23 December 1854, 10 February 1855.

24. Albert Smith Autobiography, 68, 73.

25. Ibid., 73. Others in seemingly helpless situation learned to support themselves also. David Thygerson, a blind man, learned to weave rugs that he sold for an income, and another blind man, Andrew Larsen, became a shoemaker. See Thygerson's Autobiography, *passim,* especially chapter 15;

Sanpete County Commissioners' Minutes, Book G, 105 (4 October 1921); *Manti Messenger,* 12 December 1913, 15, 24 April 1922.

26. Manti City Council Minutes, 4 December 1875; Sanpete County Court Minutes, Book A, 81 (30 January 1862).

27. Ephraim City Council Minutes, 25 February 1889; Manti City Council Council Minutes, 3 January 1898; Sanpete County Court Minutes, Book A, 83 (3 March 1862), 88 (3 June 1862).

28. *The Sanpitcher,* 29 June 1867, in David Candland, *Documents of David Candland* (Lewisburg, PA: Bucknell University, 1967), 101; *Sanpete County Court* Minutes, Book A, 81 (30 January, 1862); 88 (3 June 1862); 125 (20 June 1865).

29. Sanpete County Treasurers' Reports, 1867–96.

30. Sanpete County Court Minutes, Book C, 230 (4 June 1895); 223 (16 April 1896), 225 (7 May 1896), 240 (15 June 1896). Nielson's enthusiastic description of the Fairview site (230, 4 June 1895) contrasts greatly with his presentation of the other sites, and he personally contributed one hundred dollars toward its purchase, 251–52, 9 October 1895. For Gunnison's less attractive offer, see Gunnison City Council Minutes, 1 June 1895.

31. Sanpete County Treasurer's Reports, years as indicated.

32. Ibid., *Manti Messenger,* 3 February 1911; Sanpete County Commissioners' Minutes, Book H, 300–301 (6 October 1931).

33. Ibid., Book F, 2–3 April 1917, 1–2 April 1918; Ernell J. Mortensen to Afton Christensen, 19 November 1931, 1.

34. Ibid., Book H, 300–301 (6 October 1931),306 (3 November 1931), 312 (1 December 1931), 314 (7 December 1931), 329 (7 March 1932); *Gunnison Valley News,* 12 November 1931.

35. Sanpete County Commissioners' Minutes, Book F, 185 (5 August 1913), Book H, 324 (2 February 1932), Book G, 135–6 (4 April 1922), 143 (6–7 June 1922); *Gunnison Valley News,* 10 December 1931.

36. Spring City Council Minutes, 22 July 1872, 9 January 1873, 23 August 1879, 9 September 1879.

37. Ephraim City Council Minutes, 6 January 1883; Manti City Council Minutes, 5 November 1883.

38. Sanpete County Court Minutes, Book A. P. 53 (5 December 1859), p. 54 (5 March 1860); Manti City Council Minutes, 15 December 1890; Spring City City Council Minutes, 17 December 1875; Gunnison City Council Minutes, 2 June 1894; Ephraim City Council Minutes, 2 January 1871, 3 May 1874, 26 December 1882.

39. Barney Hyde recalled some devastating fires at Spring City during his boyhood, and blamed their destructiveness on the Mormon village

design and the community's dogged reliance on ineffectual "bucket brigades" to fight such fires. Ken Hansen, interview with Barney Hyde.

40. Manti City Ordinances, 8 July 1879.

41. Manti City Council Minutes, 16 August 1886.

42. *Sanpete Democrat,* 24 February 1900; *Manti Messenger,* 25 March 1921; *Mt. Pleasant Pyramid,* 13 February 1914; *Gunnison Valley News,* 24 June 1925, 21 June 1928.

CHAPTER 6

AGRICULTURE
AND LIVESTOCK

After four decades in the Sanpete Valley, settlers had established a diversified and extensive agricultural economy. Statistics for 1889 indicate that within Sanpete County were 414,331 sheep; 11,260 range cattle; 4,638 dairy cattle; 5,863 horses; and 4,238 swine. Sanpete fields produced 353,257 bushels of wheat; 135,077 bushels of oats; 16,091 bushels of barley; 4,170 bushels of rye; 1,726 bushels of corn; 27,985 tons of alfalfa hay; and 11,626 tons of wild hay. Dairy products included 212,522 pounds of butter and 8,180 pounds of cheese. Beekeepers gathered 61,220 pounds of honey.

The prosperity of the nineteenth century continued into the twentieth century until the end of World War I in 1918. Sanpete County experienced a modest gain in population, and the most important economic development was the rapid rise of the sheep and wool enterprises over the entire county. During World War I (1914–18), agricultural prosperity was stimulated by military needs. A somewhat ominous development was the cultivation of a considerable amount of marginal farmland encouraged by high prices and an unlimited market for agricultural products.

Men threshing grain in the Gunnison Valley, about 1915. (Courtesy LaMar Larsen)

The 1920s saw the first of the so-called "inventory depressions" of this century, as agricultural production remained at a high level while the market shrank drastically, creating huge agricultural surpluses. Farmers who had taken up marginal lands found it hard to keep up payments as prices for their produce fell. They responded by beginning a series of desperate experiments in agricultural diversification that continued until the end of World War II, when turkeys emerged as their most promising hope. Most of the experiments involved various kinds of crops: peas, carrots, cabbages, cauliflowers, sugar beets, and watercress.

The first experiments in large-scale industry occurred in 1914. Pea- and sugar-beet-processing plants enjoyed success for thirty-eight years, finally failing in the 1950s. Agricultural experiments were encouraged by a plentiful labor supply—the sons and daughters of large Mormon families who found decreasing opportunities in a shrinking agricultural economy. Statistics testify that during the 1920s Sanpete county's population dropped to nineteenth-century levels.

Though the population decline halted for a time during the 1930s, the decade was anything but prosperous for Sanpete County. The agricultural depression of the previous decade intensified as the Great Depression swept across all sectors of the national economy. Few residents of Sanpete County were in actual danger of starvation, for the Mormon church mitigated the effects of bank failures and unemployment by encouraging self-help cooperatives as well as home-gardening. Various New Deal programs also put local men to work on forest and range reclamation and public work projects. Neither church nor federal programs, however, offered much towards the solution of Sanpete County's fundamental economic problems.

World War II brought new economic life to the county as sheep provided wool for uniforms, and a parachute factory in Manti provided a beginning for a modest industrial development. In the years immediately after World War II, the turkey business assumed an important place in the economy of the county, and its importance has steadily increased to the present.

Sugar

Sanpete County farmers experimented with a variety of truck crops, particularly during the 1920s; but by far the most successful one was sugar beets. The sugar beet experiment was an ambitious attempt to build an entirely new economic base for the county, including both agricultural and industrial aspects. Among the first, and certainly the most, persistent and vocal advocates of sugar-beet cultivation was Gunnison's remarkable Bishop C. A. Madsen. Sanpete County has never had a more tireless champion of scientific and diversified agriculture, and during his tenure as bishop of Gunnison Ward around the turn of the century, Madsen began an impressive program of experimental plantings and correspondence with agricultural experts in an attempt to improve the economy of his community. In 1901 Madsen announced a prize to be awarded for sugar-beet growing and hinted that beets would soon come to replace grain as the county's main cash crop. The contest, he said, "will give an unexpected stimulus to our yet infant sugar industry, in which we venture to predict that the Rocky Mountain region will come to the front (as in 1889 when Utah took the first prize for wheat)."[1]

Madsen's idea was slow in taking root, but as early as 1904 the ambitious scheme of vast amounts of acreage committed to sugar beets to be processed at a local plant was being discussed and Sevier County was part of that plan. Six thousand acres were to be pledged for beet cultivation between Sanpete and Sevier Counties, and a firm that already had a beet factory in operation in Fort Collins, Colorado, was to be approached with promise of a crop that large, to see if they could be tempted to build a similar plant in central Utah. The plan came to nothing, but the idea remained, and in 1916 Mount Pleasant's Commercial Club appointed a committee to secure pledges of 5,400 acres for beet cultivation in Sanpete County alone. This time the plan worked, and the People's Sugar Company built a processing plant at Moroni in 1917.[2]

During its first season of operation, the People's Sugar Company plant processed 20,000 tons of beets and paid farmers $140,000. The experiment seemed to be a success, and in 1919 a similar plant opened in Centerfield, known as the Gunnison Valley Sugar Company. Both plants needed at least 6,000 acres of beets in order to make possible a ninety-day processing run in the fall, and both plants had difficulty from the beginning convincing conservative Sanpete County farmers that sugar beets were worth the risk. To tempt farmers to make the change, the plants cut their profit margins by raising their prices for beets. They provided free seed (an investment of $12,000 in 1926), and they offered bonuses and profit-sharing plans. Local newspapers cajoled their readers to commit larger acreage to beets. In 1926 the *Mount Pleasant Pyramid* noted disapprovingly that the community's initial pledge of 1,200 acres had dwindled to a mere 125 by harvest time.[3]

In spite of its initial promise, the sugar-beet industry in Sanpete County failed to become the savior of the county's economy that its advocates had hoped it would. During hard times, Sanpete County farmers seemed unwilling to experiment with new crops, preferring to ride out the Depression with a marginal existence based on familiar crops and tested procedures, rather than risking everything on chance. Farmers also faced the serious problem of an inadequate labor supply, partly because thinning beets was particularly hard work, requiring much detailed hand labor under a hot sun.

Nevertheless, the processing plants continued to hope for improvements in sugar-beet acreage and struggled along for several decades. During the 1920s, both the Moroni and Gunnison plants passed into the hands of large corporations: U&I Sugar bought the former, and the Wrigley Gum Company purchased a controlling interest in the latter. Competition between the two companies for the limited amount of beets became intense. In 1928 a sugar-beet war broke out when the Moroni company offered a price of $8.00 per ton to farmers in their area to induce them to break their $7.50 contracts with the Gunnison company. The conflict was resolved by a compromise under which U&I Sugar abandoned Sanpete and Sevier counties to the Gunnison Company, and the Gunnison company gave up its contracts in Salt Lake and Utah counties to U&I. With its Moroni competitor closed, the Gunnison plant improved profits. During World War II, U&I employed hundreds of local workers and paid taxes which helped support the local economy.[4] By 1946 the daily capacity had increased from 200 tons in 1919 to 1,200 tons.[5] After World War II cheaper sources for sugar became available. The Gunnison plant closed and sugar beet farmers in Sanpete and Sevier counties looked for other sources of income.

Beef Cattle

John K. Olsen in his history of livestock writes that "The cattle brought to Utah by the Mormon pioneers were those they had in Illinois in 1846 . . . dual-purpose cattle, good-sized animals that were good milker[s] and suitable to produce oxen with good walking ability . . . In 1860, oxen were produced from the Texas Longhorn crossed with Devon Cattle from England. . . . Oxen would walk 14 miles a day [pulling heavy wagons]. The last oxen were shipped out of Ephraim in 1902."[6] In time new cattle breeds arrived in Sanpete County replacing the oxen and Devon- Texas Longhorn breeds.

Church land-ownership restrictions and Indian hostilities in the 1850s and 1860s made large-scale livestock operations impossible. During the 1870s, however, the range cattle industry in Sanpete found footing, for these problems were resolved in that decade and made cattle (and sheep) raising possible on large tracts of what was then open range.

"Mormon derricks," like this one in Christenburg, were used to stack hay until well after World War II. (Albert Antrei)

Herefords and Aberdeen-Angus bulls were imported into Sanpete as early as the 1880s to upgrade the quality of beef cattle then available, but it was not until ten years later that Hereford cows were shipped to Chester and some Shorthorn cows to Mount Pleasant. A herd of polled Aberdeens was driven through the Sanpete Valley in October 1885. Their ultimate destination was unknown, but the reporter said they would "be at Ephraim and Manti within a few days."[7] The common herds in Sanpete in that day were probably long of horn and either red or roan colored, and some dairy cattle were probably included in the average "beef" herd. As a business with long-range objectives, purebred beef cattle were not seriously introduced into Sanpete until 1915.

The first year in which both sheep and cattle were grazed under range conditions was 1875, and the historic high point in beef production in Utah before the arrival of purebred bulls and cows came in the following decade. At this time the range was wide open, and in growing competition with sheep, local cattle herds were hard-pressed on adjacent summer ranges.

The winter of 1887–88 was unusually hard, and it brought supplemental feeding into the area for livestock for the first time. A two-year drought between 1900 and 1902 caused many failures. It affected the wild hay crop on the Sanpete Meadows as very little hay was cut that year. Cattle herds were decimated, not only through starvation, but also by forced sales. Heavy debts were incurred for feed.

Cattle permitted to graze Ephraim Canyon in 1904 had to be removed because of oak poisoning, and when larkspur also killed a large number of cattle in the early 1930s in Canal Canyon, two-thirds of their number were replaced by sheep.

World War I pressed its demands on resources just as livestock numbers were beginning to outrun the market. This has been referred to as "the best period for the cattle business." But the cattleman was quick to add that the "readjustment that hit the business in 1921 was also a serious fact." So was a severe winter that dropped two feet of snow in Sanpete during calving time in early April, followed by a week of freezing weather. That spring, cattle prices also dropped 50 percent. A slow recovery was noticeable in the decade of the 1920s, but by 1932 prices had not yet attained the 1920 level. The national economy, which went into its deepest depression ever in 1929, was ominously attended by a twelve-year drought, and the cattleman's gloom was extended until the late 1930s, during which time some of them went to the brink of despair. Said one, "I'm trying to figure out how to feed $40 hay to $10 cows. It's driving me crazy."[8]

World War II came to the rescue. It restored adequate prices and a renascent interest in the production of beef in the West. In the period immediately after World War II, the Sanpete cattle industry proved its adaptability with increased specialization, application of greater scientific knowledge, and wider national and even international contacts, with a resultant growth of self-confidence. The Hereford caught the fancy of most cattlemen as a breed with the right sort of qualities suitable for ranging in the mountains. Other cattle breeds introduced include Charolais from France and Aberdeen-Angus from the Midwest.

The purebred cattle industry of Sanpete has added vitality and a spark of biological science to an animal industry where, under the older methods of haphazard breeding, there was a tendency for herds

Fountain Green sheep herd in the desert west of Nephi in 1900. (Courtesy Flo Anderson)

to deteriorate in quality. With marked improvement of beef stock through the use of purebred sires, modern Sanpete stockmen (provided there are adequately high prices) make greater profits with fewer animals.

Sheep

The beginning of the livestock industry in Sanpete County was contemporary with the beginning of its settlement. Three periods were evident in its early history: the first, from 1857 to 1875, could be termed the pioneer period; the second, from 1875 to the creation of the Manti National Forest, was the expansion period; the third, from that event to the present, was the improvement period.

Sheep brought to Utah by the pioneers were limited in number, and after villages were established, the small flocks of sheep were pooled into a cooperative herd that was managed by a responsible man or men. Boys sometimes assisted with the smaller herds. The terms for feeding and managing individual flocks varied somewhat from town to town; but agreements were similar and were paid in kind to the owners and herders in an annual accounting. Following the Black Hawk War in 1868, vast grazing areas in the Sanpete portion of the Wasatch Plateau became accessible for grazing. This event resulted in an alteration of the prevailing custom and ushered in the second period. The forage in the mountains produced superior feed and better livestock. Individually and collectively, people began to exploit this great source of wealth, this initially free use of unsurveyed land belonging to the government.

It became necessary to enact laws to regulate branding and marking of livestock with properly registered brands and marks. Then, instead of hiring herders and managers for the co-op sheep, it was best to lease the sheep to responsible men.

Orange Seely, a well-known Indian war veteran, pioneer, and church leader, became the first lessee of the Mount Pleasant Co-op sheep herd. He was a meticulous record-keeper of herd numbers and wool production. He was also careful to record withdrawals of one-half sheep as debits or credits, or withdrawals of one-half mutton, etc. Accounts were balanced each year, and the record book attests of his honesty and integrity. The book remained with the Seely family for years.[9]

Similar methods were adopted in other Sanpete towns, and those lessees would have had to follow much the same system. With this introduction into the expansion period, a number of newcomers were attracted to the area because of the excellent forage in the mountains. The conditions were ideal for sheep, but countless herds from elsewhere (Colorado, New Mexico, and Oregon) were shipped to the Manti rail-head after the railway was built in Sanpete, or were trailed there across public-domain lands. Such uncontrolled usage was bound to abuse the range, and as sheep trailed at will they overgrazed and denuded the mountains.

Unrestricted competition spelled trouble. Overcrowding and overgrazing reduced the mountain's bounty, and heavy storms created floods. Lumber operations and fires contributed to the problem, and concerned citizens petitioned for relief. Finally in 1903 Congress created the Manti Forest Reserve. This act ushered in the third phase of the sheep industry—the period of improvement.[10]

The first man in Sanpete County to attempt an improvement program was John H. Seely. He had come with his parents to Mount

Bagged wool of the Jericho Wool Clip from Fountain Green about 1900. (Courtesy Flo Anderson)

Pleasant from California when four years of age. The Seelys were among the first pioneers to settle the town. John was thirty years old when he contracted to lease the co-op herd in 1885. His contract read that each owner should receive two pounds of wool per head and eight lambs per hundred head of mixed sheep, including ewes, lambs, bucks, and wethers.

In three years Seely began his own sheep herd with 3,800 head and gave up the co-op contract. He built his herd rapidly but knew that the way to increase his income per head would require better sheep. He imported some purebred Rambouillet ewes and rams from California and purchased breeding stock later from Ohio. Still later he began to import from France and Germany. Through the years he imported breeding stock continually and eventually built up a Rambouillet purebred herd acknowledged to be one of the best in the world. Seely, in turn, sold breeding stock in Russia, Japan, Argentina, Mexico, and Canada, and within the United States.[11]

In 1918 he sold the ram "62" for the phenomenal price of $6200 at the Salt Lake Ram Sale. By that time Seely had been in one phase or another of the sheep business for about thirty-three years. He died at the age of sixty-five on 31 July 1931.[12]

Following closely in the purebred Rambouillet sheep scene of Utah was William D. Candland. Born in Salt Lake City on 22 August 1858, he came to Mount Pleasant with his parents at an early age. He obtained his formal education in local school and prepared at first to become a school teacher through home study. After three years of teaching, however, he turned to farming. In 1889 he established the Candland Sheep Company, and Mount Pleasant became the center of his sheep and other interests. Wherever sheep were raised, Candland eventually gained recognition with his outstanding purebred stock. Some of it he sold to foreign countries, notably Japan and Russia. At this time, Mount Pleasant was on its way to becoming one of the Rambouillet capitals of the world.

Blending civic and political activities with his farming and livestock interests, Candland became the first state senator from Sanpete County after Utah gained statehood in 1896. His sons Royal W. and Guy L. Candland shared the responsibilities of the company with their father for many years. The Candland Company was probably the first of the sheep ranches in Sanpete to import Basque sheep herders.

The Candland Sheep Company was dissolved in 1938, and "W. D." died suddenly in 1940 in Salt Lake City. He was eighty-one years old.

The purebred Rambouillet sheepman who continued to produce highly improved range sheep over the greatest number of years was John K. Madsen. Born in Mount Pleasant in 1872, Madsen was conditioned to hard work by frontier life and eventually attained international recognition. He began herding sheep when he was thirteen years old for $10 a month. For nine years he worked for sheep men, eventually earning $30 monthly and taking part of his wages in old ewes. Paying "herd-bill" on them when running his employers' sheep, he was sometimes pressed to meet his expenses, often selling his "increase" to break even.

In 1897 Madsen borrowed enough money to buy more old ewes at 90 cents per head and launched his own sheep business. He hired his younger brothers to help him as herders. Some of them later also

Camp tenders from Fountain Green on their way to supply summer range sheep camps in about 1900. (Courtesy Flo Anderson)

had sheep of their own. Then in the fall of 1909, when the estate of sheepman James F. Jensen was being settled, Madsen bid on the 400 head of purebred ewes that had been brought from the East for Jensen by Jim Fisk. He acquired them by a margin of 25 cents per head and thus found himself in the purebred Rambouillet business. In 1916 Madsen was honored by being asked to consign animals to the first ram sale promoted by the National Woolgrowers Association.

For nearly fifteen years, Madsen's son-in-law, Bill Olsen, was associated with him in the management of the Mount Pleasant Rambouillet Farm, and after John K. Madsen died on 11 May 1941, Olsen continued to operate the business for another twelve years. In March 1954 the business was purchased by McBride and Swenson, and Frank Swenson operated it under the firm's original name of John K. Madsen. When McBride died suddenly in 1962, circumstances did not favor the continuation of John K. Madsen's name, and the assets were sold to various purchasers.[13]

The community of Mount Pleasant was particularly notable in

the purebred Rambouillet business, but the rest of Sanpete also carried on range sheep enterprises.

At intervals between 1859 and 1880, several of the residents of Fountain Green had accumulated small flocks of sheep, which, as in Mount Pleasant, had been kept close to home as family flocks. In 1880 a co-op herd of 600 head of ewes and bucks was pooled in the community. These sheep were taken into nearby hills during the summer months. The sheep of the earliest period of the industry in Sanpete were an inferior type of Spanish Merino, which produced from three to six pounds of wool per head. Most of the shearing in pioneer Sanpete was done by women, paid 4 cents per sheep. The owner was hardly ever able to dispose of the wool at more than 6.5 cents per pound. The wages for sheep herders amounted to about $20 per month, in addition to camp supplies, which consisted mostly of mutton, Dixie molasses, bacon and sourdough.[14]

In Sanpete, as elsewhere in a free society, it was inevitable that some individuals would show somewhat more innovation, initiative, and imagination than others. Fountain Green was no exception. Andrew J. Aagard, Rasmus Anderson, and Antone Christensen ("Dane") were the three most prominent sheep men whose names have survived. Antone was the first man to venture onto what is known as "the West Desert" of Utah with a sizeable herd of sheep for purposes of winter grazing. He did this in 1885.

As small bunches of sheep on Fountain Green grew to herds of 3000 head each, the quality of the animals and their wool improved with bloodlines provided by the purebred Rambouillets from Mount Pleasant. On 10 December 1908 the woolgrowers of Fountain Green joined in founding an association with 318 shares at $50 per share. Headed by Henry Jackson, the officers included N. P. Aagard, J. L. Nielsen, J. P. Anderson, and Warren Holman. This organization made up the "Jericho Pool," a nationally promoted clip of wool from 100,000 Rambouillet sheep, shorn at Jericho in the Tintic Valley of Juab County. It was sold under the trade label of "Jericho Wool Clip," and its quality earned for it the highest prices in western wool. In the 1940s Fountain Green was acknowledged as the "Wool City of the West," producing more wool per capita than any similar place in the Intermountain region.

The sheep census of 1940 shows that there were 2,248,000 head in Utah. In 1980 the census show there were only 507,000. In the United States as a whole, the same census showed a reduction over the same period of over 39 million head, cut back from 52,107,000 in 1940 to 12,513,000 in 1980.[15]

Poultry—Chickens and Turkeys

The chickens of pioneer Sanpete were of no distinct breed, but the leading ones were, like the earliest cattle, dual or even triple purpose. Chickens provided meat, eggs, and feathers. The Rhode Island Red, the New Hampshire and the Plymouth rock, all heavy soup-pot breeds that laid brown eggs, were the early favorites, but rarely in purebred form.[16]

In 1910 the first poultry hatchery for chickens west of the Mississippi River was built by Stanley Crawford in Manti.[17] Unfortunately, Crawford died of a ruptured appendix in February 1911, at the age of thirty-two and hence was unable to develop his hatchery business.[18]

By 1915, the only chicken eggs available were those produced in home flocks, and in that year Ray P. Dyreng and Erastus Jensen founded the Manti Hatcheries Company.[19] Encouraged by the Manti Commercial Club, Dyreng and Jensen became joint managers of the company in which other members of the club subscribed stock. In a short time they became impatient with the mother-hen process of incubating eggs, and within a few years they were heating artificial incubators with hot-water pipes warmed by a coal furnace. By the mid-1920s they were successful enough in their operations to attempt breeding with selected stock. It cannot be documented, but it seems likely that the breed in use at first was either (or both) the Buff Cochin or the Brown leghorn, both of which had been set under brooding hens by Stanley Crawford in 1910.

Not until the 1920s was the poultry industry organized. In 1923 Benjamin Brown, Clyde Edmunds, and Bert Willardson founded the Utah Poultry Producers Association in the Gunnison Valley, which offered poultry and egg producers throughout the county the opportunity of organizing sales and stabilizing prices. "In my book," John K. Olsen remarks, "those three men who started the Utah Poultry

The Manti-Apex breeding farms for white Leghorn chicks in the 1950s.
(Courtesy Morgan Dyreng)

Producers Association deserve [much] honor. Truly they are the
founders of [Sanpete's] significant turkey business."[20]

In 1929 each poultry man built a shed type of poultry house for
his hens. This was the result of a trip to visit the egg-production plans
around Draper, Utah, a visit conducted by the extension agencies of
the Utah State Agricultural College. In that year twenty-nine chicken
houses were constructed in Ephraim alone, and then more in Moroni
and Chester. However, for more than two decades and until the dis-
solution of the Utah Poultry Producers Association in the 1950s,
more than half of the prosperous egg business in Sanpete was managed by housewives.[21]

In 1923 Benjamin Brown, one of the Jewish settlers at Clarion,
was in New Jersey when he sent word back to Clyde Edmunds in
Centerfield and Bert Willardson in Gunnison: "You get the eggs, and
I'll sell 'em."[22] This, in essence, was the commencement of the Utah
Poultry Producers Association, which eventually benefited nearly all
egg producers, large or small, in the Sanpete Valley, except for a hand-

ful, who for private reasons preferred to market and buy feed through a similar association in Draper, Salt Lake County. The chicken industry in Sanpete was mainly one of commercial egg production, which required annual replacements of laying stock through baby chicks. These, of course, were produced by hatcheries from eggs produced on breeding farms.

In 1925 one of the Manti Hatcheries Company's employees, William P. Munk, joined his kinsman, L. R. Anderson, in starting a rival hatchery called the Apex Hatchery and Imperial Poultry Farm. Shortly thereafter they combined with the Manti Hatcheries to form the Manti-Apex Hatcheries.[23]

Meanwhile, the Manti-Apex became the dominant chicken-hatchery in Sanpete, and one of the largest in Utah, and certainly one of the most efficiently managed plants anywhere. In the early 1930s interests in the Manti-Apex were redivided in such a way that L. Glen Anderson, one of the original Apex stockholders, and William P. Munk were able to form a rival company, the Peerless Hatchery. All the time, however, both Anderson and Munk retained some financial interests in Manti-Apex.

In 1937 Ray Dyreng's oldest son, Morgan, bought out the interests of both Anderson and Munk, and thereupon he became manager and principal stockholder of Manti-Apex. Immediately, he made chicken breeding the most significant part of the farm's activities, concentrating especially on the White Leghorn, which by now everybody seemed to agree was the most prolific layer of large white eggs, the type most demanded by consumers in the market place.

Attending summer courses at Utah State Agricultural College, Morgan studied poultry husbandry and poultry genetics intensely. In tune with his plans, Morgan Dyreng joined Manti-Apex to the National Poultry Improvement Plan. The production of high-grade Leghorn chicks by knowledgeable breeding practices went hand-in-hand at Manti-Apex with commercial egg production until 1956. Although the plant was producing over 300,000 eggs annually by 1953, Morgan Dyreng suddenly found himself competing at a disadvantage with farms in California which were able to produce more than he could. However, closer to home, the rival Peerless Hatchery in Manti at its best was able to produce no more than 35,000 eggs a year.[24]

In time Manti-Apex thus became a "cooperative franchise" of the Kimber Chicks Farms of Fremont, California, in 1953. In 1956 Manti-Apex Hatcheries acquired another Kimber franchise at Fort Collins, Colorado, and operated it for several years in conjunction with the Manti plant. In 1965 the entire poultry and egg business became difficult to handle at any but the very largest levels, as the competition became more corporate, more mechanized, and more conglomerate. After nine years in Larimor County, Manti-Apex disposed of its Fort Collins plant in 1965.

The turkey is the only domesticated animal in Sanpete that did not arrive with the pioneers in 1849. They had been introduced, however, by 1867.[25] During the grasshopper infestation in 1865, the birds were used as predators to consume what they could of the calamity. Since few farmers in Sanpete have ever lived on their farmlands, the turkey was kept in the farmer's home yard in town as a barnyard bird, but this was found impractical because of the ranging instincts of the birds. It was decided fairly early that the turkey was a ranch type of domestic, not a farm bird. Shifting for herself on an outland parcel of range away from the farmer's house, the turkey hen, without a keeper or night roost or domestic feed arrangements, shifted for herself readily, scratching for seeds, insects, and whatever grain she would come home for occasionally to seek in the barnyard. She found and prepared her own nesting place and raised her own brood. The brood, however, was as vulnerable to predators as any other gallinaceous bird, and it is reasonable to surmise that this along with natural diseases made turkey raising in pioneer days a highly unprofitable enterprise.

Not until 1920 did the turkey in Sanpete come under closer scrutiny. Will Irons hatched some eggs under a turkey hen in Moroni that year. A year later Marion Jolley of Mount Pleasant joined him, and the two together raised 500 turkeys. Whatever these partners may have accomplished for themselves, their efforts were an inspiration to Ray S. Tanner in Indianola, who in 1923 raised a flock of 105 turkeys out of breeding flocks from Colorado and California. From these, Tanner raised 1,000 birds. He then selected 300 hens to produce eggs to hatch in local incubators. Within a year he had produced 2200 turkeys commercially and was the first grower in Utah to ship off a whole carload of them to market.

In 1927 Tanner entered into a contract with the Manti-Apex Hatcheries to incubate the eggs from a turkey-breeding farm, which he had established southeast of the Temple Hill in Manti. This arrangement continued at a moderate level until 1932 when, in the face of losses, Tanner concluded that despite occasional successes, the Sanpete Valley was too cold, especially in the spring of the year.

Turkey raising in Sanpete then experienced a hiatus for about five years, after which, when the industry was revived in 1937, growers in Sanpete began buying their young stock from the Sanders Brothers in LaVerkin, Utah. This effort by Sanders Brothers, which began operations in 1937, produced flocks specifically to lay eggs for Manti-Apex. For a few years turkey-breeding flocks were also maintained by Floyd and Arta Ottosen at Sterling, on grounds now occupied by the Linderhof Inn and the Cedar Crest Lodge. A full half of Manti-Apex facilities in Manti were used for turkey hatching in 1938. They added to their plant in 1939.

The breed of turkeys hatched by Manti-Apex was the broad-breasted Bronze, which originated with breeders on the Pacific Coast. However difficulties caused the managers of Manti-Apex to abandon the breed. The hatching bronze turkey chick had problems emerging from the egg alive. After maturing to the point of breaking out of their shells, many of the young poults died almost instantly, and even among those that managed to survive, a good percentage perished soon after hatching.

The cause was not obvious. In time university laboratory studies indicated that it was not the cold Sanpete spring which was to blame for high losses, but the valley's high elevation, which is between 5,000 and 6,000 feet. At this elevation, the oxygen content of the atmosphere is only 80 percent of that at sea level. As soon as the young bronze turkeys contacted this oxygen-deficient air, many were asphyxiated. Although this problem was eventually solved by incubation research at the University of Wyoming, the Manti-Apex abandoned all turkey-hatching efforts by early 1942, especially when they became aware that over 40 percent of their profits at that time were

Bronze turkeys in Sanpete County during the 1940s or early 1950s. (Sanpete County)

accruing from the production of baby chicks, notably the White Leghorn.

The first turkeys in the Ephraim area were grown by Leon Jennings, A. C. Nielsen, Jr., Joseph H. Thompson, Glen J. Nielson, Lee Anderson, Ludwig Olsen, Marcus Hermansen, Ray Olsen, and a few others whose names are not readily available. These growers left eggs intended for hatching at the Manti-Apex Hatcheries until that firm abandoned turkey-egg hatching completely. Mature birds were dressed out in growers' sheds or in barns, most of which were located on Second West, north of the railroad station.

In the early days of the Sanpete turkey industry, most of the birds were sold in Utah and Colorado markets, but the Utah Poultry Association shipped two full carloads to New York on 22 November 1923.[26]

One other hatchery was founded in 1950, this one by Stuart Shand, that was devoted entirely to the production of turkey poults. The Shand Turkey Hatchery, next to the old Manti pea cannery, produced 150,000 poults in 1953.[27] However, Shand's ill health prevented his developing the hatchery into a major operation, and he died in 1963, which ended the business for the family.[28]

In Gunnison Valley turkey production also began in the same simple way, usually as an adjunct to farming. Gunnison growers, however, began in 1933 to form a cooperative processing plant at Ephraim, an act which arose quite normally out of the Utah Poultry Producers Association. This group had been active since 1923 with both chickens and turkeys. Ephraim's turkey cooperative operated for two years; then in 1935 it was purchased by the Utah Poultry Producers. Bids were accepted from Sanpete towns to construct a new plant. Ephraim won the bid, and the plant was built at 275 West 100 North.

Moroni had been hit hard by the failure of its sugar factory and the closure of its bank in 1931. The city needed a new industry to revitalize its economy and employ its workers, and the turkey business satisfied these needs. The construction of a modern turkey processing plant by the Utah Poultry Producers Cooperative Association in 1935 was a boon to the area. The plant took birds from local growers and killed, dressed, cooled, and shipped them to various markets under controlled conditions. To provide needed mash feed for their flocks, the Moroni Feed Company was organized in 1937. It originally used a feed mixture prepared by flour miller Bent Monson. The turkey industry grew so quickly—from 700 birds in 1927 to 50,000 in 1937 to 375,000 in 1945—that a larger feed plant was required. The old People Sugar Company plant south of town was purchased in 1939 to house the larger facility. The growing Moroni Feed Company allied with the farmers Cooperative Service Station in 1939 and in 1940, purchased the Moroni Turkey Processing Plant. During the 1945–46 season the joint feed and processing business produced over five million pounds of dressed turkey. The turkey industry has flourished to the present time.

ENDNOTES

1. *Manti Messenger,* 9 February 1901.

2. J. Hatten Carpenter Diary, 14 December 1904; *Mount Pleasant Pyramid,* 30 June 1916.

3. *Mount Pleasant Pyramid,* 4 January 1918; 19 March 1926; 9 April 1926; *Gunnison Valley News,* 21 February 1926; 11 December 1924; 2 April 1925; 9 September 1926; 7 October 1926; 5 April 1928; 27 September 1934.

4. Sanpete Daughters of Utah Pioneers, *These Our Father: A Centennial History of Sanpete County, 1849–1949,* (Ephraim, 1949), 222–25.

5. *Gunnison Valley News,* 17 April 1942; 19 April 1928; 3 Jan. 1929.

6. John K. Olsen, "Livestock in Retrospects, Period II." (Ephraim, UT: unpublished, 1979), 2.

7. *Manti Home Sentinel,* 16 October 1885.

8. Ibid.

9. Will C. Clos, compiled by Hilda Madsen Longsdorf, "Historical Sketch of the Livestock Industry in Mount Pleasant, Utah, 1859–1939" (Salt Lake City: Stevens and Wallis for the Mount Pleasant Historical Assn., 1939), 294–95.

10. Ibid., 296.

11. Kate B. Carter. *Our Pioneer Heritage,* Vol. 9 (Salt Lake City: Daughters of Utah Pioneers, 1966), 601.

12. Clos, "Livestock Industry in Mount Pleasant," 298.

13. Pearle M. Olsen. *Nickels From a Sheep's Back* (Salt Lake City: Publisher's Press. 1976). Condensed from parts II, IV, and V.

14. Sanpete Daughters of the Utah Pioneers. *These Our Fathers,* 229–30.

15. Utah Crop and Livestock Reporting Service, September 1980.

16. *Manti Messenger.* Advertisement by Rev. G. W. Martin, 5 April 1909.

17. Morgan Dyreng, interview with Albert Antrei, 3 April 1981. See also *Song of a Century,* 90.

18. Stanley Crawford's headstone, Manti, Utah Cemetery.

19. Morgan Dyreng Interview. See also *Song of a Century,* 90.

20. John K. Olsen. "Chickens in Sanpete." (Ephraim, Utah: Unpublished, n.d.)

21. Ibid.

22. Morgan Dyreng Interview.

23. Ibid. Morgan Dyreng, General Manager and Owner of the Manti-Apex Hatcheries, provided detailed information on the egg and poultry industry verbally in April and May 1981. He also included involvement in the beginnings of the turkey industry, especially to details of turkey egg hatching. Mr. Dyreng has been the owner and operator of the Manti-Apex hatcheries for over forty years. He was also useful in bringing the narrative of egg production in Sanpete up to date. Unless otherwise noted, all signif-

icant information on the poultry industry in Sanpete was derived from conversations with Morgan Dyreng.

24. *Manti Messenger.* Tourist supplement, Summer 1953.

25. W. H. Lever. *History of Sanpete and Emery Counties.* (Ogden, Utah: 1898), 34, 35.

26. John K. Olsen. Unpublished notes on poultry in Sanpete in general. (Ephraim, Utah: 1979).

27. *Manti Messenger.* Tourist supplement, Summer 1953, 3. See also *Song of a Century,* 90.

28. Ann Shand Rasmussen. In conversation with Albert Antrei, 5 April 1981.

CHAPTER 7

ECONOMIC AND COMMERCIAL ACTIVITIES

While farming and agriculture were the foundation of Sanpete County's economy, other commercial and economic activities were important. Grist mills and saw mills were a first priority for settlers, followed by the establishment of a commercial system for the acquisition and exchange of goods. The cooperative movement was an important part of early commercial life in the county. When LDS church leaders encouraged their followers to practice the United Order, Sanpete residents complied—at least for a time. The discovery of coal near Wales on the west side of the valley brought hope for a more diversified industrial future. Coal brought the railroad into the county, putting Sanpete Valley potentially ahead, at least in terms of economic opportunity, of most of the rest of rural Utah. However, neither coal nor the railroad altered the basic rhythms of life for Sanpete residents—rhythms which focused on the farm, the Mormon village, and the LDS church.

Mills

The pioneers brought with them skills and equipment and

The Manti Grist Mill. (Utah State Historical Society)

employed them to create the earliest settlement economies. With carried-in technology limiting their initial efforts, the first attempts at manufacturing were only partially successful. In Manti the vanguard leader, Isaac Morley, built a grist mill which produced course flour and feed but not fine, white flour.

Flour milling has been essential to sustaining the county's inhabitants since the first years of settlement. Small grist and flour mills were typically the first industrial structures built in every town. They were erected along streams and used the water to turn wooden water wheels which turned heavy grinding stones. In time horizontal metal turbines replaced the upright wheels and steel rollers were installed in lieu of the old burr stones. By the turn of the century, new or remodeled mills were using this improved technology and became exporters of refined white flour. Ephraim had three such mills, among them the Climax Roller Mill on Mill Hill. Marcus Hermansen and his sons operated the mill from about 1901 into the 1930s when it became the Ephraim Milling and Elevator Company. The company also converted the 1870s Ephraim Co-op and Granary into a flour mill, producing grade "A" Velvet flour, as well as feed for poultry and livestock. After this mill closed, it remained vacant for decades before both historic stone structures were restored in the early 1990s and put to new uses as a cooperative crafts store and art gallery. Similarly, following the stone-ground milling era, roller mills were built in Fairview, Manti, Mount Pleasant, and other communities.

Charles Shumway and others erected the first sawmill which provided rough-sawn lumber for building structures. It was built during the summer of 1851 in the mouth of City Creek Canyon where it could take advantage of water power. Niels P. Domgaard made a simple, horse-powered mill that produced molasses from sugar cane, although not yet sugar. Domgaard converted his molasses mill to water-power. The flour mills were soon yielding white flour and the sawmill produced shingles, window and door sashes, and ornamental trim.

The Cooperative Movement

The theocratic economic system that prevailed in the county during its nineteenth-century developmental period was a combination of traditional American capitalism and Mormon-organized cooperation. At times forms of religious communalism, highlighted by the establishment of the United Order in 1874, were attempted as a substitute for capitalism. The purpose of the communal experiments was to distribute more equally the collective resources among the entire populace, rather than rely on the more self-interested methods of capitalism, to provide for everyone's needs. While limited cooperation, especially the tithing, ZCMI, and public works programs, succeeded during the formative decades in driving growth and development, the more idealistic, demanding communal experiments failed.

Central to the success of the Mormon cooperative economic system, beginning in the 1850s, was a network of tithing offices or bishops storehouses. These collection facilities were built territory-wide, including most of Sanpete's settlements. As late as the early twentieth century, tithing offices were built in the county, including the fine ones dating from 1905–1908 and still extant in Manti, Ephraim, Spring City, Fairview, and Fountain Green. In 1908 tithing "in kind" was discontinued, and storage houses were no longer constructed. But during the previous half-century, tithing was voluntarily contributed in the form of cash, livestock, produce, or labor. As early as 1850, the first settlers of Sanpete Valley were counseled to use their tithed labor to build "a state road and a bridge."[1] It was expected that faithful LDS church members would give 10 percent of their gross incomes, although records show that the consistency of payment varied widely, necessitating ecclesiastical reminders and even levies or assessments when income flagged and the economy became sluggish.

In order to finance the LDS church's planned public works projects in 1851, a resolution was adopted at the Mormon general conference requiring members to give a tenth of the value of the property they owned at the time. Later institutional tithing levies also were imposed on the profits of commercial shops, businesses and factories. The tithing was collected locally, and as surpluses accumulated, shipments were sent to the large General Tithing Office in Salt Lake City. In 1857, for example, Sanpeters sent a caravan consisting of 1,562 pounds of lead plus foodstuffs including 1,940 bushels of flour, 1,196 bushels of oats, and 21 bushels of barley.[2]

During the Mormon Reformation of 1855–56, members were asked to "consecrate" or donate to the church all of their property, cash and goods. Upon receiving an accounting showing the appraised value of all items given, local leaders "gave back" what they considered the donor needed to maintain his household and occupation, retaining the excess to be used for church purposes or given to the less fortunate. In this manner, public projects such as meetinghouses, schools, courthouses, roads, and irrigation canals were erected. In the same manner, new immigrants and the financially disadvantaged were cared for.

Although the church-sponsored economic system was of great significance to the growth and stability of the county, especially in its early decades, free market capitalism dominated daily economic life. Families and individuals were responsible for developing skills which would be used in producing goods and services needed in a community context. Following the biblical principle that "the laborer is worthy of his hire" (Luke 10:7), each person was paid in cash or, more typically, trade goods, based on the value established by the local society for the goods or services provided. Although there were commercial interchanges between Sanpete's settlements, and to a lesser extent an import-export relationship with cities in the territory, each town was relatively independent economically. Isolated from the larger

Manti's South Branch Co-op Store was built in the 1860s. (Courtesy of Fairview Museum)

American economy, self-sufficiency was the goal of every Mormon town and most individual households.

Sanpeters responded to economic initiatives originating in Salt Lake City, such as the 1868 movement to establish a silk industry. Silk worm eggs were imported from France and distributed to towns in the territory. Upon the counsel of Brigham Young, the Saints in Mount Pleasant raised a large number of mulberry trees and fed the leaves to the worms. Silk was made from the cocoons and then converted into fine clothing. The excess cocoons were exported to Salt Lake City.[3] While silk production was never a major factor in the Sanpete economy, it demonstrated the willingness of Mormons to experiment to determine how they might best use the resources of their intermountain environment.

The cooperative movement had a large impact on the Sanpete economy in the late nineteenth and early twentieth centuries. Every settlement participated in the endeavor.

The first cooperative mercantile institution in Sanpete County was ZCMI—Zions Cooperative Mercantile Institution. The ZCMI cooperative stores seemed to be ideally suited to Sanpete County, for they fit well with the communal tone that characterized life there, and yet they made available a diversity of manufactured products increasingly desired by a rural society passing out of the subsistence phase of frontier living.

In spite of persistent opposition from the few merchants who antedated the arrival of the ZCMI, retail cooperatives were operating in Manti and Ephraim within months of the inception of the program in Salt Lake City.[4] Eventually, nearly every town in the county had at least one cooperative, and some had several. Orson Hyde reported on 5 October 1869 that all mercantile establishments in the county were cooperatives and that all were doing well. Institutionalized cooperatives swept the popular imagination, and it appears that all residents of the county were members or stockholders in one or more cooperatives—cattle, sheep, tanning, coopering, milling, irrigating, and retailing. Peter Madsen of Ephraim had stock at one time or another in six different cooperatives. "The rule," Madsen said, "was cooperations in every thing."[5]

Manufacturing was also made possible on a cooperative basis, in fulfillment of a long-felt need. "Come, Capitalists, this county abounds with wealth," David Candland called out from Manti in 1863, in a plea for the development of manufacturing. Perhaps the most successful manufacturing enterprise was an elaborate furniture factory at Ephraim run perhaps by the Danes, who were so prevalent in that community, and for whom the creation of fine furniture has been a proud national tradition. In 1869 the Ephraim correspondent for the *Deseret News* reported that "the people have an excellent furniture shop, doing a good business, some specimens of work, especially several centre tables, being elegant in design and finish." He also reported, even more ecstatically, that "one of the brethren at Ephraim had cast and bored a brass cannon, which is a superior piece of ordnance."[6]

During the early years of the cooperatives, it was primarily the retail stores that reported profits. The Manti store paid a dividend "that gave general satisfaction" as early as July 1869. The store at Fountain Green paid dividends of 68 percent in 1870. The Gunnison store paid $3.00 per quarter on each $5.00 share during its first three quarters.[7]

Other kinds of cooperatives were successful. Philip Hurst, who ran the Fairview Sheep Cooperative, records in 1884 that their stock was worth 200 percent if all accounts were paid up. Even with the accounts unpaid, the stock was still 100 percent or face value. It was an aggressive business. Hurst wrote that he had traveled more that 1,000 miles by railroad, and had taken several long trips by horseback in the interests of the cooperative. The year 1886 was an especially good year for the cooperative movement in Fairview. The Sheep Cooperative that year declared a dividend of 33 percent, while the mercantile store paid 15 percent, besides investing $4,000 in a new grist mill.[8]

Such stories of success, however, proved to be the exception. Where a few were as eminently successful as noted and managed a long survival, the sad tale is that failure was more common. The story of the Manti Cooperative Store was typical. "The first six months were slow," H. J. Hals wrote, "because of the shortage of money among the people. When we took stock the rent was a little over $100.00 and the last six months it went a little better than the beginning. Each received $300 in shares as interest and all goods were set to lower prices." By 1876 the store seemed to be in fairly good condition, and J. C. A. Weibye gave the following figures for the store that year: "Each share was $10.00, each share earned $1.24 in interest for 1875; there was a total of 1,246 shares; total capital was $12,480; total stock on hand was worth $6,169." The store was weakened in 1878 when it decided to absorb the financially ailing Ladies' Cooperative Store. Even more serious was the decline in enthusiasm for the cooperative ideal in the 1880s, which Bishop Reid alluded to wistfully in an address to the Sanpete Stake in 1882: "There is no coercion in this Church—men can sustain it or not, as they please, that is their business. It is to help all, not to make a few rich." Although the Manti store stayed in business until 1916, it met increasing difficulty, and when its holdings were liquidated that year, they brought only $7,000 against an indebtedness of $9,000.[9]

The demise of the cooperative movement in Sanpete County may also have been aided by outside factors. In 1878 Bishop Madsen of Gunnison wrote to stake president Canute Peterson to complain that the parent ZCMI store in Salt Lake City priced its goods so high that it was impossible for local stores to maintain even their home business. The Gunnison store was dying, he wrote, because residents of Gunnison could get goods just as cheaply in Salt Lake City, even with the costs of transportation figured in.[10]

The United Order Movement

The cooperative movement barely established itself through the territory before the Mormon leadership began asking the faithful to enter into an even greater form of economic communalism by embracing the United Order of Enoch. This "United Order" was an idea of Joseph Smith's, and it was in perfect harmony with the utopian mood of the early nineteenth century which led to the creation elsewhere in North America of Brook Farm, Fruitlands, New Harmony, and similar communities. Mormons had tried the United Order before coming to Utah, but they had laid it aside temporarily during the early settlement phase. The pressures of the panic in 1873 on Utah's economy caused a renewed interest in economic self-sufficiency, and the apparent success of a United Order organized at Brigham City by Lorenzo Snow and at St. George by Erastus Snow encouraged Brigham Young to revive the institution through the territory.

Leonard J. Arrington has identified four primary types of United Orders, the distinguishing principle among which is the degree of commitment required of members. Only two of those types appear to have been organized in Sanpete County. The "Brigham City type" which was hardly more than a multi-purpose cooperative, was intended, according to Arrington, "As a device to reinforce and extend the cooperative network already in existence." The "St. George type" was identified by the willingness of all persons in the community to contribute all of their economic property to the order and receive differential wages and dividends according to their labor and property invested.[11]

Minute books exist for only two of the United Orders in Sanpete County—Fairview, which followed the St. George pattern and Mayfield, which followed the Brigham City pattern. However, it is

The Sanpete County Co-op in Mount Pleasant during the 1890s. (Courtesy Rell Francis)

established knowledge that United Orders existed in Manti, Mount Pleasant, Gunnison, and probably in other communities as well

Both Fairview and Mayfield organized their United Orders in 1874 and capitalized their stock at $10.00 per share. The Fairview Order issued 7,500 shares, and the one at Mayfield issued 5,000. The articles of association to which members subscribed upon joining was a standard contract designed for loftier potentials than the small communities of Fairview and Mayfield could manage. Their contract, for example, included such purposes as follows:

> mining, manufacturing, commercial and other industrial pursuits, and the construction and operation of wagon roads, or irrigation ditches, and the colonization and improvement of land and for establishing and maintaining colleges, seminaries, churches, libraries, and any benevolent, charitable, or scientific association, and for any other rightful objects consistent with the Constitution of the United States and the laws of this territory.[12]

The Fairview United Order, which required that members commit all of their economic property to the association, experienced problems from the very beginning. Some prospective members attempted to use the United Order as a means of escape from financial problems by committing to it not only their assets, but their liabilities as well. The board of directors did not immediately prohibit that practice, but they saw the dangers inherent in assuming a large debt at the outset. They decided at first that such persons "may join the co and put in what time and means they consistently can but reserve sufficient to settle their debts before they can become full members." Later, probably because it needed more members, the board left the way open for negotiation of such debts, specifying only that prospective members so encumbered "will accept the conditions of the Board pertaining thereto."[13]

Agricultural land and livestock were the commodities most immediately brought into the United Orders, and self-sufficiency was always the goal. In 1875, for example, Mayfield United Order provided, in addition to equal shares of new tracts of land purchased by the organization, "For each stockholder to have a pig and about a dozen chickens and receive feed from the company for them."[14] But they soon realized that self-sufficiency was eluding them, at least temporarily, and they began to expand into non-agricultural pursuits.

The Fairview United Order worked out an arrangement with the Provo Woolen Factory for exchanges of beef for clothing. At Manti the United Order ran a tannery, a shoeshop, and a canvas shop. Besides purchasing "city lots and hay land," the Mayfield United Order attempted to build a lime kiln and purchased apple trees to be planted on the town lots of their members. One of their real estate investments required the eviction of two tenants, O.C. Mortensen and Jeppe Sorensen, who were living in two houses that the order had planned to use as granaries. A motion for eviction carried the requirement for Mortensen "to forthwith take away some rabbits which he kept in cellar belonging to the company as they are undermining the house."[15]

The United Order was a short-lived experiment. By 1877 there were few left in all of Utah Territory. The Gunnison and Fairview organizations did not last through 1876, and Mayfield and Mount Pleasant United Orders expired in 1877. The renewed prosperity experienced in the national economy about that time doomed them all, but in Sanpete County their demise also illustrates the triumph of individualism over collectivism.

By the middle of 1874, the Fairview United Order was already critically short of operating capital and discussed sending a delegation to Brigham Young to "get information upon some points that were not easy to arrive at a conclusion upon." The crop failure of that year did not help, and the board reduced wages and other expenditures for that season. Hard times brought defections, and the order was hard pressed to refund the investments to those who wished to leave. In December the board voted to transfer its power to a general superintendent in the interest of more decisive action. By the beginning of 1876, it was apparent that widespread dissatisfaction was going to cause more defections than the order could bear.

> J. H. Allred made a request to be allowed to withdraw from the company, Jehu Cox spoke of the advantages that had been taken by parties drawing out thought there should be more stringent by-laws at least to make those drawing out, to pay a portion of the Company's indebtedness. Elum Cheney complained that this Capital-Stocks draw no dividend and he did not know how he could continue in the Order without consuming his Capital-Stock.[16]

After nearly three decades of economic individualism in Sanpete County the United Order movement had trouble generating enthusiasm for communalism. The ward minutes at Gunnison report:"

> The Order did not receive but a small (portion) of the property subscribed to the Order; that a reluctance to participate was apparent, almost in every effort made by the Board to stimulate action. And even men who it should be supposed that they should know, discouraged the building up of the Order . . . The United Order in Gunnison Ward, gradually dwindled into nothing.[17]

The same story comes out of Mount Pleasant: "We are not able to live in that Order," said Christian N. Lund, "and it was finally dissolved, with much loss to many."[18]

Coal Mining

Two Welsh coal miners from Merthyr Tydfil (old Wales)—John E. Rees and John Price—settled at the site of Wales, Utah, as early as

A Fountain Green blacksmith shop about 1910. (Courtesy Flo Anderson)

1854, but they did not begin serious mining efforts until the Welsh arrived in sufficient numbers for a labor force in 1859. The coal deposit there lay in an unusual geological position between two horizontal beds of limestone, and it proved easily worked because it was close to the surface and the limestone protected the mine from water seepage. It was the first coal mine to be discovered in Utah, but the initial high hopes that it generated for industrial development diminished after thorough testing of early samples. Compared with coal discovered later in Carbon County, Wales coal had a higher fuel ratio, but it was much less pure, containing high amounts of ash, sulphur, and fossil elements. The Welsh miners, who brought their Old World skills to the New, found it very good for use in blacksmith work, but tests for coking potential for general industrial purposes revealed its impurities, and the washing process required for coking was too expensive.

An English company bought out the Welsh miners in 1875, and, in 1880, in the interests of their investment, they constructed the first railroad into the Sanpete Valley in the form of the narrow-gauge "Sanpete Valley Railway" which operated through Salt Creek Canyon between Nephi and Wales, or Coal Bed. Later the rails were moved to run through Moroni. By 1904 only 400 tons of coal were extracted from the Wales mines annually, a negligible amount compared with the more than 1.5 million tons mined throughout Utah.[19]

The Morrison mines in the mouth of Six-Mile Canyon, two miles east of Sterling, were first worked in 1888, and this brought the Sanpete Valley Railroad deeper into the valley in 1894, by way of Ephraim and Manti. This coal had actually been discovered much earlier than 1888, and its quality and characteristics were similar to the coal of Carbon County, but several nagging problems persisted in the mining process. In the first place, the coal was very soft and broke easily during the extraction process, thus impairing its value. Furthermore, the deposit led to severe faults in the strata and could not be relocated on the other side of the breaks. Finally, the faults allowed vast amounts of water to run into the mine, making work difficult. An ironic source of revenue developed when the mine operators sold the water to the Gunnison Irrigation Company and the Manti Reservoir Company. The latter concern also bought water-storage rights in Funk's Lake (now Palisade Lake), from which they dug a ditch to conduct lake water to the fields of their Manti shareholders.[20] The Morrison Mine was abandoned shortly after 1900.[21]

The third major coal deposit was discovered near Mount Pleasant, but it was never seriously mined. Test samples proved inferior in their coking potential and the deposit itself was uneconomically deep, between 955 and 1,151 feet. As of now, no mining entrepeneurs have considered the Mount Pleasant fields to be of sufficiently high quality to offset the cost of extraction, although the desperate industrial needs of World War II led to serious investigation.[22] Better mines in Carbon and Emery counties were more accessible to the larger markets in the Salt Lake Valley.

The Railroads

No other event had a greater positive impact on the county's economic and cultural life in the nineteenth century than the coming of the railroad. Its arrival, especially from 1890 on, also enhanced connections with the outside world. In addition to transporting goods, passengers could travel at will and a cornucopia of literature and new ideas became available. A noticeable flourishing of commerce, cul-

The Sanpete Valley narrow-gauge railway through Fountain Green.
(Courtesy Flo Anderson)

ture, and architecture was an almost immediate result both of the
largess brought by agricultural and livestock wealth, together with
ready access to new ideas and life ways emanating from the eastern
states and beyond.

Sanpete's first railroad, the Sanpete Valley Railway, entered the
valley in 1880 for the single purpose of exploiting the coal beds near
Wales. The territory's larger cities to the north were in urgent need
of coal to run their industrial machinery and heat their homes and
businesses. Much of the coal from Coalville, Carbon County, and
eastern sources was too expensive, of poor quality, or not available
on a consistent basis. The single-track, narrow-gauge line laid up Salt
Creek Canyon from Nephi had been conceived earlier, after Indians
showed John Rees substantial coal outcroppings in 1854, but it took
an infusion of British capital and the assistance of Simon Bamberger
(later Utah's first non-Mormon governor) before the costly project
could be realized. In 1894 the initial line of the Sanpete Valley
Railroad was extended across the valley southeast to the mouth of Six
Mile Canyon near Sterling from whence it transported coal from the

Morrison mines. The track was converted to standard gauge in 1896, but the mines petered out and the line was discontinued in 1907.

Even more important to the ending of the county's geographic isolation was the Denver and Rio Grande Railway which came from the north through Thistle, reaching Manti in December 1890. Soon the cities along the line—Fairview, Mount Pleasant, and Ephraim— and those along spur lines built wood-frame stations with loading docks, making it possible for local farmers and stockmen to start exporting the county's surplus goods to outside markets. The new D&RG also provided passenger service, quickly outmoding the old stage line. For a while the older Sanpete Valley Line and the new D&RG Western were in competition, but eventually the newcomer prevailed and bought out the interests of the Sanpete Valley.

During the golden years of railroading, the county prospered as never before, evident by the fine Victorian and early twentieth-century architecture still extant from the corresponding building boom. At the same time, however, the tracks divided the towns and created the stigma of living "on the other side of the tracks." Eventually, any economic benefits were not enough to prevent railroad difficulties and eventual failure. An 1894 account reported that "the train on Tues. evening was delayed about an hour in the field north of Manti by the large number of cattle in the track. The engine struck some of the animals. The train is delayed almost every night on account of stock."[23]

Habitual lateness, costly maintenance of the line, and a declining economic climate contributed to the railroad's gradual demise. During the 1940s, sections of the line were abandoned. The last train departed Manti in 1949. In time all but the Mount Pleasant depot were razed. In 1983 the remaining trackage, which was used occasionally for hauling freight, was destroyed by the massive landslide which cut off the Thistle route. After the Thistle Dam was formed, the little-used line was not reconnected. Long before this time, however, the county's vehicular road system had been well-established.

Mail Service

During Sanpete County's first seventeen years, communications with the world beyond the valley occurred via written and verbal

The Sanpete Valley Railroad Engine. (Utah State Historical Society)

means transported by those traveling in and out of the county. Brigham Young and Isaac Morley exchanged communiques in this manner in the early years. Returning missionaries, freighters, military couriers, and others also served as messengers. Wagon trains entering Utah Territory from the Midwest brought news, books, magazines, and newspapers from the East and Europe.

Early in 1851 a postal route was developed between Salt Lake City and Sanpete County. Probate judge George Peacock served as the first postmaster.[24] Over the next eight years, five more post offices were established. Eight were founded in the 1860s and eight more came in the 1870s. Ten more offices came into existence by the turn of the century. Only a few have been added in the twentieth century due to the near ceasing of settlement activity.

Before the federal mail system was fully operational, individuals and groups contracted with the territorial government to carry mail and small packages, usually on pack mules or horseback. Several express companies operated between Utah and the states, among them Wells Fargo, American Express, and the Adams Express Company. Until 1870 Russell, Majors and Waddell was the largest freight handler, using large, ox-drawn wagons. Once the mail and goods reached Utah, local equivalents of these national enterprises operated between Salt Lake and Sanpete, bringing in imported items and exporting locally grown and manufactured goods, and exchanging correspondence.

The Telegraph

It was nearly impossible to receive current news until the Deseret Telegraph extended its line into the county. In early 1861 Edward Creighton, the father of frontier telegraphy, came to Salt Lake City to ask Brigham Young to help build the first transcontinental telegraph line. By 17 October 1861, the line had reached Salt Lake City from the east, and a week later the line from the west reached Utah's capital city. In the following years, the Deseret Telegraph Company established lines to Utah's major communities. The Sanpete line was first opened on 28 December 1866, with Anthon H. Lund as the first operator.[25] This instantaneous means of communication gave the county sudden access to all developed sectors of the territory and country and helped to ease the sense of isolation felt by Sanpeters.

Newspapers

Sanpete's journalistic tradition got its start when Frederick C. Robinson used "phonographic reporting," a new system of phonetic-based "Pitman" shorthand he learned in England, to produce the county's first newspaper, the *Manti Herald*. Using skills he had perfected as a church and civic recorder, educator, essay and song writer, and Manti correspondent to the *Deseret News*, Robinson's first issue was published on 31 January 1867, the year of his death. His paper consisted of a single, personally handwritten, legal-sized page. It went only to subscribers and carried admonitions from Brigham Young, news—including coverage of the Black Hawk War then in progress—plus local advertising. The originals of the several issues of "Volume 1" are extant in the Salt Lake City Public Library.[26]

It would be another eighteen years before Manti printed its first mechanically produced newspaper, the *Home Sentinel*. The *Manti Messenger*, forerunner of today's paper, was created by the Manti Printing and Publishing Company on 13 October 1893. The city's third paper during these exuberant expansionist times was the *Sanpete Democrat*, founded in June 1898 by L. A. Lauber.[27]

Ephraim's first newspaper, the *Sanpete County Register*, began in 1890 with James T. Jakeman as editor but ceased printing after some twenty editions. A year later M.F. Murray and Company started it up again under a new name, *The Ephraim Enterprise*. This weekly newspaper has continued under the same name for well over one hundred years. Eventually printed in Manti, the paper is widely read locally and by former Ephraimites who have moved away.[28]

Mount Pleasant's local newspaper, *The Pyramid*, first started in November 1890 by A. B. Williams, has continued until the present. In the late twentieth century, there were four weekly newspapers in the county: the *Mt. Pleasant Pyramid*, *Manti Messenger*, *Ephraim Enterprise*, and *Gunnison Valley News*.

ENDNOTES

1. Journal History, Brigham Young to Isaac Morley, 23 Dec.1850.

2. Journal History 12 February 1857.

3. *Mount Pleasant, 1859–1939,* Mount Pleasant Pioneer Historical Association reprinted by Community Press, Provo, 1939, 127.

4. Sanpete Stake minutes, 23 July 1882.

5. *Deseret News,* 5 October 1869; Peter Madsen Autobiography, 57.

6. *Deseret News,* 29 May 1963, 16 July 1969, 24 November 1869.

7. *Deseret News,* 9 August 1869.

8. Phillip Hurst diary, 29 January 1884; see also undated entries for 1886.

9. H.J. Hals autobiography, 8 March 1870; J.C.A. Weibye journal, 10 January 1876, 23 May 1881; Sanpete Stake minutes, 23 July 1882; *Manti Messenger,* 14 January 1916.

10. Gunnison ward minutes,149.

11. Leonard J. Arrington, *Great Basin Kingdom,* (Cambridge: Harvard University Press, 1958), 330–31.

12. Minutes of the Fairview United Order, 1–5; minutes of the Mayfield United Order, 1–5; minutes of the Mayfield United Order, 14 September, 20 November 1874.

13. Minutes of the Fairview United Order, 12 July, 9 November 1874.

14. Minutes of the Mayfield United Order, 2 October, 1 May, 6 March, 20 October 1875, 8 January 1876; minutes of the Fairview United Order, 7 July 1874; H.J. Hals Autobiography, 96; Joseph Hansen Family History, 27.

15. Mayfield United Order, 20 October 1875.

16. Minutes of the Fairview United Order, 21 June, 13 November 1874; 22 September, 25 December 1875; 28 February 1876.

17. Gunnison ward minutes, 1876.

18. Christian N. Lund, Mount Pleasant. n.d.

19. G.B. Richardson. "Coal in Sanpete County, Utah," U.S.G.S *Bulletin* 285, 280–83; Clark, "Coal Near Wales," 189.

20. Ernest J. Scow. Shareholder, Manti Reservoir Irrigation Company, Manti, interviewed by Ruth D. Scow, 4 December 1980.

21. Richardson, "Coal in Sanpete County," 283–84.

22. Paul Averitt, "Coal, Mineral and Water Resources of Utah" (Utah Geological and Mineralogical Survey, Bulletin 73) March 1964, 45–46.

23. *Manti Messenger,* 28 September 1894.

24. *Deseret News,* 22 March 1851 and 2 March 1854.

25. Hilda Madsen Longsdorf, *Mount Pleasant* (Mount Pleasant: Mount Pleasant Historical Society, 1939), 115.

26. Richard L. Robinson, "Frederick Charles Robinson (1826–1867)," unpublished manuscript, Salt Lake City, 1996.

27. Daughters of the Utah Pioneers of Sanpete County, *These . . . Our Fathers: A Centennial History of Sanpete County, 1849–1947* (Springville: Art City Publishing Co., 1947), 32.

28. Centennial Book Committee, *Our Yesterdays: A History of Ephraim, Utah, 1954–1979* (Ephraim City Corporation, 1981), 154.

CHAPTER 8

WATER AND THE
NATIONAL FOREST

During the first twenty years of settlement, most controversies over land involved water rights. Orson Hyde, the LDS general church authority resident in Sanpete County, would not live in Manti because in his day he found the water in Manti Creek too muddy and too unpalatable. Establishing himself in Spring City, where the spring water was more to his liking, Hyde administered a *de facto* water court. The LDS church controlled water directly in the first decades, but later mutual irrigation companies were formed to supervise the use of this most important natural resource. After ditches and canals were dug, farmers sought to increase the amount of water available through reservoirs, tunnels to bring water from the San Rafael/Green River drainage on the east side of the mountains into Sanpete Valley, drainage endeavors, artesian wells, and the use of mechanized sprinkling systems.

Early Irrigation Efforts

Manti was one of the first communities to complete an "extensive irrigation enterprise," a "canal about five miles long, six feet wide

This photograph by L. P. Christensen of Ephraim shows work on the Chester Ponds during the 1880s. (Courtesy Jenny Jensen)

and two-and-one-half feet deep," to turn the course of Cottonwood and Spring creeks "to obviate the difficulty of cutting hay in the wet swamps." [1] In Fairview the first irrigation ditch was dug by Barney Ward. He was an "old trapper" already living along the Sanpitch River north of the present townsite when the first settlers came. He had taken a small stream of water from the river to irrigate a piece of land near his house. His ditch, later enlarged and extended by the settlers, was known as the "Graveyard Ditch." As the town grew, settlers cut small ditches from Cottonwood Creek to their city lots to water their gardens. After a short time, they saw the advantage of working together cooperatively on ditch digging. As early as 17 May 1860, a committee was appointed during a church meeting to supervise the digging of irrigation ditches. The first cooperative effort was the City Ditch from the Sanpitch River. During that first year, water was also taken from Birch and Oak creeks. As the population grew, so did the number and size of canals and ditches.

In 1860 the first settlers of southern Sanpete County filed on the waters of the Sanpitch River, Twelve Mile, Nine Mile, and Six Mile Creeks. The Old Field Canal was taken from the Sanpitch in the early 1860s. It was dug by oxen pulling "plows, Vs and slush scrapes," plus exhaustive pick and shovel work. The ditch was first dug to Neil Sorensen's farm, then to Fred Erickson's farm. The ditch eventually carried 125 second-feet of water. The flow of the Sanpitch lessened as more water was taken out up stream—a source of contention for many years. In 1878 the New Field Canal Company was organized and dug a canal to take water from Twelve Mile Creek to the Gunnison-Centerfield area.

In Axtell, the county's southernmost town, attempts to bring water in from Salina Creek in 1877 were unsuccessful. The first settlers drew from Willow Creek which was divided into ten shares. Axel Einersen owned 4/10 while four others split the rest. One share watered a "good sized farm." On 17 April 1897 the Willow Creek Irrigation Company was formed. In Fayette, John James and his sons built the first canal from Warm Creek to bench land west of Fayette. The canal was later enlarged to include land three miles north. In 1893–94 a local group extended the Earns and Robbins Canal to the Fayette area.[2]

In early Wales two streams were diverted to town lots, each of which received two shares of water, the rest going to farm land. Each share was good for two hours of watering. On 15 April 1889, the Wales Irrigation Company was founded with 308 shares. Water was taken from Pete's Canyon about two miles south of town. In the same year, the West Point and Silver Creek irrigation companies were formed. The former dug a seven mile long canal from the Sanpitch, while the latter drew from a spring west of Moroni to water 571 acres of farm land plus 100 acres of pasture.[3]

In 1860, within a year after settlement in Unita Springs (now Fountain Green), water was brought in a channel from the canyon to the townsite. A plow was used to cut increasingly deeper furrows in a ditch into which stream water was diverted from its original course. In 1903 all of the various water rights and claims in Fountain Green were combined to form the Fountain Green Irrigation Company. Stock was issued in exchange for water rights. Most of the water came from Brig Springs north of town, but other sources included Log

Hollow, Water Hollow, Big Hollow, Pole Canyon, Birch Creek, and Squaw Springs.[4]

Water Shortages and the Law

While Sanpete residents cooperated in developing a network of ditches and canals to irrigate their lands, the system was not without tensions and conflicts. Livy Olsen, a Spring City settler, described the relationship of water and land in Sanpete County:

> . . . as all water was soon appropriated for beneficial use, and the land being valueless without it, land jumping was unknown, because of the fact that water rights did not apply to any one particular piece of land and land jumpers could not acquire the water rights, this method of securing a farm at another man's expense did not exist.[5]

As new settlers arrived and obtained new land and water rights, they took some of the water which had been going to previous settlers. Peter O. Hansen of Spring City lamented after his poor 1860 harvest that his crop of wheat was "so slim" because new settlers had "robbed our water when we needed it most."[6] With water rights divided and repeatedly subdivided, limited resources were sometimes spread so thin that cooperation turned to stiff competition and unity turned to contention. Some settlers, such as Oluf C. Larsen who departed Spring City for Ephraim, moved from one town to another in search of farms with accompanying water rights.[7] Often the primary claims to a source of water conflicted with secondary claims to the same source. In June 1861 a problem arose between Mount Pleasant and Spring City over the use of Cedar Creek. Spring City's claim to the water was based upon prior settlement. William Morrison said he was satisfied to be ruled by the local church leaders, but that according to the law Spring City had first rights to the water anyway. Mount Pleasant residents countered by saying that they wished to change the natural channel of Cedar Creek in order to guarantee enough water for their town. Church leaders decided that the waters of Cedar Creek should be allowed to continue their course in the natural channel.[8]

Fairview and Moroni confronted each other over the water of Oak Creek. This resulted in an arrangement by which Fairview promised to send as much good water to Moroni as the former took out. In other words, the solution was a compromise, in which the two towns simply agreed to split the stream. A committee from Moroni was allowed to visit Fairview from time to time to monitor their neighbors' compliance.⁹

Water rights for new settlers posed problems when the water had to be extended to expansion fields in various towns. In Manti the people held a mass meeting on 19 September 1864 to consider what they would do regarding water for lots opened farther from town during the past three years. In most cases of settlement acreage, the solution was to extend the system of canals and ditches to handle the demand. Moroni encountered the same problem, but they decided that the owners of distant fields had the responsibility for supplying their own water through their labor on an extension of the city ditch.

Sanpete Valley's ability to absorb new settlers ended much sooner than most had anticipated. In 1890 a survey of irrigation practices in the West reported a dismal situation in Sanpete County:

> The water supply is scanty even for one-half the land, and the right to take water from each creek, by increase of settlement and subdivision, has become so complicated and has been so extended that it is difficult even for those owning prior rights to get sufficient water to mature a fair crop. It is even worse with the later settlers, for, according to the regulations, they are only allowed the flood waters or such portions of the stream as their neighbors can not use. After a late comer has used the water for several years and has established a home it becomes a matter of great difficulty, both legally and actually, to deprive him of water, destroying his trees and fields, in order that the older settlers shall have enough, and yet, on the other hand, irrigators holding prior rights feel that it is not just for other men to come in and gradually destroy the value of their farms by acquiring the greater part of the water.
>
> Sanpete County is a good example of the evils arising from the neglect of jealously guarding prior water rights. As population increased, the older farmers, from friendship or compassion, allowed others to share their water supply, and frequently in times of scarcity good naturedly divided the scanty supply. Thus an increasingly large number of irrigators acquired certain rights to the water, until the limit has been reached, when in dry seasons all

suffer together, and at other times there is barely enough water for all, and they do not receive sufficient returns to insure prosperity or contentment.[10]

Utah irrigation law in 1852 gave county courts control of water, allowing local governments to distribute this resource in "the interest of settlements." The county then appointed water masters to distribute the water to farms, homes, and businesses. The legislature also made individual grants of streams to Mormon leaders to establish irrigation canal and milling companies. In 1865 the legislature passed irrigation district laws that authorized the establishment of districts which were empowered to tax residents to pay for building irrigation systems. When heeded, the laws were interpreted widely and adjusted to local conditions. In dry years water masters tried to ensure that everyone got some water, even if the earlier settlers did not receive as much as they needed for maximum production. In the 1880s, people began to pursue individual interests above community welfare. This change was reflected in a new law in 1880 which repealed the 1852 statute and gave authorities the power to distribute water rights to individuals. The new law "became the dividing line between communitarian and individualistic irrigation systems." Historian Thomas Alexander observes that by

> ... sweeping away the history of a people who had tried to build a covenant community, the courts used individualistic theory to justify a practice that had originated in the impulse to build Zion. By the mid-1880s, Babylon sailed high on Utah's irrigation waters.[11]

One result was that earlier settlers were often given more water than newer ones, who sometimes could obtain no water at all. The law also allowed individuals to sell water rights like a commodity without taking responsibility for the effect on neighbor's needs. Some favored irrigators were allowed to appropriate the entire flow of a stream, even if they did not need it, creating a monopoly on the resource and putting at helpless disadvantage those who depended on water but could not afford to buy it.

Beginning with the Higgins Decree of 1900, water rights on the Sevier River drainage system were gradually bestowed on a legal basis

Construction of Nine-Mile Reservoir in 1909. (Courtesy Gerald Alder)

in that area through a series of court orders adjudicating various individual disputes. The Higgins Decree was followed in 1906 by the Morse Decree, then in 1926 by a temporary action of state engineer J.M. Bacon which became popularly knows as "Bacon's Bible." None of these affected the drainage of the Sanpitch, however, despite that fact that the Sanpitch is a tributary of the Sevier. It was not until the ruling on 30 November 1936 of Judge Leroy H. Cox, who promulgated the "Cox Decree," that water rights in Sanpete County were finally given clear, legal sanction.

The Cox Decree was a profoundly conservative action; its purpose was solely to codify tradition and add the force of secular law. It was far too late in 1936 for anyone to attempt any kind of revolutionary redistribution of water that alone could have pumped new life into Sanpete County agriculture.[12]

Of equal importance to laws and traditions affecting water use was the management and control of the watershed in the mountains above the Sanpete Valley. The threat to the watershed from overgrazing and other questionable practices led to the establishment of the Manti Forest Reserve in 1903 and brought the United States Forest Service to Sanpete County.

The National Forest

The presence of national forest lands on watersheds above the Sanpete Valley is a reflection of the existence of land-use problems of a serious nature, most of which began during the 1870s. These problems were mainly ecological, but because people were involved, they ultimately became political and economic. Their complexity was suspected from the beginning, but they had to await years of scientific and political maturity for their solution. Despite scientific evidence of the success of the forest service in handling most of the basic problems, there has always been some opposition to such management because it involved restrictive regulations.

In 1891 the United States Congress passed the General Provision Act authorizing the president to designate particular areas of forested public domain as Forest Reserves. Yellowstone, the first of these, was followed quickly by several others, including the Manti Reserve. In 1897 Congress passed a forest management or Organic Act to provide for favorable conditions of water flow and a continuous supply of timber for the nation.

In 1901–1902 an outbreak of typhoid fever in Sanpete County was attributed to water used for culinary purposes contaminated by decaying animal carcasses lying in forest streams. This was one of the reasons Sanpete citizens petitioned the federal government to establish the Manti reserve. In March 1902, 8,800 acres of Manti Canyon were withdrawn from access and grazing. Despite the protest of local stockmen, Nephi Ottesen was hired that year to ride the reserve and enforce the closure. On 29 May 1903, the Manti Forest Reserve was created by presidential proclamation. President Roosevelt added 190,000 acres to the north end of the Manti Forest on 18 January 1906. The new area encompassed the land currently in the forest from Fairview Canyon to Spanish Fork Canyon. Most Fairview and Indianola residents favored this action for its protection of the watershed and timber land.

Flooding continued in several locations west of the plateau for many years. A 1908 flood washed through Ephraim with boulders estimated to weigh seventy-five to one hundred tons. Flooding in 1909 did "much damage" at seven locations in the county, four of

The aftermath of a flood in Manti about 1900. (Utah State Historical Society)

them in or near Wales. The flooding in Ephraim did $20,000 damage. Fairview had to dig out of the mud, and Fountain Green was washed over by canyon waters from the Sanpitch Mountains. Twelve Mile Creek sent floodwater through Mayfield, Axtell, and Gunnison in the south.[13] A major flood in 1918 brought boulders, rocks, and mud through town which damaged bridges and fences, covered gardens, and filled basements. Louis Oldham slipped, fell into the stream, and drowned. After the floods, prisoners from the state penitentiary were sent to help clear the Pleasant Creek channel.

Carlyle H. Ollerton, son of a forest ranger, remembers a flood that hit Mount Pleasant in the early 1920s.

> We had a large flood caused by a cloud burst on the east canyons and it did quite a bit of damage. I recall my mother gathering up the children and rushing them into the house and the neighbors rushing over to our house because our house was on high ground and was two stories, where most of them were one story homes in

that area. The flood left a lot of damage and it was some time before it was cleaned up, with the bridges being washed out and all the work and cleaning up that had to be done with horses and scrapers and men with picks and shovels.[14]

The establishment of the Manti Forest Reserve brought full- time forest superviors and managers who had to deal with a myriad of problems while developing policies and procedures that would regulate traditional practices and activities in an attempt to manage the forest resources.[15]

A pioneer forest service employee, J. W. Humphrey, began working on ranger districts in 1906 and became supervisor of the Manti National Forest in 1919. He continued as supervisor until his retirement in 1941. Humphrey left a valuable account of his career with the forest service beginning with his application for employment in 1905.

> Sometime about the middle of July 1905, some friends of mine suggested that we go to Mount Pleasant and take the Forest Ranger examination which was scheduled for July 23 and 24. At that time I was living in Salina, and the nearest Forest Office where the necessary blanks could be secured for making application was Ephraim. I lost no time in securing the blanks and filing same with the Civil Service Commission.
>
> The Manti Forest Office was located upstairs over the Christiansen Furniture Store in Ephraim. We reached the office by climbing the stairs next to the ranger's office, and walking a plank south across the greater part of the store roof, as the office was in the south side of the building. About eight months later I received an appointment as Assistant Forest Ranger on the Manti Forest, with headquarters in Orangeville, Range District #2. My appointment became effective the day of the San Francisco earthquake, April 18, 1906. A. W. Jensen was Forest Supervisor, and Parley Christiansen, David Williams, Frank Anderson, Beauregard Kenner, and Ernest Winkler were the rangers. Winkler and Arthur Jeffs were forest guards up until 1906 when Winkler was made assistant ranger.
>
> On April 18, 1906, I received a compass, a Jacob staff, a marking hatchet, a surveyor's link chain and pins, a small "Use Book" that I could put in my hip pocket, Gifford Pinchot's "Primer in

Forestry" in two volumes, numerous forms, most of which were for free use, and some stationary, including township plats and a map of the forest.

The following day I left for Orangeville with one saddle horse and one pack animal. Arriving at Orangeville I rented a pasture near the forest boundary. I had no tent so I used an open cabin on the pasture that I rented, and which I later bought. In June I hired a man to move my wife and baby into Upper Joe's Valley where I built a hog-proof enclosure which I covered with a large tarpaulin, and this served us the first year as a tent. The following year I received an authorization of $65 with which to build a cabin and to buy a stove. I hauled some homemade slab chairs and a rough lumber table from one of the old abandoned sawmill sets. This sufficed for furniture for another year or so when funds became available for a better stove and additional furniture.

In 1907 I was given the responsibility of a ranger nursery, 36 by 36 feet, enclosed with lath fencing, and shaded also with the same material. I hauled the fencing, built the nursery, and planted it to Ponderosa pine from seed secured from the Bessey Nursery in Halsey, Nebraska. I did all this alone as there were no neighbors within 25 miles, no telephone, and the road was difficult to get over with a light buckboard. It did not take me long to find out what rodents and birds could do to a beautiful little nursery. I improved a sprinkling system for the nursery by setting up a barrel to which I attached a hose. I did this only after I found that [a] friend['s] wife could not carry the necessary water from the creek to water the nursery with a sprinkling can when I was away for a few days at a time. I was furnished a shotgun to shoot the birds, and poison to kill the rodents; and we succeeded in getting about 200,000 nice little seedlings in that nursery.

. . . Sometime between 1907 and 1910, Sam Pierce was hired to trap bear that were very numerous in Twelve-Mile and adjoining canyons. As I recall, between 50 and 100 bear were taken out by Mr. Pierce. Prior to that time the bear had kept the cattle out of the high country so that the upper range began to show the effects of too heavy use. . . . [16]

Somewhat earlier than the Manti National Forest, the Payson National Forest was established by presidential proclamation on 3 August 1901. Lands were added to it by the same means on 5

November 1903 and 21 July 1905. These lands of the Payson National Forest also protected Sanpete watersheds in the northwest corner of the county. However, the Payson National Forest was eliminated on 18 June 1908 when divisions of that forest north and south of Salt Creek were combined to create a new national forest, the Nebo National Forest. In 1915 President Woodrow Wilson issued an executive order abolishing the Nebo National Forest and assigning forest lands south of Salt Creek to the Manti National Forest and lands north of that divide to the Uinta National Forest. In 1923 President Calvin Coolidge signed an executive order placing the forest lands south of Salt Creek under supervision of the Uinta National Forest with headquarters in Provo.[17]

Due to shrinking budgets and related consolidations, the Manti National Forest was joined with the La Sal National Forest of Grand and San Juan counties in 1949–50. This was described as more of a "shotgun wedding" than a consensual union.

To achieve greater administrative efficiency, the watershed areas west of Fountain Green, Moroni, and Wales, all in the Uinta National Forest, were put in the charge of the Sanpete Ranger District of the Manti-La Sal National Forest through an internal agreement in 1974.[18]

The Great Basin Experiment Station

In order to make long-range stable adjustments, it became necessary to understand the plant ecology better in the region. Determining mountain ecology and the carrying capacity of summer range in general became the specific task of the research station established in Ephraim Canyon.

First called the Utah Experiment Station, construction began in 1912 and was completed in 1914. The station headquarters were located at the base of Haystack Mountain in Ephraim Canyon, ten miles east of Ephraim along the mountain road to Orangeville. Later called the Great Basin Research Center, it was said by the government to be "the oldest research station on forest range and watershed land in America."[19] The station's office was in the Ephraim City Building, while the field headquarters stayed in the canyon. A branch of the Intermountain Forest and Range Experiment Station in Ogden, the

The Great Basin Experiment Station on 13 March 1918. (Utah State Historical Society)

agency did investigative work over a large part of the Great Basin. The main field laboratory in Ephraim Canyon served as a model for developing similar stations in the United States and internationally. The station's work included finding adapted plants and procedures for increasing production on valley and foothill ranges.

The first range and watershed studies were conducted by Dr. A. W. Sampson.[20] Beginning in 1912, ecological studies were conducted in oak-brush, aspen, aspen-fir, spruce-fir, and subalpine zones from roughly 6,500 feet above sea level to somewhere around 10,000 feet.

Sampson left the Great Basin in 1922 to become associate professor of forestry in the forestry school of the University of California, Berkeley. Even before he left the county for good, however, Arthur W. Sampson had achieved national recognition as the "father of the science of range management." His three textbooks on range and pasture management, range forage plants, and livestock husbandry on mountain ranges were being used as college texts in nearly every forestry school west of the 100th meridian.

Since the research station was established in Ephraim Canyon, it has produced a veritable torrent of scientific and practical information on range management, erosion phenomena, and Great Basin ecology. Research was done at such places in Ephraim Canyon as Headquarters of the "Spearmint" Station at Haystack Mount, and on substation sites on Majors Flat, Wiregrass, Snowberry, Bluebell, Philadelphia, and on Erosion Areas A and B at Alpine substations, where an older ranger station stood above Headquarters. Scores of technical researchers employed at the branch station have published nearly 200 articles and government bulletins, plus at least three known textbooks, based entirely or largely on investigations of phenomena between Majors Flat at the forest boundary to the head of Seely Creek, and from Horsehose Flat to Bear Creek. Some of these investigations have achieved international circulation and no little scientific distinction.

In 1960 the title of the chief research and administrative office at the Great Basin was changed from "Director" to "Project Leader." It was under this official title that A. Perry Plummer authored the most scientific papers of all research personnel at the Great Basin, thirty-eight in all. Most were of single authorship, but some were in collaboration with selected associates from the forest service, the State of Utah, or with personnel of the three universities in the state. Plummer's contributions were mainly in agronomy, shrub genetics, or in detailed phases of ecology and problems of the mule deer.

In 1971 Karen Vance of Fairview assembled materials to establish a small museum at the experiment station and twenty years later, in 1992, Snow College took over maintenance and operation of the station. The college has maintained the museum and historic laboratories, preserved the buildings, and uses the facilities for summer school classes and special conferences. The Great Basin Environmental Education Center was dedicated in 1993 and is one of the highlights along the Ephraim Canyon Scenic Drive.

As of 1999, the Manti-La Sal Forest contained 1,338,066 gross acres, of which 366,021 acres lay in Sanpete County. Of the 958,258 gross acres within Uinta National Forest, only 21,230 lay in Sanpete County, while 1,907 acres of the Fishlake National Forest are found in the county. Altogether, there are 389,158 acres of national forest lands in Sanpete, which is located in Region 4, Intermountain, of the National Forest system.[21]

ENDNOTES

1. *Inventory of the County Archives of Utah: No. 20 Sanpete County* (Salt Lake City: Utah Historical Records Survey, Works Projects Administration, 1941), 22.

2. Daughters of Utah Pioneers, Sanpete County, *Centennial History of Sanpete County, 1849–1947*, (Springville, UT: Art City Publishing Co., 1947), 165, 173.

3. Ibid., 198.

4. Ibid., 202, 208, 211.

5. Livy Olsen, "The Life Story of a Western Sheriff," 11.

6. "Peter O. Hansen Reminiscences," 141–142.

7. Oluf C. Larsen, Autobiography, 37.

8. Mount Pleasant Ward minutes, 28 June 1862.

9. Moroni Ward minutes, 2 March 1875.

10. U.S. Department of Agriculture, *Report On Agriculture by Irrigation in the Western Part of the United States at the Eleventh Census:* 1890.

11. Thomas G. Alexander, *Utah, The Right Place, The Official Centennial History*, (Salt Lake City: Gibbs Smith Publisher, 1995), 224.

12. U.S. Department of Agriculture, *Irrigation Water Management Sevier River Basin, Utah* (June 1976), 7–10; Dudley D. Crafts, *History of the Sevier River Bridge Reservoir* (Delta, Utah: DuWil Publishing Co., 1976), 2.

13. *The Pyramid*, Mt. Pleasant, 20 August 1909.

14. Sue Ollerton, "Life History of Caryle Hood Ollerton," Local History Project, Utah State University, 9 March 1977.

15. For an account of the first supervisor of the Manti Forest Reserve, see Adolf W. Jensen, "Unpublished Reminiscences" (Ephraim, 1953).

16. J. W. Humphrey, "Unpublished Reminiscences," (Ephraim, 1953).

17. Jensen, "Unpublished reminiscences."

18. Gary M. Coleman, letter to Albert Antrei, 14 July 1980.

19. Jensen, "Unpublished reminiscences."

20. Ibid., 75–76.

21. Forest Service, "Land Areas of the National Forest System," United States Department of Agriculture, September, 1996, 34, 72, 100.

CHAPTER 9

RELIGION

The history of Sanpete County cannot be understood or appreciated without comprehending the religious motivation that brought about its settlement, development, and vitality. From the moment the pioneers first set foot in the county to the present, life in Sanpete has been dominated by the Church of Jesus Christ of Latter-day Saints or Mormon church. Still, Sanpete County residents are not exclusively Mormon, and other groups, including Presbyterians, Methodists, Catholics, and even splinter groups from mainstream Mormonism have played an active role in the county's history.

Founded in Fayette, New York, in 1830 by Joseph Smith, Jr., The Church of Jesus Christ of Latter-day Saints grew rapidly while moving its headquarters to Ohio, then Missouri and Illinois, each time being expelled and exiled, before making the mass exodus to the Great Basin starting in 1847.

A core belief in Mormon theology is the concept of Zion, a word of many meanings for Mormons. It refers to God's chosen people, his church, and the places where the church and his people reside. The church collectively is Zion and its individual members are citizens of

Construction of the Manti South Ward Building about 1880. (Utah State Historical Society)

Zion. The Mormon settlement area is the land of Zion where the people of Zion live by God's laws and await his second coming. The pioneering effort was viewed as nothing less than the work of establishing Zion or the Kingdom of God on earth.

Mormon Church Leaders

Among Sanpete's most influential LDS religious leaders was Orson Hyde, president of the Quorum of Twelve Apostles for twenty-eight years. During April 1858 General Conference, Hyde was called to serve as president of the Sanpete-Sevier District of the church. Maintaining a household in Salt Lake City to which he returned on a regular basis, Hyde first located in Manti. He soon moved to Spring City, however, where he built a large limestone house (still standing) and established permanent residency for his polygamous family. The husband of seven wives and thirty-two children (of which only seventeen lived to adulthood), Hyde also served several terms as a territorial senator.

One Hyde biographer claims that "In 1860 he was sustained as the first president of the Sanpete Stake, and served until 1877, a few months prior to his death."[1] Since the stake was not officially created until 1877, however, it is likely Hyde's position was a reaffirmation or restructuring of his church district presidency. Regardless of title, Hyde was clearly the chief religious leader in Sanpete for the twenty years preceding Canute Peterson's twenty-five year tenure. During this time Hyde was overseer of Sanpete's greatest proliferation of colonies. When he arrived in June 1860, there were only six small settlements in the county. Five years later, at the beginning of the Black Hawk War, there were fifteen settlements. Hyde was a prolific speech giver, active organizer, deeply involved with Indian relations, improving irrigation, farming and local economics, and guiding the spiritual welfare of the Saints.

In poor health his last ten years, Hyde received a blow to his status when in 1875 Brigham Young rearranged the seniority of the Twelve Apostles. He subtracted the six months Hyde had been disfellowshipped during the church's move from Caldwell County to Far West, Missouri. Both Orson Hyde and Orson Pratt were dropped in seniority below John Taylor. Hyde's reaction to this demotion is not recorded, but had this correction not occurred, Hyde would have succeeded Brigham Young as church president after the latter died 30 August 1877. Hyde outlived Young by only fifteen months, passing away on Thanksgiving Day, 28 November 1878. It was John Taylor, not Hyde, who became church president.

Another important leader in the early days was Dan Jones, an extraordinary speaker and perhaps the most successful Mormon missionary of all time. Converted to Mormonism in 1843, the next year Jones was with Joseph and Hyrum Smith the night before their murders in Carthage Jail and avoided death himself only because he had been sent away to find a lawyer. The same year he became a forceful missionary in his homeland of Wales and baptized converts by the hundreds, including an entire Protestant congregation. In 1849 Jones arrived in Utah with some 2,000 Welsh converts, some of whom joined him in bolstering the struggling settlement of Manti. Here Jones helped deal with Chief Wakara, build the fort, grind wheat, and run a store. He was elected the first mayor of Manti.

In 1852 Jones was once again in Wales where he won a large number of converts to the Mormon faith and helped many of them to immigrate to America where some eventually settled in Wales, Sanpete County. Here Jones and others devised a plan to freight coal from the new Wales by wagon to Utah Lake and thence to the Salt Lake Valley by boat. The project never materialized. When he died in 1861, Jones left three wives and six children, "having lived several lifetimes in his 49 years," and having left an indelible mark on Sanpete County. [2]

One of the especially distinguished church leaders coming out of Sanpete was Anthon H. Lund who had lived in Ephraim, Fairview and Mount Pleasant. In 1889 Lund, a Dane, became the first Scandinavian apostle of the LDS church. He later served for twenty years as a member of the First Presidency, the highest-ranking body in the church.

Although he never resided in Sanpete County, Brigham Young had for nearly three decades greater influence over the county's development than any man who lived there. From Salt Lake City he supplied the creative impetus for the founding of nearly 300 communities. In a tireless effort to instruct and encourage the Latter-day Saints, Young also made dozens of major treks through the Mormon settlement area between 1847 and 1877, the year of his death. The trips were invaluable to fledgling villages, and townspeople looked forward to them with much anticipation and celebration. These visits were marked by parades, pageantry, feasts, and large meetings for which whole towns would turn out. Local men were engaged to assist the caravans or serve as bodyguards, while the women were kept busy preparing food and making accommodations for Young and his entourage of visiting apostles and other dignitaries. One historian summarizes that:

> Such visits enhanced community, unity and loyalty; they helped people to persevere in difficult circumstances; and they demonstrated that each community was considered important. Whether Latter-day Saints lived 45 miles, 80 miles ,or 300 miles from Salt Lake City, most could count on at least a yearly visit. He listened, observed, renewed friendships, counseled, instructed, comforted, motivated, scolded, strengthened and blessed. So important were

The Ephraim Tabernacle. (Utah State Historical Society)

these visits to Young and to the settlers that even as he aged and his health declined, he continued his arduous travels. These trips were one key to his leadership and to the successful colonization of the Great Basin.[3]

Young made numerous trips to Sanpete County starting with the first in April 1851 during which he organized the first high council. Two months later John Lowry, Sr., was appointed presiding bishop of Sanpete. His final trip was in April 1877, just four months before his death, during which he dedicated the site of the Manti temple.

While Young's visits focused on mass meetings and private conferences with priesthood leaders, women were also instructed on a less frequent basis by heads of the Relief Society, the auxiliary for females. With her two counselors, Eliza Roxey Snow, who presided over all women's organizations from 1866 to 1887, made frequent trips through the territory. Between March 1880 and December 1881, for example, she twice visited Sanpete County, driving her own buggy over "the most fearful roads." In Sanpete she met with women in twelve different settlements, returning for repeat visits to seven of them. Among her purposes were furthering Relief Society projects, strengthening the women's commitment to plural marriage and organizing the Primary Associations for children. The advice she and her counselors gave to their sisters was as well-received as Brigham's was by the brethren and resulted in the women's "phenomenal contribution to nineteenth century Mormon community development."[4] By 1884 there were seventeen Relief Societies in the Sanpete Stake.

The "Swedish Apostasy"

The presence of a sizeable number of non-Mormons in Sanpete County began in 1862, when a rift in the Mormon church known as the "Swedish Apostasy" resulted in the excommunication of a number of people. Scandinavian immigrants had brought their national rivalries and prejudices with them, and even a common religious enthusiasm could not erase those centuries-old traditions. The Swedes, who were a minority within a minority, thought that the refusal of church authorities to hold services in their tongue, in addition to Danish, Norwegian, and English, was unreasonably discriminatory. Two of them gave vent to their discontent too harshly and were excommunicated. The movement gained momentum as sympathizers followed the two into religious exile, either through formal excommunication or by simply letting their active participation in the Mormon church lapse.[5]

During the following decade, the number of those non-Mormons grew very little, and they remained relatively unorganized. Mount Pleasant, where the movement had started, remained its center. By 1875 the non-Mormon group had become known as the "Liberal Party," and they had begun construction of a building in Mount Pleasant later called "Liberal Hall," to be used for social gatherings and dances.[6]

On 3 March 1875 the mail wagon from Nephi stopped in front of the Mount Pleasant post office, and a young Presbyterian minister named Duncan James McMillan stepped out. McMillan was a well-educated Scotsman, who tenacious personality and Presbyterian moral resolve would prove useful in his new home. Victimized by an unspecified disease, perhaps tuberculosis, McMillan had followed his doctor's advice in forsaking his New York home for the dry air of the Great Basin. Hearing that a sizeable number of non-Mormons in central Utah were without a spiritual shepherd, he set out to try to persuade them to become Presbyterians.[7] It soon became apparent

The Manti Presbyterian Church in the 1880s. (Courtesy Wasatch Academy)

that those who elected to do so had gained a resourceful leader who would not be easily dislodged.

McMillan preached at the Liberal Hall at 3:00 P.M. the following Sunday, 7 March, and in the evening addressed the Mormons in their church. His reception at the latter engagement was not recorded, but he so impressed some of the Liberals that they began negotiations with him to secure his permanent services. The Liberals must have known that McMillan intended to stay, for the non-Presbyterians among them drove a hard bargain with him. They allowed him to use the Liberal Hall for church services and a school, and donated one-third of the cost of the building. McMillan had to agree, however, to open the school immediately, to guarantee to keep it open for five years, and to pay them the remaining two-thirds of the cost of the building within one year.[8]

In spite of his limited capacity for physical labor, McMillan made a set of school furniture, using only hand tools, and opened school on 20 April with thirty-five students. Although enrollment grew rapidly, financial pressures nearly toppled the school before the first year ended. McMillan had some meager savings of his own, but he expended them on a disastrous trip through the Midwest to secure contributions that would enable him to pay off the building by the deadline. He secured $1,000 in pledges, but realized only $350. As the deadline approached, he secured a mortgage on the building that enabled him to make the payment, but this seemed only to postpone disaster rather than avert it, since funds were only trickling in. However, when a totally unexpected check for $500 arrived from the ladies of the First Presbyterian Church of Cedar Rapids, Iowa, the Liberal Hall was redeemed.[9]

His financial problems over, McMillan went on the offensive, extending the Presbyterian missionary effort to most of the other major communities in the county. The dry Utah air seemed to have effected the physical cure he sought, for he proved to be a tireless worker, not only preaching at his own school at Mount Pleasant, but traveling constantly to preach throughout the county and creating and supervising other churches and schools. He also made frequent trips to the East to raise funds and recruit workers. On one trip he brought his mother back to assist in his work and to help keep house for him. Finding he needed even more help and companionship, on another of his whirlwind trips he married an attractive young music teacher and brought her and her new Mason and Hamlin organ out to Mount Pleasant.[10]

The longest lived of McMillan's missionary establishments in Sanpete County, with the exception of Mount Pleasant's First Presbyterian Church and Wasatch Academy (which still thrives today), was the Manti school and church. Manti was fertile ground. As the second largest community and the county seat, Manti attracted outsiders who were sometimes non-Mormon and therefore possible recruits for the Presbyterians. The railroad, for example, brought H. J. Hornung and his family, who were mainstays in the Manti Presbyterian church for several decades.

McMillan began his "assault" upon Manti almost immediately upon his arrival in the county, preaching there frequently in rotation with other communities. On Saturday evening, 20 April 1878, McMillan held services in Manti, and the congregation agreed to form a permanent church the following day and to seek a pastor. At the organizational meeting on Sunday, twelve members enrolled, most of whom were apostate Scandinavian Mormons.[11]

In his search for a pastor for the Manti church, McMillan was fortunate to secure Reverend George W. Martin, who served for many years not only at Manti, but as a sort of roving pastor for Ephraim and Gunnison as well. When McMillan moved to Salt Lake City in 1880 to set up a headquarters for the Presbyterian missionary effort in the whole region, Martin succeeded him. Martin was nearly McMillan's equal in educational background: he was a graduate of both the University of Ohio (1876) and the Union Theological Seminary (1879). He was the Manti pastor from 1879 until his death in 1919.[12] He was Manti's first full pastor—and the last. After 1919 the Presbyterian church declined rapidly in Manti and nobody was appointed to replace him.

Martin's first task was to get a church built, mainly because the Presbyterian day school, begun in 1877, was badly in need of suitable quarters. Shortly before his arrival, some of the members had solicited subscriptions "among those outside of the church of the Latter Day Saints" for building finances. Although it was said that they received $700-$800 in pledges, they had lost their list of sub-scribers before Martin arrived. His first move in reviving the plan was to recontact as many subscribes as possible, but he decided to drop the idea altogether when he discovered that some of those who had pledged money were under the impression that the new building was to be used also for "dances, political meetings and infidel lectures."[13] Martin eventually financed the building with member contributions

The Gunnison Presbyterian Church in the 1880s. (Courtesy Wasatch Academy)

and mission funds from the East, and, with "our much prized bell" in place, the first service was held on Thanksgiving Day, 1881.[14]

Other communities as well soon felt the Presbyterian presence; indeed, during the late 1870s and early 1880s, Mormons must have felt they were being subjected to a Presbyterian invasion. The Presbyterian mission in Sanpete County was divided into two districts: G. W. Martin was responsible for Gunnison, Manti, and Ephraim: and William Wilson was responsible for Mount Pleasant, Spring City, Moroni, and Fairview.[15]

It is clear that the degree of success enjoyed by the Presbyterians varied widely from one community to another. *The* [Presbyterian] *Church Review,* surveying the non-Mormon religious scene in Utah in 1895, pointed out that Ephraim, for example, "has always seemed to be hard ground for missionary work." A Presbyterian church was founded there in 1880 and one elder was ordained to oversee it, but he quit within one year, and church membership, which had reached twenty-four at one point, was down to only twelve in 1895. At Gunnison, on the other hand, the Presbyterian school opened by

Mary Crowell in 1881 had grown from an enrollment of twenty-six in 1881 to "nearly 60" in 1895, and another teacher had become necessary.[16]

Most Presbyterian institutions in Sanpete County declined and closed during the early decades of the twentieth century. The rising quality of the public schools rendered the Presbyterian schools less important, and normal attrition through death, coupled with declining immigration into the county and the general failure of the Presbyterians to make converts among the Mormons, doomed the churches as well. The Manti school for example, closed in 1909. During the 1920s, the South Sanpete Presbyterian Mission was combined with Sevier County under the roving guidance of Rev. S. T. McLeod, who held services twice a month in each of the communities under his charge.[17]

Mount Pleasant, the original Presbyterian center, has been the only community where the Presbyterians have continued to thrive. Because of innovative programs. highly qualified teachers, a low student-to-faculty ratio, and an aggressive recruitment effort, Wasatch Academy has attracted students from all over the Intermountain region and several foreign countries. Although regular support from the Presbyterian church ceased in 1973, Wasatch Academy, in its unique position as a lone Presbyterian outpost in a Mormon world, has continued to enlist the support and interest of Presbyterians through the county. Many of the buildings on its campus today bear the names of wealthy donors who may never have set foot in Utah.[18]

The Methodists also sponsored missionary endeavors in Sanpete County, although they were not as widespread nor as long-lived as the Presbyterian efforts. Theirs was a two-pronged program. In November 1882, under the direction of Martinus Nelson, who had set up headquarters at Salt Lake City for a Methodist mission to Danish and Norwegian Mormons, Methodist evangelists began preaching throughout central Utah. Peter A. H. Franklin and Martin Anderson preached in Sanpete County in the communities of Manti, Ephraim, Moroni, and Mount Pleasant. By their own accounts, both met a marked lack of interest among the Mormon rank-and-file and aggressive resistance from the Mormon leaders.[19]

Members of the Utah Gospel Mission. (Utah State Historical Society)

The other prong of the Methodist endeavor met with better success. Like the Presbyterians, the Methodists set up permanent churches and schools, in each case in the same communities as the Presbyterians. The Methodists eventually had buildings in Mount Pleasant, Moroni, Spring City, and Ephraim, most of which were built from 1885 to 1888. Also like the Presbyterians, they used their schools and well-trained teachers as their main source of appeal, hoping to win converts and church members as a by-product of their educational efforts. The schools at Spring City and Moroni seem to have been the most successful. The latter, taught by Miss Emily Anderson, enjoyed at the beginning an enrollment of thirty-seven, although it fluctuated from twenty-two to forty-two. The Methodist church at Moroni had an average attendance of about fifty in 1895.[20]

The Utah Gospel Mission

A second wave of evangelical Protestant activity began in the early twentieth century as traveling circuit preachers sent by the Congregationalists, Seventh-Day Adventists, and Salvation Army focused on Sanpete County. Congregational minister John D. Nutting, a resident of Salt Lake City, had the greatest impact. His

Utah Gospel Mission, organized in Cleveland, Ohio, in 1900, operated for half a century with the sole purpose of evangelizing Utah's rural towns. Unlike the earlier Protestants who provided the Mormons with a useful service—quality education—the Gospel Mission provided only its anti-Mormon message. Paid by Nutting through contributions he raised, his missionaries worked in teams of three for a year each, systematically combing small Mormon communities and holding meetings. The Gospel Mission received a predictably cold reception in Sanpete, a Mormon stronghold. Reece Anderson of Mount Pleasant recalls that Nutting's meetings in the 1920s, "would really get to be something. The more the old gentleman and his followers attacked the Mormons, the more they reacted to it, . . . and some rather bitter episodes would take place."[21] Anderson observed that the mission's fervent efforts had the opposite effect intended . Finding their beliefs attacked, initially curious, lukewarm Mormons responded by attending their own church in greater numbers. Few permanent converts were won and the net effect may have been a strengthening of the local LDS church.

Polygamy

Of all Mormon religious and social experiences during the nineteenth century, polygamy is easily the most discussed. It attracted a great deal of partisan rhetoric, but the precise measurement of its extent and effects is difficult.[22] Although much about the subject remains obscure, Sanpete County sources illuminate important aspects of it.

From the earliest days of settlement, LDS leaders preached polygamy as an integral part of their religion. During the settlement's first winter at Manti, Isaac Morley spoke "particularly upon the Plurality of wives and cautioned the Young People to beware of opposing the Principle and said that a curse would follow those who would oppose that principle, and showed the effects of opposing any principles which God had revealed."[23]

The 1880 U.S. Census indicated that twenty-four of the 367 Mount Pleasant households were clearly polygamous, while an additional ten households each contained only a married woman with children and were thus probably polygamous. The number of polygamous households in Mount Pleasant falls between 6.5 and 12 percent. Census data for Manti suggests the polygamous households at between 6.6 and 16.9 percent.[24] In reviewing the biographies of 722 men included in W. H. Lever's *History of Sanpete and Emery Counties,* Stanley S. Ivins, found that 12.6 percent had more than one wife.[25]

Those who embraced polygamy encountered hard times during the 1880s, for the Edmunds Act, passed in 1882, brought renewed vigor to the anti-polygamy crusade. News of the impending legislation caused angry threats of civil disobedience in Sanpete County. At a Sanpete Stake conference in January 1882, "Pres. Maiben said, More would be done by the world from time to time to deprive the saints of their civil rights. Said Congress might pass unconstitutional laws but where it was against the sentiment of the people such laws could not be executed, because the people would not regard them."[26]

After the bill became law, there was a general closing of the ranks as Mormon leaders determined to defend their institutions with renewed zeal. Impassioned rhetoric was especially prominent in the Relief Society sessions at the fall 1881 Sanpete Stake conference. Mary Ann Price Hyde, plural wife of Mormon Apostle Orson Hyde, "bore her testimony in celestial marriage said our enemies do all in their power against us, she had been in celestial marriage for the last 40 years, and never regreted. Urged both young and old to bare testimony and to act in the work that is calculated to exalt us."[27]

It was over three years before the commitment of any Sanpete County polygamist would be put to the test, but the prosecutions were intensive when they began. From 29 November 1885 until the end of the decade, the repeated raids of polygamist-hunting federal marshals were a prominent feature of Sanpete County life. For polygamists like J. C. A. Weibye, the raids meant, at the very least, a series of frustrating interruptions of regular business and "hiding up" with relatives, or in the mountains, or in hastily constructed cellars, and, at worst, a humiliating, heartbreaking, and costly term in the Utah State Penitentiary. Weibye's journal captured a sense of the disruptions caused by the raids in an entry for 8 October 1886: " . . . an Excitement was raised here in Manti about Deputy Marshals being here in Sanpete Valley from 6 to 25 in Number, so that many of our leading men hided up. I stayed with my daughter Margreth Kjar, in 4 day from Saturday Noon, till Wednesday afternoon."[28]

The following spring (1887), Weibye received a letter from Salt Lake City warning that another raid would begin soon and telling him to alert the other polygamists: "The Deputyes came here to Ephraim, Spring City, Manti and Mount Pleasant they are macking prepartion for an Attack on us in some of the Settlements, they have rented a room in Ephraim for a Week." A week later Weibye wrote that "none of the Marshals have made us any disturbance yet here in Sanpete County, but we have hided up some of us for several days."[29]

While Sanpete Mormons stood by the doctrine of plural marriage, as church leaders preferred to call polygamy, the practice did reflect and create certain problems. Olea Thompson explained that in Mount Pleasant in the 1860s

> there was a dearth of young men in Mount Pleasant as in all Mormon communities. Young men were slow to join the church, its membership was composed mostly of married people and young women, so the girls had not much choice, either they became an "Old Maid" or they married into polygamy and there were few "Old Maids" in those days.[30]

The case of Peter Madsen shows that men, as well as women, were subject to pressure to contract polygamous marriages. Madsen wrote that during the "Mormon Reformation" of the 1850s:

> we had lots of preaching and council, but some of it went to far to be from the highest authority, some of this was about plural marriage. I was obedient but not wise. I married a girl, but she did it more of fright than of love, for that reason it could not last long only about 9 months then she was divorced in 1858.[31]

Those who were able to escape unhappy relationships as easily as Madsen were fortunate. Others, like Nels Peter Madsen, were less lucky. When he went to prison to serve a six-month sentence for polygamy, he deeded his farm to one of his wives. Upon his release, he found her unwilling to allow him to deed it to his other wife, and he found himself barred by officers of the law from removing any livestock or machinery. Bitterness resulted, and he never again visited that wife nor even her children, until after she died.[32]

The Fairview North Ward Chapel. (Utah State Historical Society)

By far the most detailed and pathetic documentation of an unhappy polygamous marriage in Sanpete County is found in the diary of Elvira Euphrasia Cox Day, second wife of Eli A. Day, the schoolteacher at Mount Pleasant. Day's strategy for avoiding prosecution for polygamy was to keep the marshals from discovering that he had a second wife. As a schoolteacher, he could hardly afford to go into hiding. Accordingly, he lived with his first wife, Eliza, in Mount Pleasant and boarded Elvira (the second wife) with her brother, Abner, in Fairview. As portrayed in her diary, Elvira's marriage consisted of a succession of indignities, punctuated by brief moments of conjugal bliss during Day's rare visits. Not only was she deprived of Day's public recognition and company, but Elvira also suffered, by her account, constant vilification from Eliza and the imposition of having to serve as guardian to Ellen Day, her husband's nineteen-year-old sister, with whom she had bad rapport.

The tragedy revealed by her diary is of a deep but mostly unrequited love. Much of Eliza's hostility seems to have been a result of her frustration at the fact that Elvira bore the first of Day's sons. When Eliza finally gave birth to a boy, Elvira revealed the depth of her love for Day, together with some of her unhappiness at his rejection of her when he would not allow her to name her son after him, the father:

> I thank God that Eliza has a boy now. I can feel easier than ever before. I suppose he will have all of his father's name, which (I know I don't do right to condem) but I feel that its very selfish. I have tried to make myself believe, and have made other people, that I did not want his name—the dearest name on earth to me—but its no use telling myself I didn't want it or writing such things down here—I did want part.[33]

Eli Day did exercise great caution in his relationship with Elvira. He refused to ride with her in the same carriage to a family reunion. When he refused to dance with her in public she wrote:

> Bro. Day offered to go and help or he would not have been there, for I felt like I never again wanted to be at a dance where he was till I could dance freely with him—in fact I formed a resolve to that affect when I was refused the simple boon of a dance—just as though dancing with a person could any way possible be termed cohabitation!![34]

The arrangement proved too difficult. The marriage did not last. Elvira got her own teaching certificate, and after a long career as a teacher and author of poems and dramatic productions used in ward theatricals, she died at Manti in the 1940s.

Polygamy ended in Sanpete County, especially after Mormon president Wilford Woodruff issued a Manifesto in 1890 effectively ending the practice of plural marriage.

The Manti Temple

The crowning achievement of religious and pioneer life in Sanpete came to pass between 1877 and 1888 with the construction of the Manti temple. Not only an architectural masterpiece, the temple reflects the dedication to Mormonism of the residents of Sanpete and surrounding valleys and their ability to work together in building the most sacred of LDS buildings.

At the time of the initial settlement of Sanpete Valley, Heber C. Kimball, a counselor to Brigham Young, reportedly prophesied that

The Manti Temple looking to the north from the city. (Utah State Historical Society)

not only would the settlement succeed, but that a temple would be built to adorn the valley.[35] At a conference held in Ephraim on 25 June 1875, the prospects for a temple were discussed with Brigham Young and other local church leaders. Most seemed to favor construction of the temple at the stone quarry in Manti, although a substantial minority remained uncommitted to a specific location. Near the close of the conference, Young announced that "The temple should be built on Manti stone quarry." Nearly two years later, on 25 April 1877, Young formally dedicated the Manti temple site which had been purchased from Manti City for the sum of $54.

After the dedication of the site by Young, he went on to give instructions for the construction calling for the temple to be built by those with clean hands and pure hearts, that the building of the temple was not a matter of merchandise, and " . . . if any person should enquire what wages are to be paid for work done on this Temple, let the answer be, 'Not one dime.'"[36]

Five days after the dedication, a force of a hundred men gathered at the quarry to commence the eleven-year project. "There were those from Ephraim who walked over daily. Such a one was Andrew Christian Nielsen, the one they called Andrew Mormon Preacher, who walked over daily from Shumway's Springs, where he lived. On the other hand, J. P. .L. Brienholt walked over every Monday and back home not until Saturday night, after this sixty hours of weekly toil on his Lord's temple was done."[37]

Nearly two years were spent blasting and scraping to excavate the site for the footings and foundations of the temple. The cornerstones were laid on 14 April 1879 and work began on the walls using stone taken from the hill. Brigham Young died in August 1877 just four months after dedicating the site. Most of the construction was carried on under the administration of President John Taylor until his death in 1887. President Wilford Woodruff saw the temple completed and presided over its dedication on 17 May 1887.

William H. Folsom, who served as architect and project superintendent gave the following description of the planned temple on 26 November 1877:

> The temple is 171½ feet long and 95 feet wide outside measurements; the towers are 30 feet square at the base, the west tower will be 169 feet high. The east tower will be 179 feet higher from grade of building; the grade of the temple site will be elevated 63 feet above the street grade on the west. The main room will be 80 feet by 104 feet in the clear and 20 feet high in the clear. Middle chamber 20 feet high. The upper chamber will be 28 feet high in the clear and 80 by 104 feet in the clear between walls with self-supporting roof without columns.[38]

Local craftsmen applied their best skills to decorate and adorn the interior of the temple. C. C. A. Christensen, assisted by Dan Wegland and Martin Linzie, painted murals on the inside walls of the temple. William Asper was foreman of carpentry work and supervised the building of the magnificent five-story spiral staircase with its 408 intricately fashioned spindles, that is a favorite of visitors inside the temple. Jeppe Jefferson did much of the interior woodwork carving. John Patrick Reid was responsible for much of the ornamental hardware. Women produced beautiful carpets for the rooms including one for the Celestial Room which had twenty-seven different colors.

After its completion in 1888, the Manti temple underwent several major renovation projects, including the construction of a great stone stairway on the west side of the temple. Built in 1907, the stairway was removed in 1940. An extensive four-year renovation project was undertaken from 1982 to 1985 that included major interior restoration and repair work, the extension of the annex north for a larger foyer, the construction of a two-story addition east of the annex, replacing the roof and weathered stone, installation of new mechanical, electrical, plumbing, fire-protection, heating, and cooling systems, landscaping improvements, and other work. In the late 1990s exterior stone restoration was completed.

Standing on Temple Hill and visible from most parts of the county, the Manti temple remains a physical symbol of the importance of religion in Sanpete Valley.

ENDNOTES

1. Howard H. Barron, *Orson Hyde, Missionary, Apostle, Colonizer* (Bountiful, UT: Horizon Publishers, 1977), 221.

2. "Welshman Dan Jones was One of Zion's Busiest Bees," *The History Blazer*, Utah State Historical Society; also see Ronald D. Dennis, *The Call of Zion: The Story of the First Welsh Mormon Emigration* (Provo, UT: Brigham Young University Religious Studies Center, 1997).

3. Ron Esplin, "Brigham Young's Travels in the West." in S. Kent Brown, Donald Q. Cannon, Richard H. Jackson, eds., *Historical Atlas of Mormonism* (New York: Simon & Shuster, 1994), 102–3.

4. Ibid., 105–7.

5. WPA Utah Writers' Project, *Inventory of the Sanpete County Archives*, (Salt Lake City: Historical Records Survey, 1941), 30.

6. Samuel G. Goodwin, *Freemasonry in Utah*, (Salt Lake City: Grand Lodge of Utah F & A M, 1933), 5.

7. Ibid., 3–5. *The Church Review*, 4 (29 December 1895), 40.

8. *The Church Review* 4 (29 December 1895): 40.

9. Ibid., 41.

10. Mildred Eigenbrodt, "Proudly It Stands," *Wacademy World* 41 (Spring 1975): 3.

11. Manti Presbyterian Church Minutes, 1; J. C. A. Weibye Journal, 21 April 1878.

12. *The Church Review,* 42: Rev. Duncan J. McMillan, "Presbyterian Work in Utah," in *Addresses at the Tenth Anniversary of the First Presbyterian Church of Salt Lake City,* 13 November 1882 (Salt Lake City: Utah Printing Company, 1882), 18; *Mt. Pleasant Pyramid,* 7 March 1919.

13. Manti Presbyterian Church Minutes, 2.

14. Ibid., 32–33.

15. McMillan, "Presbyterian Work in Utah," 18.

16. *The Church Review,* 42–43.

17. Centennial Committee of Manti, Utah, *Song of a Century,* (Manti: Centennial Committee of Manti, 1949), 71. *Gunnison Valley News,* 20 November 1924, 16 July 1925.

18. See the official publications of Wasatch Academy, "A Profile of Wasatch Academy 1978–79," and "The Wasatch Academy Capital Program."

19. Arlow William Andersen, "The Norwegian-Danish Methodist Mission in Utah," *Utah Historical Quarterly* 25 (April 1957): 153–61.

20. Henry M. Merkel, *History of Methodism in Utah* (Colorado Springs: The Dentan Printing Co., 1938), 198, 199–200, 240; *The Church Review,* 1, 42; Cindy Rice, "Spring City: A Look at a Nineteenth Century Mormon Village," *Utah Historical Quarterly* 44 (Summer 1975): 265–66.

21. John S. H. Smith interview with Dr. Reece Anderson, 7 January 1972, 16–17.

22. Studies of Mormon polygamy include Stanley S. Ivins, "Notes on Mormon Polygamy," *Western Humanities Review* 10 (Summer 1956) 229–39; Kimball Young, *Isn't One Wife Enough?* (New York: Henry Holt & Co., 1954); Richard S. Van Wagoner, *Mormon Polygamy: A History* (Salt Lake City: Signature Books, 1986); Jessie L. Embry, *Mormon Polygamous Families: Life in the Principle* (Salt Lake City: University of Utah Press,1987); and B. Carman Hardy, *Solemn Covenant: The Mormon Polygamous Passage* (Urbana: University of Illinois Press, 1991).

23. Manti Ward Minutes, 19 January 1850.

24. 1880 U.S. Census, Population, tabulation available at the Utah State Historical Society Library.

25. Ivins, "Notes on Mormon Polygamy," 229–39

26. Sanpete Stake Minutes, 15 January 1882.

27. Ibid., 15 September 1881.

28. J.C. A. Weibye, *Journal,* 8 October 1886.

29. Ibid., 9 and 17 May 1887.

30. Olea Thompson, "Portrait of Grandmother," 6–7.

31. Peter Madsen Autobiography, 28.

32. Wilhemina Madsen Biography, 11.

33. Elvira Euphrasia Cox Day, Diary, 24 July 1889.

34. Ibid., 20 August 1889.

35. Manti Temple Centennial Committee, *The Manti Temple* (Manti, UT: Manti Temple Centennial Committee, 1988). This summary history of the Manti Temple is taken from this book published during the 100th anniversary of the dedication of the Manti Temple.

36. Ibid., 6.

37. Albert Antrei, *View from the Red Point* (Manti, UT: Manti Messenger Printing and Publishing Co., 1976), 35.

38. *The Manti Temple,* 23.

CHAPTER 10

EDUCATION

Sanpete County has a well-deserved reputation for its fine public and private educational institutions and its concern for education. Graduates of the three public high schools in Sanpete County—Gunnison, Manti, and North Sanpete—have gone on to distinguished careers in many professions. However, like the other pioneer undertakings in Sanpete County, education and the development of public schools was a long and difficult process.

Early School Conditions

In the first decades after settlement, children received schooling on a very irregular basis, mostly in the winter when there were fewer farm and livestock chores. Lack of funds or goods to pay teachers kept many children out of school. It was also common for parents to take turns sending one child at a time, and later another and another, as means permitted. Miles E. Johnson recalls of the man who baptized him that Elder Matthew Coldwell was also "his second school teacher for about three months. That was all my mother could pay for."[1]

School children in front of the Fairview School about 1880. (Courtesy Fairview Museum)

Schools in the early decades were typically held only two or three months a year and only a fraction of the eligible students attended regularly. Schooling was so erratic that C. C. Goodwin, editor of the then-anti-Mormon *Salt Lake Tribune,* wrote in a national magazine that the Reverend Duncan McMillan "went to Sanpete Valley where there were no schools" prior to his arrival in 1875.[2] Despite a strong response from the Mormon population, including several affidavits documenting the long time existence of many Sanpete schools, the statement about McMillan was never recanted. It seems to have been meant as a comparative claim to the effect that, using the Presbyterian schools as the standard of quality education, the Mormon schools did not pass the test. To some extent his assessment was accurate. The Protestant schools had well-trained teachers, better books and supplies, a superior curriculum, and more improved schoolhouses than their local counterparts, at least in the 1870s and 1880s. In retrospect, Sanpeters might acknowledge McMillan's positive role in provoking the locals to elevate the quality of education in the county.

In pioneer days, books, paper and pencils, desks, and other standard school supplies were scarce. Some schools had no graded text-books, while a few had such reliables as readers by Parker or McGuffy. Where paper was lacking, students were allowed to write only a few lines each day. Some students brought scriptures or their parents' books from home, but this did not allow for a uniform curriculum. The subjects taught were generally limited to "reading, writing, and arithmetic," plus geography in the upper grades. Sanpete County in 1868 had eight school districts but only sixteen schools.

By the 1870s, home-manufactured desks with seats were being made, copied from prototypes in Salt Lake City. Wall maps and chalk boards also began appearing. Other advancements came more slowly. Corporal punishment was the accepted mode of discipline, and teachers were free to administer whippings and other forms of physical force as they saw fit. Attendance remained irregular, and graduations and diplomas were rare. The teachers themselves were often only a little older than the students, and few had received any formal training. Some became teachers by passing correspondence courses. One typically qualified by taking an examination or, in some places, merely knowing how to read, write, and figure well. One disincentive was the poor pay and low social status accorded teachers. They were expected to be flawless in character and very dedicated, but most of them resorted to "moonlighting" to keep bread on the table. The situation improved somewhat after 1881 when the Sanpete Educational Institute was organized in Ephraim. A summer school for teachers, it turned out over 100 new teachers each term by the turn of the century. Many of them came from other counties, but most of those from Sanpete stayed to teach in the county.

Educational Facilities

School trustees have always been concerned with providing adequate physical facilities so that the classroom environment would enhance rather than impede learning. The first school in the county was the 20-by-30-foot whipsawed log schoolhouse built during the winter of 1850 in Manti. Jesse W. Fox, the territorial surveyor, was the first teacher, and school was held "at least six months a year" for several years. In the early decades, the main facilities concerns were for good benches, lighting, and a moderate temperature. In 1885 the district schools in Manti were furnished with thermometers and teachers were required to maintain a moderate temperature in their class rooms.[3] Ephraim teachers in 1900 were advised to keep rooms "at about 50 degrees," and to take advantage of any "north breeze, it being good for nourishment."[4] This wisdom was not always followed. In 1912 the temperature in some of the high school rooms in Mount Pleasant was "only 14 degrees above zero one morning this week." The observer tried to see humor in the situation as he commented, "never mind students, cold storage keeps us fresh."[5] School board officials in 1910 lamented the "very cramped quarters" of the two-room dwelling used as a school in Mayfield. It was noted that the drinking water was poor and that thirty-two pupils were taught in a 10-by-26-foot room, while another twenty-four were in a 12-by-15-foot room with only a single outside door.[6] Some health conditions were beyond the control of school caretakers. During the lethal influenza epidemic of 1918, many schools suspended operations. For more than half a year, the high school continued the learning process through correspondence. In early 1920 the public school in Spring City finally lifted the flu quarantine. It was noted on 27 February 1920 that "attendance is now about one-third of normal. A full attendance is expected by March 1."[7]

Throughout Sanpete County's educational history, attempts were made in each community first to provide a school facility and then to enlarge or replace earlier buildings with improved ones as population increases dictated and financial means permitted. As in domestic, religious, and commercial architecture, there was a natural progression in several steps from small, crudely made structures to today's large, well-constructed, highly functional facilities. The first schoolhouses were often literally that—classes held in private homes with students from several grades learning together in each room. Most towns had at least a private, home-taught school from its first or second year of settlement. In Centerfield, Marie Gribble and Harrie Higham were the first school teachers, both holding private classes in their homes. In Ephraim, Bishop Edwards called Agnes Armstrong on a "mission" to teach school in her one-room adobe house in the fort. The students sat on slabs of wood cut from logs and supported with peg legs. Lacking text books, the students used the

The Manti red public school building was dedicated 1 January 1894. It was razed in 1938. (Courtesy Ruth D. Scow)

Book of Mormon, Bible or books brought from home. They had no pencils, chalk, or slate. Instead they wrote or drew with pieces of soft yellow rock found near the stone quarry. In early Manti, before schoolhouses were built, classes were held in private homes, the city hall, council house, and the courthouse block. Fairview's early private home schools were run by Susan Ann Brady, Telestra Avery, and Helen Higgenson. Lacking room in its four ward school houses in Ephraim, Cordelia Dorius taught a kindergarten in Charles Christensen's house.

Many Sanpete villages began schools in their first, multi-purpose meetinghouses. These were typically primitive, one-room structures built of logs, stone, or adobe. In Centerfield's first log meetinghouse, pupils sat on wood slabs supported by dry goods boxes and log legs. Here Albert Tollstrup sat behind his desk—another box sitting on logs—or stood at the wall-mounted blackboard writing with his homemade chalk and cleaning with erasers made of rags. In Ephraim's Little Fort, the first meeting house served for school purposes with Parlan McFarlane and Edwin Tolton, both stone cutters, being among the first teachers. Mrs. Palmer and Mr. Syckle taught the first regular classes in Fayette in a log school and church house built in about 1867. A night school was conducted by Joseph Bartholomew. Before the move to its new townsite, school in Gunnison was held in its first meetinghouse, a 20-by-40-foot structure of logs sawed at Bunce's Mill. It was plastered inside and out and was warmed with a fireplace at each end. The ubiquitous slab benches were present and the teacher used a pine table as a desk. Unlike several other early meetinghouses, it featured a board floor and windows flanking the door. The children of Thistle Valley (Indianola) likewise learned their "3 R's" in a log meetinghouse. Spring City's first log meetinghouse was used as its first school, church, and social hall. The backless log benches would be pushed against the walls when dances were held. The people in Wales, drawing from the traditions of their homeland, built a "Common House," their name for an all-purpose meetinghouse. Here the first town school was conducted. Students were charged $3.00 per term, payable to schoolmaster Jonathan Midgley in cash, produce, or goods. Each child was responsible for bringing his or her own supplies. In Mount Pleasant, near the bridge over Pleasant Creek, was a long, one-room meetinghouse which served as a school, chapel, dance hall, and theater. The cold of its earthen floor was tempered by a huge fireplace used for both heat and light. The first teachers were A. B. Strickland and Mrs. Oscar Winters. Before its abandonment in 1910, Dover pupils were taught in the meetinghouse by John Redington and the Reid brothers.

The next phase in Sanpete's nascent educational history saw the building of one-room schoolhouses dedicated solely to learning functions. Virtually every town had one or more of these first "real" schoolhouses. In Axtell a log school was erected at Josias Jensen's prompting. It was finished with willow lath, plaster, and lime whitewash for Hannah Hansen Jensen Christensen, the first teacher. Chester's first schoolhouse was built of logs in about 1880 on the Neal Davis Ranch. Ellen Armstrong was the first teacher, followed by Joel Childs, a farmer. In larger Ephraim four school districts were formed in 1855, each corresponding with one of the four LDS wards established in 1859. Thereafter the wards were also called "Teaching Districts" and the schools were known as "Ward Schools." In 1859–60 three rock schoolhouses were built, with the First Ward House not being completed until 1864. Teachers were appointed and paid in wheat, potatoes, meat, and, rarely, cash.

In the Fairview fort, the first schoolhouse was dedicated 9 December 1860. A fireplace allowed for winter school which typically was a thirteen-week period during which the teachers were paid $4.50 per week. Adelia Cox Sidwell taught first, followed by William Christensen. In addition to the split log benches, desks were made by placing rough boards on wooden pegs driven into the log walls. Fountain Green's first school was built in 1860 but it became so over-crowded that another was erected in 1863. It too was short-lived, being destroyed by fire in 1865. Wanting a more permanent struc-ture, an adobe school was raised on the same ground and served for 41 years until a brick school replaced it in 1907–1908. Under the leadership of Joseph S. Horne, a new rock schoolhouse was built in Gunnison in the late 1860s and served for thirty years. Indianola's first schoolhouse was not built until 1900. Older Manti had two one-room schools built of stone after an 1866 legislative act allowed towns to assess a "levy of taxation not to exceed 30 mills," of which two-thirds went to buildings and one-third to salaries. Mantian Lily May Munk Livingston, born in 1871, later wrote of her school experiences there:

> I attended school in the old rock school house with a big round stove in the center of the room. It seemed to me that we sat with cold feet all winter long. All drawing except of maps was forbid-den. However, more or less drawing went on behind large books and slates. I remember reading the Pacific Coast Second Reader so many times that I memorized every lesson and could even repeat them beginning at the back of the book. Later I went to school upstairs in the City Hall and the last two years in the Old Council House. . . . A.C. Nelson, who later was State Superintendent of Public Instruction, was my principal teacher. I loved school and each night I could hardly wait until morning to get back to school. I recall propping my book on the fence between the stalls so I could study while milking cows. Some of the subjects those two years were Theology, penmanship, spelling, drawing, English grammar, history, geography, natural history, rhetoric, Ray's

Higher Arithmetic (really tough) and fancy work. I was valedicto-
rian. I recall seeing tears in the eyes of my teachers when I said,
"May the time, dear teachers, be short before you see satisfying
results from your anxious labors."[8]

In Mayfield where the townsite is more spread out than in settlements with concentrated grids, there were three one-room schools.
Later settled Milburn started with a one-room log school where
Tryphena Cox was the first teacher. The town built a red brick schoolhouse in 1894. As late as 1886, a one-room school with a dirt floor
and earthen roof was built in Mountainville. In Wales the revered
Common House was razed in 1892 to make room for a new brick
church. By then students attended classes in a one-room, wood-
frame school supplemented by a second wood-frame school, rooms
in the town hall, and the house of Nathaniel Edmunds. This overcrowded condition was mitigated with the construction of a new,
three-room schoolhouse in 1908.

It was during the decade of the 1890s that Sanpete's larger communities began building sizable stone and brick schools to house
their burgeoning student populations. These edifices of learning were
far superior to their crowded, uncomfortable, one-room predecessors. The new generation of schools ranged from two to four-room,
single story buildings in smaller towns to massive Victorian, two-
story schoolhouses with eight to twelve rooms in bigger cities. As
Centerfield outgrew its 1880s rock school, it erected a two-story
masonry schoolhouse behind it and converted the older building to a
church. Chester's first masonry school was a small, one-story rock
building, later moved stone-by-stone to Spring City where it was
reconstructed as a residence. In 1904 a new structure was raised and
served as the "center for school, public gatherings, dancing and worship," along the pattern of pioneer meetinghouses. The Jewish settlers
of Clarion erected a school in 1912, the year after their arrival in
Gunnison Valley. The first teacher was Royal D. Madsen.

In fast-growing Ephraim, the four small stone ward meetinghouses were soon overcrowded. The Central School House, a four-
room, rock building, relieved some of the pressure, but classes were
also held in the North Ward Co-op Store and the top floor of the

extant Co-op Building where the Sanpete Stake Academy (Snow College) got its start. After the Ephraim Ward was divided in 1877, the South Ward School House was built. In 1900, 702 pupils were attending in one of these locations. With fifty-five to sixty students in a room, it was clear that further improvising was not practical. In 1908 an immense, three-story brick and stone school was erected and situated diagonally on the corner of First South and First East. It was designed to include both the grade school and high school, but due to its unusual competition with nearby Sanpete Stake Academy, the high school did not enter the building until 1923.

In Fairview the 1874 rock school building was expanded in 1884; but by the turn of the century, it could no longer serve the increased number of students. In 1900 a two-story, eight-room, "greystone" (actually limestone) school block was erected. Dedicated 2 February 1901, it became the Fairview Museum in 1982. Fountain Green followed suit in 1907 with its tall, residential-looking brick schoolhouse and its school on the north side, also two stories and brick but of modern design, erected in 1912–13.

Also taking advantage of the economic largess and new educational ideas of the time, Gunnison built a new stone schoolhouse, Washington School, in 1899. The next year Mayfield built its two-story building. The first "modern" school in Mountainville was its brick structure of 1917–18, used only until 1920 when students were bused to Mount Pleasant. One of the most architecturally remarkable schools from this era is the two-story, brick and stone elementary in Spring City. Still extant but vacant, it is unique in design, a Victorian Eclectic masterpiece of arches, stepped gables, massive chimneys and rusticated walls. A similar and even larger schoolhouse in Manti did not survive. The monumental "Red School" was built in 1893 at a cost of $20,000 but was razed in 1936. Considered one of the finest schools in Utah at the time, it was perhaps the largest Victorian-era building of its type in the county. Even so, it was soon overcrowded, necessitating the erection of the newer "White School" next to it. Similar in size was Mount Pleasant's new central school, Hamilton, a three-story masonry giant erected in 1896. More long-lived, by 1947 it housed 350 students in six grades with twelve teachers and staff. Sterling's brick and rock school, erected in 1898–99, was

The Spring City School under construction. (Utah State Historical Society)

another late all-purpose building abandoned for a new elementary in 1915. It was in turn left empty in 1956 when students were first transported to Manti.

As educational philosophies, organizations, and economics changed, beginning with consolidation efforts in 1915, smaller communities began transporting students to the nearest larger town. Chester's students were transported to Moroni starting in 1934, and in the same year, Milburn and Indianola children were bused to Fairview. Beginning in 1939, Fayette's pupils were sent to Gunnison. Mayfield students were at various times at either Gunnison or Manti. By covered wagon, bobsleigh, and later a covered truck, Mountainville's children were hauled to Mount Pleasant. The schoolhouses in these smaller villages, some of them almost new, were abandoned, while even the large Victorian structures in places like Gunnison, Manti, Ephraim, Mount Pleasant, and Spring City proved too small to accommodate the swelling student bodies. Eventually, most of the grand schools were destroyed and replaced with lower, but larger and more functional brick structures.

Following school consolidations in the 1920s and 1930s, new schools were built throughout the county. Manti High School was designed in 1922, as were elementaries in Ephraim, Mayfield, and Spring City, as well as a gymnasium in Ephraim and additions to the school in Centerfield.[9] As education became more diverse and specialized, shop buildings were designed for the high schools in Manti and Gunnison in 1938. A mechanical and domestic arts building was erected in Ephraim in 1939–40. Ephraim's large, all-grade school of 1908 was demolished in 1965 in favor of a new facility housing both elementary and junior high students. Seventh to ninth graders were also transported to Ephraim from Manti and Sterling as a result of consolidation. Similarly the impressive Hamilton School in Mount Pleasant was razed in the 1960s to make way for a more modern building.

Secondary Education

In Wasatch Academy, which graduated its first high school students in 1887, and in Sanpete Stake Academy, which graduated its initial class in 1889, we have two of Utah's first secondary schools. The Sanpete Stake Academy has been touted as Utah's "first public high school," although its association with the LDS church raises the question of whether it was entirely "public." It was, in fact, organized two years before the state's oldest public, non-religious secondary school, Salt Lake City High School, now called West High. Sanpete's public nature is indicated by its later becoming a state institution, as well as being the precursor of Snow College and Ephraim High School. Whether first or later, both Wasatch and Sanpete academies were progressive for their era, there being only five public high schools in all of Utah in 1900.

The next four-year high school was Manti's, created in 1905 as a project of the Manti Board of School Trustees. As early as 1887, editorials in the Manti *Home Sentinel* raised the need for a high school. The two main organizational promoters then—the Ladies Literary Club of Manti and the Arrapine Commercial Club—stayed with the idea for the next eighteen years. In 1905 these two groups, joined by the Farmers Institute and three trustees of the Manti School District, organized meetings which resulted in the passage of a $12,000 bond issue to fund the project. Initially the new high school had a principal, D. H. Robinson, but no building. School was held in the annex of the Manti Tabernacle using chairs, desks, and tables donated by townspeople. By the start of 1906, an impressive, three-story building of white brick had been erected next to the "Red School" of 1893–94. The lower floor of what came to be called the "White School" housed overflow students from the grade school. The modern design features included indoor restrooms with running water (just then available), a kitchen, principal's office, an auditorium, wide staircases, several large class rooms, and a nearby shop building. The curriculum included English, algebra, "physiography" (physical geography), history, and bookkeeping. The first class graduated in 1909. Graduation was not easy to achieve as failing grades were given for inadequate performance. During the 1915–16 school year, grades were changed from numerical percentages to the letters used today.

It was probably the existence of the high schools in Manti and Mount Pleasant that prompted the creation of the two current school districts with headquarters in those two cities. On 8 June 1911, the Sanpete County school superintendent, A J. Rees of Wales, began organizing the South and North Sanpete High School districts. Correspondingly, the two high schools were named South and North Sanpete. Each of these four-year schools was given supervisory responsibilities over the two-year schools in their areas. The creation of secondary schools brought changes in administrative structures and policies. After requiring the advanced payment of tuition in 1922, the South Sanpete School District reversed the policy the next year after it realized that compulsory education and forced tuition were incompatible.

As in the nineteenth century, state law created educational structures without accompanying funding, a problem left with the districts. Undaunted, the two districts and their new school boards took up the task of locating two-year high schools. They left the matter in the hands of the electorate. Voters in late 1911 chose to have one such facility in Gunnison. Because they already had the Sanpete Stake Academy, the people in Ephraim and Mayfield voted against any new high school in South Sanpete. However, the larger district support for the Gunnison school prevailed, and a two-year high school was organized in Gunnison on 20 April 1912, with Louis Peterson as principal. At first, it rented three rooms in the Washington School. The nomadic school continued to change locations almost annually until it became a four-year school and erected its own building in 1922.

In Manti where the 1906 high school existed, the South Sanpete School District rented the building from the Manti Public School District, its builders, and its owners. Both of these types of organizations were dissolved in March 1915 when, throughout Utah, they were combined to became the "Common School Districts of the First Class." In Sanpete these were the two general school districts, North and South Sanpete. The North Sanpete School District administers all the schools north of Ephraim from its headquarters in Mount Pleasant. From Ephraim south school matters are governed by the South Sanpete School District out of Manti. Several attempts to further combine the two districts into one county-wide district have failed.

Although the principle of consolidation was generally accepted in 1915, its meaning in the 1920s was interpreted in various ways as expressed by its inconsistent application in Sanpete's schools. The schools experimented with various grading arrangement formulas. They ranged from 6–2 (grades 1 through 6, followed by 7 and 8) in Manti and 6–3 in the North Sanpete District junior highs to 8–2 in Ephraim and Mayfield. In Ephraim at the time, students in the last two years of high school attended classes at Snow Junior College, amounting to a 8–2–2 system. These arrangements, which varied mostly according to the presence of junior or senior high school buildings, were modified again in the 1970s when the "middle school" concept became popular. This system called for placing the ninth grade back in the high schools and replacing it with the sixth grade to create middle schools from what had been junior highs. The new arrangement was essentially a 5–3–4 formula.

Another change during this era was the enforcement of compulsory attendance laws which had been on the books since 1852. Because students had received their education so sporadically, the first graduation class from Manti High School in 1909 included

Freedom students were transported by a horse-drawn wagon in the 1890s. (Courtesy Ida Donaldson)

pupils in their twenties. By the 1920s, attendance monitors had increased the frequency and consistency of attendance and lowered the average age of the graduates. This was achieved in part by consolidating schools and transporting students from the outlying smaller towns into bigger city schools. This "busing" policy started in 1915 when children from Mayfield and Sterling were driven daily to Manti. Cars had been on the scene for only a few years, and some students were transported in horse-drawn wagons. Others found a little more comfort in an automobile modified to add extra rows of seats and a canvas "convertible" top. Such a "bus," owned by the Manti Motor Company, was leased to the South Sanpete School District until 1918 when a "real" bus was purchased. Other concerns of the time involved combating "the cigarette evil, the movie craze and the moral situation in general."[10]

School consolidation and the presence of two school districts often created dissention in the county. Jealously and confrontations arose over the locations of schools, distribution of funds, and busing issues. Others were more concerned over the quality of education and the lack of enthusiast support on the part of both parents and students. Critic Alonzo Morley lamented the conditions in Moroni during the 1920s. In Duck Springs in the northwest part of town where there were large families, the "majority of children in this section quit school at an early age" and "strong gang organization is present. . . ." He continued to observe that "educational standards are also comparatively low. Pure science and art are shunned by most students and the 'just get by' attitude is characteristic. Most students go to high school more for pleasure than for conscientious study. The school majors in basket ball in which it receives hearty support from the town."[11]

Morley continued his criticism of Sanpete schools observing that

Superficial activities at the school are prevalent. One of the strongest traditions is the locking up of school teachers on April Fools Day. This sometimes results in serious accidents. Last year one of the teachers became enraged and nearly choked one of the pupils to death; two of his fellow teachers could hardly pull him off the student. This year one of the teachers had an artery cut in his wrist pulling him through a door. Such hoodlumism is valued more highly than scholastic attainment.[12]

Morley did conclude his appraisal on a more positive note, commenting that the school board is "bracing up the curriculum to raise the standard" of education.

In 1923 Manti dedicated and opened a new high school building. In 1956, the year of the "South Sanpete War of Consolidation," Manti received Ephraim's students after sixty- eight years of attending high school in Ephraim, usually in competition with Snow Academy. At the same time, Mayfield's children were sent to Gunnison instead of Manti. A third high school building was constructed in Manti in 1980–81. Today its serves students attending grades 9–12. Also in 1980–81, Gunnison saw the construction of its new school, designed to house grades 7–12.

Consolidation dilemmas did not seem so perplexing in the North Sanpete School District. Although a high school was in operation in Mount Pleasant, it had no major building nor any construction funds. A bond election on 19 January 1911 to raise $25,000 for a new site and school proved successful, and additional funds were borrowed on three more occasions to fund the new, state-of-the-art facility, completed by the year end of 1911.

In mid-September 1911, the newly organized school board considered the question of how many high schools should be located in the North Sanpete School District. The board recommended three, one each in Mount Pleasant, Moroni, and Fairview, but decided to leave the matter for the voters to chose. The votes were nearly unanimous in favor of only two schools, the one in Mount Pleasant and a new one in Moroni. The citizens in effect reversed this decision in March 1912 when they defeated the bond election that would have funded the Moroni school. Thus Delbert Draper, the first principal of Moroni High School, began his school year of 1912–13 without a building. His fifty-six students were compelled to improvise in the overcrowded grade school.

After years of experimentation, heated debate, and confusing advances and retreats by the municipal and high school districts, the differences were resolved legally with the administrative consolidation of the high school with the lower schools in both districts. On 12 July 1915, the North and South districts had all their schools consolidated into a "Common School District of the First Class." In 1957 the high schools in Moroni and Mount Pleasant were consolidated into the larger school in Mount Pleasant. At the same time, the North Sanpete Junior High School and Moroni Junior High School were joined in the former high school building in Moroni. Again this change caused controversy, but it eventually settled down. Similar pains were felt in small towns like Wales when the school board voted to close the elementary school and bus students to Moroni.

The Protestant School Movement and Wasatch Academy

The Protestant schools of the mid-1870s through the early twentieth century provided a good, alternate education for Presbyterians, Methodists, a few Lutherans, and those Mormons who felt safe in entrusting their children to gentile teachers. One reason for Mormons taking such a calculated risk was that the Protestant schools provided a better overall education. The teachers were formally trained in Eastern colleges or teachers academies. The curricula

A class of the Manti Presbyterian School about 1890. Teacher Sarah B. Sutherland is in the center of the top row. (Courtesy of Wasatch Academy)

they offered were more varied and rigorous than in the ward or district schools. With better funding from out-of-state sources, they were well stocked with graded textbooks and supplies. As the popularity of the schools increased, they built sturdy masonry or wood-frame schoolhouses in each of the county's larger communities. Typical of the mission schools was the one established by the Presbyterians in Gunnison in 1881. The church sent teacher, Miss Mary Crowell from Ohio, first to open a school in a small house. The next year they purchased a city lot and built a fine limestone chapel and school. Measuring 25 by 45 feet, it had a belfry with the town's first bell, and was dedicated in April 1886. In 1884 Mrs. M. M. Green and her daughter Alice moved to Gunnison to run the school. Mrs. Green was also a nurse and preached sermons in the absence of a regular minister, thus tripling her value in the community.[13]

Reverend Duncan McMillan's religious motivations for establishing a Presbyterian school in Mount Pleasant in 1875 were discussed in the previous chapter. By the end of the first term of that school year, 109 students were attending classes in Liberal Hall, still extant on Main Street. Despite its initial success, the school later struggled and was on the verge of closing due to lack of funds. It was saved more than once, the first time through a timely donation from a missionary society in Cedar Rapids, Iowa. The school was put on a firmer financial footing after McMillan left in 1880 when it was taken over by the church's Board of Home Missions.

In the early years, Mount Pleasant Academy, as it was first known, offered education only for the lower grades. It soon provided a high school curriculum, however, and graduated its first class of two students in 1887. The next high school graduate came in 1895 and graduates have been advanced nearly every year since. After fifteen years in Liberal Hall, the facility proved too small for the swelling classes, so plans were developed to build a new, two-story, masonry school and administrative structure. Led by the Sanpete County Co-op, a group of local businessmen subscribed $2,000 for the impressive Victorian building called Hungerford Hall, completed in 1891–92.

As its reputation grew, Wasatch Academy began to attract students from out-of-state and by 1896, a boarding department had twenty-four students enrolled. By this time school administrators had begun to piece together adjacent parcels of property to create what eventually became the present campus. At first the campus consisted of Hungerford Hall and a few older buildings on lots scattered about nearby in the southwest quadrant of town. The boarding boys lived in Hungerford, while the girls stayed in a house a block away.

To strengthen its scholastic offerings and its academic standing, the academy continued to expand its facilities and curriculum in the early twentieth century. During the principalship of Charles W. Johns, which began in 1911, much of the present campus land was secured, making it about the size of a city block. Hungerford Hall was enlarged and the nearby brick school house and grounds were acquired, as were the two Victorian houses which became "Lincoln" and "Indiana" halls. In 1913 the first major dormitory, "Finks Memorial Hall," was built for boarding girls using contributed money raised nationwide. Three years later the boy's dormitory, "Darlington Hall," was built thanks to a donation from Mrs. Charles F. Darlington

of New York City. In 1917 the school purchased the gymnasium corner and the Johansen cottage, making a block-and-one-half campus
in a favorable location just south of the business district. The
"Frances Thompson Memorial Infirmary," a small health care center,
was erected in 1921, and the next year stately, round-arched "John's
Gymnasium" was built and named for the school principal. The
building boom continued in 1923 when the "Olivia Sage Memorial
Hall" was raised. After Johns resigned in 1924, construction continued during the long tenure of principal W. K. Throndson. Honoring
the school's founder, "Duncan J. McMillan Memorial Hall" was built
to house several teachers and the superintendent.

Progress at Wasatch Academy was temporarily interrupted on 4
April 1933 when fire destroyed beloved Hungerford Hall. For the balance of the year, classes were held in Darlington Hall and other buildings, adversely effecting the next year's enrollment. In the midst of
the Depression and out of funds, administrators again discussed
school closure. The academy was saved a second time when, in the
spring of 1934, it was learned that building funds had been made
available through the estate of Miss Alice Craighead, whose father
had been a friend of Dr. McMillan. As a child, Alice had listened to
the reverend's stories of his work in Utah. Impressed, she later listed
the academy as one of the recipients of a gift in her will. Instead of
closing its doors, administrators took a risk and expanded the school.
Craighead Industrial Hall was built in 1934 to house the manual arts
and homemaking departments. By early 1935, the large, brick, two-
story Craighead Administration Hall was built on the old stone foundation left from the Hungerford Hall fire.

The academy received additional boosts when similar schools,
Hungerford Academy in Springville and another Presbyterian boarding school in Logan, were closed and consolidated with Wasatch.
During the two mergers in 1912 and 1934, Wasatch received equipment, students, and a few faulty members. In the late 1930s, a few
more houses were purchased and razed for a new girls dormitory
funded from the Craighead estate. In 1938 the historic Seeley House
was obtained to serve as the principal's residence. The next year the
school counted a staff of twenty-four, accommodations for about 160
boarding students, equally divided by gender, plus a day-time enroll-

An early photograph of Wasatch Academy. (Utah State Historical Society)

ment of more than 80 pupils, allowing a total potential enrollment of approximately 250.

Wasatch Academy was a major contributor to all future Utahns in helping to develop a free Mount Pleasant grade school. Some Utah

educators view it as the precursor of the state's present public school
system. "Brigham Young had set a tone of church opposition to tax-
supported schools which resulted in few districts availing themselves
of the right to levy school taxes as provided by territorial law. Young
fostered a system involving community financing of school building,
with the operation of such schools to be supported by per capita fees
paid by a student's parents."[14]

The academy dropped its lower grades to become solely a high
school by 1958. Most pupils are boarding students. Often competing
against larger schools, the "Tigers" of Wasatch Academy have won
numerous academic and athletic awards. Many of the graduates have
become community leaders and distinguished in their professional
careers. Students today come from "a variety of religious, racial and
cultural backgrounds . . . from isolated western mining towns, Indian
reservations and overseas nations lacking high school programs for
American parents serving diplomatic missions."[15] In 1988, the year
headmaster Joseph Lofton was appointed, students came from twelve
states and five foreign countries. Lofton, a graduate of the University
of Texas and Utah State University, has directed considerable progress
during his ten-year tenure.

The campus now exceeds two blocks in size, including some
buildings on the periphery. The school is non-denominational,
although it retains a spiritual kinship with the First Presbyterian
Church. In the mid-1990s, funds were raised for a state-of-the-art,
$2-million math and science building. Master-planning has identi-
fied and prioritized future projects such as the updating and restoration of the now-historic buildings and construction of a new dining
hall.

Sanpete Stake Academy/Snow College

Prior to the establishment of public high schools, colleges, and
universities in Utah, the LDS church provided upper level education
though twenty-two academies founded between 1875 and 1911. All
but six of these were closed after similar state-supported schools were
created and took hold. Of the six survivors, three of the old schools
remained church facilities while three others, including the Sanpete

Stake Academy in Ephraim, were transferred to the state and continue to operate.

The college is co-named for Lorenzo Snow and Erastus Snow, both among the first Mormon missionaries to the Scandinavians who immigrated to Sanpete County. Lorenzo Snow was also the president of the Church of Jesus Christ of Latter-day Saints when the school was renamed Snow Academy in 1900. The fifth church president, serving only from 1898 to 1901, Snow believed in the academy's future and authorized construction of the main school and administration building (later named the Noyes Building) which was started in 1899 and completed ten years later.

Founded as the Sanpete Stake Academy in 1888, the year the Manti temple was completed, the school may have been established partly to provide an educational alternative for Mormons who were being attracted to the Protestant schools thriving county-wide in the mid-1880s. The idea for the school is said to have developed from dinner table conversations at which stake president Canute Peterson approached LDS general authorities about the advantages of establishing an academy. Peterson officially proposed the school for advanced studies at a stake conference in Mount Pleasant. It was approved on the condition that church president Wilford Woodruff and the Council of the Twelve also give consent. They did, and the new school conducted its first classes on 5 November 1888. In the two large upper rooms of the Relief Society Hall in the Co-op, benches and tables were installed for students enrolled in one of three levels of course work: Preparatory, Intermediate and Normal. The first group included grades 7–9; the second 10 through early college; and the Normal division, lower level college teacher training. The categories overlapped somewhat and were not as well-defined as they are today because of the irregular, part-time attendance of rural students then.

Alma Greenwood was called by church leaders to come from Fillmore to serve as the first principal. He was assisted by Carrie Henrie Payne and for the first few years, they were the only teachers. The position of teacher was initially much like that of missionary, and early teachers served with little or no pay.

Under the moniker "Holiness to the Word," the *Circular*, a four-

Snow Academy on Founders Day, 5 November 1902. (Courtesy Manti Daughters of Utah Pioneers)

page catalogue for the "First Academic Year, 1888–1889," offered classes in theology, reading, grammar, composition, orthography (spelling), arithmetic, penmanship, singing, and hygiene. The "Advanced Department" had the same classes, using higher level books, and added an "elocution" class.[16] The inaugural class of the academy contained 121 students aged eleven through thirty. Two-thirds were from Ephraim, while most of the others came from the county. Students of both genders paid tuition ranging from $4.00 to 6.00 per term. In 1938 Fannie G. Thompson, a charter member of the Snow Academy alumnae, described how the school's first students

> . . . had finished the courses given in our public schools and were able to pass the examinations given before they could be enrolled. Most of the younger ones were placed in the advanced (Intermediate) grade as we had attended school for perhaps 6 or 7 years in succession and had at least learned our 3 R's, while some of the older ones had perhaps gone only a few years, and many of them were placed in the Preparatory grade.[17]

The academy refined its curriculum to a regular four-year high school program in 1894 while maintaining its Normal courses for the 13th and 14th grades. To accommodate its larger student body, still in the co-op (Society Hall), the school also held classes in the North Ward meetinghouse starting in 1896. Two years later business classes were started in rooms above the Progress Market, and dressmaking classes were held above the Ephraim Market. Conducting classes for students spread across town in several locations was not an efficient mode of operating. It was during the progressive, twenty-nine-year administration (1891–1921) of President Newton E. Noyes that much of the present campus property was obtained. The school traded some church property for some city-owned land used as a stock corral and park. On this half-block—the beginning of a permanent campus—the cornerstone of academy building was laid on 17 May 1899 by Anthon H. Lund. This was the school's first major building, and it housed both classrooms and administrative offices. It was dedicated on Founder's Day, 5 November 1909, although it had been occupied for several years prior to its completion. Still the architectural centerpiece of the college, the three-story, masonry, neoclassical building was built at a cost of approximately $70,000, $15,000 of which was given in donated materials, labor, or cash.

By 1900 the Sanpete Stake Academy had advanced sufficiently to be included in the church's school system and receive regular appropriations. This allowed for the construction of additional facilities including the original gymnasium, now called the Dee Anderson Building, erected in 1912. In 1922 the school's name was changed to Snow College. Along with the name change was a change in Noyes's title from principal to president. The college had at that time fifteen salaried teachers and 400 students in its high school and college divisions.

The creation of the college in Ephraim had one negative side-effect—the slowing of growth of the town's high school. For its first thirty-four years, the academy accepted both high school and college level students. To alleviate the conflict, the Church Educational System (CES) stopped accepting high school students in 1922. The next year the 9–12 grade pupils were transferred from Snow to the South Sanpete School District where they formed Ephraim High School in the school year of 1923–24. During the same period, Snow College held classes for grades 1–4 of the local elementary school to give college students "in house" practice as school teachers.

A manual training class at Snow College. (Utah State Historical Society)

Wayne B. Hales, an academic and physicist, was the college president at this time. He expanded the physics and chemistry departments as well as the library. During his regime scholastic standards were raised to the extent that the school received accreditation from the State Board of Education. Additional accreditation as a junior college was gained in 1931 during the Milton Knudsen administration. That same year the Utah State Legislature passed House Bill 101 by which Snow College went from the church's school system to the state's. Snow came close to meeting the fate of the other extinct colleges, but P. C. Peterson (son of pioneer leader Canute Peterson) talked Ephraimites into keeping the school when the church wanted to give it up in 1932. He is said to have given legs of lamb to "bribe" fellow legislators into voting for the state to take over the school. The bill passed by a single vote—cast by Peterson himself.[18]

In 1937 the college created another high school program, this time for students in the 11–14 grades. In 1941 the Snow College Vocational Agriculture Department established a farm at which students researched remedies to diseases in cattle, sheep, turkeys, and other animals and poultry important to the local and state economy. In 1952 it became headquarters for the Utah Agriculture Experimental Station Project 389. The latter was changed to the Snow College Farm in 1956, and then to the Snow Field Station in 1959, after which a weather station was established there.[19]

As a state junior college under the seventeen-year (1936–52) presidency of James A. Nuttall, Snow experienced significant growth. In 1938 the Vocational Arts Building was constructed, followed by the first girl's dormitory, Greenwood Hall, on the site of the old Presbyterian church. During World War II, sixty-eight acres were added to the campus for athletic fields and a vocational agriculture complex. From 1941–47, a new gymnasium was completed, partly with state funding. Post-war construction included new dormitories, a cafeteria, new heating plant and bleachers, along with the first renovation of the Noyes Building. In 1950 radio station KEPH was installed on campus. In 1953 a new auditorium was commenced as one of the concluding landmarks of President Nuttall's prolific administration. Curiously, he left the school under somewhat mysterious circumstances. At about the same time, Governor J. Bracken Lee was attempting to transfer all two-year state colleges back to the LDS church. Senate Bill 39 passed both houses with nearly unanimous votes on 15 December 1953. A referendum followed, however, and the state's citizens voted in favor of state support for the junior colleges by removal of their high schools divisions. Thus Snow College was spared from this regressive fate and instead became the Snow College Branch of the Utah State Agricultural College. Then-president Lester B. Whetten was given a new title, "Director." In 1956–57 Snow was reaccredited as a two-year junior college by removing the high school program it had begun in 1937. The school underwent still another name change when, in 1969, the legislature reverted to its previous name, Snow College.

ENDNOTES

1. "Miles Edgar Johnson Autobiography," Utah State Historical Society Archives, 7.

2. *Harper's New Monthly Magazine,* October, 1881, 768.

3. *Manti Home Sentinel,* 20 January 1885.

4. *Ephraim Enterprise,* 25 August 1900.

5. *Mt. Pleasant Pyramid,* 13 December 1912.

6. *Manti Messenger,* 14 October 1910.

7. *Mount Pleasant Pyramid,* 27 February 1920.

8. Lily May Munk Livingston, "Memoirs." (Manti, UT: unpublished. 1871–1967).

9. Architectural drawings in archives of Sanpete County Courthouse.

10. Minutes of the South Sanpete School District, 28 August 1917..

11. Alonzo Morley, "Community Psychology of Moroni," 1924.

12. Ibid.

13. Most of the information for this section is drawn from W. K. Throndson's "History of Wasatch Academy," in *Mount Pleasant, 1859–1939,* Hilda Madsen Longsdorf, compiler, (Mount Pleasant Pioneer Historical Association, 1939), 262–66. Also see, "Wasatch Academy," *Mount Pleasant Pyramid,* 17 April 1975 (Wasatch Academy Centennial) for an account of the 1875–80 era.

14. "Utah State Historical Society records," quoted by Jack Goodman, "Wasatch Academy at Mount Pleasant is Sanpete Magnet," *Salt Lake Tribune,* 11 December 1988.

15. Ibid.

16. "Circular of the Sanpete Stake Academy, Ephraim City, Utah for the First Academic Year, 1888–1889" (Manti, UT: Home Sentinel Printing, 1888).

17. Fannie G. Thompson, Speech given at Golden Jubilee Founder's Day Celebration in Ephraim, 1938.

18. Gary B. Peterson and Lowell C. Bennion, *Sanpete Scenes, A Guide to Utah's Heart,* (Eureka, UT: Basin Plateau Press, 1987), 63.

19. *Our Yesterdays: A History of Ephraim, Utah, 1854–1979* (Ephraim City Corp, 1981), 76.

CHAPTER 11

SOCIAL AND CULTURAL LIFE

The social, cultural, and recreational aspects of life in the Sanpete Valley are rich and varied. While many activities have been passed on from one generation to another since the early pioneer days, new activities have been introduced over time, some remaining in fashion only a short time, others acquiring a permanant place along side those inherited from pioneer days. Ellis Day Coombs and George F. Olsen, in reflecting on the pioneer culture of Fairview, provide a description applicable to all Sanpete towns.

> One of the outstanding characteristics of the Mormon Pioneers was their ability to make the best of their surroundings. No matter how gloomy the outlook, they always found something to help the situation and were prone to see the bright side of the picture. One way in which this was accomplished was through their amusements.
>
> The early settlers of Fairview were not exception to this rule. As soon as they had planted their crops and built their shelters, they built the schoolhouse which was used as a community center. They held dances in this building form the first. These dances were

typical of the early days. The people wore clothes in homespun, which served for the best, as well as everyday apparel. Some of them danced in homemade shoes and some had no shoes at all but danced as merrily as the rest.

The music was furnished by a fiddler. Warren P. Brady and James Stewart were the first to play for the dances in Fairview. The old time waltz, schottische, polka and quadrille were the dances used, and they were danced with a vim which left no doubt as to the enjoyment of the occasion. Often then dancing would be interspersed with a program or refreshments. They often danced until morning. The dance ticket was not often paid with money, as that was very scarce, but wheat, vegetables, meat, and produce of any kind was received. Very often three young men would haul a load of wood which would be accepted as ticket for the three of them.

The desire of the young people to dance was often capitalized by leaders in the town to get services performed that otherwise would have been less readily given. For example, an emigrant family arrived in Fairview and a log house was put up for them upon an unfenced lot. The boys of town were told that they would be given a free dance if they would get post and poles to fence the property for these newcomers. The response was immediate, and the poles and posts were soon on the lot. The dance was given to the boys. Later, they were proffered another dance if they would build the fence. A small army of willing workers soon had the fence in place and the promised dance was enjoyed by them. Someone then suggested that these poor people had no team or tools with which to work, to clear, and to plow a garden spot, so the women promised a big supper and the men promised another dance and the lot was soon cleared of brush, plowed and level ready for the spring planting. Many a widow was supplied with winter wood and the bishop's wood pile was always replenished by the boys who loved to dance.[1]

The earliest pioneers offered "readings" and recited verse, along with singing soul-stirring campfire renditions of "O My Father" and "Come, Come Ye Saints" in their need for both entertainment and religious revival. Their need for such outlets of feeling was dire, to take both their minds and their bodies away for a time from the all-pervading, almost overwhelming reality that wracked them on the

The Sanpete County Fair—early September 1920. (Utah State Historical Society)

demanding frontier. A theatrical company was organized when Manti was first settled (1849–50). This drama company styled themselves "The Amateur Thespians," which they undoubtedly were.[2]

Activities they had cherished in their former lives in the East and in Europe were carried on in their new wilderness communities. For instance, "football matches were played [in Manti] with Springville on Saturday and Monday; 1100 people saw the second game. There was a dance Saturday night in honor of Springville."[3] Also, "the Mount Pleasant and Ephraim town bands had a contest. The Mount Pleasant boys came with cash in hand, and bets were placed up to $1000."[4] Town bands were items of pride all over Sanpete.

We are informed by the press that "baseball games are enthusiastic times as local teams vie with teams from other towns of Sanpete . . . Many folks go to the mountains for outings. Some . . . hike, maybe to stay as long as a week. Other[s] have outings [in] Salina Canyon, Fish Lake, etc. (including Castille Springs in Spanish Fork Canyon)."[5]

One of the most interesting outings, begun in 1911, was the

social gathering and games between citizens of Sanpete and Emery counties on top of the Wasatch Plateau at various places. From 17 July to 5 August, for example, it was held on Twelve-Mile Flat east of Mayfield. In 1913 the event involved 500 people.[6]

The young women of Sanpete did what they generally could to influence both the social and cultural values of the valley. The "Musical Maids" would perform whenever and wherever requested in Sanpete County. They were an all-female orchestra.[7]

R. P. Larsen of Moroni went to Salt Lake City with two violins he had recently made of Utah wood. He valued them at $500 each and declared that beyond question violins manufactured from Utah maplewood were superior in tone and strength over those made from imported Italian woods. Larsen came from Denmark in 1881. He said he lived and worked on a ranch in Sanpete County because he had to and that he made violins because he loved to. He had made seventy-two violins. It took forty days, more or less, to make one. On the back of each instrument made by Larsen appeared the word "Mareah," the name of his wife which he used as a trademark.[8]

In a different vein, E. J. Conrad of Chester spearheaded a movement for a Sanpete County Fair in 1897.[9] Ephraim celebrated "American Indian Day" on 4 September 1929, with song and declamation, observing that the time had come to recall the debt of this nation to the original inhabitants of this continent.[10]

The most celebrated of all holidays in Sanpete are in tune with the rest of Utah. Christmas and New Year's are important, but John K. Olsen tells us about the Fourth and Twenty-Fourth of July:

> I remember the way we celebrated the fourth and Twenty-Fourth of July before Ephraim's first automobiles. In those days most folks stayed within a few miles of home for want of ways to travel. Each community had its own brand of celebration. We did not want to miss one bit of excitement and had to be present for all happenings; the parade, the meeting or program, the races, pulling matches and even the afternoon dances. We had saved what money we had been able to earn, and the popcorn, home-made root beer, and candy pieces were enjoyed.
>
> I also remember at the day's close: how, after a wonderful day of enthusiasm and participation, we trudged homeward or rode

The interior of the Ephraim Tabernacle in 1906. The tabernacle was demolished in 1953. (Courtesy of Ruth D. Scow)

with our parents in a buggy, a two-seater (which had lost its white top) pulled by my father's pride . . . two bay mares. We were tired but happy as we wearily fed the chickens and gathered the eggs, milked the cows, fed and watered the livestock, ate bread and milk for supper and finally tumbled into bed.[11]

In time Palisade Park became one of the most popular resorts in central Utah. Shortly after 1873, Daniel B. Funk, one of the original settlers of Sterling, created a small lake dedicated entirely to recreational purposes. Funk's Lake immediately became a favorite spot for weekend gatherings and provided welcome respite from the harshness of pioneer life. Funk even installed a small steam-powered launch, and early photographs show fashionable young ladies and dapper gentlemen boarding it for excursions around the lake. Tragedy struck in 1881 when rough water capsized the launch and eleven of its panic-stricken passengers drowned. The resort fell to disuse and disrepair after Funk's death, but the recreational boom of the 1920s led to is restoration. By 1923 it boasted electric lights, a baseball diamond, an outdoor dance pavilion with a maple floor, three row-

A Fourth of July celebration in Mount Pleasant. (Utah State Historical Society)

boats, and a six-passenger launch. The resort became known as Palisade Park in 1929, and although it fell into disuse again during the Second World War, it was restored in 1946 and has remained in use since.[12] Palisade State Park has since become part of the State Park and Recreation Department, which maintains it as a campground and a place for fishing, adjacent to a nine hole golf course.

Outdoor dance pavilions were nothing less that a mania in Sanpete County during the 1920s. Dancing has always been a favorite form of recreation for Mormons, but the Gatsby-like taste for unrestrained festivities and the new freedom of the automobile made the pavilions remarkably popular. Young men picked up their dates in neighboring towns and perhaps drove to yet a third town to dance. The pavilions were relatively cheap to build, requiring little more than a vacant field, a concrete or hardwood floor, and an inexpensive lattice-work enclosure; virtually every town in the county had one. During the summer months, there was a dance in at least one of them for five or six nights a week.[13] It was a colorful interlude that few who were young during those years can ever forget.

In the fields of art, music, and literature, several Sanpete residents stand out—some of whom earned national reputations. C.C.A. Christensen left a legacy of paintings on canvas. Many of his paintings are still extant, and one of them is the only known view of Temple Hill at Manti almost twenty years before construction of the temple was begun. From a point southeast of the hill, the painting shows a knoll in front of the foothills of the Wasatch Plateau. There is nothing elegant or promising about the vista, a green-grey and bare slab of oolite rock with some desert shrubs growing on it. In the foreground is a group of Indian tepees in a grove of trees and figures of Indians, three of them on horseback. Two white horsemen approach from the left. Temple Hill is just across a rise, sloping gently westward to a precipitous drop-off.[14] At the foot of the temple-less hill is a circle of covered wagons.

Carl Christen Anthon Christensen was born in Copenhagen on 28 November 1831, the first of four sons of Mads and Dorothea Christiane Christensen. The family was very poor, and when he was eleven years old, C. C. A.'s parents found it necessary to commit him to a state-managed institution for the raising of destitute children. In English translation, this government boarding school was the "Institute of Benevolence." In 1846 he was confirmed in the Lutheran church, an official act in Denmark, and in the same year he was apprenticed under contact to a carpenter. He was released from that contract in 1848 to become apprentice to the master painter Carl Rosent, who accepted him through a sponsor-benefactress, Ane Sopie Bruun, the wife of a Danish admiral. In 1853 he was declared "journeyman painter," and in the meanwhile (1850), C. C. A. and his mother and brothers had been baptized into the LDS church by Erastus Snow. Henceforth the Mormon church and his art became equally significant in his life. He served a four-year mission in Norway (1853–57), and in 1857 he was in Liverpool to board a ship for the United States. On 24 April of that year he married a Norwegian convert, Elise Haarby, aboard the ship on its way to America.[15]

C. C. A. Christensen and Elise traveled from Iowa City to Salt Lake City pushing a handcart, and ended their three-month journey in September 1857, "destitute for everything but faith in God and hope for better days." His mother (deceased before 1857) and two brothers were already in the valley, and for a year, until 1858, C. C. A. and Elise lived in a one-room cabin with his brother Frederick's family in Fairfield, forty miles southwest of Salt Lake City.

To support himself and his wife, C. C. A. became a hod carrier because, as he put it himself, "the paintpots were dry and empty." In his first few years in Deseret, C. C. A. also tanned hides, made charcoal, farmed, painted houses, and painted scenery for the old Salt Lake Theater.

The year 1858 found him and Elise in Ephraim, where his three sons were eventually born. The paintings for which he became so famous were not begun for another twelve years. For a few years his activities were ephemeral and somewhat unstable.

In 1859 he helped found Mount Pleasant and lived there until 1865, when he served a second mission to Norway. While in Norway, he tried some portrait painting and furthered his art studies. He returned to Mount Pleasant in 1868 and lived in Ephraim in 1870. He helped in the settlement of Fairview in 1871.

His most famous work, The "Mormon Panorama," was painted to use in an illustrated lecture on LDS church history. All twenty-three canvases were sewed together into a scroll, wound on aspen poles, and rolled with a crank by an assistant, usually Frederick Christensen, who in 1880 had become principal of the district school in Fairview. The entire scroll of twenty-three paintings was about 175 feet long, and it was held erect at lectures by a wooden-legged tripod.

As C. C. A. grew older, the entire lecture process became a heavier burden. Sometime before 1906 the scroll was stored in a storeroom at Brigham Young University, where it reposed, almost forgotten, for a number of years.

Charles John Christensen, the oldest son of C. C. A. and Elise, eventually purchased the works from his father for $100 and returned them to Ephraim, where they were stored in his home. Charles died in 1928, leaving them to his wife, who, at her own death in 1944, bequeathed them to the Christensen family, the paintings themselves to be housed by Charles' oldest son, Seymour.

Seymour arranged occasionally to have the paintings exhibited at Christensen family reunions and some social gatherings in Sanpete and Emery. One relative, Lars Bishop, a seminary teacher, was sufficiently impressed to have them shown to students and teachers of religion at Brigham Young University. In 1953 Dr. William E. Berrett, administrator of Seminaries and Institutes, requested that the paintings be brought to Provo for photographing in slides and filmstrips. The originals are now permanently at the Brigham Young University.

Then, in the late 1950s and early 1960s, Carl Carmer arrived in Utah to gather material for a book on the church. Mr. Carmer proved to be the catalyst that brought the paintings of C. C. A. Christensen to national attention. The magazine *American Heritage* used twelve of the paintings to illustrate an article by Mr. Carmer, and in 1970 the art periodical *Art in America* called C. C. A.'s paintings "the art of discovery in America of 1970." After that, the Whitney Museum of American Art, through its director, John I. H. Bauer, asked permission to exhibit them in the museum's galleries in New York City.

The accomplishments of C. C. A. Christensen go far beyond his reputation as an artist. Like so many others involved in Sanpete pioneer life, C. C. A. began with nothing. His "paintpots were dry," but his innovative spirit and creativity were not. He obtained his colors from native clay and plants, even as the Indians did. He mixed them with whatever oil he found available, and after about one hundred years of existence, his colors in his paintings have proved fast and true.

Perhaps the most remarkable development in the cultural history of Sanpete County is the regularity with which its history has provided themes for creative literature. The raw humor of the Danes, the hardships of the early years of settlement, the charm and the provincialism of small-town life have all attracted writers, and some of the Sanpete County literature ranks among the best to emerge from Mormon country.

C. C. A. Christensen, Sanpete County's first artist, was also its first literary figure of more than local renown. Christensen died in 1912, after a career of some thirty-five years as a major figure on the Utah cultural scene. His reputation rests first on his paintings interpreting scenes in Mormon history and theology, and second on a prolific stream of letters containing news, poems, and comments from Ephraim to *Bikuben,* the Scandinavian newspaper founded by Andrew Jenson, the church historian in Salt Lake City.[16]

The Ephraim Carnegie Public Library built in 1938. (Utah State Historical Society)

C. C. A. Christensen still has no equal in Utah literature as an interpreter of the culture of Danish immigrants. William Mulder, the leading student of the history and culture of the Scandinavian immigrants, point out that C. C. A.'s preoccupation with the people and region he knew best went deeper than a surface interest in the "local color" of character and scene. The broadly humorous treatment of a variety of themes does not, perhaps, make for depth of magnitude, and the subject matter may be trivial. But C. C. A.'s work leaves a total impression of importance because it is such a genuine and spontaneous representation of his own people. He wrote for them and about them, but he never forgot that he was himself of them.[17]

Virginia Sorensen is the first professional writer to come out of Sanpete County, and in every way except interpretation of the humor of the Danes, she is clearly the best writer the county has produced. The great appeal of Sorensen's Manti novels and stories is that she writes as an insider, but with an outsider's perspective as well. She clearly loves Manti, but she loves it enough to criticize it. Her books, *On This Star* (1946), *The Evening and the Morning* (1949), and *Where*

The German-born musician George Brox with his zither about 1912. (Courtesy Stanley Brox)

Nothing Is Long Ago (1963), are all set in Manti, while *Kingdom Come* (1960) interprets the lives of Danish converts to Mormonism in the 1850s.

Many people in Sanpete write poetry. Some admit it and some do not. Most of the best of these poems, with some short stories and essays, are published annually in a small paperback volume called *The Saga of the Sanpitch*. Edited and published locally, this little book is supported entirely by sales. The four LDS stakes in Sanpete lend moral support to the effort. This publication is popular because it is of, by, and for Sanpete people, wherever they may be now, and it attempts to entertain, reminisce, and instruct nostalgically. Nearly always, the book comes close to clearing out its annual editions. Begun in 1969, it continues still, changing editors every few years.

Musicians in Sanpete have been appreciated from the start. One of the most enthusiastic of Sanpete's musicians was a German immigrant, George Brox. Born in the Rhineland in 1860, he immigrated to Utah in 1890 and settled in Manti where he organized a German men's choir. Early in September 1911, he left the Manti City Power Plant, where he was manager, at 6:00 A.M., on horseback, for Ferron in Emery County. He later told his community about his trip in the *Manti Messenger.* He first stopped at Mickelson's sawmill at 8:30 for a rest, he wrote, then continued up Manti Canyon to Works's campground, which he reached at noon. Here, "there was a house with a stove, a table and a bedstead made of lumber, also a stable for his horse." The trees round-about bore the carved names of Lee Hall, Joe Nielsen, and others. Hearing the happy voices of children and campers, George took his trumpet out of his saddlebag and blew a tune. He was invited to dinner by Will Heath and Niels Nielson, who were camped nearby. Brox had also brought his zither along, and he played it, too. At 9,000 feet of elevation, the sounds must have been loud and clear across the coves just west of the Skyline.

He crossed the mountain at 11,000 feet, where he saw horses feeding. A snowbank was on the north side of the mountain. There was much good grass, and some rain fell. He stopped at Works's sawmill. In the evening they held a musical program with Kenneth Bird playing his violin while Brox played his zither. He spent the night here with Thomas Hansen.

The next morning he continued his journey to Ferron. That morning he heard the noise of sheep and heard their bells. It was Frank Hall's herd. Brox stopped at Petty's sawmill. The beauty of the mountains nearly overwhelmed George, and occasionally he sang and played his musical instruments out of pure joy. He found Jens Hansen and other men repairing a bridge. Teamsters were making a new road through some timber. Brox rode past Ferron Reservoir and Harmonica Point. "I kept winding in and out and down and up again. Then I could see . . Ferron through spyglasses." He was invited by somebody to stay for supper, but he politely declined. "On I went over bridges and washouts. Met boys and girls on horseback." He also provided the *Messenger* with a description of Ferron Canyon, its rock formations, the road, and finally the big tree that had fallen across the road. He crossed the creek seven or eight times. His horse was tired. As he approached the Peter Faulner house in Ferron, it was almost 9:30 P.M. "Taking my horn out, I played 'The Watch on the Rhine.'" People came out to meet him, and with another zither player, Mr. Eberstein, they arranged a musical part, featuring zither duets and German voices ringing up Ferron Canyon with *Deutshe Lieder*.[18]

This seems to have been the only motive Mr. Brox had for riding a horse two days across "the Manti Mountain" to Ferron.

It is rumored that the first piano in Sanpete found home with Francis M. Jolley, at the "Jolley House" in Manti in the 1870s. The piano was well established in Sanpete by 1900, despite the size of the instrument and the difficulties in moving it so far.

Most of the emphasis in music in Sanpete since 1849 has been on group singing and most of the inspiration found root in religious hymns of the LDS church.

The musical leader who was most influential in choral singing in the early years was Adam Craik Smyth. Born in England in 1840, he was a graduate of the London Conservatory of Music. He migrated to Utah in 1864 and soon associated with musical groups in Cache Valley. Baptized into the LDS church in 1873, he moved to Salt Lake City in 1875, and for seven years taught music and directed operas there. About 1880 he homesteaded around Fountain Green, pushed out of Salt Lake City, it was said, "by the jealousy of other musicians who were closer to the authority of the Church."[19]

In Manti Bishop William T. Reid obtained the position of recorder in the temple for Smyth, two years before the building was completed. This was in 1886, and by this maneuver Smyth became the director of the Manti Tabernacle Choir, a group which was first organized in the 1860s by "The Westenskows," a singing family.[20] Smyth held this position of Manti Tabernacle music director for fifteen years, but in 1901 a dispute over salary demands led to his resignation. Smyth died in 1909.[21]

William Fowler, a native of Australia and composer of the lyrics to one of the most popular Mormon hymns, "We Thank Thee O God

The Gunnison Co-op and Casino (Star) Theater in 1921. (Courtesy LaMar Larsen)

for a Prophet," died in Manti in 1865 at the age of thirty-five after five years' residence in Sanpete County.

John and Louisa Hasler departed their native Switzerland early in 1869, and by way of Liverpool and New York they traveled to "Zion" by steamer and the new transcontinental railroad. Arriving in late summer or early fall, they were met in Salt Lake City by Louisa's sister and her husband, who lived in Mount Pleasant. It was a four-day journey by carriage to Sanpete.[22]

Hardly a week in Mount Pleasant, John Hasler learned that Brigham Young had called for a military drill in the fields between Ephraim and Manti, and to his notion this called for a military band. Having taught himself to play most band instruments, he brought all he had out of his trunk. In three weeks' time he had assembled both enough instruments and enough musicians, and had copied enough musical parts manually, to effect a brass band. His printed and bound edition of band music was "probably the first one in Sanpete County." After 1869 his band, rehearsed and ready, was in demand for holiday celebrations, political rallies, and special performances.

Soon he was called to lead the choir in his ward, a position he held for seventeen years." A choir was not new to Mount Pleasant, for James Hansen had led one for years; however, the bishop was amazed that John Hasler expected the meetinghouse to be lighted and heated the night of choir practice. Singing was like preaching, to be unrehearsed and spontaneous, "according to the inspiration of the spirit." But Hasler insisted that *his* choir would rehearse with both light and heat. In order to be assured of accompanists, he also taught three women of the ward to play the organ.[23]

In ensuing years Hasler contracted typhoid fever and pneumonia, not uncommon occurrences in Sanpete in the nineteenth century. Rheumatic fever finally crippled him permanently, to the extent that he used a cane for the rest of his life. He went on a mission to Switzerland sometime in the late 1870s. During his mission he organized a choir in every Swiss branch, arranged their music, and "wrote a number of hymns for an L.D.S. German [language] hymnbook."

When Hasler returned to Sanpete, he began a program of applied music that drew students from near and far in central and southern Utah. He installed three organs in as many rooms in his home during the 1880s and gave organ lessons for a fee of $15 to $20 to four to six rooming-and-boarding students at a time over a six-week period. These lessons were usually proffered during the summer. He also taught group and individual lessons all day long.

"Mina Hasler Sorenson, the youngest daughter in the family (nine children were born in Sanpete, four whom died in childhood), vividly remembers lessons beginning at six o'clock in the morning and organ music coming from every room all day long, all summer long!"[24]

Among Hasler's most successful students were John J. McClelland and Anthony C. Lund, both of whom were associated with the Mormon Tabernacle Choir for many years.

In 1890, as a salesman for the Crown Piano Company, John Hasler began traveling around an eight- or nine-county area by horse and buggy, selling pianos and organs door-to-door. As part of the sales contract he agreed to teach one member of the family twelve tunes with the purchase of an organ or twenty-four tunes for a piano. Lessons were given on his regular monthly rounds. Sometimes he returned to Mount Pleasant with payment in kind—cans of molasses, slabs of cheese, or even an occasional horse or cow tethered to his buggy.

C. W. Reid, formerly a music instructor at Brigham Young University, once said that "no other man helped to bring music into the homes of so many people over so large an area as did John Hasler."

John sustained his activities until he was seventy years old, when he "retired" to a small farm near Mount Pleasant. Music did not cease being important for him then, but in trying to organize a male chorus in the high priests' quorum he experienced the greatest test in patience. "Those old men had no ear for music!" he complained.

His death at seventy-five on 10 January 1914 was accompanied by an interesting coincidence. On the morning he died, his Swiss cuckoo clock stopped short, and reportedly no clock repairman could make it go again. The musical legacy in the form of piano and organ music that John Hasler left in nearly every home in Sanpete County, however, has continued.

The composer LeRoy Jasper Robertson was born 21 December 1896 in Fountain Green, Utah. The eldest child of Jasper H. and Alice Adams Robertson, he grew up in a family of three sisters and two brothers. His childhood and early youth were spent in activities common to the other boys his age, with one exception, his compelling interest in music.

His first music came from his homemade violin and the family organ. The violin was whittled out of rough lumber and equipped with strings from thread in his mother's sewing basket, and the hair for the bow came from the tail of one of his father's horses.

With practically no musical training, he began to play tunes by ear on his home-made violin and the reed organ. He was in the seventh grade when he became the proud owner of his first "store" violin, which his father brought from Omaha, where he had taken lambs for sale. It cost the sum of nine dollars. Each week for some time thereafter, the boy would walk from one end of Fountain Green to the other to take a lesson from Ben Williams at a cost of approximately twenty-five cents a lesson.

At this time he began to compose his own music. When he showed some of it to a Mr. Bartlett, who directed the town band, he was told that while he had real talent, he needed training in harmony and music theory to succeed as a composer.

His desire for futher study was fulfilled when he left home to attend high school and to live with his grandparents, William H. and Melissa Jane Adams, in Pleasant Grove. He procured a better violin and was able take private lessons and receive help in harmony and music theory. Four years at Brigham Young University provided him with additional opportunities to develop musical knowledge and skills. From B.Y.U. he went to Boston, where he studied and graduated from the New England Conservatory of Music in 1923. While there he completed the normal four-year course in composition, violin, and public school music instruction, plus three years of work on the piano, in the record time of two years.

Still eager to improve his composition skills, he later studied composition with some of the world's leading composers, such as Ernest Block in San Francisco and Switzerland, and with Hugh Leichentritt in Berlin. He received his Ph.D. in composition from the University of Southern California in 1954.

The gifted teacher served for twenty-three years as professor of music at Brigham Young University and later moved to the University of Utah. He also became head of the Music Committee of the Church of Jesus Christ of Latter-day Saints.

Robertson's more serious compositions, including two symphonies, three concertos for violin, piano, and cello, several chamber music numbers, the *Book of Mormon Oratorio,* and others, have been performed around the world by the world's leading artists and orchestras.

With all the emphasis on choral and choir music in Sanpete, it is no surprise that out of the high valleys of Sanpete County some solo voices emerged. Nearly every town in Sanpete has its recognized bassos, tenors, altos, and sopranos, but one stands out so clearly above the others that eventually it was heard as far away as Milan, Italy.

Glade Peterson grew up as a farm boy in Fairview, although Lowell Durham called him "the Fairview cowboy."[25] He graduated in 1947 from North Sanpete High School, where he had been active in both music and football. A running back, Peterson was fast and hard to catch, especially if he got past the secondary. He ran "a damn fast hundred yards" on the track team, say his old schoolmates, but with all that, his main interest was music, according to the same friends.

Statue of Mr. and Mrs. Peter Peterson sculpted by Avard Fairbanks. Born in Fairview in 1860, the Petersons were married for 82 years and lived all of their lives in Fairview. (Sanpete County)

This interest took noticeable first root in the Fairview Junior High and continued in North Sanpete High School.[26]

To achieve further training for his voice, Peterson went to Salt Lake City and from there to New York, where he made his debut with the N.B.C. Opera Company in *Madame Butterfly*. His professional itinerary from there included the La Scala Opera House in Milan and the Zurich Opera in Switzerland.

Another Sanpete original, "Sheepherder Sam" made his appearance in 1952 as a regular, daily, one-frame cartoon in the *Salt Lake Tribune*. Sam was the creation of Christian Jensen of Ephraim.[27]

Born in Roecslev, Island of Fyn, Denmark, in 1901, Chris Jensen was only seven months old when he came to Utah with his parents, Knud and Mary Jensen, settling in Ephraim, where Chris grew up.

His father was a farmer and wanted Chris to become a horticulturist. His mother was a mathematician of sorts and played mathematical games with Chris in his boyhood. In Ephraim, Knud Jensen planted fruit trees, and neither parent thought of Chris as an artist. Chris himself did not take an art career seriously, but for years filled pads of paper with practice sketches. He took his first lessons from a series of articles on the fundamentals of drawing in the magazine *Lone Scout*. As a young man, he "bummed around a lot," was camp tender for a sheepman, held some railroad jobs, did some sign-painting, and was a "retouch artist" with the old *Salt Lake Telegram*.

"Sheepherder Sam" was the archetype of the Sanpete sheepherder. He was straight-forward and could be caustic. He took things in stride, worried very little, and got on with life as he found it.

There was a serious side to Christian Jensen. An orchard of fruit trees painted by Jensen evoked nostalgic warmth in the memory of an art critic in Salt Lake City. Jensen's paintings speak eloquently of the desert of Utah of the 1920s, 1930s, and 1940s. A lean sheepherder on a horse, with trailing pack of animals, shown against a lowering distant sky, is a typical Chris Jensen rendition of a lifestyle in Utah now almost gone. Jensen painted a thousand things of human experience in nature now almost forgotten, even by the residents of rural Utah.

ENDNOTES

1. Ellis Day Coombs and George F. Olsen, *History of Fairview*, 50.

2. *Manti Messenger*, 10 December 1909.

3. Ibid., 3 November 1893.

4. *County Reporter*, 25 September 1895.

5. Ibid., 28 July 1911.

6. *Ephraim Enterprise*, 25 July 1914.

7. *Manti Messenger*, 20 July 1917.

8. *Ephraim Enterprise*, 8 September 1922.

9. Ibid., 27 January 1897

10. Ibid., 6 September 1929.

11. John K. Olsen, "Fact and Fiction About Sanpete's July Holidays," *Saga of the Sanpitch*, 13, 1981.

12. Daughters of the Utah Pioneers, Sanpete County. *These Our*

Fathers, A Centennial History of Sanpete County, 1849–1947 (Springville, UT: Art City Publishing Co. 1947), 46; *Manti Messenger,* 8 June 1923.

13. Halbert S. Greaves, interviewed by John S. H. Smith, 13 January 1972, 11–12; Reece Anderson, with John S. H. Smith, 7 January 1972, 13. Utah State Historical Society.

14. *Song of a Century,* 17.

15. *Improvement Era,* May 1970.

16. Carl Carmer, "Here Is My Home At Last" *American Heritage* 14 (Febuary 1963): 26- 33.

17. William Mulder, "'Man Kalder Mig Digter'; C. C. A. Christensen, Poet of the Scandinavian Scene in Early Utah" *Utah Humanities Review* 16 (1 January 1947).

18. *Manti Messenger,* 8 September 1911

19. Harry A. Dean. "A. C. Smyth and His Influence on Choral Music in Central Utah," M.A.thesis. Brigham Young University, 1938.

20. *Song of a Century,* Centennial Book, 1849–1949, 94.

21. *Manti Messenger,* 26 January 1909.

22. Marilyn M. Smolka. "Mount Pleasant's Very Own Music Man" *Beehive History* 6: (December 1930) 13–15.

23. Ibid.

24. Ibid.

25. Lowell Durham. *Salt Lake Tribune,* 17 Nov. 1965; John Fitzpatrick. *Salt Lake Tribune,* 9 April 1967.

26. Wayne G. Beck, Sanpete County Clerk; Yvonne A Howell, Sanpete County Assessor, in interviews with Albert Antrei and Ruth D. Scow, May 1981.

27. Christian Jensen, *Sheepherder Sam Cartoons* (Salt Lake City: University of Utah Press, 1978).

CHAPTER 12

THE BUILT ENVIRONMENT

Τ he nature of the county's built environment—its buildings, bridges, canals, roads, fences, and other human-built elements— derives from a complex combining of influences and resources. Although this chapter will emphasize the county's architecture, the character of any built or made object can be understood in terms of its function, materials, cost, design, and craftsmanship, all of which reflect a place's locale, culture, ethnicity and economy. Thus we can read the history of a place not only by studying books, but also by observing and interpreting the built products of its people: the design of its towns and architecture.

A perusal of old photos or a tour of any Sanpete town will reveal volumes of knowledge about that town's past. One will observe in each place generations of community growth, development and change, as one sees a variety of building ages, uses, types, materials, and styles. Any single structure will prove informative, and a collection of buildings in relationship to one another and in the context of an overall town plan will communicate how a people worked, played,

One of Utah's oldest houses is this limestone dwelling built in 1851 in Manti. The heavily molded cornice, cornice return and medium-pitched roof are typical of Greek Revival styling which dominated Sanpete architecture until the 1880s. (Allen D. Roberts)

worshipped, learned, governed, and lived together cooperatively as they built a permanent, productive, healthy, and beautiful society.

Early Building Material and Methods

The pioneers of Sanpete brought their architecture with them in the form of skills, tools, books, and their experiences with buildings before the arrived in their new homeland. Those who had been first-generation Mormons helped build impressive stone, brick and wood-frame edifices, stores, and homes in Kirtland, Ohio, Nauvoo, Illinois, and perhaps Salt Lake City or other early towns in the Mormon Corridor. Since the 1830s Mormons had been erecting thoughtfully designed, well-built structures such as the Nauvoo temple, Masonic Hall, Seventy's Hall, *Times and Seasons* Building, and Nauvoo House.

In the Great Basin, the same American styles and building types, built from the same builder's guidebooks and employing the same hand tools, produced adobe versions of their earlier Federal and Greek Revival counterparts.

Built in 1854, the John Patten house is typical of Sanpete's first generation, unstyled, vernacular residences. It is now a museum of the Daughters of Utah Pioneers. (Albert Antrei)

In the late 1840s and early 1850s, the Salt Lake Social Hall, Council House, Tithing Office, Mint, and permanent residences featured the stately symmetry, fancy cornices, small-paned windows, and orderly design seen in their Nauvoo precursors just a few years earlier. Repeating what they already knew and liked, the settlers of Sanpete towns constructed similar Federal/Greek Revival buildings, this time translated into stone and adobe. Only the lack of building technology and limited finances prevented them from building sophisticated, high style buildings during the settlement years.

The first pioneer-built structures in the county were twenty-seven dugouts cut into the talus slopes of Temple Hill in Manti in 1849. These quickly built, primitive dwellings were soon accompanied by a few equally rough, windowless log cabins with dirt floors. This temporary survival architecture was intended mainly to provide shelter against winter weather. The pioneers knew that if they could built well enough to survive, they could apply their talents and imported equipment to better effect in the spring.

Before mills and quarries were available to produce finished lum-

This rare, heavy timber structure with adobe infill in Mount Pleasant suggests an Old World building tradition. (Allen D. Roberts)

ber, shingles, moldings, and cut stone, structures were made with indigenous materials, especially logs, field stone, clay, and lime. Other materials like iron for nails, lintels, columns, and beams, would not be available in sizable quantity for several decades. The buildings constructed with native materials typically employed plain, utilitarian, vernacular architecture. Local field stone or river rock was used for foundations. Nearby lime was slaked, mixed with sand and water, and converted to a soft mortar with which to set foundation stone and adobe walls. Following the example of Salt Lake City where an adobe yard was established only three weeks after the vanguard part of pioneers entered the Great Salt Lake Valley, Sanpeters found adobe literally "dirt cheap," and it soon became a popular substitute for more durable but less easily obtained masonry units such as stone and brick.

Soft gray clay was mixed with sand, water, and sometimes straw, animal hair, or pebbles as binder, in an "adobe pit" using a man- or animal-powered auger. The pliable mud was then packed by hand into wooden forms, usually 4 by 5 by 12 inches in size. The uniformly

While designing the Manti Temple, architect William H. Folsom also designed other LDS edifices, including the majestic Manti Tabernacle, recently restored for continued use. (Sanpete County)

Sanpete's best example of Romanesque Revival architecture in the Gothic Revival mode, is the beautifully crafted meetinghouse or tabernacle in Spring City. The 1970s addition of matching oolite stone is exemplary for its design compatibility. (Utah State Historical Society)

shaped blocks were then placed on smooth ground to "bake" in the sun for a week or so. The dried blocks were then laid up in walls with lime mortar, usually with two courses running lengthwise in a stretcher bond with every fifth or seventh course turned perpendicular into the wall to connect the parallel courses together.

In the early 1890s, Judge Jacob Johnson added a flamboyant Victorian wing to his 1870s central passage house, then plastered both to resemble finely cut stone. The two towers are distinctive, the giant stone barn, stone law office and granary and the indoor plumbing—the first in Spring City. (Utah State Historical Society)

Using an adz, which looked like a sharp-edged hoe, logs were either squared for cabins, structural timbers, or planks, or shaved flat on one side to create "puncheons" which became floor and ceiling supports. Supple willow branches would be fastened to the inside walls and ceilings and plastered with a mix similar to lime mortar. The interior surfaces were then whitewashed with a liquid made from water, lime, and calcimine. Later lead and oil paints were imported and applied to plastered ceilings and walls as well as wood trim. The Scandiniavians used different color schemes than their American counterparts, distinguishing their buildings by color and style as many immigrant homes were constructed in the Danish pair-house style.

Before shingles were available, roofs were covered with logs, branches, and sometimes mat of twigs, straw, or other plants. Sod or

The Frederick C. Jensen House, built in 1891 in Mount Pleasant, is an exceptional example of Carpenter Gothic architecture, wherein a Gothic Victorian decorative vocabulary is executed entirely in wood rather than stone. (Allen D. Roberts)

plain dirt would be the topping material. Such primitive shelters would not always hold out the rain, but they offered considerable protection against the wind, heat, cold, snow, animals, and other intruders. To a lesser extent, log cabins served the same function. Connected at the corners by a variety of notching types depending on the training and/or ethnicity of the builder, these one-or two-room dwellings rarely exceeded one story, often had dirt floors, and had strips of scrap wood called "scantlings" secured to the spaces between the logs to keep out the weather.

Because glass was easily broken crossing the plains in wagon trains, only small panes, typically 10 by 12 inches in size, were packed along. When glass was not available, window openings were covered with thick paper vellum, or thin animal skins. Before mills could cut boards for doors, flooring, and trim, tanned leather skins covered door bays, floors had packed dirt or animal skin rugs, and buildings were trimless.

The groups colonizing Sanpete contained masons, millers, and

Often overlooked are Sanpete's many styles of Bungalow architecture built between 1910 and 1930. (Allen D. Roberts)

carpenters. This was a distinct advantage in providing solid structures. Because of Manti's stone masons, limestone buildings appeared there from the first year of the town's existence. A few stone dwellings dating back to the early 1850s remain, among them the a Greek Revival house on the northwest side with "1851" carved on the fireplace mantel, the south section of the Black/Tuttle/Folsom House (1851), and the John Patten House (1854). Masonry was the material of preference in part because Brigham Young so favored it over less permanent wood construction. He wanted to build a religious community with a physical environment durable enough to last to the Millennium.

Still, lumber was needed for many building purposes and the first non-residential structure built in each settlement was usually a sawmill. The pioneers brought with them from the East, Midwest, and Europe milling irons and saws. Lumber from the earliest mills was in great demand but was especially useful in erecting greatly needed grist mills and meetinghouses. Once structural needs were satisfied, lumber was used for a lesser number of plank and

Five of the county's historic tithing offices remain, all built between 1905–1908, including this one in Manti. (Allen D. Roberts)

horizontally-sided buildings. Outbuildings were often made of log and lumber and typically had vertical siding.

Written descriptions and the rare photographic views of Sanpete County during its settlement decades show small, rural towns with wide streets and large blocks laid out in a grid oriented to the cardinal points of the compass. Irrigation ditches, wood fences, and rows of fast growing Lombardy poplars and black locust trees line the streets. The one- and two-story buildings are of log, adobe, or stone construction. The gabled, boxlike forms are of either vernacular or simplified Greek Revival styling. Nearly everyone lived in town in houses clustered in low density around a small town center where a meetinghouse/school and a few commercial buildings stood. This scene was not only ubiquitous for Sanpete County, but existed for hundred of miles in every direction as the Mormon Landscape, an appearance common among the pre-railroad Mormon settlements but unique in the larger panorama of American life.

The Influence of Architects

The existence of fine architecture in the county before the advent

The Carnegie Library in Mount Pleasant is one of Utah's best examples of Prairie Style, an architecture created by American master Frank Lloyd Wright and executed here by Ware and Treganza, a Salt Lake City firm. (Utah State Historical Society)

of professional architects can be explained by the presence of experience local builders and the indirect influence of architects whose drawings appeared in widely circulated books and builder's guides. Observant of examples of similar buildings elsewhere in the territory, and capable of copying or modifying designs in print, local craftsmen created many derivative yet worthy structures. Thus the two-story, Greek Revival Council House in Manti, built in 1855–56, looked like the 1852 Social Hall in Salt Lake City, which in turn resembled Joseph Smith's "Red Brick Store" of the early 1840s in Nauvoo, Illinois.

During the county's earliest decades, the architectural profession was very different than it is now and very few buildings were designed directly by architects. Only a dozen or so men in the territory described themselves as architects during the pioneer period, and nearly all of them were employed primarily as builders, either as masons, carpenters, or joiners. What distinguished them from other builders was their ability to design buildings and draw simple construction plans. There was no schooling or licensing of architects in

The multi-arched "Tiger's Den" is one of the several historic structures grac-
ing the campus of Wasatch Academy, Utah's oldest boarding high school,
founded in 1875. (Allen D. Roberts)

nineteenth-century Utah. The term "builder-architect" best describes
the role of historic "design-build" professionals.

Despite the presence of many handsomely designed and well-
crafted churches, business and government buildings, and residences
in pre-railroad Sanpete County, no local designers advertised themselves as architects during those decades. If there were local architects,
they remain anonymous. The one exception is William Huggins of
Fountain Green who in 1871–73 was listed as "architect" in a territorial business directory. Huggins was born in New Jersey in 1811,
came to Utah in 1853, and thereafter assisted in bringing immigrants
to the state. His practice of architecture in the 1870s corresponded to
the construction of several well-designed brick houses, business, and
public buildings in the Fountain Green-Moroni area during that
period.

When architects did appear, they came mostly from out of the
county. The first designer of prominence to work in the county was
Manti temple architect William H. Folsom. The planning of the temple had begun in 1875 under Brigham Young's direction. His eldest

The ruins of Milburn's 1880s general store and social hall await possible restoration, as do hundreds of other vacant but picturesque structure throughout the county. (Allen D. Roberts)

son, Joseph A. Young was selected to design the edifice but died suddenly while visiting the site during the summer of 1875. Blessed with a fertile visual imagination, sixty-two year old Folsom was chosen to replace Young. Due to the extent of his Sanpete commissions, Folsom purchased a small, limestone house in Manti two blocks west of the temple site. To the north he built a two-story, four-room addition from which he could watch the most important architectural project of his career. A polygamist who eventually had to sell the Manti house to pay a bigamy fine, Folsom included a cleverly disguised hideout or "polygamy pit" under the new stairway. The house is still extant. From this headquarters, the gifted architect designed and supervised construction of the temple (with the help of assistant architect Frank Y. Taylor) as well as two impressive tabernacles in Manti and Moroni. While residing in Manti, he also consulted on the design of the Salt Lake temple and designed tabernacles and meetinghouses in Provo, Panguitch, and Mona.

Following the completion of the elegant and resplendent Manti temple, the ailing Folsom returned to Salt Lake City where he died in

1890. Shortly thereafter, another accomplished architect, Richard C. Watkins, began designing numerous churches, schools, commercial buildings, and houses in Sanpete. Sparsely educated in England, Mormon convert Watkins came to Salt Lake City and found employment with Utah's then-leading architect, Richard K. A. Kletting, designer of the Utah State Capitol. In 1890, asked to oversee the construction of the Territorial Insane Asylum in Provo, Watkins noticed that there were no architects to serve the cities in the central counties of the state. Establishing an office in Provo, he was especially popular in newly wealthy Sanpete County where he designed the Romanesque revival tabernacle and Victorian eclectic elementary school in Spring City, many impressive business houses along Main Street in Mount Pleasant, and others. In his long and distinguished career, Watkins designed 240 schools, many of which survive.

Another out-of-town architect with a clientele in Sanpete County was Kirtwood Cross of Provo. Among his commissions was the large, Victorian style residence built in 1894 for the James G. Crawford, Jr., family in Manti. Still extant on Second South and Main Street, this impressive two-story, brick and stone dwelling included a two-level frame carriage house, a rarity in the county.

The pattern of hiring architects from the more populated northern counties persists to this day. During the World War I era, Andrew Carnegie donated funds to build over a dozen city libraries throughout the state. Three of the most architecturally impressive ones were the masterful Prairie Style library in Mount Pleasant, and the more classically influenced designs in Ephraim and in Manti designed by the eclectic firm of Ware and Treganza Architects in Salt Lake City. The firm also designed the North Sanpete High School in Mount Pleasant and other educational facilities in the county.

CHAPTER 13

SANPETE COUNTY IN THE TWENTIETH CENTURY

If the nineteenth century had been the pioneer era in Sanpete County's history, the first decades of the twentieth century brought a new period of maturity and modernity with the completion of town water systems, the arrival of electricity, telephones, and the automobile. A network of roads emerged, and local politics took on a more national character as candidates of the national Republican and Democratic parties vied for local and state offices. Community organizations, such as the Lions Club, American Legion, and Women's clubs, appeared and helped to break down some of the remaining barriers that grew out of religious and ethnic differences. Above all, the experience in national and international events such as World War I, the Great Depression, the New Deal, and World War II showed that Sanpete County's future was tied to that of the nation and the rest of the world.

Water, Electricity, and Telephones

As livestock grazing on the Wasatch Plateau became more common, Manti residents realized the health hazard posed by their open culinary water supply. In 1882 F. R. Kenner pointed out that "we have a great deal of mortality among us—more than should be," which he blamed on the "posonous" water, and called for the installation of pipes to protect the water from pollution. By 1891 Manti had acted upon his recommendation and the system of wooden pipes had reached town, an event that called for "a feast with dinner, music, speeches and fun until at night." During the next decade, Manti homes gradually made connections to the new water main.[1]

The new water supply was anything but free from problems, however. In the first place, the impermanence of the wooden pipes meant that problems of sanitation would reappear. In 1915 a state inspector blamed six cases of typhoid at Manti on the decaying pipes and the unprotected creek above the inlet to the pipes. Although the water supply was later exonerated, it was apparent that improvements were necessary. Gunnison faced the same problem, and finally voted a $30,000 bond issue to replace its wooden pipes with metal ones.[2]

Increasing population and greater use of water created new water problems. By 1926 Manti found it necessary to install water meters to curb the excessive use of culinary water. The ordinance drew an angry protest from "A Citizen," who thought that residential consumers should be allowed an unrestricted supply while livestock men and other big users should be metered, but the ordinance stayed in effect. Gunnison metered homes in 1929 and businesses in 1932.[3]

Electricity was somewhat slower to arrive because of the great expense and more specialized technology it required. Serious discussion of electricity in Sanpete County did not begin until 1897, and, although Mount Pleasant was able to begin limited electrical service that year, the other communities had to wait for the new century before installing power plants. During the years 1901–1903, Manti, Fountain Green, Fairview, Spring City, Wales, Sterling, Mayfield, and Gunnison all acquired electrical power in at least enough quantity for rudimentary residential lighting and, in some cases, street lighting. Some of the smaller communities such as Axtell and Chester did not receive electricity until 1930.[4]

To modern readers accustomed to continuous, dependable electrical power in virtually unlimited quantities, the history of electrical service in Sanpete in the early years of this century is curious and amusing. Power was at first available only from 5 P.M. to midnight, although Manti began continuous service in 1904. Billing and collecting procedures varied. Some homes had meters, while others had to purchase light bulbs from the power company and were billed monthly according to the size and number of their bulbs, rather than the amount of time they were used. Some customers cheated, of course, privately purchasing and installing more and larger bulbs. Electric ranges were available, but they were sold by the city at cost and had to be installed by the city electrician. The city electrician was a busy man, since he had also to read the meters and collect the money due at the time he read them; no bills were sent by mail. One month's delinquency resulted in disconnection, no doubt because of the city's lack of bookkeeping, rather than their harshness in denying credit. To be reconnected, one had to pay a one dollar fee, the amount in arrears, and one month's minimum rate in advance.[5]

Most of the power plants in Sanpete were hydroelectric, and the variable water supply thus affected the electrical supply. Drought or ice caused power outages, and spring floods could destroy the ditches and even the entire power plant. At times the lights might be on for only three days in the week, drawing sharp censure from businessmen, whose livelihood depended on electrical power. Manti found it necessary to put the street lights and the residential lights on different circuits, so that in times of power shortage, the power demand could be reduced by eliminating less important uses.[6]

Electric lights were such an improvement over former lighting methods that the residents of the county generally did not mind the inconveniences and were willing to pay heavily to continue and improve their electrical service. After attending an LDS stake conference at Manti in 1903, J. Hatten Carpenter noted that the tabernacle was lighted electrically for the first time, and remarked that it "looked so clean & fresh & warm it was a pleasure to go to meeting." To ensure continued adequate supplies of electricity in spite of increasing population, the communities used steam or diesel generators as supplements to their outdated hydroelectric plants. Some built new hydroelectric plants at tremendous cost ($23,000-$27,000 estimated for the new plant at Mount Pleasant 1912—a huge sum at that time for a small community). Others signed contracts with Telluride

Power Company to purchase extra power during peak load periods. During the 1930s, the federal government provided some assistance. Manti, for instance, received a Progress Works Administration (PWA) grant of almost $16,000 for construction of a new hydroelectric plant.[7]

With electrical service installed, telephones were not far behind. Utah's first telephone was a private wire run between George A. Lowe's store and warehouse in Ogden in 1879. By 1883 telephone companies had been established in Ogden and Salt Lake City, including the Utah and Rocky Mountain Bell systems, which served other counties, among them Sanpete.

The telephone came to Sanpete Valley in 1900. On 27 October a phone was installed in the Allred Brothers store in Chester. A week later the first line was run into Spring City, and soon several businesses and residences signed up for the service provided by the Rocky Mountain Bell Company. In addition to this commercial system, city officials installed an intercity telephone network connecting City Hall, the city power plant, the roller mills, and the homes of key leaders.

On 3 January 1901 the Rocky Mountain Bell Telephone and Telegraph Company began operations in Mount Pleasant. At first, when Fairview had no telephone system, messages were wired there from Mount Pleasant by telegraph. Later, in 1901, a privately owned system was started in Fairview with four phones. In 1903 Rocky Mountain Bell extended its line to Fairview, and in 1904 phone and power lines were built in Fairview by the Telephone and Electric Light Company. About 220 phones were installed.[8] In 1907 telephones became available to the citizens of Manti when a local telephone company was organized with a capital of $10,000.

The usual arrangement was for the local telephone company to handle all local service, yet be connected to a larger company for long distance calls. Before long, telephone companies found the demand greater than they could supply, and Manti, for one, had a long waiting list of people wanting telephones.[9]

By providing greater access to the world outside Sanpete County, the telephone altered the outlook of those whom it served, and it also changed the outward appearance of the communities. With both electrical and telephone wires and poles being extended through town, the communities they served lost much of their previous rural appearance. At first, poles were placed in the center of the streets. Soon traffic hazards and the esthetic shortcomings of this placement became obvious, and poles were removed to the sides of the streets, or to less-used streets and alleys.[10]

Roads and Highways

The giving way of the "horse and buggy" era in favor of "tin Lizzies" began in Sanpete in the second decade of the twentieth century. Close on the heals of the advent of the automobile, the Utah State Road Commission was created 10 May 1909, part of a larger national "good roads" movement. The commission established four geographical areas, each directed by a member of the commission. Sanpete County was in the district administered by Richard R. Lyman, also a Mormon general authority. Lyman visited the county and met with local officials regarding the improvement of existing roads and planning, funding, and building of new routes

In July 1914 the road commission sponsored a traffic survey in Sanpete County. One of the findings was that horse-drawn traffic was still as prevalent as motor-driven vehicles, leading to legislation requiring wagons on state highways to be equipped with wide tires, presumably to protect roadways against damage and ruts. It would not be long, however, before automobile traffic would dominate the roadways and dictate their design. Concrete and, later, asphalt would gradually replace older compacted-earth-and-gravel roads which were hard on motorized vehicles. The first paved road in Sanpete County was constructed in 1914, running from Pigeon Hollow, north of Ephraim, south to Manti.

The advent of the automobile meant nearly limitless contact with others in the county, state, and beyond. Just as the railroad gave Sanpeters access to remote markets, gasoline-powered vehicles not only vastly improved transportation of all types, it eased the labor burden of farmers, ranchers, businessmen, and industrial workers. It also gave younger generations greater exposure to the enticements that lay beyond the county's borders. That migration from the county corresponded to the era of the automobile seems more than coinci-

The Gunnison Valley Sugar Company Factory. (Utah State Historical Society)

dental. Cars allowed for instant escape, whether short or long term. They also brought many changes to the face of the local landscape as paved roads, gasoline stations, and mechanic's shops appeared countywide. The small, frame station in Spring City, complete with drive-through *porte cochere* and a single gas pump, is one of the earliest remaining remnants of the onset of motorized vehicles.

Trucks became an important part of the transportation scene in Utah in about 1905. More versatile than the railroad, the trucking transport industry blossomed with "for hire" truckers hauling freight by contract and private truckers hauling for their own companies.

Beginning in 1916, several federal-aid highway acts brought funds to the state. The first money spent in Sanpete that year was for the Ephraim-to-Orangeville forest road project. The Federal Highway Act of 1921 brought additional road money to Sanpete. In 1921–22 a federal-aid construction project paid for a thirteen-mile road from Manti to Pigeon Hollow. By the 1920s the county's network of roads was well established and has not been much modified since.

Still the most important trafficway is U.S. Highway 89 which runs through the center of the entire length of both the county and the State of Utah. It enters the county from the north, just west of Indianola, having passed through Spanish Fork Canyon in Utah County. Moving south, it connects Sanpete's largest cities, including Fairview, Mount Pleasant, Ephraim, Manti, and Gunnison. Highway 89 exits the county south of Axtell on its way to Sevier County. The smaller towns of Indianola, Milburn, Spring City, Chester, Sterling, Centerfield, and Axtell also depend on Highway 89 as the nearest arterial connection to neighboring cities. Sanpete's northeastern towns, Fountain Green and Moroni, are tied to State Highway 132 which leads to Nephi along the first pioneer route into the county. Fayette relies on State Highway 28, while Mayfield is along State Highway 137. State Highway 31 goes from Fairview over the Wasatch Plateau to Huntington in Emery County.

The county's forests have hundreds of miles of roads developed in the twentieth century with the help of forest service funds. The best known of these, and the highest road in Sanpete, is Skyline Drive, which runs north-to-south along the top of the Wasatch Plateau, providing panoramic views of Sanpete Valley and picturesque access to the county's many mountainous recreational areas. The road can be taken from Tucker on U.S. Highway 6–50 in Utah County south to Ferron Reservoir, a length of seventy-seven miles. The drive also may be accessed by canyon roads running east from Fairview, Mount Pleasant, Spring City, Ephraim, Manti, and Mayfield. The three routes from Fairfield, Ephraim, and Mayfield cross over the plateau to Castle Valley in Emery County. Built along forests of dark spruce and lighter aspen, wild-flowered meadows, ponds, streams, and rock formations, Skyline Drive passes near South Tent Mountain, the county's highest peak.

Politics

The fading of conflict into consensus during the twentieth century is most evident in the field of politics. The political history of Sanpete County during the nineteenth century contained a remarkable degree of strife for a community that prided itself on its cultural unity and common interests. The Mormon church's domination of political life in the county preserved at least a facade of unanimity until near the end of the century, when the emergence at first of Mormon-gentile factions, then of political parties, formalized and solidified political differences. The process was accompanied by considerable bitterness and bewilderment, and it seemed to forecast a long period of political turbulence during the present century.

For a time that forecast proved to be true. In reporting the strife within the Republican Party in 1902 over the postmaster's job at Mount Pleasant and the party's seeming inability to choose among that town's "two or three candidates" for state senator, the *Sanpete Free Press* noted that "matters between the Republican faction of Sanpete county are about as peaceful as they are between a bulldog and a tomcat." The two factions, led by Lewis Larson and A. H. Christensen, clashed later that year at a mass meeting in Manti when Larson tried to compel the participants to nominate his slate of delegates. After a fierce struggle, the Christensen faction won by a slight margin. "It was midnight before they were thru,'" wrote J. Hatten Carpenter, "& Lewis seemed somewhat chagrined at turn of events as he had spent considerable time & expense to work up his side, but such methods are new here & not much liked."[11]

Rivalry between communities around the turn of the century loomed as large in politics as in personal factions. The most vexing question, by far, was the location of the county seat. At one time or another practically every major town in Sanpete Valley advanced its claim to become the county seat, and residents of beleaguered Manti must have felt at times as though their political life was being spent in defending their incumbency. On 4 August 1890, for example, Mount Pleasant's bid was defeated in an election, and the next night Manti celebrated its victory with a huge torchlight parade, complete with fireworks, cannons, speeches, and no fewer than two bands. Ephraim mounted its assault in 1904, and the *Manti Messenger* unleashed its sarcasm in portraying the relative backwardness of the rival town: "Ephraim has eight telephones, against forty telephones for Manti. Ephraim has no waterworks systems, insufficient hotel accommodations, no electric lights, no bank, and not even a first-class public school building." Once again Manti emerged victorious, but the harshness of the battle took its toll in diminishing the goodwill and cooperation between the communities. "It is a sorry thing," J. Hatten

Carpenter observed, "& a great pity it was ever stirred up to divide the people . . . Manti is behind or out some 700.00 for County Seat expenses & Ephraim over 1000.00 thus the people have to pay for their folly."[12]

The rivalry resurfaced in 1911 over the location of the South Sanpete High School. Once again incumbency proved decisive, and Manti won the election, but it was rumored that Ephraim had tried to conspire with Gunnison against Manti, and further ill will between the communities resulted. The only real winners, it seemed were the Manti high school students, who had had a high school since 1905. They "built a bonfire & paraded the town with horns, drums cow bells &c. & made night hideous with their yells of joy."[13] Jubilant, they gave their principal a ride in a wheelbarrow.

The most sustained, though no doubt, overly embittered, analysis of political rivalry and corruption both between and within Sanpete County communities is Alonzo Morley's 1924 study of Moroni.[14] It is difficult to corroborate much of what Morley says, but some of his allegations (for instance, when he calls Sanpete County "a haven of dissension among towns") echo more reliable reports. Government appropriations for roads and schools, he says, were particular bones of contention during the 1920s. Moreover, the town of Moroni itself was internally divided into three geographic divisions: "Duck Springs," the northwest part of town along the road to Fountain Green; "Frog Town," in the southwestern section near the railroad track; and "Dry Town," in the northeast. While the children from each of these sections fought in gangs, Morley says, the adults bickered over "civic improvements . . . An improvement in one section meets with bitter opposition from the other unless a counter improvement is designated for their particular section."[15]

Some degree of bitterness described and exemplified by Morley is probably endemic to small-town life, and sharp differences sometimes surface even today in Sanpete County politics, but the dominant trend since the 1920s seems to have been toward the kind of unanimity that the original settlers sought and occasionally achieved. Christian Jensen recalls that ideology and party organization in Ephraim during his youth in the 1920s generally yielded to the character of the man running for a particular office. People tended to vote for those they knew, regardless of party affiliation, and if the incumbent had done a good job, he would generally by returned to office. However, Vero Aiken notes a general decline in political activity during the twentieth century in Spring City:

> The Democrats and the Republicans would have their rallies and appoint their representatives and all, It's died down quite a bit now. There's not much politics, don't have much effect here now. That is, the different political parties. It don't matter who they were much. Not according to their politics. They know everybody and regardless of their politics why they vote for the man and not for the party, most of them do. Some think they're politician and still stick to their party, but then politics don't have much effect on this town.[16]

World War I

With the entry of the United States into World War I in April 1917 as an ally of the French and British and enemy of Germany, mass meetings and rallies were held throughout the county. On the eve of the war declaration, residents were urged to decorate their homes and businesses with the American flag or bunting until they could obtain one. At a mass rally in Manti on 31 March 1917, the meeting began with the singing of the "Star Spangled Banner" and concluded with the song "Columbia the Gem of the Ocean." Patriotic speeches were made and a resolution was adopted that affirmed the loyalty of Manti's citizens and proclaimed, "We stand ready to respond in any manner whatsoever within the limits of our capabilities, to help uphold the institutions of the great Republic and defend its rights."[17] The next week, after war had been declared, a parade made its way down Manti's Main Street to the tabernacle where Major Brigham H. Roberts, chaplain of the governor's staff and an LDS church general authority, gave a speech with the title, "Are You With Us?"[18] The mastheads of local papers indicated their loyalty and commitment with headlines that read, "This paper has enlisted with the government in the cause of America for the period of the war," "There is but one business for Americans today," and "Germany can be defeated, Germany must be defeated, Germany will be defeated."[19]

Support for the war effort focused on six areas—increased pro-

A crowd at the Ephraim Railroad Station awaiting the arrival of Utah Governor Simon Bamberger. (Courtesy of Doris Larsen)

duction, conservation, encouraging young men to enlist in the armed forces, support for those in the service, subscription to liberty loans, and demonstrations of loyalty and patriotism.

Local newspapers admonished young men about their duty to serve and urged them to act quickly to enlist. Part of the motivation to join the Utah National Guard was the understanding that the unit would remain together and those who joined would be able to perform their duty alongside neighbors and friends.[20] The papers also carried regular reports of the numbers who had registered for the draft and the names of those who had joined. Later letters from Sanpete soldiers were regular features in the local papers. Letters came from across the United States—California, Washington, Texas, New Jersey, and New York—as well as France, Germany, Russia, and "somewhere in the Atlantic."

C. Juan Boyden wrote in a letter dated 1 September 1918 to reassure his family that he was receiving enough to eat.

Speaking about the grub will say, especially for mother's benefit, that it would be worth at least $1 in a cafe. For dinner we had regular chicken, mashed potatoes with gravey, potato salad, peas, good bread, coffee, and ice cream and cake. Of course that's Sunday dinner but if you can make a comparison we won't have to worry about the eats.[21]

Evan Peterson wrote to his mother and family on 2 February 1918 from somewhere in France:

> We are in a town of fine people. They try to talk with us, but about all we can do is laugh, and drink wine. They sure have the real stuff, and plenty of it, and all want to treat us. And of course we never turn it down.
>
> Now as to what would be of use to me that I can't get here: First of all, and the most important is cigarettes. We can get tobacco here all right, the French stuff, but it don't appeal to the boys at all. . . . I don't think you have anything over on us for we are having real summer days here, just chilly enough at night for good sleeping.[22]

Clarence Anderson arrived in France during the summer of 1918 and wrote of the reception in England and France in a letter dated 2 July 1918.

> In England the kids would sing the "Star Spangled Banner" and in France they yell "Viva La Amerique" and ask you for a penny at the same time. Patriotic as the deuce and at the same time with a good eye for the more substantial things of life. You can't blame them tho for the poor little cusses have it hard enough I guess.[23]

Mervin Billings also wrote of a good reception in France in a letter dated 5 August 1918, asking his family to " . . . picture me with my feet dangling from a box car door with an American-French book in my hand and a French soldier on either side? It is a slow method of talking but we make each other understand. I have taken quite a fancy to the Frenchmen. They are a jolly good-natured bunch of fellows."[24]

Most soldiers wrote little if anything about combat and conditions at the front. Manly A. Newman hinted at the difficulty in doing so. "I have seen some real war and also the trenches. I can tell what the artillery can do, or what they did do, and the machine guns, and most anything else in the line of war, but there is a great many things I can't tell in a letter that I can tell whan I get home."[25]

Clarence Anderson wrote of the celebration in France that followed the signing of the armistice on 11 November 1918.

> I never saw such a sight in all my life and never expect to see such another. Why the people just went crazy.
>
> The lights were turned on, the City Hall was all outlined in torches and electric lights, cafes opened everywhere and thousands of French and Americans on the streets and in the public square, where our marine band was playing our national, and the French national airs. People shouting "Viva les Americans," clapping you on the back, shaking hands and shooting off fireworks, fire crackers, sky rockets, roman candles and flares that owuld light up the city. Oh that was a sight worth seeing and I never expect to see one which will affect me as that one did. . . .
>
> You have no idea how these people appreciate the Americans. This morning I went over to the cafe for a cup of coffee and the place was filled with Frenchmen. When I came in they all got up and yelled "Viva les Americans," and sang me a song about Berlin and the war being finished. I shook hands with the whole bunch and then had my coffee. These are great times you bet. Old men chasing around like kids again. Everyone happy and noisy. An American is some personage these days, let me tell you.[26]

Approximately 21,000 Utahns served during World War I. Six hundred sixty-five died during the war, including sixteen from Sanpete County. Of those who died, 219 were killed in battle or died from wounds suffered on the battlefield. Captain P. B. Christiansen, Ephraim, was one of three Utah officers who died in battle. In addition, Kimball C. Peterson of Ephraim, Henry M. Zabriskie of Mount Pleasant, and Diamond L. Larsen and William O. Thompson of Sterling died in battle. In addition, nine other Sanpete County men died of disease while in the military. They include: Meldon Byergo, Ephraim; Harold A. Cox, Arthur L. Mower, and Percy D. Tucker, Fairview; Alvin G. Peterson, Gunnison; Dewey H. Ottosen, and Abraham Ruesch, Manti; Alvin P. Carlson Mayfield; John R. Draper, and Nathan Faux, Moroni; Jacob Hafen, Mount Pleasant; and Raymond D. Sorenson, Spring City.[27]

Others were injured or wounded during military service, including Lawrence O. Perkins of Fairview who was gassed and Ardray Wintch who was wounded on 28 September 1918 when a large German shell landed in the midst of his gun crew killing five of his buddies and breaking one of his legs while blowing the flesh off both calves. Wintch was taken to a hospital for medical attention, and shortly after he arrived "A shell fell in their midst and the explosion killed all the doctors and nearly all the men present. For four days the wounded lay in their helpless condition before aid could reach them. Infection set in in Ardray's broken leg and it became necessary to remove two inches of the bone."[28] After six months in a hospital, Wintch was sent to Ft. Douglas, Utah to continue his recovery.

At home citizens were urged to alter their diet as part of the effort to conserve food and other resources vital to the war effort. The *Manti Messenger* admonished readers that the rules were simple: "Less wheat, meat, milk, fats, sugar and fuel. More fruit, vegetables, foods that are not suitable to be sent to camps or firing lands. No limiting the food of growing children. Not eating by any one or more food than is needed. Buying food that is grown close to the home." The article outlined general rules for conserving food issued by Herbert Hoover, United States Food Commissioner. They included: "Buy less, serve smaller portions. Preach the 'Gospel of the Clean Plate!' Don't eat a fourth meal. Don't limit the plain food of growing children. Full garbage pails in America mean empty dinner pails in America and Europe."[29]

The war time measures brought temporary changes to local business practices. Because of the restrictions on quantities of food that could be delivered, the Manti Grocery Company abandoned the practice of allowing customers to obtain goods on credit and went on a "strictly cash basis."[30] The store published a list of nearly forty commodities that were controlled by the U.S. Food Administration. The list included bread, butter, cheese, eggs, fruits, molasses, oatmeal, poultry, raisins, rice, salmon, sardines, and sugar.[31] Millers were ordered to increase the production of flour by making forty-five pounds of flour from a bushel of wheat instead of the usual procedure which produced only forty pounds from a bushel. This meant a darker, coarser flour.[32] Recipes for making rye bread were distributed, and food preservation demonstrations were offered for women that included instruction in the use of pressure cookers.[33] Wheatless and meatless days were instituted and Sanpete County joined with the rest of the nation in observing day light savings time to " . . . release all employees 1 hour earlier and thus leaving them 1 hour more in the afternoon for war gardens, or whatever work, or play they may desire." Residents were urged to plant gardens and produce as much of their own food as possible.[34]

The war effort led to the organization of a Red Cross chapter in the county with branches in each of the communities. By war's end there were over 2,000 members of the Red Cross in Sanpete County ranging from 543 members in Ephraim to 13 members in Fayette.[35] Members attended classes in first aid, but spent most of their time making clothes. Zada Mellor reported:

> Every machine in the Red Cross sewing room is busy every day and we are proud to say that nearly every woman in the city is doing their patriotic duty by going there to sew. Some of the sewers are making pajamas, caps, underware, etc, while others are making knitted articles.
>
> The members of the Junior Red Cross of the public school and high school are also very busy. They are making clothing for the Belgium children. Bandages, washrags, towels and other useful articles are also being made.[36]

Red Cross members knitted mufflers, sweaters, and socks, and assembled packages that were sent to county soldiers. Old clothing and shoes were collected for shipment to war-torn Europe.[37]

The end of World War I brought relief and celebrations—especially as Sanpete's sons returned from the battlefields of France and other assignments. When word of the armistice signed on 11 November 1918 was received, Sanpete residents spent the day in celebration. An article in the *Manti Messenger* records the events in that community.

> The first alarm to notify the citizens Monday morning was the blowing of the engine whistles at the depot, which started at 8:30 o'clock.
>
> The clanging of bells soon joined in the chorus and the city at

once became electrified. The people realized the war was over and with their hearts in their throats they rushed into the streets. They wanted to yell but the tears came instead. Tears of joy and tears of sadness. Joy for what the occasion meant to the world, sadness for the thought of the price the world had paid.

The crowd gathered on Main Street and noise-producers were in great demand. Shotguns were requisitioned but soon became too mild and dynamite was added to the uproar. An effigy of the kaiser was soon constructed and "hung" at the Library corner, where it remained till later in the day when it was burned. . . . All business houses were closed, the brass band was secured and a parade several blocks long, taking in practically everybody on the street, marched up and down the streets, the band playing the people cheering and yelling. . . . The parade wound up at the Library corner again where an impromptu program was held consisting of band music, singing, and talks by Joseph Judd, A. H. Christensen, Dilworth Wooley, Bishop Peterson and P. P. Dyreng.

The school campus was turned into a general play ground and while the huge fire was roaring and crackling in the pit, volley ball, horseshoe and indoor baseball staged outdoors—furnished amusement for all. By the time the married men had played the boys a game of baseball, and the married ladies the Hopless club, the cheffs began slicing off the beef and the crowd surged around the sandwich table from then till dark.

After the feast, bonfires, marching, singing and cheering were the order until 10 o'clock when the crowd began thinning, but a number stayed till a much later hour.

The weather could not have been ordered any better. A warm day of perfect sunshine and not a breath of wind to stir up the dust to interfere with the high jinks for the full fourteen hours.[38]

The first large contingent of Sanpete County veterans arrived at the end of January 1919 and were met at local railroad stations by local bands, family, and friends. In subsequent days more soldiers returned, and programs, dances, free moving picture shows, and dinners celebrated their return.[39] Local veterans resolved to keep the friendships and memories of the experience alive by organizing local posts of the American Legion where "a complete history of each member's service is to be kept for reference."[40]

The Flu Epidemic

In 1918–1919 an international epidemic of Spanish Influenza swept across the United States killing thousands of Americans. The first flu cases in Sanpete county were reported in October 1918. Citizens were urged to wear gauze masks as a precautionary measure. When four cases of influenza were diagnosed in Manti on 12 October 1918, town officials declared a quarantine that closed " . . . churches, Sunday schools, public schools, theatres, ward meetings, picture shows, fraternal meetings, dances, in fact all public gatherings."[41] Conditions worsened, and the first deaths caused by the epidemic were reported later in October. In November stricter measures were instituted that included limiting crowds in and out of doors, restricting funeral services to thirty minutes or less, taking precautions to prevent informal gatherings at the post office, stores, shops, and garages, and asking parents " . . . to see to it that school children do not congregate, neither to study lessons nor to deliver them to the teachers. They should study at home, and avoid others on the street."[42] When twenty-five families were placed under quarantine in Manti, schools were closed for a week in March 1919.[43] Deaths continued until at least April 1919, when the epidemic abated and residents were able to resume attending public gatherings.

Community Organizations

The Ephraim Lions Club was first organized in September 1924 with thirty members. From the first, the Lions Club has been a service organization conducting community improvement projects. For example, the Lions sponsored the Miss Ephraim contest, managed the invitational track meet held each year at Snow College, and sponsored Little League and Pony League tournaments. Manti's Lions Club received its charter 17 April 1935.

Several Sanpete communities have their own Rotary Clubs to promote local business. Manti's Chamber of Commerce handled a variety of different issues such as the impact of the railroad, the establishment of the Manti City Savings Bank, and the promotion of a better culinary water system. Beyond that, in Manti the Arrapine Commercial Club sponsored projects like the Carnegie Library, a National Guard unit for Manti, and a new high school building.

Posts and auxillaries of the American Legion were organized in the aftermath of World War I to promote patriotism, community service, and preserve wartime memories.

Each town had its own women's and special interest organizations. The Spring City Alethia Ladies Literary Club was organized in 1916 to provide a forum each Friday afternoon for the discussion of great books. The Billy Club was a social club for women in the southeastern part of town. The women gathered to practice dancing, listen to music, and enjoy other cultural activities. Besides two amateur dramatic clubs, a Widow's Union, the Home Economics Club, and the M.C.U. Circle, local LDS Relief Societies provided the social and cultural activities many women desired. Ephraim's Aucourant Club was similarly a club formed originally with young women whose husbands had served in World War II. The club's name, Aucourant, is French for "up to date, fully informed, in the current," a name well suited to the ambitions of this group of young women who considered themselves civic servants.

Ephraim also had a number of clubs devoted to specific pursuits. The Junior Literary Club met each month to study particular subjects, while the Culture Lore Club chose for its motto: "Knowledge and Action." Ephraim's Garden Club sponsored projects for beautifying the town's streets. Manti's Ladies' Literary Club and the Bryan Ladies' Club both brought women together eager for self-improvement and enlightenment.

Each Sanpete community has its own Daughters of Utah Pioneers camp. These groups were formed with the ambitious goal of preserving the history of the Mormon pioneers in their areas. Much of the local and informal history of the pioneer era has been preserved by local DUP Camps. In addtion, some DUP units have Relic Halls where artifacts are preserved and displayed.

The Great Depression and New Deal

The Great Depression began with the collapse of the stock market in October 1929. This event was curiously out of step in Sanpete County. In the first place, the agricultural sector of the national economy, which included Sanpete County, had not shared in the otherwise general prosperity of the 1920s, so the onset of a general depression was less noticeable in rural areas.[44] Sanpete County has always been less dependent upon a cash economy than most areas, and the fact that most residents were able to grow most of their own food rendered the Great Depression, for the most part, less of a catastrophe for this area than elsewhere.[45]

It was well into the 1930s, in fact, before Sanpete County began to feel the effects of the Depression. For several years after the stock market collapse, local newspaper editors spoke of the Depression as something external, a quirk in already degenerate Eastern and urban life that would soon pass. In 1930, for example, the editor of the *Manti Messenger* wrote that most of the complaints of unemployment were coming from idlers who would not work even if jobs were available, and that any serious economic dislocations that did exist would quickly disappear if everyone would simply pay their bills. The editors of the *Messenger* and the *Gunnison Valley News* were both Republicans and accepted the Republican explanation of the Depression as merely a passing phase, the seriousness of which had been exaggerated by radical agitators. In 1932 the *Messenger* discredited the recent hunger marchers on Washington as dupes of leftist political groups seeking to embarrass the Hoover administration and warned that "we should be thanking our lucky stars that we have a Herbert Hoover at the head of our government."[46]

The *Gunnison Valley News,* assessing the general economic condition of that community at the beginning of 1931, indicated that while certain effects of the Depression were evident, the economic life of the community seemed fairly normal:

> In our valley, where there was once bounteous harvest, there has been no suffering, and neither has it been necessary to maintain a breadline or solicit funds for the needy and unemployed. Work has been sufficient to maintain those seeking employment for the support of families. During the Yuletide season, and following the custom, church and civic societies provided well-filled baskets for the widows and orphans.[47]

By 1932 the effects of the Depression were evident all over the county. The family of J. Hatten Carpenter provides an excellent case study in the widespread effects of hard times in Manti. On 11 March

1932 Carpenter expressed his outrage at the measures proposed by his son's employer for coping with the Depression:

> The [Farmer's Equity] Directors do not seem satisfied [with the previous year's business] & expect him & Fay to work for abt 6.00 a month & share the losses of the Co. with them. A most unreasonable proposition & no other employee would stand for such.[48]

Later that month Carpenter's daughter Edith was forced to move from Salt Lake City back to Ephraim after schools in Jordan School District, were her husband taught, were closed. In June a son, Edwin, cashed in a bond for less than its mature value, in spite of the fact that it had matured. The company wanted another two years to pay the full value and took over three months to pay even the partial value after Edwin had requested payment. Carpenter thought that Edwin was "fortunate to get it out of them at all." In July, Carpenter found that even his position as recorder in the Manti temple was not safe against the depression. He received a letter that month from the First Presidency informing him of a 10 percent cut in all church employees' salaries. Even his wife's chickens began producing at a reduced rate, and Carpenter noted with irony that she "only got 30 chicks out of 300 eggs a 10% hatch in keeping with other industries of the time."

Those hit earliest and hardest by the Depression depended on wages or other cash exchange for their livelihood—banks, businesses, teachers, and farmers who grew cash crops. Both Mount Pleasant banks, which had invested too heavily in sheep ventures, succumbed early. The Commercial and Savings Bank, for example, expired in July 1931 in spite of $30,000 in personal loans from its directors to try to keep it solvent. The Bank of Fountain Green succumbed to bankruptcy and was purchased by the First National Bank of Nephi. President Roosevelt's 1933 bank holiday rescued the banks of Manti and Gunnison, though the Gunnison bank, which had merged with the Centerfield Bank and the Gunnison City National bank in the 1920s, took an even longer holiday and reopened only after negotiating a limited withdrawal agreement with its depositors.[49]

Tax delinquencies quickly crippled city governments. Manti was relatively fortunate; the *Manti Messenger* reported that in 1934 only 64 percent of levied taxes were paid, but in 1935 the figure went up to 75 percent, and in 1936 up to 82 percent. Moroni found itself in a much poorer condition. Only a little over half of the taxes levied in 1931 were paid, and the *Mount Pleasant Pyramid* predicted a gloomy future for Moroni residents:

> With a deficit reported in the city water department, due to defective pipe, outstanding accounts, large pumping bills, and a curtailment of expenses necessary to carry on city government for the next year, it was decided to cut the lights off the streets, if an agreement with the power company cannot be reached within the next month.[50]

Declining city revenues forced cuts in teachers' salaries. An especially graphic example is that of Halbert S. Greaves. In 1929 Greaves was teaching English in Ephraim for an annual salary of $1,300, and in 1930 he received a raise to $1,350. During 1931–32, he left to earn a master's degree at Northwestern University, but he found that his earning power was even less when he returned, for he taught high school in Carbon County for $1,100. When he resumed his old job at Ephraim in 1933–34, the highest salary he could command, even with his new degree, was $1,200. His father-in-law, who was teaching at Snow College in 1934, had to accept a 50 percent salary cut when the Mormon church, tired of losing money on the school, sold it to the state. The South Sanpete School District discovered in April 1933 that it had only enough money to keep its schools open for eight months, and asked teachers to work the last month for forgiveness of the 1932 delinquent taxes in lieu of salaries.[51]

Finally, the farmers found it hard to stay in business, especially after many years of severe drought that began in 1923. According to the *Manti Messenger*, 1934 was the climax of several bad years for agriculture and brought farmers to desperation:

> The estimate of farmers is that our crops will be about 20 percent of normal. Coming as it does this year as a climax to the past seven years of reversals, this year's drought is practically a knock-out blow. Men are out of employment and there is very little hay to feed the livestock that will be held over.[52]

Confronted with economic disaster, Sanpete County fought back with local and county relief measures. Spring City may have been the first community to start public works projects for unemployment relief. In 1930 the city put unemployed men to work graveling streets and sidewalks. The following year the county began a similar project in cooperation with the state. Unemployed men were put to work improving the Gunnison-Levan road. It was a measure obviously devised in desperation, for the men were paid only for every other day's work at the rate of three dollars per day. Those furnishing teams received five dollars. Manti began work relief projects in 1932. A dance held in January raised money to put men to work on a new pipe line for the culinary water supply, and a similar project in the fall employed others on the Manti Canyon road. In order to ensure that public money thus expended was kept at home to revive the local economy, the county passed an ordinance in 1937 requiring licenses for itinerant pedlars. The Mormon traditions of self-help and cooperative community endeavor were major factors in all of the local relief measures, but the church became directly involved as well through Seventies Quorums' gardening projects that encouraged each household to grow its own food. When Manti's city-appointed garden inspector, W. Lee Hall, finished his evaluation of the program in 1932, he found a total of 458 gardens in the city, all of which he rated as successful; only one city lot lacked a garden.[53]

Prior to the Emergency Relief and Construction Act of 1932, welfare needs had been satisfied on a local level, primarily through service provided by religious groups. From the mid-1930s, federal and state agencies infused financial support in an effort to relieve the growing number of welfare cases in Sanpete. In 1938, 779 (5 percent) of the county's 16,000 residents received welfare assistance. Railroad cars of food and goods were dispensed locally by the Red Cross.

An indicator of the Depression and drought-caused economic decline was the shocking drop in assessed valuation of real estate and taxes paid, together with the increase in delinquent tax payments. In 1932 the 5,129 delinquencies in collections left county government short of the funds it needed to help ameliorate the effects of the Depression. LDS welfare services, which originated in the 1930s, provided some relief, as did several newly founded self-help cooperatives. Sanpete was one of the first counties nationally to take advantage of matching funds from the U.S. Department of Labor and the State of Utah to create such enterprises. A sawmill employing sixty-five part-time workers was operated by the Sanpete Self-Help Cooperative centered in Spring City. Manti and Mount Pleasant had similar organizations, although none of them had a long-lasting economic impact.

The seriousness of the Depression, however, proved to be so great that local relief measures dependent upon restrictive city and county budgets were of only limited effectiveness. When President Roosevelt's New Deal programs made federal funds available for unemployment relief and other economic recovery plans, Sanpete County took advantage of them. Actually, federal assistance to Sanpete County antedated the New Deal, for the Reconstruction Finance Corporation (RFC) of President Hoover made loans to the county as early as 1932. A loan of $40,000 in the fall of that year, for example, was distributed among the towns and used in work-relief programs. The largest share of federal assistance came from New Deal agencies, particularly the Federal Emergency Relief Administration (FERA), and the Civil Works Administration (CWA replaced FERA for a time during the experimentation of the early New Deal years), the Public Works Administration (PWA), and the conservation and reclamation programs funded by the Civilian Conservation Corps (CCC) and the Works Progress Administration (WPA). The FERA projects listed by the *Gunnison Valley News* in 1935 give a good sample of all New Deal accomplishments:

> street and sidewalk improvements in Gunnison, tennis court construction; road and building improvements . . . ; park landscaping at Fountain Green; waterworks construction in Spring City and Logger's Reservoir 10 to 12 miles east of Manti; new school buildings at Manti, Moroni and Mount Pleasant; food preservation, nutrition, and sewing projects for the women of the county.[54]

One of the most popular and successful programs was the Civilian Conservation Corps which provided jobs for unemployed young men, most from eastern cities and the rural South, but local men as well. Their activities on the forest included building and repairing fences, developing springs and other watering places for livestock, fighting fires, aiding technicians in range surveys, gather-

ing data for research workers, repairing roads and buildings, and
working as "jacks-of-all-trades," always under foremen or under trade
and technical supervision.

Besides the work-relief programs directed generally at the unemployment problem, the New Deal offered special programs for various businesses and professions. Businessmen in Gunnison and
Centerfield, for example, eagerly embraced the wage and price
restrictions necessary to qualify for federal assistance under the
National Recovery Administration (NRA) and displayed in their windows the NRA eagle with its "We Do Our Part" slogan. Teachers
received assistance from a federally-funded adult education program,
though the *Mount Pleasant Pyramid* warned at the inception of the
program that not more than half of the thirty applicants could expect
to get jobs. Sanpete farmers were eligible for subsidies under the
Agricultural Adjustment Act (AAA), and the Farm Security
Administration (FSA) made 3 percent loans available late in the
decade under the Bankhead-Jones Farm Tenancy Act.[55]

The cumulative effect of the New Deal was to place Sanpete
County in a position of depending heavily upon federal aid. In fact,
the county's reliance upon such programs was much heavier, at least
in some instances, than the state average. In September 1934 an
investigation of the importance of PWA funds relative to private
employers in providing work relief showed that while Utah at large
had only 1,395 PWA employees as opposed to 1,577 placed in positions with private businesses, the situation was reversed in Sanpete
County, which had only eighteen people placed with private businesses and thirty-one on PWA projects.[56] Between 1933 and 1939,
$4.4 million was spent by the federal government in Sanpete County
in an attempt to preserve "some decent standard of life."[57]

World War II

American entry into World War II brought Sanpete County,
along with the rest of the nation, out of the Depression. In addition
to a revitalized market for agricultural products, the war brought to
Sanpete County the first promise of industrial development not
directly related to agriculture.

Shortly after America's entry into the war, a parachute manufac-

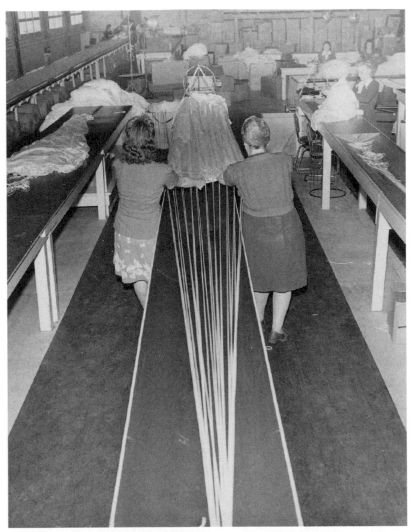

Workers at the Manti Parachute Factory during World War II. (Utah State Historical Society)

turing plant was established at Manti, and for more than two years Sanpete County's labor surplus, coupled with the urgent demand for parachutes, made the plant a successful operation. For a time it seemed that there was more than enough work to go around.

Work began in May 1942 and a Sanpete Parachute Workers Association was organized with Reva Anderson, president. The association negotiated hours and wages with the company. Two shifts were established—one from 6:00 A.M. to 2:30 P.M. and the other from 2:45 P.M. until 11:15 P.M.—for a total of 48 hours a week. Workers were paid straight time for the first 40 hours and time and a half for 8 hours. Wages started at 40 cents an hour but were increased to a minimum of 45 cents in September 1942. Promises were made to increase wages to 50 cents per hour on 1 January 1943 for those who had been on the payroll six months or longer. In addition, Thanksgiving and Christmas bonuses were offered.[58]

A new building was built and a grand opening celebration held on 24 October 1942 with speeches, a barbecue and a dance.[59] In 1943 the plant sent out a request for 350 new workers and asked mayors to provide lists of all women between the ages of eighteen and forty who could work. "Card clubs will be made into parchutes handles," the *Manti Messenger* proclaimed, "and bridge clubs are in a 'blackout' for the duration."[60]

Fired with economic optimism based on wartime conditions, many hoped to convert the parachute plant to peace-time production and continue the wartime gains into the postwar years. Even before the parachute factory finished its last contract in July 1944, the Reliance Manufacturing Company purchased it for the manufacture of military clothing.[61] But the business shrank almost immediately and never recaptured the success of the parachute plant. Carlisle Manufacturing Company bought Reliance out in the 1950s and operated plants in Ephraim and Gunnison for twenty years afterwards. Its successor, Pacific Trail Sportswear, arrived in Manti from Seattle in February 1961 to purchase Carlisle's Manti operations.

World War II touched the lives of every resident of Sanpete County in some way. With a total of 1,803 residents who served in the armed forces between 1 October 1940 and 30 June 1946, Sanpete County ranked eighth of the twenty-nine Utah counties in the number of residents serving in the armed forces. Of the 1,803, 1,106 had been inducted into the service while 697 had joined.[62]

Sanpete residents served in all parts of the world. Local newspapers carried articles about those who gave their lives, those taken as prisoners of war or missing in action, and—as they had done during World War I—printed letters from those in the armed forces. Donald

Dyreng wrote after the battle of Kwajalein in the Marshall Islands, "I've seen the horrors of war, of our own dead and that of the enemy. I was on a burial detail, and we buried better than 200 enemy dead, so you see, war is not pleasant in the long run, nothing was left untouched, and the devastation was awful."[63] Bill Peterson, writing from somewhere in the South Pacific, reported, "It rained last night and the hole I had dug in the ground to sleep in filled up with water. I have had four birthdays in the army: one in the U.S., one in Australia, one in New Guinea, and one where I am now—I hope I never have to spend another birthday like the last one."[64]

Wilbur Braithwaite, who graduated from high school in 1944 and immediately entered the army, was wounded in February 1945 while fighting in Germany. After he returned home to recuperate, he reluctantly described for a newspaper reporter the incident when his company entered a mine field that was electrically controlled.

> Just before dawn when one of the enemy saw the Americans were in the field the switch was turned which set off a terrific explosion. The boy in front of Wilbur was killed. One behind was blinded. Another was hit in the back. Wilbur had both legs broken, some fingers were broken, and he received other wounds. Fortunately no main arteries were broken altho he was bleeding profusely. . . . Because of German shelling of the position medics could not get up at once to remove the dead and wounded. Wilbur lay there for approximately six hours. Then medics got a jeep within two blocks, and when they came and found him alive the first thing they asked was his name. Altho delirious he distinctly remembers spelling the name to them letter by letter with each letter standing out as something big. They carried him to the jeep on a stretcher. Then the jeep took him to an ambulance. The first thing he was given was a blood transfusion. These were continued daily for sometime. At first the doctors were going to amputate one of his fingers. One doctor said he could save it and did, although Wilbur will go for another operation to further straighten it. He can now bend the broken knee and says he will play tennis again.[65]

The death of each serviceman was regretted and the county mourned as some of its best young people gave up their lives in service to their country including four who had been presidents of the Manti High School student body.[66]

Martha Alice Duncan, a young lady from Manti, recalled life at home during the war years.

> The girls at home got together once a week to show off diamonds, sew on trousseaus, tell about sweethearts, have social life, and keep up our spirits, as well as finding new ideas to keep up the spirits of our servicemen. When we couldn't get hose, we painted our legs with makeup so it looked like we had on hose.
>
> Music kept spirits high and enthusiasm going. There was patriotic, sad, fun, dancing, marching, and other types of music that had a beat, a rhythm, and a message to keep up our spirits and give us an outlet for emotions. We were able to get a few big bands to come down for rallies, but they too went to war.
>
> If we had a serviceman from our home, we hung a panel with a star on it in our window. If we had two servicemen, two stars were on the panel, and so on. This way everyone knew who had someone serving in the military from that home. As the boys began to die, the white stars were replaced by a gold one.
>
> When the boys began to get killed or missing in action, the whole town would mourn. It left a vacant spot in our lives and our communities. We sorrowed with the families and tried to encourage them by telling them that the boys died for a good cause. As they were brought home to be buried, it relieved the families, and going to the graves often gave them the strength to accept it. But the families of boys missing in action and bodies that were never brought home to rest in peace had a harder time accepting their loss. They somehow lived with the hoe that they would return after the war.[67]

When the end of war came, there was not the jubilant celebration that accompanied the end of World War I. Perhaps the reason was that the conclusion of the war came in two stages—the first with the defeat of Germany in May 1945 and the second with the surrender of Japan after the dropping of atomic bombs on Hiroshima and Nagasaki in August 1945. The *Manti Messenger* headlines for 11 May 1945 noted "V-E Day Observed Quietly At Manti," and went on to record that "A thoughtful and quiet attitude predominated in the meeting held Tuesday evening. . . . This same spirit had been felt throughout the day—a feeling of rejoicing that at least on one battle front the guns had been silenced, coupled with a determination that there could be no letdown in our efforts until the war in the Pacific had also been won."[68]

ENDNOTES

1. Sanpete Stake Minutes, 5 November 1882; J.C.A. Weibye Journal, 31 July 1891, 14 August 1891; H. J. Hals Autobiography, 110; C. N. Lund Autobiography, 159.

2. *Manti Messenger,* 1 October 1915, 10 November 1922; *Gunnison Valley News,* 26 April 1928, 14 May 1931.

3. *Manti Messenger,* 13 August 1926; *Gunnison Valley News,* 11 April 1929, 22 September 1932.

4. Soren Peter Sorenson, "Pioneer Personal History;" Manti City Council Minutes, 1 and 15 March 1897; *Sanpete Democrat,* 25 July 1900; J. Hatten Carpenter Diary, 19 September 1900, 17 March 1901; *Manti Messenger,* 26 January 1901, 6 April 190; *Sanpete Free Press,* 26 November 1901 4 March 1903; 17 June 1903; Ellis Day Coombs, et al., "History of Fairview," 36–37; *Gunnison Valley News,* 20 March 1930; J. Emil Jensen, "Record of the Chester Ward," Section E, 1.

5. J. Hatten Carpenter Diary, 30 August 1904; *Manti Messenger,* 12 October 1901, 10 September 1903, 28 January 1909, 25 June 1915, 10 September 1927, 25 January 1929; *Mt. Pleasant Pyramid,* 24 September 1926.

6. J. Hatten Carpenter Diary, 9 August 1901; John S. H. Smith, interview with Ferdinand E. Peterson, 24 January 1972, 21–22; *Manti Messenger,* 11 December 1914, 19 February 1915, 16 October 1931; *Mt. Pleasant Pyramid,* 19 November 1915, 29 September 1916.

7. Ellis Day Coombs et al., "History of Fairview," 36–37; J. Hatten Carpenter Diary, 21 November 1903; *Manti Messenger,* 2 April 1915, 2 December 1938; *Mt. Pleasant Pyramid,* 19 July 1912, 2 August 1912, 12 July 1929; *Ephraim Enterprise,* 20 October 1944, 15 December 1950; *Gunnison Valley News,* 29 September 1922.

8. Minute Book, Vol. E., 173.

9. *Sanpete Democrat,* 21 November 1900; Coombs, *"History of Fairview,"* 32; J. Hatten Carpenter Diary, 13 September 1910; *Manti Messenger,* 24 September 1926.

10. *Manti Messenger,* 8 October 1915; *Gunnison Valley News,* 27

September 1934; 20 August 1935, 14 April 1938, 30 June 1938, and 21 August 1941.

11. *Sanpete Free Press,* 23 July 1902. Also J. Hatten Carpenter Diary, 19 Sept. 1902.

12. Azariah Smith journal, 10 Aug. 1890; J. Hatten Carpenter diary, 5 Oct. 1904; 7 and 9 Nov. 1904; *Manti Messenger,* 20 Oct. 1904.

13. Carpenter Diary, 5 and 9 December 1911.

14. Alonzo Morley, "Community Psychology of Moroni" (n.p.: n.p., 1924)

15. Ibid., 1, 11.

16. Vero Aiken, interviewed by Cindy Rice, 11 April 1974, 14.

17. *Manti Messenger,* 6 April 1917

18. Ibid.

19. Ibid., 22 February 1918.

20. Ibid., 25 May 1917.

21. Ibid., 13 September 1918.

22. Ibid., 1 March 1918.

23. Ibid., 9 August 1918.

24. Ibid., 13 September 1918.

25. Ibid., 6 December 1918.

26. Ibid.

27. Noble Warrum, *Utah in the World War* (Salt Lake City: Utah State Council of Defense, 1924), 157–65

28. *Manti Messenger,* 9 May 1919.

29. Ibid., 13 July 1917.

30. Ibid., 19 January 1918.

31. Ibid., 25 January 1918.

32. Ibid.

33. Ibid.,22 February 1918 and 4 March 1918.

34. Ibid., 4 March 1918 and 22 March 1918.

35. Ibid., 7 February 1919.

36. Ibid., 15 March 1918.

37. Ibid., 27 July 1917 and 29 March 1918.

38. Ibid., 15 November 1918.

39. Ibid., 31 January 1919, 26 May 1919, and 3 and 18 July 1919.

40. Ibid., 27 June 1919.

41. Ibid., 18 October 1918.

42. Ibid., 29 November 1918.

43. Ibid., 21 March 1919.

44. As early as 1921 J. Hatten Carpenter saw economic hard times ahead: "Things are very uncertain & we do not know what is coming next." (Diary, 9 Aug. 1921).

45. John S. H. Smith, from interviews with Dr. Reece Anderson, 7 Jan. 1972, 6–7; with Halbert S. Greaves, 13 Jan. 1972, 15–16; and with Christian Jensen, 9 Dec. 1971, Utah State Historical Society.

46. *Manti Messenger*, 25 July 1930 and 22 January 1932; *Gunnison Valley News*, 19 June 1930.

47. *Gunnison Valley News*, 1 Jan. 1931.

48. Carpenter Diary, 11, 24, and 31 March, 28 April, 4 June, and 8 July 1932.

49. Keith Anderson, Gunnison Valley Bank, Gunnison, Utah, 9 December 1981.

50. *Mount Pleasant Pyramid*, 17 July 1931.

51. Halbert S. Greaves, interview with John S. H. Smith, 5–6; *Gunnison Valley News*, 20 April and 25 May 1933.

52. *Manti Messenger*, 29 June 1934.

53. *Mount Pleasant Pyramid*, 5 December 1930; *Manti Messenger*, 29 January 1932, 22 April 1932, 2 September 1932; *Gunnison Valley News*, 5 November 1931, 22 July 1937, John S.H. Smith, "Sanpete County Between the Wars," *Utah Historical Quarterly* 46 Fall 1978: 368.

54. *Manti Messenger*, 4 and 18 November 1932; *Mount Pleasant Pyramid*, 24 November 1933, 8 December 1933, and 15 June 1934; *Gunnison Valley News*, 3 November 1932, 31 January 1935 and 21 February 1935.

55. *Gunnison Valley News*, 10 August 1933 and 3 August 1939; *Mount Pleasant Pyramid*, 24 November 1933.

56. *Gunnison Valley News*, 25 October 1934.

57. Smith, "Sanpete County Between the Wars," 368.

58. *Manti Messenger*, 4 September 1942.

59. Ibid., 16 October 1942.

60. Ibid., 17 September 1943, 21 July 1944.

61. Ibid., 30 July 1944.

62. Allan Kent Powell, *Utah Remembers World War II* (Logan, UT: Utah State University Press, 1991), xii. A total of 71,172 Utahns served in the armed forces during this period. Of those, 41,950 or 58.9 percent were

inducted, and 29,222 or 41.1 percent enlisted. For Sanpete county, the percentages were 61.3 percent inducted and 38.7 percent enlisted.

63. *Manti Messenger,* 24 March 1944.

64. Ibid., 21 July 1944.

65. Ibid., 1 June 1945.

66. Ibid., 6 July 1945.

67. Martha Alice Duncan, in Powell, *Utah Remembers World War II,* 185–86.

68. *Manti Messenger,* 11 May 1945.

CHAPTER 14

FROM HOMESTEADING TO HIGH TECHNOLOGY

Contemporary Sanpete County, 1978–1999

Sanpete County is evolving from an era of isolated farm towns into a diverse contemporary culture.[1] This shift from rural society to cosmopolitan community is a recent phenomenon, beginning about the mid-1970s. Since then, an influx of outsiders has brought diversity to the local population, adding minorities, non-Mormons, artisans and professionals to the bedrock of Mormon farmers and laborers. While Sanpete has continued producing agricultural products these past twenty years, it also has been modernizing and diversifying itself to embrace manufacturing, technology, and telecommunications business.

The most rapid and pronounced changes in Sanpete County have occurred during the last two decades of the twentieth century. For a little over twenty years, Sanpete has been experiencing a long term period of recovery. From all-time historic lows in the early 1970s, the county population and economy began turning around in the mid to late 1970s and have steadily increased to the present.[2]

Today, due to the combination of historic isolation and rapid recent changes, life in Sanpete spans styles from the pioneer period to the computer age. The county reveals its community evolution from historic to modern times through a juxtaposition of the old and new side by side. "Everywhere you look, vivid segments of history coexist with contemporary forms, incongruities struggle and blend, anachronisms abound."[3]

As Highway 89 meanders through Sanpete's historic pioneer towns, aging features offer vivid glimpses into Utah's past. At the same time, a growing number of new homes, businesses, modern facilities and computers lend glimpses of Sanpete's future.

Today the lifestyles of Sanpete residents range from pioneer era homesteading to high technology of the information age. Log cabins with wood stoves and hand-tilled vegetable gardens exist next door to modular homes with satellite dishes and Internet computers. From cabins without electricity to contemporary houses wired for fiber optics cable and high-speed digital data, local lifestyles embrace over 100 years of history.

In Sanpete high technology is emerging mainly in the realm of communications. Since 1990 hundreds of people in the county now use cutting-edge computer technology, but few businesses manufacture it within the county. However, the county has a state-of-the-art telecommunications infrastructure able to support a computer industry and thus hopes to attract more technology companies. A few technological manufacturing businesses have moved to Sanpete and more may follow. Sanpete's rural landscape is an ideal location for people who want to live in a pristine environment and work in environmentally-friendly technical industries.

What has caused the rapid changes during the last two decades? The causes are both external and internal. A primary catalyst has been the influx of outsiders moving in, buying and building property. Another factor has been the county's need for economic development. A third has been the slow infusion of new businesses gradually giving Sanpete an economic second wind.

Meanwhile most newcomers will agree on one thing. What attracts outsiders to Sanpete is its quaint beauty and slow-paced rural lifestyle—a bucolic, backwater escape from urban sprawl in an isolated, safe, old-fashioned environment.

Sanpete County has been isolated and self-sufficient for nearly 150 years, hidden away from Wasatch Front communities behind the Sanpitch range. Today Utah's main corridor, Interstate 15, does not enter Sanpete County. The only inroads are Spanish Fork Canyon (US 89) and Salt Creek Canyon (Utah 132),or the long Levan cutoff (Utah 28), or south from Gunnison (US 89).

This isolation has always fostered independence among the county's people and communities. Even now, there is no center of Sanpete County—-each town is its own world, ruggedly individual and competitive. A historic rivalry among Mount Pleasant, Ephraim and Manti continues today.

The county is roughly divided into north and south aspects, reflected in some county services such as education and health departments. But in reality Sanpete has three distinct regions. The north takes in vast stretches of terrain from Indianola to Spring City, Fountain Green to Chester, with the social center in Mount Pleasant. Mid-county with its rolling hills and farmlands is focused around the sister cities of Ephraim and Manti. And the south county with its hints of reddish rock peaking through steep or curving inclines includes five tiny towns gravitating around the city of Gunnison.

An important new trend in the 1990s is an emerging collaboration among these individualistic towns, linking efforts, resources, and services to create a more unified county. These rural communities are learning that survival and success in the demands of twenty-first century culture will require strategic civic planning, organized management, and cooperation.

Ask residents which aspect of contemporary life in Sanpete is most important and you will get different answers. Some say growth and business, others say jobs and young people, some say preservation and quality of life. Perhaps all of these are equally vital to the county's health and future.

This chapter describes contemporary Sanpete County by considering the crucial aspects of religion, education, politics, economy, heritage, social and cultural life, diversity and future challenges.

Religion

Historically one religion has dominated in Sanpete. However, the past twenty years have seen new faiths and congregations emerge in the area. Meanwhile the dominant Mormon faith has increased its numbers as well. Today there are about sixty-five ecclesiastical congregations in Sanpete County, providing a half dozen options for religious affiliation, including the Church of Jesus Christ of Latter-day Saints (LDS or Mormon), Catholic, Presbyterian, Baptist and Jehovah's Witness.

In spite of the high percentage of Mormons, the county still reflects some national trends. Most worshippers participate in formal church congregations. Yet every town has dropouts from organized religion who either disbelieve entirely or prefer private, personal forms of spiritual observance, often in a context of nature. At the same time, a few lost sheep are finding or returning to some form of worship. Examples of all these categories are evident in the local culture.

Whether Mormon or not, believer or atheist, most residents of Sanpete have an opinion about religion. Opinions are often polarized, pro or con. When it comes to religion, Sanpete residents tend either to participate or react. Few people are apathetic, likely because there is nowhere to hide. Religion is perhaps the strongest presence in the county, providing a backdrop for nearly every aspect of social life.

In spite of the predominance of the LDS faith with its extended culture, and a more general common denominator of Christian orientation, spiritual diversity does exist in Sanpete. Baptists, Catholics, Seventh-day Adventists, and Presbyterians co-exist with atheists and agnostics. Even among Mormons, devotion ranges from the pious to the pragmatic. Today religious practice in Sanpete spans a spectrum from large church congregations to the private, individual spirituality of one.

The Church of Jesus Christ of Latter-day Saints

Today 77 percent of Sanpeters are Mormon, as opposed to 86 percent in 1989, and 90 percent in 1979. This decrease in the percentage of LDS people over two decades is likely due to the influx of

Funk's Lake above Sterling is now known as Palisade Park. (Sanpete County)

non-Mormons into the county. In 1998, out of 23,000 people in the county, 18,500 were numbered on LDS Church records. However, 36 percent of those are inactive—which means that less than 12,000 Mormons (half the county population) now attend church regularly.[4]

During the past twenty years, the total number of Sanpete Mormons has increased, along with the county population, remaining near 90 percent until the late 1980s when county population began to swell. With both populations, growth is concentrated in the last twenty years, with the most dramatic rise in the mid-1990s.

For example in 1979 when the county population was 14,000, there were 12,600 Mormons in twenty-nine wards, grouped into four stakes. Yet these four stakes were over fifty years old: Mount Pleasant, Manti, Moroni, and Gunnison stakes all were formed in the 1920s.

Ten years later in 1989 the county population increased to 16,000, and the LDS population rose to 14,537 members, in forty-one wards and six stakes. The Snow College First Stake and Ephraim Utah Stake were added in March 1985.

By 1998 Sanpete had 23,000 inhabitants and the LDS church reached 18,500 members in fifty-three wards and eight stakes, using twenty-one meetinghouses. A new branch emerged at the Utah State Prison in Gunnison, while Snow College and Mount Pleasant each added a second stake containing nine wards each.

In addition to these congregations, the LDS church operates three seminaries for high school students and a large religious institute at Snow College. Directed by John Van Orman, the Snow Institute has the highest percentage of college students in any LDS institute. These seminaries and institute serve as educational arms of the church, offering classes in scriptural studies, church history and doctrine, and related topics. Currently, 1,450 students attend the seminaries and about 1,600 attend the institute.[5]

The Mormon church in Sanpete also operates a clothing distribution center, several family history centers, libraries, bishop's storehouses, and a cannery—all providing a variety of support services to church members.

Meanwhile the spiritual center of Mormon religious life in Sanpete County is the LDS temple, situated high on the east bench above Manti. In this sacred shrine, Mormons receive the highest ordinances of their faith. One of eleven temples in Utah and nearly one hundred worldwide, the Manti Temple serves Mormons living in Sanpete County and central Utah as well as visitors from other places. In the early 1980s the 100-year old temple underwent extensive restoration and remodeling; a meticulous refurbishing of the exterior and interior included restoration of historic wall murals and wood detailing. After weeks of public tours, the temple was rededicated in June 1985.

Beyond religious observance and instruction, the LDS church also provides an elaborate network of church-related meetings, organizations, duties, and social events. All together, the Sunday meetings, weekday instruction, service callings, scouting, youth programs, group projects, and socials keep Mormons extremely busy. This Mormon preoccupation with church can be interpreted by non-Mormons as aloofness. Newcomers to Sanpete often comment that their Mormon neighbors "ignore" them, are "distant," "unfriendly," or even "hostile." "If you're not Mormon, you don't fit in," said one woman who has lived in Mount Pleasant for five years.

"Even new Mormons have a rough time blending in here," explained another local woman. "These folks don't just open their arms to newcomers." Meanwhile a city employee laughs about the local insularity. "I've lived here for twenty years and I'm *still* considered a newcomer."

Conversely, one LDS transplant who has lived in Sanpete for twenty-three years says she feels like she belongs. "We get along fine at church," says Lee Bennion of Spring City. "Sure, we're different, but we still share the common denominator of faith." For her, Mormonism bridges other cultural gaps.

Still, many Utahns agree that "Mormonism is a little different down state." Urban Mormons tend to exhibit more diversity, while rural Mormons seem more homogenous.

When presented with criticisms, Sanpete Mormons are surprised and perplexed. They don't see themselves as unfriendly at all, but as rural folk willing to lend a hand to anyone in need. They describe themselves simply as "busy," distracted by consuming responsibilities of work, large families, and unending church involvement.

Although individual views are relative, Mormonism clearly delineates people in Sanpete County. In any society one group is usually seen as normative and others are non-normative. In Sanpete being Mormon is normative. Yet most everyone agrees that the real issue is how people deal with that.

Meanwhile, not all Mormons are anxiously engaged in the cause. Whether due to burnout, apathy, or disillusionment, over one third of LDS people stray into inactivity, and a few even cancel their membership. Among LDS people in Sanpete, as elsewhere, one finds categories like orthodox/conservative, liberal/progressive, fundamentalist, inactive, and excommunicated.

Mormon Liberals and Excommunicants

While it is impossible to know how many Sanpete Mormons consider themselves liberal, it's obvious that quite a few fit that description. A variety of liberal and progressive Mormons emerge in

Sanpete community affairs, government, and business; several leaders are liberal or even lapsed Mormons.

Many liberal and inactive Mormons say they generally get along fine with their orthodox counterparts. They may disagree on politics and social values, but they relate on a human value level- perhaps because they still share a common denominator of Mormon background and heritage.

Even among active Mormons, differences arise. One orthodox LDS woman described being snubbed by church members when she became a local activist. "I don't want to alienate people since we all know each other, but I don't want to let others silence me either."

Liberals gravitate to the north end of the county, especially around Mount Pleasant. This may be due to Mount Pleasant's long history as a liberal or non-Mormon town, with its Presbyterian influence and Wasatch Academy. An interesting variety of liberal and inactive Mormons is scattered from Milburn to Ephraim, having one important quality in common—an independent streak allowing self-definition apart from the norm.

Meanwhile, a number of excommunicated Mormons live in Sanpete County. These people either don't conform to LDS codes of conduct and are excommunicated or cease believing and voluntarily remove their name from church rolls. Some have abandoned all religious affiliation, while others have joined new churches.

One excommunicated member in the county, who was expelled for homosexuality, related that while the expulsion itself was an unpleasant experience, being out of the church was enjoyable by comparison. Once out of the church, expectations and judgement from Mormon neighbors became less intense. "The neighbors still give me strange looks once in a while," this heretic noted, "but they're used to me now, so it's no big deal. They work in their yard and I work in mine, and we talk over the fence about the weather."

Meanwhile the majority of excommunicated Mormons in Sanpete are fundamentalists.

Mormon Fundamentalists

At least three segments of Mormon fundamentalists exist in Sanpete. Some who belong to the Manti church; some are remnants of the Johnson community; and the rest are a variety of independents.

Orval Johnson, a son of LeRoy Johnson—prophet and leader of the Short Creek, (Colorado City) Arizona fundamentalist group, moved to Manti from Short Creek during the 1950s. Johnson bought property and at least three houses for his families in Sanpete County where he and his sons were involved in construction work and sheep shearing. When Jim Harmston arrived in Sanpete County, Johnson and his families were directed to move back to Colorado City.

In 1990, Jim Harmston moved from Salt Lake City to Sanpete County believing that Manti is the place where the Lord will gather his people. After arriving, Harmston received "the keys of priesthood apostleship" from a visit of four angels in November 1990.

Harmston and some friends began meeting in his Manti home to study early LDS teachings, such as polygamy and "the true order of prayer." Six to ten families attended these study sessions for the next two years. They expressed concerns with the LDS church and began performing temple rites privately in homes. A council of high priests was formed.

When Mormon church leaders learned of Harmston's private temple ceremonies and unorthodox meetings, participants were summoned by LDS bishops and stake presidents. Mormons who embrace early teachings like plural marriage and "the United Order" are called "fundamentalists" and are seen by the church as "apostates."

Church excommunications of study group members began in late 1992 and cascaded from there. Members were excommunicated in Fairview, Manti, Fountain Green, and Ephraim, nearly every town. One by one the devotees were expelled, about fifty families in all, and excommunications continued through 1993 and 1994.

The emergence of a major, new LDS fundamentalist group from among orthodox Latter-day Saints was a historic, controversial event. News media from all over the county and world began descending on Manti, examining these converts to polygamy and their excommunications from the LDS church.

Undaunted, Harmston and his followers formed the "True and Living Church of Jesus Christ of Saints of the Last Days" in May 1994 with 110 members. They remodeled Bart Malmstrom's barn in

Fairview as an "endowment house" where they performed temple rituals. And they purchased a two-story brick storefront on Main Street
in Manti where church meetings are held. Word began circulating in
1994 that the "TLC" was practicing polygamy.

Trouble came in summer 1995 when a split occurred in the TLC.
The practice of polygamy was rapidly catching on, but a disagree-
ment arose. A power struggle ensued between the church's high
council and its prophet to see who had greater authority. Harmston
won and 150–200 members left the church, resulting in a loss of 40
percent membership.

Meanwhile, many locals worried about potential violence.

Since forming in 1994, new members have continued to join as
well as leave the TLC. From 1995–99, membership has fluctuated
between 250–300 adherents. During that period, the church prose-
lyted by advertising over the Internet, sending out missionaries, and
giving hundreds of high profile media interviews. While a trickle of
people continued to join, a few families became disillusioned and
either left or were excommunicated. In 1999 the TLC withdrew from
all public association believing that God is about to visit destruction
upon the earth's inhabitants. Meanwhile, the church continues to
hold services, operate a private school, and perform rituals and ordinances for members.

The Catholic Church

St. Jude's Catholic Church in Ephraim is the only Catholic congregation in Sanpete County. The church is a recent innovation,
emerging quickly during the past two decades. Prior to 1983, there
was no Catholic church, only St. Jude's Mission, serving Catholics
across central Utah.

From 1977–79 St. Jude's Mission conducted Catholic mass once a
month at Snow College. A handful of students attended along with a
new local contingent of Mexican-Americans who came to Sanpete in
the late 1970s to work at Moroni Feed. Between 1980–83 the influx
of Mexican laborers helped the Catholic mission grow rapidly to
somewhere between 50–100 people. The group began meeting in the
roomier Snow College Student Union building. Catholic Mass was

A farm scene in Spring City. (Utah State Historical Society)

recited in English, with some Spanish elements added to the liturgy; the local clergy could not speak Spanish, but they tried to improvise.

The exuberant Mexican contingent soon outgrew the college space, so in 1983 the mission bought a modest brick house across the street from Snow College, which became St. Jude's Catholic Church. For ten years a congregation of Mexican laborers and college students squeezed into the small residential quarters for Mass on Sundays.

However the biggest move toward establishing a real Catholic church came in 1987–88 when a Spanish-speaking priest arrived. Father Clarence Sandoval began offering a full Spanish mass, in addition to an English mass on Sundays.

Father Sandoval provided vision and stability for the growing congregation. In 1993 Sandoval began work on a spacious, modern chapel attached to the house, completed in 1994. Yet as soon as he finished these tasks, he left Sanpete for a new assignment.

Since 1994 two congregations attend mass in the large, white, airy chapel. One mass is spoken in English, attended by a small group of 50 or so Anglos, mostly students, a few families, and some retirees. The earlier mass is given in Spanish, often with assistance from parishioners, and hundreds flock to participate. The parish priest, Mike Scimbato, also ministers to congregations in hospitals, at the prison, out of town, and performs parish duties out of the county. St. Elizabeth Parish takes in Sanpete County as well as parts of Wayne and Sevier counties.

Meanwhile, the two masses at St. Jude's are administered with the help of a deacon from Richfield, Jim McElfish, and a Mexican server from Moroni, Fernando Montano. Fernando is the first local Mexican-American to recite the mass. A young husband and father, he delivers mass in Spanish and hopes to become a deacon, while also pursuing a degree in social work at Snow College.

Today if you attend Spanish mass at St. Jude's, all 200 plus seats are filled, with people crowded down the aisles, wedged-in at the back, and sometimes spilling out the front doors onto the steps out-side. About 250 families and 100 singles from Moroni, Ephraim, Mount Pleasant, Manti, Gunnison, Fountain Green, and other towns in Sanpete attend. Most members of the congregation work at the Moroni turkey plant. Others come from as far away as Provo and Salt Lake to hear Spanish mass at St. Jude's.

Presbyterian Community Church

The Presbyterian church in Mount Pleasant has been a continu-ous presence in Sanpete County since 1875. For decades it provided the main and only alternative to Mormonism, and continues to be a strong presence in the county.

Prior to 1980, Presbyterians met in Manti at a small church now used by the Veterans of Foreign Wars. According to Pastor David Boge, who arrived in the mid 1980s, church membership has remained about the same since 1980, averaging between thirty and fifty members.

Built about 1921, the First Presbyterian Community Church in Mount Pleasant is a dark brick, gothic-style structure. In the 1970s the church dissociated itself from subsidizing the Wasatch Academy school which it had owned since 1880.

Being the Protestant alternative to Mormonism and Catholicism in Sanpete, the Presbyterian church is "a catch all." With so few choices in Sanpete County, those who fall outside of Mormon, Catholic, and Baptist denominations often are lumped together. "We get some Lutherans, Episcopalians and Methodists since they don't have services in Sanpete," said Minister David Boge. "We even get some lapsed Mormons, some liberal Baptists, and some Catholics who come here for the English service. We try to serve them all."

Though the congregation is small in numbers, averaging about fifty to sixty people on a regular basis, it's extremely diverse in the people and geography represented. In addition to people from a dozen different faiths, the congregation includes students from Wasatch Academy and Snow College who come from all over the world. And the church draws people from across Sanpete County, as well as from Utah County and Salt Lake.

Today the church provides more than an ecumenical community for church goers on Sunday. The Presbyterian church is a strong cultural and social presence in the county, providing fellowship and cultural events for a wide variety of occasions.

A plethora of performances and concerts open to the public are staged in the church's chapel with its ideal acoustics. Visiting choirs and music groups perform religious or spiritual programs on Sundays and holidays.

The chapel is home of the Wasatch Bell Choir which performs for special occasions during the year. Originally the Youth Bell Choir, it includes more LDS members than Presbyterians because so many Mormon students are interested in playing the bells. Pastor Boge says, "It's so meaningful to me to see these kids participate and enjoy being in the choir. They are very faithful about it too, and their parents are supportive."

Boge is proud of the ecumenical participation at his services and says his congregation gets along with Mormons very well. He says, "When people come together for music, the barriers between denominations fall." Many of the choirs who come to perform are mostly LDS students. Wasatch Academy uses the chapel for its student services on Wednesday mornings, when students from a variety of countries and faiths fill the church.

In addition, the church sponsors summer Bible school for grade school and junior high children, drawing participants from a mixture of Presbyterian and other faiths including Mormons.

Baptist Congregations

The Baptist faith is another recent addition. Baptists came to Sanpete County in 1983 when about thirty faithful began meeting in the basement of the Mount Pleasant library. In 1984 they moved to another location, then in 1988 a Baptist mission was established in Mount Pleasant. The congregation remained small, with twenty-five to thirty-five members.

In 1989–90, with help from a group in Texas, the First Southern Baptist church was built on highway 117 between Mount Pleasant and Spring City. Soon after the small congregation of thirty dwindled in numbers when its pastor moved away. Later, in the mid-1990s, Pastor Bill Jones arrived, bringing people back to church, and the group has since thrived.

Today the congregation fluctuates between twenty and thirty-five members who come from the surrounding area, including Ephraim, Mount Pleasant, Moroni, and Fairview. The church is affiliated with the conservative Southern Baptist Convention.

According to Pastor Jones, his congregation is small but friendly. A few Mormons visit his church now and then, along with one or two travelers and tourists who stop in during summer months.

Another Baptist church, but affiliated with the Independent Baptist churches, is the Ephraim Church of the Bible. This church provides the only alternative to Mormon and Catholic services in Ephraim for students at Snow College and local residents.

A third Baptist congregation is the First Baptist Church in Centerfield, which provides a Bible-based service for people in the southern part of Sanpete County.

Jehovah's Witnesses

Sanpete proves the notion that no matter how isolated a place may be, the Jehovah's Witnesses will call to visit. The Witnesses first arrived when a "pioneer minister" came to the area in the 1950s and started witnessing door to door. A small group began congregating about 1960 at a modest meeting hall in Mount Pleasant.

For Jehovah's Witnesses, like Baptists, the Bible is their charter. Yet unlike other denominations, witnessing is a way of life. Witnesses are trained in door-to-door missionary work and public speaking; even their Sunday meeting is a public lecture.

By the mid-1980s local membership reached twenty to twenty-five people who then built their first Kingdom Hall in Mount Pleasant. When their numbers expanded to forty-five in the early 1990s, the group built a new, larger hall. Soon after, the congregation lost a few members who moved away.

Today the Jehovah's Witness congregation numbers thirty-six people who meet at the Kingdom Hall in Mount Pleasant. The presiding overseer is Blake Rosenlof, who was born and raised a Mormon in Mount Pleasant and was converted about 1984. Because the Witnesses are basically a proselyting religion, most local members are converts from the LDS faith.

One such convert is Ted Draper, owner of the Fairview Market, the town's only grocery store. Born and raised a Mormon in Mount Pleasant, he converted from the LDS faith in the 1950s, when Witnesses first arrived in the area. Eventually most of his family joined, including his own children.

How do two religions so focused on winning converts get along? "We don't have the same beliefs, of course, but we get along real well," says Draper. "Mormons are very hospitable when we proselyte, because they too have missionaries out there. They want their own to be treated well, so they try to do likewise." "Some are opposed to us, but a minimal few. There are a lot of fine people here in Sanpete," says Ted. On this point, at least, he and most Mormons would agree.

Education

Just as education was a primary focus of Sanpete social life in the nineteenth century, it continues to be a central concern of the county today. As with all other aspects of life in Sanpete, educational programs have grown and developed most dramatically in the past two decades.

The major features of Sanpete education today are its two public school districts, the state-owned Snow College in Ephraim, and the privately-owned Wasatch Academy in Mount Pleasant. In addition, Sanpete has a few private schools and several continuing education programs.

Sanpete County is divided into the North Sanpete and South Sanpete School districts. Today Sanpete is one of few counties in Utah having more than one school district. These two districts are comparable in curriculum, number of teachers, students, and capacity of classrooms.

A population boom beginning about 1980 created a sudden need for more classrooms and teachers. This need has continued, especially in the mid-1990s as the number of students has increased dramatically.

In 1998 Sanpete's two districts provided public education for more than 5,300 students in grades K-12. All of Sanpete's thirteen schools were built after 1960 in an effort to provide updated facilities on a par with other districts in the state. Together they offer a total capacity for 6,000 students.

North Sanpete School District

The North Sanpete School District has seen a steady increase in students since 1980, moving from 1 percent to 5 percent growth. As of 1998 the district serves 2,550 students from the towns of Indianola, Milburn, Oak Creek, Fairview, Moroni, Wales, Chester, Fountain Green, Mount Pleasant and Spring City. The district office, located on Main Street in Mount Pleasant, operates seven schools valued at $30 million. Six of the seven schools have relocatable units for changing demographics and space needs.

The district's lead school is North Sanpete High, with 781 students housed in a building valued at $11 million. North Sanpete Middle School was built in 1982–83 and currently enrolls 430 seventh and eighth graders.

North Sanpete has five elementary schools educating 1,252 children. The largest and oldest is Mount Pleasant, built in 1962 and expanded in 1995, serving 425 pupils in grades K-6. Fairview elementary school was built in 1980 and enrolls 281 students. Moroni elementary had a serious fire in 1993, so a bond was passed to rebuild the school. Spring City elementary, built in 1986, serves 138 students. A new elementary in Fountain Green was built in 1997 and houses 162 students.[6]

In addition to standard curriculum, the north district is caring and innovative with its students and the community. The district offers free and reduced-price lunches to children who live in poverty or poorer homes. And in 1998 the school board donated land for a senior citizen's center in Mount Pleasant.

In partnership with the community of Mount Pleasant, North Sanpete district built a softball complex with four fields east of the high school. In 1999 a recreation building, concession stand and P.A. system will be added.

Also in 1999 the district launched an alternative program for challenged or troubled students. Known as the "North Sanpete Transitional Learning Center" in Mount Pleasant, this alternative school teaches socially and emotionally challenged middle and high school students. Through the job training offered, the program helps students move more easily into the workforce.

The district uses strategic planning to direct its entire educational efforts five years in advance. The goal is to improve student achievement, enhance teachers' ability, and help teachers improve curriculum. The mission statement of the North Sanpete District is "learning for all through the efforts of all."

On SAT scores in 1998, fifth grade students ranked slightly below the national average, while eighth grade students ranked slightly above and eleventh grade students slightly below.

Sanpete is among the poorest counties in the state; local business, income, and tax base are low and school budgets are slim. At the same time, the state wants to equalize school districts and bring weaker districts up to par with stronger districts. This requires more money for school programs like elementary arts and music. So far the solution lies in grants and tax levies.

South Sanpete School District

The South Sanpete School District enrolls about 2,960 students from the towns of Ephraim, Manti, Sterling, Mayfield, Fayette, Axtell,

Centerfield, and Gunnison. This is an increase of 600 students since 1987 when enrollment was 2,330. Growth averaged about 100 students per year between 1987 and 1993 when it reached 2,900, leveling off after for the next six years with an average of 2,942 students between 1993 and 1999. As in other arenas, recent growth is a major issue here.

The district operates six schools, all constructed after 1960, collectively valued at $27.5 million. Five schools depend on relocatable units to accommodate expanding enrollment. Most recently, the district is finishing a $13 million building program to add facilities at four schools in Gunnison, Ephraim, and Manti.

Manti (South Sanpete) High School enrolled 625 students in grades 9–12 during 1997 in a building erected in 1980 and valued at $7.3 million. Gunnison Valley High School serves 594 students in grades 7–12, housed in a school valued at $7.3 million, built in 1961 with additions in 1991. A brand new competition gym will be completed in 2000.

Ephraim Middle School enrolls 412 students in grades 6–8 using a structure built in 1984 and 1991. A new middle school in Gunnison will begin operating in fall 1999 with a capacity of 500 students. The school will take sixth graders out of Gunnison elementary and seventh and eighth graders out of Gunnison high school.

The district's three elementary schools include Gunnison Valley with 506 children, and Manti elementary and Ephraim elementary with 350 pupils each. A new classroom and library addition was completed at Ephraim elementary in 1999.

The motto of South Sanpete School District is "Learning Today for Tomorrow." The pupil-teacher ratio is twenty students per teacher, just under the statewide ratio of twenty-two students per teacher. Of the faculty, forty-eight have a bachelor's degree, seventy-six have a B.S. with graduate work, and sixty-six have a master's degree or higher. As for teaching experience, nearly a third have one to five years, while one third have six to ten years, and over a third have eleven years or more teaching experience, with half of those having twenty years or more.[7]

In addition to its six schools, the district manages the Sanpete Academy at Snow College, as well as operates an adult day school at the Gunnison Prison that provides high school education and other courses for prisoners who want to earn a diploma.

The striking thing about South and North Sanpete School districts is how much they accomplish in spite of a lack of funding. South Sanpete has the lowest assessed valuation per student in the state. And Utah already spends less money per pupil than any other state in the nation, with a valuation of $187,339 per student. Within Utah, Park City is the richest district ($858,632 valuation) while South Sanpete is the poorest ($88,282 valuation). "This makes us the poorest of the poor—in the nation," laments district business manager Paul Gottfredson. "For the past twenty-five years, South Sanpete has been at the very bottom." North Sanpete isn't far above, being second or third from the bottom ($103,755 valuation).

The possibility of consolidating the two districts was considered in 1988 when the state legislature required a study to evaluate the potential for a merger. The study revealed that it would not be economically feasible to consolidate the two districts, mainly because their debt structures, tax rates, and tax bases were different. Both districts would like to see more equalization in funding for schools throughout the state.

District Partnerships

North and South Sanpete districts have an ongoing partnership to jointly operate educational projects. One such project is an alternative high school known as Sanpete Academy, held on Snow College's west campus. Created in 1994, this academy is an extension of the high schools in both districts. Students who are having difficulty achieving in regular programs have an option to attend this school. The academy offers regular high school credits in the core subjects as well as in vocational training, automotive school, woodworking, and other applied skills. "Our academy is working very well," believes Dennis Mower. "It's keeping kids in school and giving them a useful education."

Another partnership between north and south districts is a pilot program launched in 1997, known as the Extended Year Program.

Sanpete County has two of only five projects in the state using this extended year format. The program creates an optional term during the summer months offering additional classes for students. The program is open to all students, regardless of achievement level. It operates in all schools, grades K-12. So far approximately 1,000 students are enrolling each summer.

These extended summer classes provide both remedial and accelerated learning, enhancing the regular curriculum and giving students the option to augment their education. The program helps to offset poor retention, lets students graduate early, allows opportunity to take languages, offers field trips, and invites experts and volunteers who teach special workshops.

As an outreach to the community, both districts offer adult education programs at the high schools, including satellite EdNet courses from the University of Utah and Utah State University. In 1990 82 percent of Sanpete residents had a high school diploma compared with 74.2 percent in 1980. Through EdNet, juniors, seniors, and adults can take a full year of college courses, while concurrently enrolled in high school classes.

The north district also cooperates with Wasatch Academy on driver education and school busing of students.

Private Schools, Home Schools, and Pre-Schools

Pre-schools in the county include the Krayola Kampus in Moroni and the Treetop Preschool in Mount Pleasant.

As far as the school districts are aware, comparatively few students are home schooled in the county. State law requires that home school students still register with the school district. Between 50 to 100 students are registered with the North Sanpete District as being home schooled.

The True and Living Church Academy is a private school operated by the fundamentalist TLC group in Manti. This religious group privately educates eighty children from grades K-12 in three schools—elementary, middle, and high school. The academy was founded in 1996 and holds classes in two storefront brick buildings on Manti's Main Street, where church meetings are held on Sundays.

TLC leaders emphasize that their academy is not a home school but an accredited private school. Most of the teachers are certified and previously taught in other Utah school districts. A couple of teachers are former college professors. The faculty create their own curriculum which includes basic Utah educational requirements as well as courses in culture, history, and religion.

Wasatch Academy

Founded in 1875 by Presbyterian minister Duncan J. McMillan, Wasatch Academy now occupies more than two city blocks in the heart of Mount Pleasant. The school has a staff of twenty-four talented and dedicated teachers from in and outside Utah, as well as a student body of almost 200 who come from ten states and several foreign countries.

When the Presbyterian church divested itself of Wasatch Academy in 1980, the school became a privately-owned institution managed by its own board of trustees. This ended 100 years of ownership by the church, as well as the dominance of one faith among students and faculty. As a result, since then the Academy has become more diversified in every way, from student body, to religious faith, to teachers, to classes.

With this shift came the retirement of headmaster Roger Hansen in 1981, who had served in that post since 1955 and taught since 1936. The Roger Hansen Endowment was established then in honor of Hansen's long service to the school. Don Chin became headmaster in 1981, later replaced by Joseph Loftin in 1988.

Under the leadership of Loftin between 1988 and 1999, the academy has doubled it student population from 68 to 136 boarding students and tripled its annual fund. During this period the school developed its "prefect system," designed to involve students in the disciplinary program in a positive, reinforcing manner.

The academy has an honors program for high achievers and a Learning Strategies Program to help advance students with learning difficulties into main stream curricula, and a diverse offering of athletic programs.

In 1990–92 Wasatch implemented a computer network and lab which led to the installation of a sophisticated fiber-optic dual platform system. For this innovative system, the school received national recognition in the *Wall Street Journal*.

The year 1993 brought major renovation to the campus and

school buildings, including the soccer field, the F.C. Jensen home, and the new math/science building.

A successful pilot program was launched in 1995, called Interdisciplinary Interim week, which takes students into a field of learning for practical experience. Also in 1995 the headmaster and board of trustees adopted a zero tolerance drug policy for students.

In 1997–98 fiber optic lines were laid to and from buildings, dorms, and faculty house, linking them to a multi-server computer network system. The academy began using the InterActive GradeBook, which enables students, teachers, and parents who may live long distances away to interact via computer in real-time dialogue about grades, assignments, and learning strategies.

Snow College

Founded in 1888, Snow College is a state-owned, two-year junior college with 2,740 students, whose average age is nineteen. The college offers two-year associate degrees and one-year certificates. Two thirds of the students are enrolled in the transfer student program, which prepares them to finish a four-year degree elsewhere; while the other third pursues vocational studies. There are 85 full-time faculty members and about 145 full-time staff, plus part-time faculty and staff.

The college campus has over 120 acres on the east side of Ephraim, including a farm. Twenty-five buildings house five major academic divisions offering sixty-seven areas of study, and include student housing. The college also maintains the largest, most complete library in the county.

Enrollment has grown every year, except 1998, drawing students from across Utah, the United States and several foreign countries. About 85 percent of the students are LDS while the other 15 percent are mostly Catholic, Protestant, Buddhist, or other. Only 6 percent or 150 students are minorities. About 100 are international students, of which 75 percent are Asian, while the rest are Tongan, Latin American, West African and Thai. In the 1980s there were more Middle Eastern students, such as Palestinian, Iranian, Pakistanis, and Indians.

Snow is the most residential college in Utah. More than 90 percent of its students live outside of the county. "This is an advantage," says president Gerald Day, "in that we provide very high-quality academic and vocational programs in a friendly, residential setting."

The college provides educational, cultural, athletic, and economic resources that enrich Ephraim and Sanpete County. Campus growth since 1970 includes the new Science Building, Willardsen Media Center, multipurpose complex, and Activity Center. In 1990 the new west campus site was dedicated as the Technical Education and Economic Development Center where the Trade and Industries and High Technology buildings were erected. Among recently completed or renovated buildings are the Humanities and Arts Building (1993), renovation of the Phillips Library (1995), the $8 million Greenwood Student Center, and restoration/ renovation of the Noyes Building (1998).

Like its peer colleges, Snow has a full compliment of forty student clubs and organizations. These include academic clubs, athletic clubs, Greek, service, and special interest clubs, ethnic clubs, and performing groups. The Snow forensics team placed in the top three teams nationally five years in a row, and took national championships in 1995 and 1998.

Since the mid-1970s, the "Summer Snow" program has highlighted the talents of art and music students. Snow has an honors program and offers developmental courses for older students. Athletic successes have been numerous, including a perfect 11–0 season and National Junior College Championship in football in 1985.

Members of Snow's forensics team took individual "First Place" honors in the 1985 national competition and the 1998 forensics team won the national championship. The science department may be the school's strongest; many graduates go on to become top students at the University of Utah, Utah State, and Brigham Young University. Several Sanpete County doctors began their higher education at Snow. The music, theater and arts programs are "second to none" among junior colleges. There are eleven musical groups on campus, and the school stages four major productions annually.

Today there are five academic divisions: business and technology; humanities; fine arts; natural sciences and mathematics; and social and behavioral science. Courses are offered in sixty-seven major sub-

jects ranging from entomology, microbiology and radiological technology, to building construction and management, to the old Sanpete
stalwarts, agriculture and range science. A variety of academic support services, financial aids, and scholarships makes learning more
accessible than ever before. The school's outreach and community
programs also help students experience the essential relationship
between learning and living in an increasingly challenging world.[8] On
the threshold of the twenty-first century, today's students are aided
by a variety of electronically-delivered courses. A wide selection of
university tele-courses are available to Snow students via the EdNet
system. The college offers a variety of evening classes, from science to
art. Adults take classes at Snow College, both day and evening.
Interestingly, the number of Sanpete residents with a bachelor's
degree rose from 13.7 percent in 1980 to 15.6 percent in 1990.

An innovative program launched in 1997 is the Traditional
Building Skills Institute. Students learn traditional crafts such as
adobe and brick-making, stone masonry, log construction, lime plaster making, and furniture making. Students then practice these crafts
on local projects.

The past two decades have brought other unique courses in pri-
vate programs taught around the county. Some of these include the
Central Utah Gymnastics Academy in Manti, Kosan Youth Ballet in
Gunnison, Showtime Dance in Manti, and Royal West Central
Martial Arts in Ephraim.

In summary, education like other aspects of Sanpete culture is
diverse and growing. From the "poorest of the poor" in public school,
to the privileged few at Wasatch Academy, or from the higher curriculum at Snow College to the vocational training of alternative high
school—Sanpete education is ever improving and vital to the matu-
ration process of its citizens. Education will always be a crucial element of county life.

Politics

Like most counties in Utah, Sanpete's politics are dominated by
Republicans. This has remained true despite infusions of outsiders
which nearly doubled the total number of registered voters—from
6,737 in 1978, to 11,501 in 1998.

However the Republican majority shows signs of decreasing. In 1978 nearly 90 percent of the county's voters registered as Republican, while twelve years later in 1992, still 86 percent were listed as Republicans. But by 1998, the population admitted to being 75 percent Republican and 25 percent other, which includes Democrats, ultra conservatives, libertarians, and independents.

Sanpete County is located squarely within the central-southern region dominated by rural conservative legislators known as "the cowboy caucus." This Utah caucus votes conservatively on nearly all issues and vehemently opposes new designation of Utah public lands as "wilderness."

The "cowboy caucus" has a marked effect in the Utah senate, and clearly controls the Utah House of Representatives, likely due to the fact that the state legislature is mostly Republican and Mormon. Yet the caucus has had even more influence on federal issues than on state legislation. They are actively involved in all battles and government decisions over public lands, wielding political clout in the ongoing conflict between environmentalists and ranchers.

Some call Sanpete "a one-party county" where partisan elections are a foregone conclusion. Each election year when the caucuses from both parties make plans to meet, the Democrats have a sense of humor about their lack of numbers. Since their party doesn't need much room to convene, they advertise "the Democratic party will meet in the phone booth."

State senator Leonard Blackham says, "This has never been a single party county—Democrats get elected too." While it's true that Democrats do get elected in the county, few Democrats have ever been elected to represent Sanpete in the Utah state legislature.

The last and only Democrat in twenty years elected to the Utah legislature from Sanpete county was state representative Ray Neilsen from Fairview. Ironically, he was an unbeatable Democrat, respected and well-loved, serving from 1972–1992. Having a Democrat in that position constituted half of Sanpete's representation, since the county had only one shared state senator and one state representative.

State representation from Sanpete changed with the 1990 census reapportionment. The county was divided into three legislative districts, two of which overlap into neighboring counties north and south with the majority of voters there. Theoretically, this gives Sanpete County three representatives as of the 1992 elections; however, two usually come from adjacent counties. Meanwhile, the state senator slot represents eight counties: Juab, Millard, Beaver, Sanpete, Sevier, Wayne, Garfield, and Piute. This powerful position has been held from 1992 to the present by Leonard Blackham from Moroni. He originally was elected in 1991 as a state representative from Sanpete, but after the district division, Governor Michael Leavitt asked him to take the senate seat.

At the county level, more Democrats are elected and serve in high positions. However, only two Democrats have been elected county commissioner in the past two decades. Keith W. Sorenson served as a Democratic county commissioner for two years from 1979 to 1980, while J. Newton Donaldson of Moroni served as a commissioner from 1979 to 1986. No Democrat has been elected since.

While the county elects more Republicans than Democrats, there is a smattering of the latter category found in several county offices. In 1982, four Democrats took county positions. The 1990 elections saw three Democrats take office. In 1998 Democrats filled three county positions including county clerk Kristine Frischknecht who is serving her third term. Other Democrats elected in 1998 were the county assessor Steven Kjar, and county sheriff, Claude A. Pickett. Previous to Pickett, the last Democratic sheriff was Kennard Anderson from 1976–86.

Still, Republicans dominate in Sanpete politics, filling the majority of county and civic positions. Leonard Blackham suggests, "It wouldn't take much to change that—people will vote primarily for the person, not the party." Others agree, including county commissioner Bruce Blackham, and even Gary Parnell, the Democratic party chairman since 1993.

Clearly, Republicans do have an advantage because most voters are registered Republicans. "If they don't know the candidate, they vote Republican," admits Parnell, "but if they know the candidate, they'll vote for whoever they think is best." However, when the highly qualified and dedicated county Director of Economic Development, Joe Blain, ran for the Utah House of Representatives in 1994, he lost to the Republican incumbent who was from Millard County.

While state and county elections are partisan, many city positions are not. Theoretically, many city positions do not depend on or reflect political parties. Blackham says, "The more local the government is, the less involved is partisanship. At the city level it's pure service."

Several Democrats serve in city positions. For example, the Ephraim City Council currently has three Democrats—Bart Nelson, Lorna Larson and Cliff Burrell. And the previous mayor of Mount Pleasant, Amoir Deuel, was not only a Democrat, but a woman.

Need may be the reason why there are more Democrats at the city level; many city positions are volunteer. Often, the person who gets a job is simply the one most willing or able to spend the time. And, generally speaking, those willing to serve are needed to fill two or three positions in town. For example, Republican Bruce Blackham was Gunnison mayor before becoming a county commissioner. Ephraim Mayor Gary Anderson, another Republican, doubles as the county agent. In Sanpete many layers of community service mingle and overlap.

A high level of volunteerism exists in city services too, providing EMTs, firemen, the ambulance association, as well as chairpersons of organizations, events, and celebrations. Often there are not enough staff and resources to cover public projects and services, so time and materials must be donated. An example is the Moroni Opera House restoration which has received $50,000 worth of donated time and materials from locals. This community spirit of collaboration is a hallmark of Sanpete County towns, echoing all the way back to their origins. Community labor on the Moroni Opera House today mirrors the 1890s when locals cut pine trees and sold them to pay for travelling actors and local businesses provided stage props.

Constituency

The partisan imbalance in government is not as extreme among voters. Today about one-fourth to one-third of Sanpete voters register as Democrats, creating a constituency with a 3 to 1 ratio of Republicans to Democrats. Yet 100% of Sanpete's state legislators are Republican, and two-thirds percent of the county leaders are

Republican. Thus political leadership doesn't reflect the political affiliation of its constituency.

Most Sanpete Democrats live in the central to north end of the
county—the "liberal half" of Sanpete. Ephraim, Spring City, Mount
Pleasant, Fairview, and Milburn all have contingents of liberals and
progressives, as well as environmentalists. A number of attractors
draw liberals to these areas: Snow College, the arts communities,
preservation, progressive projects, Wasatch Academy, liberal enclaves,
bohemian networks of artisans and craftsmen, vacation homes, and a
sporadic nonconformist attitude.

Conversely, the south half of the county is staunchly Republican.
Gunnison Valley is more than 90 percent Republican, with few if any
Democrats or liberals. According to Commissioner Bruce Blackham,
"It's very conservative here; liberals and Democrats would likely feel
out of place."

However, the partisan perspectives in Sanpete may not always be
reflected back to elected officials—if constituents don't give feedback.
Only the squeaky wheel gets heard. Leonard Blackham says, "People
catch me on Sunday at church and ask, 'Are you taking care of me?'
meaning, 'Are you representing me?'"

He acknowledges it's easier to represent Mormon Republicans
like himself because they already have the same philosophy and
understand each other's views, problems, and needs. While his con-
servatism sometimes gets him into hot water and bad press in Salt
Lake, he gets few complaints in Sanpete.

"Oh, maybe twenty to thirty negative calls per year," Blackham
estimates. But as for the liberal element in his constituency? "I'm not
aware of their presence or concerns because they don't communicate
with me. I like to think I'd listen and consider them, incorporate their
views."

Regardless of party, Blackham doesn't hear much from anyone.
Beyond an occasional comment or two, Blackam says, "Local citizens
don't really get involved. They don't have time; that's why they have
representatives—to deal with politics for them. I don't think people
need to feel guilty about letting someone else represent them," reflects
Blackham. "That's the way the system works."

Many voters in Sanpete have little time to spend on politics due to the demands of life in a rural area. "People are too busy trying to make a living," says Blackham. "They have two or three church callings and civic duties like the volunteer fire department. Most people are barely managing to keep up with work, church, their family, and extended families."

Blackham likes to illustrate with a story from the 1980s, when Governor Norman Bangerter came to Sanpete for a one-on-one meeting with the locals. He recalls, "The Governor's assistants kept telling me to prepare plenty of chairs and questions, but I kept telling them not to expect much. So the governor came down for a big meeting. And two people showed up. It was the middle of summer and everyone was outside working."

Political Conflicts

In Sanpete County the most hotly-debated political issues in the past twenty years deal with land use, such as environmental regulations and zoning/development. Interestingly, the first battle tends to be partisan, while the other is not.

Hot environmental issues include designation of wilderness lands, impact statements, environmental compliances, mitigation plans, and control of applications such as fertilizers, chemicals, pesticides, and herbicides. Zoning issues include county and city master plans, annexation of unincorporated lands, subdivisions and development. Zoning can regulate both the development of property and sale of lands. And in Sanpete County, land is everything.

During the past twenty years, environmentalists and ranchers have argued bitterly over whether additional BLM lands in central and southern Utah ought to be declared "wilderness area." These two groups are philosophically at odds, with perceptions miles apart. One wants to protect land from disturbance, the other needs to disturb it. One sees environmental limitation as a given, while the other sees limitation as a sacrifice. Clearly the only solution is a compromise, but what's unclear is how "compromise" will be defined.

The battle tends to fall along party lines: environmentalists are liberal Democrats, and ranchers are conservative Republicans. On one side of the power struggle is the cowboy caucus; on the other side is the Southern Utah Wilderness Alliance.

The Utah wilderness issue seems like a moot point in Sanpete County, where no BLM lands have been declared a wilderness area. In Sanpete all public lands are either BLM lands, national forest, or division of wildlife reserves. The closest wilderness areas are Mt. Nebo in Juab County and the San Rafael Swell in Emery County.

However, the wilderness debate can affect Sanpete ranchers in two ways. First, many Sanpete ranchers have grazing permits for their sheep and cattle in neighboring counties on BLM lands being contested, and thus are affected by the debate. Second, there is a chance more land may be designated as wilderness, outside as well as inside Sanpete County. If this happens, the conflict may become a statewide fight.

When it comes to the grazing lands, Leonard Blackham speaks for many Sanpete ranchers. "Environmentalists aren't pragmatic, they're idealistic because they don't farm the land. We farmers have to deal with the reality. They think they have a greater respect and love for resources, but we're trying to protect living things, too. When you have to scrape to make a living on the land, you don't want to see resources go to waste."

Currently within Sanpete County, one problem is "ghost roads" where avid recreators drive over public forest lands with off road and other recreational vehicles. Due to population growth and new technology in recreational vehicles, ATV's are prevelant in Sanpete, along with motorcycles and four-wheeler cycles. Obviously, this is not part of the forest management plan; recreators are supposed to drive only on designated roads. But it's hard for many free-wheeling four wheelers to resist the temptation of testing out their new equipment on rugged natural terrain or steep inclines. The forest service has responded by putting signs on ghost roads asking people not to drive there, warning to ticket drivers if caught. Tickets have been issued.

Meanwhile there are other environmental protections that directly affect Sanpete, such as increasing agricultural regulations and pesticide controls. Many farmers resist new controls. "If we don't treat sick trees, then the beetles will spread," Leonard Blackham explains. "Our approach is to catch infestation early, control it, minimize its effects. We learn to act fast, then accept what comes. We're realistic because we know we're not in control of nature—it can throw you. We're small, we're just a part of it."

Weed control has been a major concern of farmers in Sanpete during the 1980s and 1990s. In 1985 there were ten to fifteen prominent "noxious weeds" which posed a danger to farm crops and range, such as a serious Musk Thistle problem. The state created a weed law requiring farmers to remove weeds on their own land. After a long and concerted effort coordinated by Commissioner J. Keller Christenson, several noxious weeds in Sanpete have been brought under better control. In fact, Christensen won the 1999 state award for "#1 Weed Control."

Meanwhile as the Food and Drug Administration creates tougher standards for food production, this directly affects poultry and other agricultural industries. "Too much regulation takes the tools away from agriculture to do its job," explains Blackham. "Consumers want the government to guarantee safety but it's just not possible. That's a personal responsibility."

Other environmental issues are difficult to solve. Those concerned about protecting wildlife say Sanpete used to be a mecca for pheasant hunters, but in the last twenty years the pheasant population has gone way down. They point to changing agricultural practices, using pressurized sprinkling systems to water fields. These systems heavily wet down pheasant nests until hens abandon them, leaving the eggs to die.

At the same time, the appearance of red foxes and raccoons is alarming as they infest Sanpete and impact ground-nesting birds. The numbers of foxes and raccoons have climbed tremendously in the past twenty years.

Water use may become a hot issue in coming years, as the local population continues to proliferate. Concern is being voiced already by some locals that stream flows are way down. Sanpete water usage is higher today than in 1980, due more to agricultural uses than to culinary needs. In Sanpete adequate water for agriculture is crucial. Thus some farmers are trying different watering systems to cut back water use.

Another water conflict lies between Sanpete and Carbon County, along the Gooseberry Creek. This creek arises in the Price River drainage system on the Carbon side of the mountains, but within the boundary of Sanpete County. An existing tunnel called "the narrows" could be used to transport Gooseberry Creek water over into Sanpete. This would deliver water for agricultural and municipal uses in northern Sanpete county, where eventually the demand for municipal water will exceed the available supply and water for agriculture is inadequate during late summer.

The "Narrows Project" would build a dam to store Gooseberry Creek water in a reservoir on the east side, and transport it through the tunnel to the west side for use in Sanpete County. Recreation facilities would be developed at the Narrows Reservoir as well as a fishery. Carbon County does not like this plan very much. In this case, an odd coalition of environmentalists and ranchers have joined forces in Carbon County, opposing Sanpete's water project. They both want to stop the building of the Narrows dam and reservoir, scheduled for construction in 1999. Carbon ranchers worry it will take more water away from them, while environmentalists worry it will flood riparian habitats.[9]

Meanwhile other changes in the land are coming rapidly as population grows and new stresses emerge. Waste disposal has become a growing concern since the county had to create a new land fill in 1985. Located south of Mt Pleasant, the new fill was expensive, costing about $150,000, and the county wants to avoid filling it too soon, hoping to make it last as long as possible. Ironically, this has created an economic need to recycle, which has brought about the positive effect of increased recycling in the county. Now city services are collecting yard waste from residents to grind up and deliver for use elsewhere. Aluminum and office paper are also recycled by city services.

Development, Zoning and Subdivision

In the 1990s zoning and subdivision ordinances have become extremely important as land development has escalated. County zoning and subdivision ordinances govern all land outside of city limits, and define the power and duties of county officials to regulate that land use much of which is farmland. Zoning regulates the usage and development of land and buildings.

Prior to zoning and subdivision ordinances, in the 1970s and early 1980s, the county allowed recreation subdivisions with reduced requirements on services. During this time approximately 20,000 acres of recreation subdivisions were recorded. Most development was in the north end, from Spring City to Indianola. The north end has more privately-owned land; there are few recreation subdivisions in the south end where much of the land is state land or national forest.

Then in 1980–82 the county began to strategize planning between towns. At this time towns were realizing they needed to work together; councils saw a need to network on zoning processes, civic services, municipal services, solid waste, and building inspection.

The first Sanpete County Development Code regulating land use was adopted in 1981. It established acreage zones and zoning for the entire county. It stipulated guidelines for development, zoning, and subdivision geared to handle the lesser stresses of Sanpete population and development in the late 1970s and 1980s. The code discouraged some subdivisions and developments. But by 1990 the code was inadequate to meet new growth.

By the early 1990s, the influx of population forced the towns to take an even more pragmatic look at growth and county infrastructure. The towns decided to collaborate on four main areas: solid waste and sanitary landfill; a county building inspection office; economic development; and a county master plan.

After a decade of study, discussion and work by county officials and employees, a new county master plan was developed in 1998. Sanpete was almost the last county in Utah to create a master plan, enticed by state funds to do it. Along with the master plan, new zoning and subdivision ordinances were written and adopted in 1998, designed to manage rapid growth in the county. In spite of the new county zoning ordinances, demands for development have continued increasing since 1990. Urban sprawl in Utah County leaves people willing to commute or do whatever is necessary to find green space, including comply with zoning. Since the mid-1990s, the Skyline Mountain Resort and Aspen Hills developments above Fairview expanded rapidly; by 1998 with approximately 27,000 acres of subdivision recorded as taxed pieces of property. Meanwhile the county's 1998 zoning and subdivision ordinances are far more elaborate and detailed than its basic 1981 code.

The new ordinances regulate mini-subdivisions; they also set up specific steps of obtaining building permits for residential structures. They dictate requirements for individual parcels, building on vacant land, well permits, and other changes to property.

Although county commissioners favor the new zoning, many local citizens do not. The new zoning and subdivision ordinances was adopted over the protests of the Sanpete Citizen's Committee for Responsible Government. This group was formed in 1998 to monitor and dialogue with elected officials to ensure public review and repeal or change repeal of laws and ordinances that undermine citizens' rights.

On the positive side, commissioners assert that the county master plan, the zoning ordinances, and subdivision ordinances together create a conscientious management of organized growth. These documents protect the county from overdevelopment and ensure proper infrastructure, health, and safety. They provide consistent rules, better oversight, protect green space, ensure sensitive development, regulate subdivisions, and protect heritage.

On the negative side, critics say the ordinances are too specific, difficult to understand, too restrictive of personal rights, too detailed and invasive of property, grant county officials too much power and decision, and in some aspects may be illegal. The ordinances give power of oversight and decision-making to the county commission, county planning, building inspector, and often require public hearings. Critics say too many regulations apply; everything on the property is regulated—water, wells, sewage, crops, animals, and number of people on the premises.

In 1998 the Citizen's Committee submitted a referendum petition to put both ordinances on the November 2000 ballot for a general vote. If the vote fails, both ordinances will be scrapped and the county will revert back to the previous development code drafted in 1981. The citizen's goal is to scrap the new zoning and subdivision ordinances and start over again. They also want the public more involved in protecting their rights. Deanna Hart said, "If the citizens don't get involved, the county is going to pass an ordinance they don't like."

Even retired county commissioner J. Keller Christenson has problems with the new zoning and subdivision ordinance. "It's too nitpicky," Christenson argues. "We need orderly growth—in the past we've had some bad examples of no planning. But this has too many restrictions on development. It's over-detailed."

However, Christenson doesn't want to see the new ordinances totally zoning repealed. "It's too much work to do over again; we just need to fix the bad spots, chisel away at the ridiculous ordinances."

While the county zoning battle rages, city zoning and subdivision regulations govern property within city limits and are determined by each city, usually the city councils in each town. Thus city ordinances vary from town to town.

Interestingly, most towns have kept to their original pioneer grids, still intact with few or no suburban features like curved streets and cul de sacs. The exception is Ephraim, which has a number of suburban neighborhoods. Also, in most towns, the original five-acre pioneer block of four lots (1.25 acres each) allows for each lot to be subdivided into quarter lots of 10,000 sq. ft. each. Yet Spring City passed an ordinance in the 1980s disallowing this subdivision and keeping lot size at 1.25 acres. Old timers in the town supported the ordinance, opposing subdivision; most people wanted to keep large lots and have animals on their lots. Most towns still allow farm animals, although Fairview changed that policy in 1981. Meanwhile Ephraim and Gunnison do allow subdivision beyond the 10,000 square foot limit.

Annexation and zoning changes of unincorporated lands can be an uphill battle for some towns, while much easier in others. For example, in Spring City, the town held a public hearing that was 99 percent against annexing property on the south end, even though it was within city limits. They also held a public hearing about trailer park expansion and development, with an overwhelmingly negative response. But in Ephraim, about seventeen acres on the north end were easily rezoned from agricultural to commercial property, then annexed by the city. The process moved quickly to accommodate construction plans of a new Wal-Mart superstore in 1999. A few

Ephraim citizens vigorously fought the annexation and rezoning with little success.

Many people, including county officials, cringe at seeing development of farmlands. They fear losing the green belts around the towns. They don't want to see Sanpete highways become giant strip malls where storage units and businesses line the sides. But the social, environmental, and economic issues are complex. Commissioner Keller Christenson asked the question whose responsibility is it to provide the green space explaining that economic considerations were important because "For farmers, the land IS our retirement."

Ultimately, perhaps neither farming nor business will moderate itself. Both are ever-growing. Agriculture requires the use of open lands and resources to nurture the continual growth of plants, animals, and production. Development usually gets what it wants via money, persistence, and an overload of the procedural apparatus. Preservation may be the only guard against the excesses of both.

County Services

Each town has its own fire department staffed by volunteers from the community. An effort has been made in recent years to upgrade and improve firetrucks and equipment. For example, the Gunnison fire department has a modern, well-equipped department due to its isolation in the southern tip of the county. Since 1989 Gunnison has begun to collaborate and share its fire department services with other towns in the county.

The county also operates 911 emergency service and an Ambulance Association staffed by certified EMTs and volunteers. 911 calls go to dispatchers at the county sheriff's office in Manti and are referred to police and deputies in the locale of the crisis.

The county also has search and rescue teams to locate and assist people in danger who are lost, stranded, trapped, or injured. These crews are also staffed by volunteers, some with training, some without. Teams use special rescue vehicles, such as four wheel drive trucks, snow cats, and rescue 1 trucks that enable teams to extricate the injured from damaged vehicles.

In some cases, these emergency service volunteers overlap and serve on two or three types of emergency teams. While no women serve as firemen, there are a number of female EMTs. There are also a few midwives who deliver babies in the county, including one or two who are also registered nurses and/or EMTs.

Three medical clinics now serve the county. Fountain Green Medical Clinic serves the northwest county. IHC Health Center in Ephraim serves Ephraim area. Manti Medical Clinic serves the Manti area.

Two major improvements in county emergency and medical services are the county's two hospitals, in Gunnison and Mount Pleasant, and its two health clinics in Moroni and Manti. Compared to most rural counties, Sanpete has a strong, modern healthcare system. Serving the south county, the old Gunnison Valley Hospital was replaced by a new one in 1980, then underwent extensive remodeling and upgrading in 1990. The hospital now has eight physicians, one surgeon, a radiologist and a half dozen visiting specialists. It houses twenty-one beds, including acute care facility, physical therapy, women's service, twenty-four-hour emergency room service, radiology, surgical services, and home health agency.

Sanpete Valley Hospital was established in 1949 as an LDS Church-run hospital. The hospital was acquired by Intermountain Health Care and moved into new facilities in 1984. The facility has six physicians, one surgeon, two physician's assistants, one CRNA and a half dozen visiting specialists. The hospital houses twenty beds, including acute, long-term and skilled care, physical therapy, women's services, twenty-four-hour emergency room, radiology services, surgical services, lab services, and specialties like podiatry and optometry.

In the past two decades Sanpete has added and improved a variety of emergency services to aid citizens in crisis. Founded in 1976, the Central Utah Counseling Center offers mental health services and substance abuse treatment. Patients are seen at the clinic in Ephraim which has a staff of therapists, a psychologist, and a psychiatrist.

The Division of Child and Family Services in Manti offers assistance for domestic problems including domestic violence, spouse abuse, and all forms of child abuse. The officed also provides protection, counseling and education for victims of domestic violence.

An important, progressive trend has emerged in Sanpete County services since 1989. At that time the county began coordinating more efforts, resources, and services between individual cities, and consolidating some programs as countywide services. More than just smart planning, this trend has been crucial to city and county well-being by creating a more unified county. While historically the towns had to be independent in order to survive, the opposite is true today. Small rural towns are learning that if they want to succeed in the challenges of twenty-first century society, they must network and share management and funding. This new, growing cooperation between Sanpete town governments and services is a major shift in civic administration, and one that will continue helping the county become stronger and more viable.

"The county services had to join together for common good and common goals," explained Commissioner Eddie Cox. "There is more cooperation between city and county government now. The towns are realizing they can't stand by themselves."

Although the towns were slow to team up, they're getting better at it, working together on a variety of projects. In the past there has been a distinct barrier between north and south county, especially with regard to government and schools. The main rivalry has been over allocation and use of county funds—but now the attitude is, what goes to one, goes to all. Traditionally, competition arose between Mount Pleasant and the Ephraim/Manti area, and again between those towns and Gunnision area. Rivalry with Gunnison is particularly longstanding due to Gunnison's isolation. The southern town is separated from the others by geography and has ties to Sevier County. The upper towns saw Gunnision as a rebel that did not cooperate, while Gunnison felt abandoned, having to fend for itself with no help from the county. Now Gunnison is sharing its services with upper towns. "As we grow, we see how hard it is to be independent," admits former mayor, Bruce Blackham. "The problems of growth have forced us to cooperate."

Competition for county funds was especially intense when it came to schools, with the north district vying with the south district for dollars. But this gap has been closing since 1989, and now the two school districts work closely together on educational projects like alternative high school and extended year classes. Other new collaborations among the cities and county include cooperation among city governments, creation of a county fire district in 1989, county building inspection, county master plans and zoning ordinances in 1997, county sheriff and deputies, creation of county Drug Task Force in 1999, and weed control.

Crime

Until recently, crime statistics have not been readily accessible. But in 1998 the Sanpete County Sheriff's office purchased a new computer system and began updating its computer files to report information on crime and other statistical data. Meanwhile there are some trends evident in Sanpete crime.

Crime has increased dramatically during the 1990s over the 1980s, according to the county sheriff. The county jail population has grown every year since 1990, when it averaged three to four inmates; today the jail averages about twelve inmates. The rise in crime has exceeded the rate of population growth, the crime increase is not simply caused by increased population, but other factors.

Sheriff Claude Pickett attributes the rise in crime to increasing drug and alcohol activity, as well as a lack of discipline and accountability among youth.

Not only has crime increased but its nature has changed. "Now it's a different type of crime we see," explains Pickett. Offenders' motives were different over a decade ago, prior to the drug focus. Then crimes were based more on need—farm and property burglaries, stealing things like batteries, equipment, and gas. Those crimes are still happening, but now the motive is usually the drive to support a drug habit. "Users are stealing high dollar items from high dollar people." There are more cabin and vacation home burglaries— partly because more cabins are being built. There are also a higher number of the typical farm and residential burglaries.

Crime is now more visible than ever before. This is partly due to an increase in police who are catching more law breakers. Sanpete County employs one-third more deputies now than in the 1980s, and there are twice as many city police today. In 1999, Sheriff Pickett assigned an information officer to provide press releases on crimes, making information is more readily available and thus reported more often in the newspapers.

Although crime is on the rise in Sanpete, the county still has a relatively safe rural environment, with far less crime than the urban areas on the Wasatch Front. Still, drugs are a growing concern. Early in 1999 approximately $50–60,000 worth of drugs were passing through Sanpete County every week. 68 Drugs in the county tend to be methamphetamines and pot, along with some cocaine, LSD, and heroin, as well as prescription drug abuse.

Sanpete does, however, have homicides, albeit drastically fewer than in Salt Lake County. Yet even the few homicides have increased in number. There were approximately two homicides in the 1980s, while at least four have occurred in the 1990s. Interestingly, the motives were varied, attributed to family revenge, armed robbery, religious execution, and lovers' quarrels.

The Floods of 1983–84

The Utah flood year of 1983–84 was a pivotal experience for the town of Manti. Spring runoff overwhelmed canyon creeks which caused mudslides and flooding in Manti Canyon. Water came rushing into downtown Manti, flooding streets. Residents used sandbags to reroute water channelling it like a canal and eventually, a river—which cut the town in half. The labor required to protect homes and businesses from flooding created an intense community bonding that radiated out to a countywide effort including the National Guard. The flood united residents, Mormons and non-Mormons, like nothing else. Whenever the water rose and more sandbags were needed, the Manti fire station siren signaled the community that is was time to fill sand bags. Everyone pitched in, working day and night to protect the town. For many, the flood became a time marker in history, with all local events categorized as being either before or after the flood.

What's left of Thistle rests fourteen miles north of Sanpete County , on a short stretch of Highway 89 connecting to Spanish Fork Canyon. The heavy spring runoff of 1983 triggered a freak landslide in Spanish Fork Canyon just north of Thistle, it dammed the Spanish Fork River creating a natural reservoir at the base of Billies

Mountain which soon became known as Thistle Lake. The lake inundated the houses of Thistle as well as the main line Denver and Rio Grande railroad tracks and the Marysvale branch tracks which ran south from Thistle through Sanpete and Sevier counties to Marysvale in Piute County. The lake also covered part of Highway 89 closing an important route into Sanpete County and southeastern Utah for months until a new road was constructed across Billies Mountain.

Economy

For nearly fifty years, Sanpete never seemed to recover from the economic depression of the 1930s. Even after World War II, the economy remained depressed; from then to the 1970s, Sanpete population and economy were in a state of decline. The early 1970s saw all-time lows in the county and concern for its future.

However, in the late 1970s, Sanpete population, economy, and hope finally began taking an upturn when new business emerged in the county. In the twenty-year period since, Sanpete has been experiencing a long, slow, but steady period of economic progress. Some critical factors have influenced this development: new mining and extraction operations, the Moroni Feed Co., new industrial firms, the Gunnison prison, major population growth, and creation of the Office of Economic Development. Originally known as the Office for Economic Concerns, this important county service was established in 1986 to help chart a course for county economic strategy. It evolved into the Sanpete County Economic Development Committee with Eddie Cox, of Central Utah Telephone, serving as chair. In 1989 it became the Sanpete County Office of Economic Development. In 1992 Spring City native Joe Blain returned from Boston and took on the directorship, bringing to the office his professional background as a banker.

Today the Sanpete County Office of Economic Development collects and disseminates economic data, forecasts trends, and proposes solutions to the challenges facing Sanpete. With help from other county offices, the OED has created a number of important publications including the *Sanpete County Action Plan*, the *Sanpete County Overview* of county services, the *Sanpete County Economic Development Survey 1998*, a marketing strategy plan *Sanpete County:*

The Moroni Feed Company Plant. (Utah State Historical Society)

The Way It Was, a 1997 promotional and travel brochure *Utah's Sanpete County: An Adventure Into the Past,* and the useful, up-to-date *Sanpete County 1999 Business Directory.* The Office of Economic Development also collaborates on many projects, publications, and efforts, including tourism, historic preservation, and developing the Sanpete heritage industry.

Agriculture

In Sanpete today, as in the nineteenth century, agriculture remains the county's economic foundation. About 50 to 55 percent of the total earnings in Sanpete County are from agricultural industries and services. However agriculture's prominence and ability to sustain the local population have faded somewhat. Sanpete has gone from a totally farming culture to a mixed-industry culture, where the percentage of farmers has dwindled to 22 percent of the work force.[10] Today most farmers are part time, holding other jobs as well.

Between 1982 and 1996,the number of farms actually decreased from 772 to 696, while the number of acres cultivated increased from 423,918 to 447,463. The amount of irrigated land increased by almost 40 percent, as did the market value of both farm products and livestock and its products. In human terms, today one farmer uses the land previously farmed by three.

The total number of sheep, as well as cattle, hogs and pigs, have all decreased since 1982. Dairy farms have been larger but fewer in number because of consolidation. While the sheep business was successful for decades and although Sanpete is still Utah's largest wool and breeding sheep producer, the sheep industry in Sanpete is now one tenth of what it was at its peak. In the past twelve years the number of sheep declined 30 percent.

The number of turkeys increased from 3 million to 4.5 million between 1982–94. The amount of wheat, corn, and barley produced dropped significantly, but the tons of alfalfa hay increased between 1980 and 1994.

A pattern seems to be that agricultural and livestock production are decreasing in diversity and quantity except for turkey raising, which is rapidly growing and perhaps compensating for the industry.

Today, instead of farm crops, turkey production is the cornerstone of the county's agricultural base. Sanpete is one of the top ten turkey-raising counties in the United States, producing 5 million edible birds per year.

Celebrating its sixtieth year in 1999, the Moroni Feed Co. is a uniquely successful agricultural industry. In a day when most farmers sell their products to middle men and never see the profits, Moroni Feed keeps the profits to itself. Another unique aspect is the company's longevity, having developed and grown continuously over sixty years, with many third-generation growers now participating. Moroni Feed not only provides business for Sanpete, but has kept independent farmers in business.

Moroni Feed is a co-operative, which means that it's owned, controlled, and managed entirely by its producers—from turkey breeders to growers to marketing, all are members of the co-op. "All profits from the turkeys are returned to the turkey growers for the benefit of the farmer, not some stockholder in New York City; it's the only reason we're successful," explains Leonard Blackham, chairman of the board.

The turkeys are all natural, 90 percent free-range birds. The company specializes in the "big tom," a rare breed of bird known as the Orlopp turkey which is larger with less fat and more meat. Moroni is the only large producer of that bird in the country, which is popular with hotels and restaurants on the east coast.

In 1980 Moroni Feed produced 40 million pounds of turkey, making a good profit. The years from 1983–86 were also good years, during which U.S. consumption of turkey was 9 to 16 lbs. per person. Over the next ten years, from 1985–95, the company made average profits and continued to grow. The years 1995–98 have been the least profitable years since 1970, due to an oversupply of birds nationally. However, there is optimism that 1999 will be a good year. "Agriculture is always a struggle, but we're optimistic and expanding," said Blackham.

Currently, Moroni Feed captures only 3 percent of the national market, with about 5 million turkeys or 75 million pounds per year. But plans for a major expansion are underway; with a $350,000 loan from the state's Industrial Assistance Fund, the plant will begin processing year round with a goal of producing 100 million pounds of turkey per year. "To survive in this business, we need to be able to gain economies of scale by producing 11–12 months a year," explained David Bailey, a turkey grower who is president of the company.

With 925 employees and sixty-five turkey producers, Moroni Feed is the largest single independent employer in the county, thus providing an important key to the economy. Each year in February, Moroni Feed celebrates its success by feting a huge turkey dinner for growers, vendors, suppliers, buyers, patrons, and government officials. About 600 people attend.

While Sanpete has diversified and expanded its rural economy, gradually it has been developing new business, manufacturing, and technology. As the county population in 1992–93 finally exceeded the previous zenith reached in 1920, the number and type of businesses have also increased, reflecting industry fluctuations, population growth, consumer changes in lifestyle, and technology of modern times.

New Employers and Businesses

The 1970s brought four new employers who helped bring an end to deep depression. About 1980 the new Gunnison Valley Hospital opened, hiring 120 employees. This was an enormous boost to the Gunnison area because it created a stable business with permanent jobs. The hospital's presence encouraged growth and stability for existing businesses.

At the same time, Sperry Univac located a new plant in Ephraim, employing 400 people to manufacture computers. This high-tech business and its prestige gave the central county an economic boost.

A noticeable shift occurred around 1978, when three new coal mines opened in the mountains east of Sanpete Valley in Carbon and Emery counties providing hundreds of jobs. The Deer Creek and Valley Camp opened in 1975. Utah Fuel opened mining operations in 1980, hiring 400 employees.

The new mining operations gave a huge boost to county employment. Many of these mining jobs were quickly taken by employees from the Moroni Feed Co. turkey plant who were seeking better wages; their mass exodus to the mines left Moroni Feed Company without workers. Unable to find locals willing to work for minimal wages, the feed company imported Mexican laborers who accepted low pay. Thus the mines and the feed company together provided hundreds of new jobs and economic momentum.

New manufacturing enterprises in the 1980s included the production of trailers and coaches in Ephraim. Sportswear makers emerged in Manti. A jewelry maker located in Spring City. A steel fabrication plant began operating in Fairview then moved to Moroni. One attraction to Sanpete is a cheap labor force of locals who are accustomed to a lower income. Meanwhile sand and gravel were being quarried from the Centerfield area by Cox Enterprise; coal and lumber were gathered from Moroni by Moroni Coal and Building Supplies; and azomite, a colloidal silicate clay, was quarried south of Levan by the Azome Utah Mining Company of Sterling.

Another contributor to the economy was a group of experimental natural gas wells, although one well in Joe's Valley was abandoned in 1981. Meanwhile a traditional income-producer, forest products

such as logs and lumber, were still coming from sawmills run by
Lavon D. Nielson Logs of Ephraim, the Ephraim Sawmill Company,
Hansen Lumber Company in Fairview, and Draper Lumber
Company in Mount Pleasant. The sawmill in Fairview was the
county's largest, a Class III facility producing 1–5 million board feet
of lumber per year. It was well equipped with a circular saw head-rig,
sash gang, edger, and planer.

Hermanson's Roller Mills in Gunnison and the Moroni Feed
Company continued to produce feed for poultry. Meat products
came from the Moroni Locker and Processing Company in Fairview,
while Ephraim's Hi-Land Dairy continued to provide milk.

By 1980 there were twenty-three manufacturing businesses
located in the county. An important new development was the creation of major industrial parks. In 1980 there were three: two forty-
acre parks in Ephraim and Gunnison and a 200-acre park in Mount
Pleasant, the largest one between Fillmore and Springville.[11]

Unfortunately an unexpected down shift came in the late 1980s
when Sperry Univac pulled out of Sanpete, laying off 400 employees.
Due to national market changes in the demand for computers, Sperry
couldn't compete with the IBM/PC. Since the departure of Sperry, no
new computer manufacturer has emerged, likely because the Sanpete
population is not large enough to provide high numbers of skilled,
corporate laborers needed for technology companies. Also no other
high-tech computer firm is located nearby to provide local support.

The arrival of a large welding company in 1989–90 helped, but it
could not quite absorb the loss of Sperry-Univac. Fortunately, 1990
brought a vital infusion of new business growth to Sanpete County.

Perhaps the biggest factor in the southern county's economic
recovery and continuing health was the arrival of the Central Utah
Correctional Facility in 1990. Located on the north end of Gunnison,
this prison is a satellite expansion of the overcrowded Utah State
Prison near Salt Lake City. Gunnison's facility is the same class of
prison with the same classes of prisoners: some are maximum security, 80 percent are medium security, and some are minimum security. But there are no death-row inmates.

The prison was an enormous boon to Gunnison area, bringing
new jobs and economic stability to the area, which bolstered

The restored Ephraim Cooperative Mercantile Institution Building. (Allan Kent Powell)

Gunnison's preexisting but sometimes struggling businesses. After the prison began operating, other businesses in the area prospered as the prison fueled the local economy without competing with any existing businesses.

However, the coming of the prison was not without controversy and resistance, which occurred in two waves. First came the general resistance in 1988–89 against the decision to site the prison in Gunnison. Local people feared the idea of housing criminals near their town, but Mayor Bruce Blackham worked with the community to educate people about the prison facility, explain its impact and advantages, and help foster acceptance.

A second battle came after the prison was built. Intense local opposition arose when plans were publicized for building a mini-mum security modular dorm outside of the prison fences and perimeter. The dorm would accommodate new prisoners who could work on crews outside the prison grounds. Immediately, locals balked at having 200 inmates working outside prison fencing, fearing some might escape into the community. Although the dorm could have been built inside the fencing, early publicity set the townspeople against it, so all plans were dropped. Prison officials did not want to upset the community.

Currently the prison has completed one phase of its three- phase design. Construction has begun on phase two which will bring 192 more beds and a 288-bed dorm. Phase three will begin after phase two is finished. All three phases will be constructed inside the security fencing.[12]

In addition to local jobs created by the prison, inmates themselves contribute to the economy by creating useable products and donating wages. The inmate labor force creates cost-effective quality goods and services. They process milk, meat, and other agricultural products, make license plates, recycle used printer cartridges, provide data entry and micrographic records management, refurbish computers for schools, provide printing services, asbestos handling, community work crews, sign shops, furniture refurbishing, sewing, marketing, office work, and light assembly.[13] Utah Correctional Industries also provides another invaluable byproduct: redemption. Rehabilitation of non-violent offenders is a growing national trend in prison reform focusing on encouragement, education, vocational training, employment, and alternative sentencing such as drug court, rehabilitation programs, counseling, halfway houses, intervention programs, therapy, and substance abuse treatment.[14]

Another boon to the economy in Gunnison during 1990 was the renovation and upgrading of the Gunnison Valley Hospital, which not only brought medical services up to par, but created new jobs for area residents. Like the prison, the newly revamped hospital has been a stabilizing force in the southern county economy.

Recent Efforts

Meanwhile, also beginning in 1990, came the arrival of three new high-tech, manufacturing companies. Interestingly, these three businesses abandoned the Wasatch Front to relocate in Sanpete due to a need for greater acreage and more affordable land than what was available in the rapidly urbanizing Provo-Orem area.

The first company was Applied Composite Technologies, arriving in Fayette during the early 1990s. The company manufactures high-tech artificial limbs made of graphite. These graphite prostheses are in high demand due to performance advances created by the high-end graphite. In fact, 96 percent of amputees who compete in the olympics use this product.

Second came Wasatch Technologies in 1996 to Gunnison. They produce fiberglass columns used in architecture, which are made from the same pneumatic tubes used in amusement rides, light poles, and fiberglass. Latest in 1997 came the Auto Meter to Ephraim, which makes testing equipment and gauges for high-performance vehicles.

These three new companies boosted and diversified the Sanpete economy by hiring 400–600 employees. Together, they provide a more stable economic base, because if one company should fold, it won't set the county employment back too far. Still, it took Sanpete until 1996 to bounce back fully from the economic slump created by Sperry-Univac's shut down.

Conversely, since 1996 Sanpete economic growth has slowed a bit. Some mining has been reduced, laying off workers; for example Utah Fuel is down from 400 original employees to 100 in 1999. Also Wasatch Front businesses are staying put, waiting to see the effects of business growth and the massive I-15 reconstruction, due to be completed in 2002. Those business owners who might tend to relocate in rural areas are waiting to see how urban construction will change the Salt Lake area and how their commerce will fare.

About 1992 the Sanpete Office of Economic Development began publishing its annual "Sanpete County Action Plan." The plan analyzes the status of economic factors and indicators, then outlines a new economic strategy. The following strategies were selected: 1. Develop a positive in-county attitude that will enhance our out-of-county image. 2. Establish a county business retention and expansion program. 3. Protect agricultural and value-added opportunities. 4. Attract new firms to Sanpete County. 5. Increase the length of stay and amount of money spent by tourists in the county. 6. Develop a methodology for protecting Sanpete County's historic resources. 7. Review and update this action plan.[15]

Meanwhile the Sanpete Office of Economic Development hopes to attract new companies, businesses, and manufacturers from out of state who will create sustainable wages, stable long-term jobs, and products that can be sold outside the county. To this end, the county offers incentives such as "enterprise zones," allowing companies to get state tax credits and industrial park space with adjacent land available for use.

A popular economic strategy in the late 1990s has been for small towns to court small, "clean" businesses and industrial firms that might otherwise locate in larger cities. Gunnison, for example, succeeded in attracting Satterwhite Log Homes of Longview, Texas, a firm that will employ two dozen workers when it moves its manufacturing plant from Gypsum, Colorado. Satterwhite will pay its employees an average of $31,800 a year (before benefits), more than twice the county average of $14,000.

Gunnison city administrator Ray Limb explained that "We only want employers that will bring twenty to forty good-paying jobs at a time. We don't have the population base for larger employers, and we don't want to be forced to grow to accommodate one. If some company comes in with, say. 200 jobs, as we build the city accordingly, if they leave we are destitute. If we have several small businesses and one leaves, we won't be as hurt."

Telecommunications and the Internet

One aspect of high technology that is emerging in Sanpete County is the computer Internet. Beginning in 1995, the arrival of Internet service in Sanpete has rapidly advanced communications technology, closing the distance to the outside world. Internet providers bring increased opportunities to residents, as well as increased business to county phone companies.

Of thirteen independent phone companies in Utah, five are in Sanpete. It's unusual to have so many phone companies in one county, but when U.S. West would not take its service to the little towns, enterprising individuals started their own companies. The oldest is Central Utah Telephone, formed in 1961 from the Fairview Telephone Company established in 1903. It includes Skyline Telecom and serves the north half of Sanpete, as well as Spanish Fork Canyon. The giant U.S. West only serves Ephraim and Mount Pleasant, while Manti Phone Co. serves just Manti and Sterling. Gunnison Valley area is served by Gunnison Telephone. Additionally, there are three cellular services in the county: Cellular One, Air Free Wireless, and Comnet Service.

As early as 1981, telecommunications companies and equipment were making a new mark on Sanpete County. After the first telephone company in Sanpete began billing on computer in 1979, it paved the way for three phases of computerized telecommunications.

First, in 1981 came digital switching. Gunnison was the second town in Utah to have it, then in 1986 Fairview followed. In 1993 U.S. West brought it to Mount Pleasant and Ephraim. Digital switching ushered in the information age by allowing phone lines to handle more information and features, as well as making all lines more reliable.

Second came the installment of fiber optics in 1994. Third was the arrival of digital switching Internet service in 1995–96. These three innovations allowed Internet services to begin operating in Sanpete, which brought six Internet providers. First came Burgoyne and Cisna. Then came Central Utah Communications, the only high-speed Internet in the county, currently serving 600 customers in the north end. Then came Manti with 150 customers, and Gunnison with 150. Last came U.S. West.

Today in 1999 there are at least 1,000 Internet customers in Sanpete County with access to the latest computer technology for home, pleasure, work, business, and communication. People are beginning to operate home businesses over the Internet. With the computer, Internet, and communications technology available in Sanpete today, people are able to work where they want to live, in a beautiful natural environment. All the same telecommunications services available in urban areas are available in Sanpete via telephones and computer services.

In addition, many existing Sanpete businesses are beginning to use computers and the Internet for transactions, marketing, and sales, in- and outside- the county. With the computer, Internet, and Web sites, as well as voice mail, a small business can look like a big business; a home or cottage industry can be international.

The possibilities for electronic commerce may eventually compensate for the lack of traditional business in Sanpete, especially if

Sanpete county maximizes its potential for selling heritage products over the Internet.

In 1997, the Sanpete Office of Economic Development reported a "robust" economic boom and a 6 percent increase in new jobs, in spite of a high jobless rate.[16] Meanwhile, the office has teamed-up with the Utah state business recruiting team to help attract out-of-state businesses to Sanpete.

An impressive selection of small, privately-owned heritage businesses has emerged since the late 1970s. Only a few are mentioned here.

Horseshoe Mountain Pottery, owned by Joe Bennion, was established in 1977. Bennion and his wife Lee, an artist, came from the Wasatch Front to Spring City where they bought a house and set up a pottery shop. Visitors can watch Bennion hand throw clay on the wheel or buy from the assortment of handmade stoneware fired in Joe's kilns.

The Ephraim Co-Op and Central Utah Arts Center occupy two prominent historic buildings on Main Street. Both were restored in the early 1990s to preserve local heritage, promote art, and sell crafts. The co-op sells a wide variety of local craft items made by residents. The arts center main floor is a gallery for the work of Sanpete artists, while art classes are held in the basement.

Peel Furniture Works was founded in 1991 by Dale Peel of Mount Pleasant. A carpenter and wood worker, Peel creates exact replicas of early Utah pioneer furniture. Using antiques and photographs for models, he uses native lumber to create the same designs and colors used by Mormon pioneers. He sells furniture from his shop in Mount Pleasant, as well as other locations around the state.

Paul Hart Violins is a violin making school on Main Street in Mount Pleasant established in 1999. The shop produces fifteen to thirty instruments per year, including violins, violas, cellos, bases—all made in the traditional Italian method. Students enroll in this program from all over the United States, paying $400 per month for a three-year program. This school is only one of four in the country, with the others in Salt Lake, Chicago, and Boston.

Native Wines, also in Mount Pleasant, is another heritage industry opened in 1999. This intimate, organic winery is owned and operated by Bob Sorenson and Winnie Wood in the town's historic laundry building on 5th West. Using local fruit, juices of apples, pears, and strawberries are fermented in huge oak barrels and available for tasting and for sale. Of the four wine labels in Utah state, Native Wines is the only winery to ferment and bottle its own wine, use local fruits, and exclude grape wines.

Employment

Today in Sanpete County, government has replaced agriculture as the county's biggest employer, although the largest private employer is still agricultural business.Generally, the county's economic health has been hampered by high unemployment rates and low per capita income, Sanpete has ranked fairly high in poverty statistics.

In 1986 Sanpete had the highest percentage of unemployed work forces, 14.9 percent, of any county in the state. In the ensuing years, the percentage of workers with jobs increased, with only 9.1 percent unemployed in 1990. The rate rose to 10.1 percent in 1991, however, still placing the county among the state's leaders in unemployment. By September 1996, the rate had dropped to 6.0 percent still twice the state average.[17]

According to census figures, the public service agencies—including government, schools, Snow College, the prison, and civic workers—employ the highest total number of workers in the county. Agricultural workers still account for the highest number of employees hired by private business in the county. The next largest employers are manufacturing and the wholesale and retail trades.

In 1990, of the county's 6,149 workers, 2,920 worked in agricultural pursuits. Another 1,660 worked in government positions. Of the remaining work categories, 864 were employed in manufacturing, 824 in the trades, 423 in service professions, 141 in construction, 125 in transportation, communications, or utilities, and 98 in finance, insurance, or real estate.

In 1995, 40.57 percent of the county's non-agricultural workers were employed by governments, 20.08 percent in trades, 15.23 percent in manufacturing and 14.23 percent in services. No other category accounted for more than 4 percent of the total.

In all major categories, local wage rates lagged considerably behind the state rates. Between 1991 and 1993, however, county income increased by an impressive 44 percent, suggesting that overall economic health was improving.

A review of statistics over the past two decades may not reveal much about *personal* progress. For example at Moroni Feed, 60 percent of employees are Hispanic laborers most of whom were not U.S. citizens in 1980; yet over the years many have stayed in the area permanently and given rise to second-generation workers. In the mid-1990s, more were becoming United States citizens and spreading out into county, taking other jobs in the agricultural community and service areas. Today many own homes in Moroni and Ephraim.

To help rural communities overcome the disadvantages of depending on single economies, Governor Michael Leavitt instituted a rural resettlement program in 1995. The state's Department of Community and Economic Development also provided financial assistance to help rural counties like Sanpete attract out-of-state and urban in-state companies to establish branches or expand into rural areas.

Population Growth

In some ways Utah County has been the bane of Sanpete's existence, both harming and helping its growth. Sanpete's close proximity to the Provo area caused main streets to suffer in the 1960s and 1970s when automobiles, new roads, and shopping malls lured people out. People began moving out as well because, according to many, "there was nothing here for them." As a result, county population reached an all-time low of 10,976 residents in 1970.

This process finally leveled out in 1978 when, for the first time since the pioneer period, newcomers began entering the county and former residents returned. In 1980 there were over 14,000 people living in the county.

The growth in population brought signs of hope for the economy. Sanpete's unique offerings began attracting more visitors, students, and residents. People were moving to Sanpete to attend Snow College or Wasatch Academy, or to work in the turkey industry or labor in the mines. Others were discovering Sanpete's secluded, pastoral settings offering inexpensive property, historic buildings, farm land, a nature retreat, or privacy. As a result, people were buying houses and prices took off in the late 1980s.

Newcomers moved to Sanpete for a variety of reasons. While some were laborers who came for jobs, others were retired Utahns returning from Salt Lake or California, looking to retire in pleasant surroundings. Others were skilled workers, artisans, or professionals who wanted to get away from urban areas. Some incomers were originally from Sanpete, who wanted to reinvest themselves back home where they had roots. Some were younger couples looking for a place where they could own property or homestead.

The most dramatic population growth in Sanpete came after 1990. Since 1990–91 the county population has grown 3–4 percent every year for eight years running. From 1990, when it hit 16,300, it began to climb dramatically to 17,500 in 1992, 18,800 in 1994, 19,999 in 1996, and 23,000 in 1998.

As a result of record population growth, Sanpete is seeing a boom of new homeowners and construction, along with some historic preservation. Tourism, vacation homes, recreation, home businesses, and heritage industries are growing. While population and development have taken off, business still lags, hoping to catch up.

Between 1990 and 1995, the value of the county's residential land and buildings nearly doubled, while the value of its commercial, industrial, and agricultural land and buildings remained the same, suggesting that the county population is growing at a much faster rate than its various businesses.

Where is the population growth going? Newcomers are appearing all over the county in every town, but most are locating in the north county, which is closer to Utah County. Between 1990–94 the towns with the highest percentage of population growth were Gunnison, 55 percent; Fountain Green, 29 percent; Fairview, 26 percent; Sterling, 23 percent; Spring City, 17 percent; and Mount Pleasant and Manti, 11 percent.

New residences have been built in every town since 1992 with Ephraim, Manti, and Mount Pleasant accounting for the most.

The Skyline Mountain Resorts are an enormous vacation home development implemented in the 1990s. They follow the lower half of the Skyline Drive—a road along the ridge of the mountains dividing Sanpete from Emery County. This major resort development is planned in two phases. Phase 1 created 1,057 lots of one acre each, designed to nestle in the hills and canyons flanked by acres of green space. Lots of one-half acre are available on the golf course. Lots range from a lower elevation near the resort entrance above Fairview, to much higher elevations in the hills where residents must use a four-wheel drive or snowmobile to travel during winter. So far, 770 lots are sold and 200 homes have been built.

The second phase called Skyline Heights will create 600 lots ranging in size from 1.5 to 6 acres. This development will be wedged in between the two main prongs of the phase one resort. The Skyline resorts total 1,657 home lots accompanied by a golf course, club house, pool, and stables for horses.

These developments are all designed to be "low density" vacation homes and getaway cabins that will preserve open space. Yet taken together with another resort, Aspen Hills just to the south, these three developments encompass 6,000 acres of land and constitute a major influx of new population, equivalent in size to another town.

Other vacation home developments include Pine Creek and Cedar West near Mount Pleasant, and Hideaway Valley and Indian Ridge near Indianola.

Progress vs. Preservation

Some residents do not like the idea of economic development because they fear urbanization, suburbanization, and commercial encroachments into the rural historic nature of Sanpete's unique villages. "I'm against economic development because it will change things," said one local man. "We didn't move here to find new businesses—we moved down here because we were tired of seeing vinyl covered houses."On the other hand, "Many locals don't care much about historic preservation—they don't see the cultural charm of this district," said one city official. "It is really the outsiders who recognize the value of preservation."

Prior to 1980 most Sanpete stores were modest, local enterprises. Grocers were small, and retail outlets were dime stores. Restaurants were small cafes like City Cafe in Ephraim and Casey's Cafe in Mount

Pleasant, or hamburger stands like Roger's Dairy Freeze. Unfortunately, many small businesses that provided local services and products have vanished.

Since 1980 several new chain store businesses have popped up in every town and many seem to be taking hold. Small branches of Utah banks have arrived including: Zion's Bank in Manti and Gunnison; Far West Bank in Fairview and Mount Pleasant; and First Security Bank in Mount Pleasant and Moroni. Locally owned financial institutions have also thrived including Gunnison Bank, the Bank of Ephraim, and the Moroni Feed Credit Union.

Where before only small, older motels could be found, now modern motels are available along with nearly a dozen bed-and-breakfast establishments—many located in historic homes—throughout the county. Revenues from hotels and lodging more than doubled between 1990 and 1996.

Restaurants have always been few and far between in Sanpete, but a demand for more options in food brought new establishments to Gunnison, Ephraim, Mount Pleasant, and Fairview.

Two major supermarkets came to Sanpete in the late 1980s when Terrel's opened in Mount Pleasant and Thriftway opened in Gunnison. Recent fast food additions are McDonald's, Hogi Yogi, and Subway Sandwiches all in Ephraim. Gas and food marts have proliferated since the mid-1980s and do a steady business.

A viable way to generate money in the county is through retail shopping and to this end, the Office of Economic Development produced the first complete and professional Sanpete County Business Directory in 1999. Director Joe Blain stated the goal of the directory was to "support Sanpete County businesses and consumers" hoping they would "use this directory to help locate area businesses." He plans to continue publishing the directory annually.

Ultimately, the attraction of new business to Sanpete, especially retail business, is a complex issue. New business is needed, but new retail stores are a dilemma. New retailers offer more choices to keep residents shopping locally, but they take business away from existing stores. However, many residents leave the county to shop, taking retail tax dollars elsewhere. There is a desperate need for business capable of producing high volume revenues; but if huge retail stores come in, they can kill smaller local stores. Small businesses do not generate enough revenue to fuel county jobs and health, so if larger companies don't come, stagnation will result. And if business does not come to Sanpete but to nearby towns outside the county, such as Nephi, the result is even worse, because it both hurts Sanpete stores and pulls money out of the county. This delimma is evident in the recent controversy over building a Wal-Mart store in Ephraim.

Wal-Mart

When Wal-Mart announced plans to build a 109,000 sq. ft. superstore in Ephraim, the national drama of the huge corporation vs. independent business arrived in Sanpete.

Response was immediate. In summer 1998, an activist group formed to fight the new development. Citizen's for Responsible Communities quickly informed residents about the perceived negataive impacts of Wal-Mart.

Why did Wal-Mart select Ephraim? "We were impressed with the level of local support," said company spokesperson, Daphne Davis.

The company initially sought property on the south end of Ephraim, near a proposed multi-plex movie theater; unable to secure a sale, Wal-Mart bid on farmland at the town's north end, adjacent to the historic cemetery. "That was the best location," explained Davis, "with enough acreage."

No retail store larger than Terrel's groceries had ever come to Sanpete County, and even that was recent. Wal-Mart represented the turning of a corner, leaving Sanpete's historic rural identity behind, for the look of urban suburbs across America.

"It's not just a development," protested Sherron Andreason, Ephraim resident and member of the Citizens for Responsible Communities. "We're losing a way of life—and we don't even realize it. We're inviting urban sprawl to a wonderful haven."

Yet city officials said the majority of residents favored Wal-Mart. "Between 85 and 90 percent of the city want it. They support having increased choices for shopping," said Ephraim Mayor Gary Anderson. Wal-Mart spokeswoman, Daphne Davis concurred. "The numbers were in favor of Wal-Mart."

The citizen's committee made several complaints against the proposed development. The store would be disruptive to the pastoral north end of town next to the cemetery. Located in a pasture where sheep graze, the colossal red, white and blue cinderblock building with blaring 24 hour lighting "would be like putting a bulldozer in a flower garden."

Equally important was the concern that Wal-Mart will compete with existing local stores, driving them out of business. The potential negative effects on local business prompted three studies in 1998, evaluating impact of the coming superstore. One study was a Brigham Young University survey of the county finding that 70 percent of the residents favored Wal-Mart.

Another was the "Sanpete County Economic Development Survey" revealing that a majority of Sanpete residents prefer to shop outside of the county. Product selection, price and quality are the most important determinants. Wal-Mart would significantly affect out of county shopping but only divert some of the shopping away from local merchants.

The third study, "Potential Impacts of the Proposed Wal-Mart Development" by Wikstrom Economic & Planning Consultants concluded that the store would capture some business leaving the county, but would also draw customers away from local merchants.[18]

With ground-breaking scheduled for 1 July 1999, Wal-Mart symbolizes the changes and challenge facing contemporary Sanpete County in the future.

Sanpete's Heritage

Heritage and Sanpete County are nearly synonymous. The landscape is dotted with hundreds of nineteenth-century buildings—many well preserved, others weathered or crumbling. And the county is filled with examples of work and products typical of the nineteenth century.

Sanpete County contains the best-preserved group of pioneer communities in Utah. "It's the best representation still existing of early settlement life in Utah," according to historian Tom Carter. Sanpete has often been compared to the Amish settlement in

Pennsylvania. Today, in spite of increasing convenience stores and homes, the county still possesses the nature of a historic district.

Sanpete offers an ideal match of well-preserved pioneer culture and tourism. Sanpete County may be the best place in Utah to see historic architecture.

Mormon pioneers' commitment to long-lived communities is reflected in their buildings, many of which persist from the first three decades of Sanpete's settlement. Many buildings are listed on the National Register of Historic Places or the Sanpete County Register of Historic Sites.

Preserving History and Culture

The county, along with the state, has evolved through four phases of preservation effort. In the first phase, various ad hoc efforts were created to save individual buildings around the county and state. An example is the work by historian Tom Carter or architect Allen Roberts, describing and listing historic buildings in Sanpete County during the 1970s and 1980s. In the second phase, the state historic preservation office allocated funds through the certified local governments program (CLG) to fund preservation projects at the county and city levels. An example is the preservation of Ephraim Co-op in 1980.

The third phase came in 1994 when the state launched its Mainstreet Program to save historic downtowns. Bim Oliver coordinated this program, producing a guidebook entitled, *Shaping Liveable Communities*. The Mount Pleasant historic Main Street was one of four pilot projects, restored between 1994–96 and serving as prototypes. The fourth phase of historic preservation is the creation of county and city preservation councils.

Formed in 1996, the Sanpete County Heritage Council is a new and energetic organization that coordinates all heritage projects in the county. It promotes preservation and economic development from a heritage perspective. The council includes two representatives from the cities of Mount Pleasant, Spring City, Ephraim, Manti, Fairview, Moroni, and Fountain Green, along with a representative from the county.

The heritage council works in partnership with over a dozen state agencies and several county offices to fund and produce projects. These include the Department of Agriculture, Utah Travel Council, Utah Arts Council, Utah Heritage Fund, Department of Community and Economic Development, Division of State History, Division of Commerce, Division of Business Development, Department of Natural Resources, Division of Parks and Recreation, and Snow College.

The council focuses on four project areas: preservation of historic buildings/business districts, interpretation of county history for the public, tourism/marketing, and business development. Regarding preservation, the council has worked closely with several historic renovation projects, including the Mount Pleasant Main Street project and preservation of the 1890 Denver & Rio Grande Railroad depot, the Moroni Opera House, Fountain Green Main Street, the Bishop's Storehouse in Ephraim, the old Spring City School, and other community buildings in the county. Regarding interpretation, the council has worked hard to help create educational projects promoting appreciation of county history and tourism. Four projects have been completed so far and others are in process.

Working with Brigham Young University, the heritage council created a video documentary about the 1860s war between Ute Indians and Mormon settlers in Utah. *Cultures in Conflict: Utah's Blackhawk War* tells the story of a conflict that began in Sanpete County, but spread out statewide as white settlers and native Utes clashed over land in early Utah. Dozens of descendants were interviewed on both sides of the conflict. The video, produced in 1998, is an informative tribute to the struggle of early Utahns. Another recent documentaray in 1999 was Dennis Lyman's *History of Manti Hill.* Both documentaries were aired on Utah television.

In conjunction with several other county and state departments and organizations, the council sponsored creation of a Sanpete tour book in 1998. *Getting Together With Yesterday: A Tour of Sanpete County Historic Buildings* describes in words and pictures the attributes of 156 historic structures in the county. The book has a chapter about each city, including a map of the town with a guided tour of several intact historic buildings. There are brief descriptions of the architecture and a history of each building.

The heritage council also coordinated production of a county audio cassette tape tour. Visitors can put the tape into their car stereo and be guided by a narrator to various sites and interests. The tape describes folk arts, history, folklore, and points of interest.

The county and the state are working together on development of a Heritage Highway along U.S. Highway 89 from Spanish Fork to Kanab. Similar to the national heritage highway project "Route 66," the Utah Heritage Highway will draw tourists to take a leisurely, scenic route through the countryside as an alternative to speeding down I-15. Along the way, tourists will be able to visit and appreciate the heritage corridor of Utah with its many charming sites, stops and products. In 1998 the state allocated $50,000 seed money to get the project going.

Museums

In the past two or three decades, Sanpete County has established or upgraded a number of museums to capture the past and make it available for education. Three are in Manti: the Patten House, the Manti Art Museum, and History House on Heritage Corner. Two museums in Ephraim are the Central Utah Art Center and the Pioneer Relic Museum. The Mount Pleasant Relic House and Wasatch Academy round out Sanpete's selection of historic repositories for artifacts and objects. Additionally, historic photographs can be found in the Ephraim Library.

The Fairview Museum of History and Art, established in 1965 by Golden G. Sanderson and Lyndon Graham, offers the county's largest, and most varied if not eclectic collection or art and historical artifacts. The museum is housed in the restored 1900 Fairview Elementary School and its companion, a new exhibition hall completed in 1995. The new building provided exhibition space for the Huntington mammoth discovered in 1988 in Sanpete County. The building also houses other collections including the art galleries. The new building also generated greater interest in the project, attracting wider support from the community. The museum also contains a wealth of Utah and Sanpete art, historic artifacts, and photographs documenting local, state, and natural history.

Challenges

There are many challenges to preservation. The first is the fact that historic structures are in decay and represent the eroding of the past. "Pioneers came in here and transplanted western civilization," commented one preservationist. "Now it's all broken down or knocked down. Buildings made by our grandparents are replaced with sheetmetal structures. Sanpete is in decline from its origins, its original nature."

Another challenge to preservation is opposition, including criticism and resistance. The first category includes those who dismiss or thwart heritage concerns, and those who eschew projects that are unauthentic. For example, most artisans believe heritage projects should be authentic. The second category includes developers and others whose efforts are considered adversarial to preservation.

Some fear that some landmarks will become pretty facades rather than living restorations. For them, preserving heritage means productive reuse. Artisans say preservation should create genuine products, employ local craftsmen, and have a self-existent life or "living heritage. Authentic heritage products include local wool products from local sheep, handmade rugs, quilts, furniture, bricks, pottery, stonecutting, dairy products, weaving, and wine making. Authentic rural arts preserve pioneer tradition while allowing craftsmen to market their skills.

In any community evolution is a delicate balance between preservation and progress. If either one suppresses the other, it can be destructive to the community. While caution feeds preservation, money drives development."Development and preservation have values that are incompatible," according to Bob Sorenson, a local craftsman. "Developers aim for the lowest costs and demand rapid construction to meet deadlines, while authentic stone masonry and carpentry require quality, time, and patience."

The Sanpete Heritage Council sees preservation and development as highly compatible, needing each other in order to succeed. According to Monte Bona, director of the Sanpete County Heritage Council, "Preservation equals sound economic development." He along with many artists, carpenters, and masons, seek better collaboration between local skilled labor and county heritage projects. An example is the Fairview Museum.

Two local programs aspire to create more collaboration. One is the Central Utah Art Center which sponsors grants and programs to have artisans teach their crafts to interested students and apprentices.Another is the Traditional Building Skills Institute at Snow College, co-sponsored by the Utah State Historical Society. Here trained artisans teach traditional crafts such as adobe and brick-making, stone masonry, millwork, log construction, lime plaster making, pioneer furniture manufacturing, and related skills. Students practice the crafts on local historic buildings needing restoration. After training, students may stay and work in the county on historic restoration or leave to seek work outside. Ultimately, whether the heritage industry of Sanpete County will be successful, it remains a crucial focus—as a growing, promising, indigenous, traditional, and potentially lucrative economy for residents.

Social and Cultural Life

Yesterday, the historic social halls of Sanpete each provided a community social center; but today many of the old halls or their use are gone. With one or two exceptions, those that remain await restoration. Meanwhile what has arisen in their place?

At first glance, social and cultural life in Sanpete seem scarce. Most social events are tied to family, church, special events, the college, the library, the schools, or town festivals. The dominant influence on social and cultural life in Sanpete is the LDS church through its well-organized network of meetings and activities. Today churches serve as the equivalent of old social halls for Mormons and many others. In fact, when it comes to social and cultural events, Mormons will attend others' churches and vice versa.

At the same time, secular centers for Sanpete society and culture are diverse and evolving. Town halls, high schools, and community centers provide meeting space for events. Also several historic buildings offer charming surroundings for cultural gatherings. And local shops and businesses sometimes host events.

A surprising variety of social and cultural activities occur around the county, if you look closely. An economic benefit is that these events attract outside visitors to the area, who often stay long enough to enjoy the hospitality of the county's quaint shops, eating establishments, and lodgings.

A general observation of the county is that the principle towns of Sanpete each has a unique cultural identity. For example, Ephraim is the most culturally diverse town and the center of education. Manti is the power center of government and church. Gunnison, the third largest, is independent and alone, with an identity as the prison town. Mount Pleasant, the fourth in size, has always been the liberal town, and the home of Wasatch Academy. Spring City is the quintessential Mormon village with a sprinkling of artists. Moroni will always be the turkey town, and Fountain Green the lamb town. Fairview with its museum of historic artifacts is a town that evokes the past.

Another superficial glance divides the county in half with two cultural/educational centers. Wasatch Academy is the cultural center for the north county, while Snow College is the cultural center for the south. Ephraim is a focus of educational and ethnic culture, as well as the visual arts. While Wasatch Academy is an oasis of education, culture, and open-mindedness.

Wasatch Academy is a cultural magnet, with a venue of sophisticated performing arts events open to the public. It hosts multi-cultural music programs, such as black gospel singers or music storytellers and performance poets who come almost monthly. A remarkable, innovative arts education program and desk-top publishing facilities bring much to the community. The Wasatch student literary and art magazine placed first in the United States.

Snow College sponsors cultural activities ranging from educational events to entertainment. Concerts and stage performances attract audiences from all over the county. The theater department performs four major stage productions per year. The music department sponsors five choirs and two orchestras, as well as a couple of bands and jazz ensembles, all of which perform concerts. The dance department fetes performances of modern and traditional dance. And the college hosts out-of-state performers and speakers, as well as hosting large pop music concerts.

Ethnic and foreign students at Snow College bring cultural diversity to the Ephraim area. For example, the Polynesian Club has sponsored an elaborate luau since 1990, with an authentic Polynesian feast and traditional dancing performance. Festivities draw 1,000 people from all over Utah and raise money for Polynesian students' tuition.

International students hold a food festival in April creating unusual dishes from every culture around the world. People from the community who have lived in other countries contribute dishes as well. Hundreds of people attend the event. The same is true of the Pinata Festival sponsored by the Spanish Club every December. And the language club holds an international Christmas party featuring music performed in native languages and holiday food from European countries. All these events draw a high percentage of participants from the surrounding communities.

Dance and Theater

The Snow College theater department stages student plays and performances every semester. All shows are open to the public.

Dances in the county are held at Snow College twice monthly, as well as in the high schools, junior highs, and local churches. Private groups also sponsor dances in community centers. One particularly fine dance venue is the historic Ephraim Social Hall on Main Street.

Two prominent historic buildings in Sanpete once served as the two major social centers of the county. Both have been preserved and renovated for use as social halls today. The Ephraim Social Hall and the Moroni Opera House preserve the idea of the pioneer social hall and offer it to us still. Today they represent the social evolution from pioneer times to a contemporary society.

Said to be "the finest dance hall in the state outside of Salt Lake City," in 1911 the Dreamland Dance Hall or Ephraim Social Hall housed a fine orchestra and community dances every weekend. Today this imposing three-story, two-floor brick hall is one of the two most prominent historic buildings in Ephraim. The first floor originally housed a general store, and the second floor was the dance hall, with a twenty-two foot ceiling and vast dance floor, made of maple hardwood. The building was remodeled and refurbished in 1987, with Fat Jack's Pizza parlor on the main level and a dance hall on the second floor. The original dance floor is intact, as well as the full-length windows and full-length French beveled mirrors which once reflected light from several large tungsten lamps. This immense hall is used today for dances on weekends, as well as dancing lessons, parties, receptions, reunions, and other events.

Built in 1891, Moroni Opera House is a two-story, one floor brick theater—the oldest public building in Moroni. It is one of only three surviving opera houses from nineteenth-century Utah (the others are in St. George and Beaver) as well as one of the few remaining pre-movie era theaters in Utah. It had a very high ceiling and unusually spacious stage for a rural theater, at thirty-five by twenty-five foot. There was an orchestra pit and main floor seating for those who came for live theater, musical theater, operas, and plays performed by home-grown talent and traveling vaudeville, theater groups, and stock companies. It was also used for "general amusements" as well as town meetings and political events. Movies were shown for a time. About 1930 the house was remodeled as a flour mill; the stage was torn away and all props were destroyed. In 1994, it was purchased by the Moroni Heritage Development Committee which is renovating the building and the stage. The hall will function as a social center for theater, musicals, and dances, hopefully attracting performers from outside. Sanpete Community Theater began performing about 1971 at the first Scandinavian Days Celebration. Conceived as a fundraiser to put a roof on the Ephraim Co-op, it became the county's annual community theater. This amateur troupe is dedicated to supporting all performing arts, and welcomes anyone from the community who has an interest in participating. It is staffed by volunteer members from each town; but occasionally professionals are invited to perform. Members put on all types of performances, including murder mystery, dinner theater, plays, musicals, comedy, drama, song and dance, children's productions, variety shows, solos, readings, and puppeteering. The troupe stages at least four productions per year, renting halls all the way from Gunnison to Fairview, including Manti Auditorium, North Sanpete High School, Gunnison High, Fairview Dance Hall, and various churches. Without a permanent home to store their sets and costumes, they hope to call the Moroni Opera House home when it's completed.

Gunnison Casino Theater is a stunning example of the beaux arts style from 1912. Built by a local promoter and owner of the

Gunnison Co-op, this theater was used for live stage shows as well as movies. It was the center of commercial entertainment in the Gunnison area, billed as "one of the most attractive amusement halls outside Salt Lake City." The theater operated continuously for 80 years, then, after a brief period of inactivity, resumed showing films and staging plays. Today it's used for live stage plays and movies are run every week.

The North Bend Entertainers are a theatrical group, started in 1983. They produce a highly anticipated play every year, namely the July 24th Melodrama. For the first seven years, the Entertainers staged their melodramas in the old Fairview Junior High School, since then the troupe has staged its performances in the old Fairview Dance hall, which was fire damaged in the 1890s but restored 100 years later in the early 1990s. Other events at the hall include dances, weddings, reunions, craft fairs, and the city Christmas party.

A fairly large scale dramatic interpretation was the sesquicentennial Mormon wagon train in 1999 that journeyed from Nephi to Manti. Mormons dressed as pioneers walked alongside conestoga wagons retracing their ancestors' steps all the way from Nephi. Upon arriving, they made dugouts on the hillside and camped as did their early settler ancestors in November 1849.

The largest and most famous theatrical production in Sanpete county is the Mormon Miracle Pageant, performed on the Manti Temple grounds. Sponsored by the LDS church, this event first began in 1972 and has grown every year. The play depicts stories and dramatic scenes from the Book of Mormon, with elaborate costumes and state-of-the-art, concert quality sound equipment. Audiences come from all over Utah, out of state, and foreign countries creating enormous crowds that block all traffic in Manti. Yet the pageant is amazingly well managed. In 1998 the crowds reached a maximum of 20,000 in one night, with a total of 94,000 for the season. Performances are held on Tuesdays through Saturdays, traditionally in July; however beginning in 1998, the performance dates were moved to June.

Music

Live music performance is a Sanpete tradition going back to pioneer days when traveling performers came through the county and entertained locals with opera, musical theater, recitals, and chorus. Today residents are continuing this tradition in a variety of ways.

Snow College offers public music performances by its choirs and bands, as well as major music concerts featuring pop entertainers during homecoming season. Snow College concerts are always well attended.

At North Sanpete High School, Roy Ellefsen is the choir director who teaches music and French. Roy conducts a top notch choir that performs for special occasions. He also directs a musical at the high school every year. This school actually has the best auditorium in the county, and, with 350 seats, it competes with the one at Snow. Even the Utah Symphony has played here. Roy also teaches music education. Meanwhile the elementary schools are trying hard to get some grants for music and art.

The Wasatch Bell Choir at the Mount Pleasant Presbyterian church performs on special occasions, interpreting classical, religious, and popular music. This ecumenical choir is half LDS, half Presbyterian, and alternates performances in both churches. The choir is a cultural bridge between religions.

Beginning in 1980, David Rosier began organizing a music concert series in the beautiful Spring City chapel with its ideal acoustics. The choir performed a capella and chorale music for the public on a Friday night once each month for six months, fall through spring. People from all over the county came to hear these musical performances, until objections to applause in the chapel brought the concerts to an end.

In 1998 a new acoustic music shop specializing in bluegrass and folk music opened in Fountain Green. Owned by Russ and Sharon Evans, the store inhabits an historic building on Main Street restored by Russ and Sharon. The store sponsors free music concerts on a regular basis, hosting folksinger and bluegrass artists from around Utah. Performances are always sold out, drawing 75–80 people. The store sponsors a bluegrass festival in Fountain Green every July.

Art

Art, artists, and art projects are a vital force in Sanpete County culture. The Fairview Museum of History and Art has the largest collection of Avard Fairbanks sculptural works in one location. The museum has seven galleries for exhibition of art. The museum is building a permanent collection of two and three dimensional art works.

A variety of gifted artists and artisans have located in Sanpete during the last twenty-five years, and have created a network of people with remarkable talent.

The Central Utah Art Center was founded in the 1992 to foster and support the work and teaching of artists in Sanpete County. Located in the restored Old Relief Society Granary next to the Ephraim Co-op, this center is open from Tuesday to Saturday, and exhibits local art as well as works from outside the county. Funded by grant monies, it sponsors classes in painting, drawing, pottery, sculpture, and bookmaking. Classes are held in the basement, where groups of artists meet for life drawing, pottery, painting, and children's art classes. The artists instructing will teach anyone who is interested. Classes are a chance to gather for art.

Kathleen Peterson, who came to Sanpete in 1976, oversees the Art Center and teaches art classes there as well as at Wasatch Academy. A visual artist who works with oils, watercolors, pastels, and batik, she travels and teaches all over the world.In 1999 the center received its first grant to host art workshops and art education. Each workshop features a local artist teaching his or her skill to students.

The Gunnison Valley Arts Council formed in 1987 to bring arts programs to south Sanpete. The council sponsors arts events such as visual arts, readings, lectures, and musicial performances. The council also sponsors art shows, funds art projects, and supports arts education. Snow College also sponsors art workshops taught by watercolorists Osral Allred and Carl Purcell.

Sanpete County has a long roster of talented artists. A few of them include painters Lee Udall Bennion, Ella Peacock, Susan Gallacher potter Joe Bennion, painters Randall Lake, Mike Woodbury, Ron Richmond, Carl Purcell, and Osral B. Allred at Snow College, sculptor Benson Whittle, Randall Lake, Susan Gallagher, Mike Workman, Nickle Lauritzen, Ella Peacock, Brad Taggert, Brad Aldridge, Ron Richmond, Rick Gate, the late Max Blain, and Chris Jensen.

Literature

One might be surprised to learn that Sanpete has more than a few authors. The most famous is Virginia Sorensen from Manti, well-known for her novels published in the 1940s and 1960s. Pearle M. Olsen wrote *Nickles From A Sheep's Back* in 1977. Fairview researcher Norma Vance wrote a local history called *Moccasins and Wooden Shoes* in 1989. Wilmer Tanner from Milburn authored at least three books, *Plant Carbohydrates* in 1981, *Snakes of Utah,* with Douglas Cox, in 1995, and *Enjoy the Journey Along Your Marriage Highway,* 1998. A variety of local writers contributes every year to the annual *Saga of the Sanpitch,* a collection of stories recording local folklore and creative writing, published yearly since 1969.

The Milburn area seems to inspire unusual creative work. Lifelong resident Randy Brunger wrote a curious book in 1984 entitled *The Spy Who Wasn't,* detailing his years in Russia as an agent for the CIA. Sculptor and scholar Benson Whittle wrote a satirical book, *Le Petit Richards* printed in 1978, satirizing himself as an erudite Mormon misfit. Whittle also authored a book about medieval European stone sculpture entitled, *The Barbaric Carver,* and has published several articles and papers, including a "Review Essay of Early Mormonism and the Magic World View" and a monograph on "The Sunstones of the Nauvoo Temple." His wife Patricia Hatch, a medieval scholar, is co-editor of *The Journal of Magic Realism* and publisher of a small press.

Recent histories of Sanpete abound, adding to the collection of volumes about individual towns. Examples include *History of Sterling,* by Grace Funk and Rose L. McIff, 1983; *Life Under the Horseshoe: A History of Spring City,* by Kaye Watson, published in 1984–86; and the 1939 history of *Mount Pleasant* by Hilda Madsen Longsdorf reprinted in 1999. These histories are full of details and anecdotes. Recent books about Sanpete families include *The Dorius Heritage,* by Earl Dorius, 1979; *The Shoulders on Which We Stand,* by DeMont Powell in 1982; and *Denmark to Manti,* by Joseph Anderson in 1990.

Albert Antrei has written two books about Manti—*View from the Red Point* (1976)and *High Dry and Offside* (1995). He and Ruth D.

Scow compiled the 1983 county history, *The Other 49ers: A topical history of Sanpete County, Utah 1849 to 1983,* published in 1982.

Tom Carter has published several articles about Sanpete, and two architectural studies, *A Way of Seeing: Discovering the Art of Building in Spring City* and *Building Zion: Folk Architecture in the Mormon Settlements of Sanpete County,* 1984, revised 1994.

Likely the most popular and well-used book on the county is *Sanpete Scenes: A Guide to Utah's Heart,* written by Gary B. Peterson and Lowell "Ben" Bennion in 1987—full of pictures and details about Sanpete. A colorful tour guide to historic buildings in each town is *Getting Together with Yesterday: A Tour of Sanpete County Historic Buildings,* by Karen Graser, Maxine Hanks and Allen Roberts, 1998. Edward Geary's, *The Proper Edge of the Sky: the High Plateau County of Utah* appeared in 1992, and *Sanpete Tales: Humorous Folklore of Central Utah* by Edgar M. Jenson and William Jenson Adams, published in 1999.

A few professors at Snow College have published books in recent years, including *Uncommon Common Sin* by Lynn Poulson in 1993 and *The Bible as Literature* by Roger Baker in 1995. Don Breakwell and Allan Stevens authored a biology text, while religion faculty David Wilmore wrote *The Journey Beyond* and *When the Spirit Whispers* with the help of Michele R. Sorensen. Most recently in 1999 came *A Handbook of Riparian Management for the Conservation of Neotropical Migratory Birds in Utah,* by Paul Gardner, Richard Stevens, and Frank Howell.

Additionally, Snow College publishes a student literary magazine entitled *Weeds* as well as the *Faculty Studies* journal, both annually. Student journalists also publish a weekly newspaper, the *Snowdrift.* Snow College also sponsors a lecture series open to the public, featuring speakers from around Utah and outside the state. Wasatch Academy also publishes a student journal for literary and artistic work.

The county's four newspapers and several publications are the main and vital source of public information and cultural discourse in Sanpete. These publications create a focus for daily events and provide a place where citizen can exchange their views, including disagreements. The papers may be the only forum for clashing perspectives in Sanpete to actually meet and deal with each other.

The *Gunnison Valley News* serves the south end of the county. The *Manti Messenger* began in 1885 also publishes the *Ephraim Enterprise*. The two papers use much of the same material, but are slightly different, catering to the separate readership of these two sister cities. The editor is Max Call, assisted by his wife Beth. The *Mt. Pleasant Pyramid* serves the entire north county with a circulation of 3,000. Koleen Peterson and Penny Hamilton served as editors in the 1980s through 1998, when Cheryl Brewer took over.

The *Horseshoe Trader* is a pithy little publication produced in Manti and available in every business in Sanpete. Containing a fascinating array of display and classified ads. Also known as *The Universal Impression,* such is the flavor of *The Horseshoe Trader,* distributed all the way from Park City to Hanksville.

Horseshoe Mountain Pottery News is published quarterly by Joe and Lee Bennion and hand mailed from Spring City. You could call it the arts paper of Sanpete. In its pages the Bennions share news of the city, family, and friends. They update patrons on their works in progress and cultural events.

Holidays and Festivals

Sanpete festivals are lively and unusual, drawing energetic support from locals and bringing visitors from all over the state. Each is centered on heritage in some way.

On Memorial Day weekend, the last Saturday in May, two events compliment each other. Ephraim's Scandinavian Festival, founded in 1980, celebrates the Scandinavian heritage of pioneers who founded the county. It includes a parade, food, crafts, concerts, and a rodeo. Spring City Heritage Day offers a tour of twenty historic houses,the historic church, thatn finishes with a dinner hosted by local LDS wards. The tour is sponsored by Friends of Historic Spring City. The group, organized in 1990, is a nonprofit organization dedicated to various historic preservation projects in Spring City. Local artisans sell their rugs, pots, furniture, tin, and soap on the street next to Joe Bennion's pottery shop. The tour actually began back in 1982 as the D.U.P. Historic Home Tour. It has had a profound effect on Spring

City, where half of the homes on the tour have been bought and restored by people who came and took the tour. It is a fundraiser for historic projects, and a vehicle for education and preservation.

The first weekend in June is Centerfield Founder's Day. Regular events include softball, pot-luck dinner, and a mud rally.

In mid-June comes the Manti Mormon Miracle Pageant, the spectacular outdoor dramatic play performed on temple hill. The audience sits on grassy lawns while scenes from the Book of Mormon are played out under spotlights near temple walls.

On July 4th weekend, the Gunnison City Old Fashioned July 4th is a two-day celebration with a parade, car show, carnival, dinner, concert, and fireworks. Moroni City's "Red Hot July 4th" is a home town celebration that begins with a fun run and flag ceremony, lots of homecooked food, and ending with fireworks. Mount Pleasant's "Hub City Days" celebrates the 4th with parade, rodeo, pioneer activities, and fireworks display. Manti City's traditional family Fourth of July celebration includes free swimming, greased pole climbing, and fireworks.

Mid-July brings two unusual festivals. Fountain Green celebrates its "Lamb Days" with a huge picnic in the park featuring barbecued lamb sandwiches. It also sponsors a talent show, softball games, parade, rides, entertainment, prize drawings, craft fair, and dance. The Black Hawk War Commemoration is everything the name suggests.

July 24th may be the biggest holiday of the summer because it celebrates the arrival of the Mormon pioneers in Utah and tends to last a whole week. Fairview's Pioneer Days includes fun runs, parade, craftshows, rodeo, and the unforgettable Demolition Derby. Spring City's Pioneer Days is a old-fashioned, historic celebration including parade, games, food, entertainment, and prizes.

The July 24th Demolition Derby in Fairview is a sight to behold, drawing sell-out crowds every year. The derby occurs at the Fairview Rodeo Grounds, although the first year it was held in a field. People camp in line the night before to get tickets, which go on sale at 9 A.M. and are sold by 10 A.M. Locals with frustrations they need to release and cars that are ready for the graveyard enter the derby, usually thirty to forty vehicles. Upon the signal, cars start gunning for each other and smashing fenders until two lone wrecks survive, and drive to the death.

As summer winds down in August prior to the start of a new school year, two celebrations bid the season goodbye. Mid-August brings the Jazz festival at Snow College offering an impressive collection of jazz performances. The season finale is the Sanpete County Fair which runs for over a week in Manti, known as "the biggest little fair in the state of Utah."

In addition to community celebrations, church and school activities, there are youth groups for teens in the county including Youth Council, 4-H, Boy Scouts, Girl Scouts, Jr. Jazz Basketball, Utah Boys Basketball, and Utah Girls Basketball.

Additionally, there are at least eight types of civic groups in Sanpete County, with branches in twelve cities. These include the Daughters of Utah Pioneers, Sanpete County Heritage Council, American Legion, Legion Auxiliary, Chamber of Commerce, Lion's Club, Rotary International, and Veterans of Foreign Wars. There are senior citizens centers located in the seven largest communities.

Diversity

The overwhelming majority of Sanpete residents are Anglo-American, conservative Mormons. Sanpete is a white, Mormon county.

Yet non-Mormons, liberals, and ethnic minorities have lived in Sanpete County from the beginning and have always played a role in its culture.

Sanpete county contains a wider variety of people than many realize. Many variations on the dominant theme exist, creating a diverse culture of people in Sanpete. In 1994 there were 116 Native Americans, 880 Hispanics, 312 Asian/Pacific Islanders, and 22 Blacks in Sanpete County. A total of 1,330 minorities compared to 17,470 non-minorities.[19]

A cursory look at *types* of people (not race or ethnicity) in the county results in an interesting set of polarities. There are insiders and outsiders, Mormons and non-Mormons, natives and transplants, middle class and poor, anglo and ethnic, polygamists and monogamists, conservatives and progressives, newcomers and old timers urbanized and rural, young and aging, traditionalists and bohemians, locals and tourists, professionals and laborers, local workers and commuters, leaders and citizens, preservationists and developers and so on.

With so many categories coexisting within the population, every person in the county can find at least one aspect of society that he or she has in common with another person, no matter how different they may seem on the surface.

Artist Lee Bennion says, "People have accepted us here. Maybe it's because we try not to see division lines, we try not to categorize." Yet for many others in Sanpete, division lines do exist.

Mexican Americans

Mexican-Americans have a community apart from others. "The first families to arrive from Mexico were greeted with cookies and casseroles and curious Mormon welcome committees. . . . now it's possible for a Mexican from Guanajuato to come . . . and feel like they are right back home again. The trailer park community is like a little Mexico."[20]

Language, housing in trailer parks , workplace, low end jobs, culture and society all serve to keep Mexicans apart from whites or culturally still "across the border."

The 1990 census listed 880 Hispanics living in Sanpete County. Of these, twenty-three held administrative or managerial jobs; three held professional jobs; two held technician jobs; and nine held sales jobs; five held administrative support jobs; nineteen held service jobs; twenty-four held production/craft/repair jobs; twenty-three were machine operators; eight worked in transportation or moving; and sixty-three were equipment handlers/helpers/laborers.

Most Hispanics work at Moroni Feed Co. Their co-workers speak Spanish with them and they go home to tortilla dinners. Few ties to the non-hispanic community exist outside of work. But attempts are being made to bridge the gap. One is the annual pinata festival at Snow College. Some doctors at local health clinics provide free medical care for those in need.

Ephraim may serve as the best example of ethnic cultural experimentation in the county. It is the most ethnically and culturally diverse town, and the most involved in creating multi-cultural events. Yet an assessment of Ephraim may actually describe the current status of cultural diversity countywide. "The community is struggling to overcome cultural differences enough to better understand their neighbors while still retaining their cultural identity."[21]

ENDNOTES

1. This chapter was written by Maxine Hanks and is taken from a longer study on contemporary Sanpete County a copy of which is available in the Utah State Historical Society Library In the Spring of 1999 the author interviewed the following county residents and others whose responses are included in the text of this chapter without individual endnote citations: Gary Anderson, Sherron Andreason, Lee Bennion, Bruce Blackham, Leonard Blackham, Joe Blaine, Monte Bona, J. Keller Christenson, Eddie Cox, Daphne Davis,Ted Draper, Peter Godfredson, Jeff Hanks, Dennis Mower, Claude Pickett, and Wynne Smith.

2. *Sanpete Action Plan,* Executive Summary of Sanpete County Economic Situation, Office of Economic Development, 1990

3. Karen Graser, Maxine Hanks, Allen Roberts, *Getting Together With Yesterday: A Tour of Sanpete Historic Buildings* (Sanpete County Heritage Council, 1998)

4. LDS Statistical Membership Records and Church Directory, 1998 About 63.8 percent of Sanpete Mormons are active in church, compared to 60 percent of Salt Lake Mormons.

5. Church Educational System, Records, 1999

6. Utah State Office of Education, "1997–98 Annual Statistical and Cost Supplement to a Report on School Buildings in Utah," (Salt Lake City, May 1998) 34

7. South Sanpete School District Annual Report to Parents, 1999

8. Snow College Academic Catalogue, 1998–99

9. "Draft Environmental Impact Statement for the Narrows Project, Utah" United States Department of the Interior, March 1998, s-1, s-2

10. Utah Agricultural Statistics and Utah Department of Agricultural and Food Annual Reports

11. Wayne L Wahlquist,ed., *Atlas of Utah,* (Provo, UT: Brigham Young University Press, 1981) 204, 222

12. Sherry Waters, Division Administrative Assistant, and Warden Administrative Office Files, 1999

13. *Inside Our Fences,* Utah Correctional Industries, Second edition, 1997

14. "Crime and Punishment: Assessing the Status Quo," seminar, 13-15 May 1999, Salt Lake City

15. "Sanpete County Action Plan," 1992

16. "Sanpete County: A Notch at a Time," Fourth Quarter, Economic Report, 1997

17. "Stataistical Abstract of Utah," 1993

18. *Ephraim Enterprise,* 6 August, 13 August, 27 August, and 3 September 1998

19. Utah Population Estimates Committee, 1994

20. Rugh Peterson, Peterson, Dorret, Alvarez, "Running Head: Mexican Americans," unpublished paper, sociology department, Brigham Young University, 14

21. Ibid, 15.

CHAPTER 15

THE COMMUNITIES OF SANPETE

Axtell

The Axtell area, first known as Willow Creek, was first farmed by Lars Peter Fjeldsted and his family in 1870. Here, along the Sevier River in the southwest part of current Axtell, a cooperative herd of sheep was kept by the pioneers. Fjeldsted was called to settle in Emery in 1878, but by then the family of John Bosshardt, Sr., had homesteaded in what came to be the south central part of town. Others farmers, mostly from the Centerfield-Gunnison area, gradually came and stayed to form a village spread out on an east-west line along Willow Creek, and later along the north-south-running Highway 89. John Bosshardt, Sr., and his family located in the south central area in 1874, planting the first alfalfa seed. Axel Einerson, who settled in the east part of the hamlet in 1875, was a tireless developer of the place. He raised sugar beets, ran the post office, a store, and a blacksmith. Above the store was Axtell's first dance hall.

A townsite of gridded blocks was never established in Axtell. Instead, it was divided into large, half-mile squares, defined by country roads. There is no town center, commercial district, or high density. The village grew slowly, being enlarged gradually by the addition of a few more farm families each year. Named after territorial governor Samuel B. Axtell, the village's name change occurred in 1891, a momentous year for the town with the arrival of the railroad.

Sanpete's southernmost town has always been a small agricultural community. The arrival of the railroad in 1891 did not result in a commercial district given Gunnison's dominant status to the north. A few other industries have been explored, among them Al Tuft's salt mines in the foothill outside of town. Tuft extracted, boiled, refined, and sold the salt to other Sanpete villages. Sugar cane was raised starting in 1876. A molasses mill was operated by Axel Einerson. His workers produced as much as 4,000 gallons a year. Attempts in the 1870s to bring water from the creek into town and its fields were not successful. A reservoir begun in 1883 allowed Axtell to store its water. The Willow Creek Irrigation Company, organized in 1897, capitalized to build an irrigation system. Willow Creek Reservoir, located in the foothills about five miles east of town, is useful for both water storage and as a wildlife refuge.

The first school was built of logs in 1888. Hannah Hansen Jensen Christensen was the first teacher. The first Sunday (or Sabbath) school started in 1891, led by Gustov Johnsen. Until the railroad came, settlers had to retrieve their mail from Gunnison. A substantial new stone school was erected in 1898 in north-central Axtell, followed by a larger, brick school built in 1912 in the center of town. Starting in 1936, the hamlet's students were bused to Gunnison. Still in use, the brick school was converted to the LDS wardhouse yet in service.

In the mid-twentieth century, Axtell, like the other southern Sanpete villages, raised sugar beets plus peas and corn for canning. Today hay and stock are the main products. It remains a pastoral, rural entry to the county from Sevier County to the south.

Cedar Cliffs

Cedar Cliffs is not found on any modern map because its population has entirely abandoned the area. It was settled in the late 1880s by James C. Livingston, a polygamist from Salt Lake City. His son, who lived in Fountain Green, probably told his father of the available site, located on Birch Creek about three miles south of Fountain Green. The federal prosecution of polygamist men was very active, then and it is likely that Livingston settled in the small, remote place to provide protection for some of his families. The place grew large enough to build a schoolhouse and for an LDS Sunday school to be organized, but it never sustained continued growth after the polygamy issued was settled and Utah obtained statehood. Today a few empty but substantial homes and trees remain as a reminder that not all Mormon villages possessed the resources to sustain them indefinitely into the future.

Centerfield

Centerfield, so called because of its location in the middle of a fine field, began after 1869 when people left the fort in Gunnison and moved south to the Field. The land owners set up and agreed to rules and regulations for the government of the Field. Three men—known as the Field Committee—were appointed to make a plot, number the lots, and issue certificates to the owners. New entries and transfers were recorded for the sum of $.25. Owners were required to make fences and keep them in good repair. Noxious weeks, such as black-seed, were to be destroyed.

This was the beginning of Centerfield as it is today. It was not until 1871, with the beginnings of co-operative farming, that the first families moved into the Field, as Centerfield was called then. In the next few years, the Field grew considerably. The first three families to settle were those of Chris Sanders, Michael Nielsen, and William Childs.

When the United Order was instituted in 1874, the large 1,200 acre U.O. Farms No. I, II, and III were located in the Field. In 1875 the land was appraised at $4.00 to $5.00 per acre. Axel Einerson, John Christensen, and L. Lubin were the foremen of the U.O. farms.

In November 1876 the men of the Field considered it too cold and dangerous for their children to walk the three miles into Gunnison for school and church. They asked no monetary reward from Gunnison, they just wanted to be allowed to form their own school district. At first school was taught in private homes. Then, in

1882, the first school and community hall was built just south of the present town hall. It was fashioned of logs and had a dirt roof. It was heated in the winter months by a cobblestone fireplace. The people of the Field were generally happy about their new schoolhouse. There were those who didn't think this log cabin was good enough and continued to walk the three miles into Gunnison.

In the early 1900s, more and more settlers came to the Field. Many new homes were built. Some were of adobe and some were of log. The last commercially owned and operated adobe hotel was east of the sugar factory and was owned by Thomas Nielson until 1904.

House logs and lumber were hauled from Twelve Mile Canyon. Often families accompanied the men to the narrows for a full week of fun and work.

According to Hannah Thunnison, "A good deal of furniture was made for our own and other settlements." Bedsprings were made of rope. Mattresses of straw ticks or featherbeds. Home spun blankets and quilts were made from worn clothing. The mother of the home usually was responsible for all the family's clothing. She carded the wool to make her own thread and material. She colored fabrics using common berries and plants.

Field residents loved to have fun and dance—especially at a home warming. This was done just after a house was built and before the new residents moved in.

In 1885 Albert Tollstrup came to the Field to teach. He had fifty students—some older than himself. Winfred Fjeldsted, Soren Anderson, Lizzie Jensen, and George Peterson were some of the students. Tolstrup's pay was $10.00 a quarter, usually paid in gold. For this he walked the two miles to teach in any weather. He was responsible to keep the school room clean and the fire made.

In 1886 residents wanted to built a new school and church house. Money was scarce, so labor, hay, and grain were donated and sold to purchase the needed materials. Chris Tollstrup and Gustav Nielsen cut and laid the stone. The building was finished by 18 January 1889 when a picnic was organized to benefit the organ fund.

Before the school was finished, tragedy struck in the form of a

Centerfield Church. (Utah State Historical Society)

diphtheria epidemic. Death visited nearly every family—some two or three times. It was especially hard on the children and many died.

The Centerfield Elementary School was built in 1941 and used for nearly twenty years when the children were then taken to the Gunnison Elementary School. The Centerfield school was destroyed by fire. The present town hall was also used as a school and community center from the time it was built in 1908 until the elementary school was built behind it in 1941.

On 10 June 1891 school was let out and the children walked to the Rio Grande Western railroad tracks to watch the train make its first run through Centerfield. A siding called "Grove" was put in early in the 1900s to help with the loading of farm produce.

In August 1897 the front of the Fields rock church neared completion. It still stands with its distinctive mansard roof. Andrew C. Fjeldsted was sustained as bishop and Sylvester Whiting and Charles E. Embley as counselors of the Centerfield Ward in 1897.

The following are some of the events and businesses important in Centerfield's history. Centerfield was granted a post office in 1898 and was operated out of a private home for seven years. About 1904 A. L. Fjeldsted bought a store on the east side of the highway from John Edwards and the post office was located in the store.

In 1909 the Gunnison Telephone was incorporated and lines to Centerfield and Axtell were hung on Mountain States poles for a rental fee of ten cents per pole per year.

High school basketball games were played in the Centerfield Opera House in 1912. The Walter Christensen's Stock Company put on plays in the Opera House. The Opera House had a curtain painted with a beautiful forest scene that rolled up with ropes. Later the Opera House was used for roller skating and dances—especially those held at Christmas and on the Fourth of July. The Opera House burned down on 5 October 1927. The fire destroyed the barber shop, a confectionery, and a pool hall. Brooksbanks Photography Studio was located to the north of the Opera House. Also north of the Opera House was a grocery store run by Henry Stiminson.

Another store was located across the street. James Beck had a store just south of the Old Rock Church. The Barlows bought it after Beck died. All the old stores used their own script. Eggs were brought to the stores and exchanged for goods and script.

Centerfield received electricity in 1913, and a culinary water pipeline was laid from a spring north of Mayfield in 1914. In 1922 the old streets were graveled and street lights were installed. Sidewalks appeared in 1924 and major improvements of the water system occurred in the 1930s.

In 1919 Alred L. Fjeldsted built a joint bank and theater building on the east side of the highway in Centerfield where S&H Heating is currently located. Many stock company shows, local plays, and silent movies were performed and shown in the theater. After Fjeldsted's death, the bank merged with the Gunnison Valley Bank in 1926.

On 19 September 1919 everyone assembled at the newly con-structed sugar factory for the grand opening. The factory was located south of Centerfield. Wages were forty cents an hour, and during one eighty-eight-day campaign, 43,307 tons of beets were processed. The sugar factory was controlled by William Wrigley, Jr., the gum manufacturer. He made extensive improvements and the railroad spur was officially known as Spearmint. Many benefits were realized from the sugar industry as farmers had a handy market for their sugar beets and as many as 200 men were employed during the sugar campaign.

Centerfield is primarily an agricultural village dependent on water development. An early water venture was the New Field Canal Company organized in 1878. It brought water west to Gunnison Valley from Twelve Mile Creek. Locals participated in the building of Gunnison Reservoir beginning in 1889 and the forming of the Gunnison Irrigation Company in 1888, capitalized with $250,000 in stock. The Gunnison Highland Canal Company of 1896 further expanded local storage and irrigation systems. Grain and alfalfa hay were the town's major crops and enough was raised to maintain an export business. In the early-to-mid- twentieth century, sugar beets, cabbage, and peas were successful, along with beef and turkey. High quality, purebred milking cows and bulls were imported from the eastern states staring in 1913 to strengthen a local dairy industry commenced about 1905. By 1947, 80,000 pounds of milk products were being shipped out daily from the local creamery. Beef cattle did well on the lush fields of wild hay, although thieving was common. After the Willow Creek Grazing Association was started, the strain of beef stock was upgraded and production improved considerably. As the amount of local hay, grain, and beet pulp increased, so did the feed to cattle. The timely arrival of the railroad brought wealth to Centerfield's productive farmers and stock raisers. The same became true of the poultry business, especially after the formation of the Utah Poultry Association in 1922 energized the industry. Many began raising chickens and turkeys in large numbers. Some, including Mr. and Mrs. B. K. Tuft of Centerfield, pioneering new poultry raising methods that revolutionized the business in Sanpete County.

Chester

Close to the geographic center of the county and the only town located in the Sanpitch River bottomlands, Chester is situated at the rural crossroads of Utah 117 and 132, four miles south of Moroni and about five miles west of Spring City, a little west of Highway 89. Unlike Sanpete's largest towns, Chester is a collection of widely scattered homesteads reminiscent of farming ares in the eastern and midwestern states. Since its founding in 1870, Chester's population has varied from about 170 to 270. Known as "The Bottoms" and called Chesterfield by David Candland, one of its first settlers, the name was shortened to Chester in 1877 by the postal department. Candland and Hans Beck first homesteaded the area of lush wild hay in 1870 but due to Indian troubles, did not move their families there until 1875. Using a "brush puller" of logs and iron teeth, the colonists removed the sagebrush and ran water from the river to their newly planted wheat fields. In addition to the river, springs were abundant and some incorporated them into their homes. Thanks to the plentiful water and the virgin soil, agricultural pursuits were successful.

As settlements upstream began taking more water out of the Sanpitch, it was decided a reservoir was needed to protect Chester's interests. Hans Beck led the effort to build the reservoir in 1879. It was so successful that four others were built thereafter. The Chester-Sanpitch Canal Company (later the Chester Irrigation and Ditch Company) was organized in 1891. In 1900 three brothers, Henry, George, and James Sumsion, English converts from Springville, arrived and founded a construction company.

An LDS ward was founded in Chester in 1878 with Reddick N. Allred its first bishop. Three years earlier a Sunday school had been established, conducted under an open-air bowery. Ellen Armstrong was the first teacher in the village's initial school held in a log cabin. Taking advantage of the town's stone masons such as Joseph Bagnall and Lars Christensen, a rock school house was erected in 1893 and served for ten years before growth required a new school, constructed of brick in 1904. This multi-purpose building was also used for church, civic meetings, and socials. After twenty years of fundraising, a modern church meetinghouse was built in 1961. The building was razed twenty years later as the Saints were absorbed into a ward in Moroni. The 1893 rock edifice also was razed, but it was moved stone-by-stone and rebuilt in Spring City as a private residence by Paul and Ann Larsen. As the population later decreased and new schools were built in Moroni, Chester's students were transported there.

The first telephones came to Chester in 1912, followed by an electrical power system in 1930. In 1915 the ward built a recreation hall with a hardwood dance floor, stage, kitchen, and banquet facilities. Known as "The Hall," it was popular as the main social gathering place.

Joseph Bagnall built the town's first store, followed by a larger one established by Charles Allred. Here the postal and telephone offices were located. The store was also run by Wilford Allred and Sam Martin, but after the latter's death, Chester was without a store. The Chester Cash-Store was opened in 1942 and the hamlet still has a store at the crossroads today. It seems the town did not benefit much commercially from being linked to a branch of the Utah Southern Railroad in 1880. A line of the Denver & Rio Grande came into town in 1890, allowing for the export of crops and stock. Much as it does today, the early economy depended on farming, stock raising, and related businesses such as the Chester Creamery. A pea vinery was built in 1924, sending peas to the Ephraim Canning Company eight miles south for canning. By the mid-twentieth century, Chester's population had dropped to 170 but it survived on the strength of its sheep, Hereford cattle, dairy, poultry and hay production. In 1981 the Sutherland Dairy relocated from overcrowded Utah County to the Chester area.

Christenburg

Christenburg has been described as "a dispersed hamlet in Gunnison Valley at the confluence of the Antelope Valley to the north and the Sanpitch River northeast which leads through low hills into Sanpete valley." It was settled by three Christensen brothers—Herman, Julius, and Theodore, and their families. The settlers had some early success at raising and selling large crops of fruit, but eventually the site proved too cold for reliable fruit production. The area was also once a major raiser of local Cotswold-Marion sheep. For a time a chalk mine extracted the resources of Landmark Chalk Hill, and a roller miller produced fine flour from 1895 into the 1920s. After being bypassed by a highway realignment in the 1930s, the remaining impetus for retaining a community diminished. Descendants of the original families still inhabit the area, relying mostly on alfalfa and grain for their livelihood. Never built on a typical Mormon village grid, Christenburg's spread-out appearance was made more so after the Sanpitch River flood of 1983 washed through its bottomlands.

Clarion

Located three miles west of Gunnison, only a few graves with Hebrew characters remain of a failed Jewish experiment to live cooperatively in Sanpete. Clarion's history may be the most unique, though short-lived of Sanpete's villages. Taking advantage of a farming district called West View watered by the West View Canal started in 1895, members of the Jewish Agriculture and Colonial Association of Philadelphia purchased 6,000 acres from the State of Utah and planned a new settlement. A preparatory group of Benjamin Brown and ten others first arrived in 1911. Over the next few years, eighty-one families, urban Jews joining the "back to the soil" movement of the time, tried the experiment of leaving their city ghettos to live off the land.

The settlers built homes, a school house, and a common store house, and put 1,500 acres under cultivation. Each family lived on a forty-acre parcel, all strung out along the north-south-running road through town. The meager crop the first year was still cause to celebrate a Harvest Day on 18 August 1912. Under a large bowery erected for the occasion, Governor William Spry praised the Jews for their accomplishments. By the spring of 1913, 213 people lived in Clarion, sharing machinery, buying and selling cooperatively, and expanding the tilled land to 2,400 acres. Their efforts were thwarted, however, by a broken canal which flooded their fields, and an early frost. During the third year, insufficient water, some of which was said to have been drawn off illegally by other farmers, resulted in a third year of poor crops.

Although some remained encouraged by the hope of exploiting waters from the State Canal of 1913–16 and the promised Paiute Canal, most left in 1915 with the enterprise failing to achieve its goals, despite seemingly interminable toil. Aside from the obvious

Governor William Spry speaking at a harvest celebration in Clarion on 18 August 1912. (Utah State Historical Society)

culture shock, Clarion's residents suffered from inexperience, inadequate water, under capitalization, and internal dissent. Alkaline soil and the deaths of two infants and an adult, Binder, further dampened Clarion's spirits. The post office, opened in 1915, closed the next year. Unable to make its loan payments, the colony declared bankruptcy in 1917. A few stalwarts stayed on into the 1920s but finally left, fearing that their children would lose their Jewish heritage through assimilation in the local culture.

The best known Jewish name identified with the settlement of Clarion is that of Maurice Warshaw, founder of the Grand Central chain of retail stores in northern Utah. Benjamin Brown was the founder of the Utah Poultry Producers Association, considered by many to be the foundation of the significant egg, chicken, and turkey industries in Sanpete in later years.

The book on Clarion was not closed with the departure of its Jewish settlers. They sold their land to local Mormon farmers who either moved into the homes or moved them to Gunnison, Centerfield, or Redmond. By 1919 an LDS branch had been established to serve the 140 members who met in the old schoolhouse. Growth continued and a ward was created in 1925. P. L. Frandsen was both the first presiding elder and bishop. The ward lasted until 1934, but a prolonged drought starting in 1933 caused the Mormons to also abandon the place. In 1921 several Japanese families moved into area. They were successful at truck farming, raising lettuce, cabbage, cauliflower, and celery, along with grain, sugar beets, hay, and peas. By the middle of the twentieth century, Clarion was described as one of the richest farming sections in the valley. World War II, however, again changed the dynamics of the population.

Few people live in the Clarion area now, although the best land is still cultivated. Some of the old houses remain in deteriorated condition, along with concrete foundations of others which have been moved. In the little cemetery are two graves with inscriptions in Hebrew.

Dover

After its founding by a substantial group of forty-five families in 1877–78, Dover flourished on the bench land west of Fayette across the Sevier River. The settlers first depended on spring water to irrigate the good soil but soon dammed the river to bring in additional water. The town's future seemed even brighter after the West View Canal was dug. By 1879 a one-room multi-purpose meeting house had been erected of adobe and a post office had been established. A branch of the LDS Church was organized with William Robinson as branch president. Two general stores, one a cooperative, operated in healthy competition with payments often made with "in kind" goods. Still an active community at the time Utah achieved statehood, townspeople celebrated the important occasion by exploding dynamite with a well-driving hammer (in the absence of a cannon). The hammer, however, blew apart and injured several people, dampening the ceremony.

While most other Sanpete towns managed to survive the droughts and Depression of the 1930s, Dover did not. Doverites lost land to the waters of the same dam and reservoir built by Millard County interests that caused Fayette residents to abandon this area. The others left due to the droughts which were especially severe in Gunnison Valley. While droughts destroyed the town's agricultural livelihood, epidemics of the time deflated their spirits. Out of necessity, the people sold their property if they could and moved away, some taking their houses with them. Other buildings were torn down for salvage as the town soon became a "ghost town." Some concrete foundations and deteriorated frame structures remain, along with an unmaintained cemetery, but these humble remnants belie Dover's now-forgotten half-century as a viable Sanpete village.

Ephraim

Isaac Behunin and his family were the first to live on Pine (or Cottonwood) Creek in 1852. Though he claimed forty acres and built a dugout where he and his wife and nine children spent the winter of 1852–53, he moved to Manti in late 1853 for protection against the Indians. When others like Calif G. Edwards tried to settle nearby, Behunin discouraged him, claiming there wasn't enough water. Since the Behunins' effort was an individual one rather than one of collective or group community building, and since there was no continuity between their short stay and the serious village-making that started in 1854, one might best chose 1854 as the year Ephraim was founded.

In February 1854 James Allred left the fort at Manti with approximately fifteen families, including Isaac Behunin and family, and moved seven miles north to Pine/Cottonwood Creek. With Allred and some of his sons presiding, the groups started a fort and named the place Fort Ephraim. The Allreds stayed until the spring of 1859 when they moved back to Spring Town where they had originally settled in 1852. Many of the Danish immigrants who had fled to Manti also moved to Ephraim and stayed after the Allreds left. They enclosed a 1.5 acre lot where the Ephraim Co-op and tithing office now stand. The first fort, the Little Fort, had walls seven feet tall with cabins on all four sides. Included in the fort was a church-school, Seventy's House, bowery, sawmill, tannery, tithing office, and stone cutters shop, among others, built of logs, adobe, and stone. The creek ran in, through, and out of the fort in two little streams.

In spring the colonists planted fields of wheat, oats and potatoes north and west of the fort, and vegetable gardens inside the fort. Isaac Behunin built the first sawmill on Pleasant Creek and a road was put up the canyon for retrieving logs. On 4 August 1854 Henry Beal was elected the first magistrate of the Fort Ephraim Precinct. Mormon priesthood groups were organized the same year, just as a new influx of Danish converts arrived. Most went to Ephraim, while the others located in Manti. The Little Fort proving too small, a much larger Big Fort enclosing seventeen acres, including the Little Fort, was built. Its north wall was fourteen feet tall and four feet wide at the top, built of stone. Finished in 1855, the other walls never reached more than seven feet high as the fort was never attacked directly. The forts gave protection and some stability, as did the stone tower on nearby Guard Knoll from which observers could watch activities in the valley. These safeguards were not foolproof, however. Ambushes in October 1865 cost the lives of several whites in Ephraim Canyon. In financial terms, the new fort cost $13,000 and many hours of cooperative effort, diluting the farming effort. Constructed across a sizable creek, the platted Fort Ephraim offered protection and some modest growth outside of the fort until the end of the Black Hawk War in 1872. So many Danish immigrants sought refuge in Fort Ephraim that they comprised a majority by 1860.

The first years were hard times as the pioneers struggled to irrigate, farm, log and feed new immigrants in the face of Indian raids and devastating grasshopper attacks such as the one in 1854 which devoured many crops.

From 1854–59 and again in 1866, Spring City's and Mount Pleasant's losses were Ephraim's and Manti's gains as settlers flocked to the strongest forts for protection. Some who arrived never returned, choosing instead to stay in the safer confines of the larger communities. Ephraim's growth increased after the arrival of Canute Peterson and the end of the last Indian-Mormon war. People moved out to the townsite, surveyed in 1860, and built houses and outbuildings.

Ethnic, economic, and water conflicts among the Mormons eventually caused church leaders in Salt Lake City to send outsider Canute Peterson, a Norwegian, to serve as the fourth bishop. Arriving from Lehi in 1867, his strong leadership helped bring an end to hostilities with the Indians and within the white community. Growth and prosperity followed. Ephraim became an incorporated city in 1868. In the 1870s the Saints built an impressive tabernacle, a two-

Ephraim Main Street. (Utah State Historical Society)

story co-operative store, a large granary, and a city hall, all of well-crafted limestone.

With Brigham Young's selection of Canute Peterson to serve as Sanpete's first stake president in 1877, Ephraim became the seat of the church for the county's Mormons. It also made possible the creation of the Sanpete Stake Academy, a church-sponsored educational venture promoted by Peterson and others in Ephraim. After a humble beginning with classes held throughout town and in the second floor of the co-op, the school moved into what came to be called the Noyes Building, a stately, neo-classical structure and the first building on the academy's new campus east of downtown. After the church turned the school over to the state in 1932, it became an accredited two-year college and its name was changed to Snow College. The school now has a campus of more than 120 acres, a full-time faculty and staff of about 220, and a student enrollment of 2,740. The economic impact of the college in Ephraim rivals that of agriculture—the longtime economic mainstay. It has also brought youthful enthusiasm, diversity, and networking to various statewide programs and institutions. The growth of the college has gradually altered the composition of Ephraim's population which by 1880 had reached about 90 percent Scandinavian.

Throughout most of its history, Ephraim has competed unsuccessfully with Manti and Mount Pleasant, its north and south-flanking members of the "Big Three" triumvirate, for the status of being Sanpete's most populated city. Finally, in 1960 Ephraim surpassed the other two in size and it has gradually increased its lead since, reaching 3,363 citizens in 1990. Ephraim has competed successfully in other ways through the years. While Manti became the seat of county government and Mount Pleasant captured Wasatch Academy, Ephraim became the home of Snow College, As it grew, Ephraim's grid of square, platted blocks and wide streets filled with fine homes and outbuildings. Main Street—also U.S. Highway 89—developed a significant commercial district with a great variety of stores and shops, a new stone city hall, stake center (replacing the tabernacle), a Carnegie library, social hall, tithing office, theater, bank and hotel. Most of the buildings are still in use. Despite efforts to raze the vacant Co-op and stone granary, they were saved and restored. The co-op returned to its original use—a cooperative handicraft store with a public meeting hall above. The three-level granary became the home of the Central Utah Art Center. The social hall was also restored, and several historic homes have been converted into bed and breakfast establishments. To celebrate the town's Nordic heritage, a few locals started a Scandinavian festival in 1976. It is still held every year on the weekend before Memorial Day and draws many out-of-towners and former Ephraimites to enjoy events held on Ephraim Square.

Fairview

Located at the confluence of the Sanpitch River and Cottonwood Creek, Fairview is the largest town in the northeast end of the Sanpete Valley. Founded in 1859, soon after the resettlement of nearby Mount Pleasant, Fairview was one of the first towns established during the second wave of Mormon settlement in Sanpete Valley. Receiving permission from Brigham Young, Warren P. Brady, Jehu Cox, and several others planned the colonizing of what was first called North Bend in October 1859. Twenty families led by James N. Jones joined the venture, and by the end of 1860, a townsite had been surveyed and a large log meetinghouse had been erected to accommodate early church, school, and social functions. Rows of poplars were planted, streets were graded, and fences were constructed as North Bend took on the appearance of the ubiquitous Mormon village. In 1864 the town obtained a post office and forsook its original name in favor of the more descriptive name Fairview, because it "commands an excellent view of the great granary extending south even beyond Manti, thirty miles distant."

During the Black Hawk War of the 1860s, some Fairview residents moved to Mount Pleasant for protection after a few men were killed in deadly skirmishes. Those who remained complied with Brigham Young's instructions to build a fort. By the end of 1866, a thick rock wall ten feet high enclosed the center of town. Within a few years, the conflict was essentially over and aggressive settlement and community development commenced. In the course of the ensuing decade, Fairview's population burgeoned to more than 1,000, making it the fourth largest in Sanpete by 1880. In 1900 and again in 1940, the town exceeded 1,700 people; however in 1980 the population had declined to just 916, ranking Fairview sixth among the county's twenty or so active communities.

Fairview shared with its neighboring villages the fact of its Mormon origin and governance, together with its significant ethnic makeup. Yet by 1880 Fairview had the smallest percentage of foreign-born, married adults (50.3 percent) of any of Sanpete's major towns in a county which averaged 72.2 percent foreign-born. Fairview was distinctive in other ways as well. Initially the "child" of larger Mount Pleasant only six miles to the south, Fairview eventually became its rival, competing vigorously for land, water, timber, grazing rights, and a fair share of church and government funds. The town's Mormon bishops sometimes found themselves in the center of bitter disputes with leaders of other communities, much to the dismay of local apostle and stake president Orson Hyde, who was assigned to arbitrate disputes and settle contentions.

Yet despite their strong-willed and independent natures, the people of Fairview took full part in the cooperative society of their times. In 1874 they enthusiastically followed church counsel and established a United Order. Stock certificates (7,500 shares) were sold at $10 each to fund the enterprise. But like most of the other orders in the territory, Fairview's was doomed to rapid failure. Poor crops and under-capitalization nearly forced its demise in 1874 after only a few months of existence. Despite gallant and creative efforts to keep it alive, the order was discontinued by 1876.

Fairview's economic base has always depended largely on agriculture and the livestock industry. Following trapper Barney Ward's lead, irrigation ditches were dug and reservoir sites identified soon after settlement. Food crops, hay, and grains were planted, and, in 1870, the town's first flour mill was constructed south of town. Livestock raising, ranging from beef and sheep to chickens and turkeys, has persisted throughout the town's history. Because of its proximity to canyon forests, sawmills were established in the early decades to support a lumber industry and a healthy export business. By the turn of the century, there were half a dozen steam sawmills in the mountains east and north of town.

Beginning in the 1860s, Fairview developed a one-street commercial district along the old territorial road running through the middle of town. In 1869 a Zion's Cooperative Mercantile Institution or ZCMI was started. Other stores, shops, and businesses followed, so that by 1900, Fairview's downtown could boast of a library, several general stores, a furniture store, creamery, harness shop, butcher shop, and two hotels. In 1881 a Presbyterian mission school was founded, with a chapel being erected in 1894. A good public school system was established in the 1890s; 498 of Fairview's 1,800 population in 1898 were students. Recreational needs were accommodated in a social hall and the Eclipse Pavilion.

The arrival of the Denver and Rio Grande Western Railroad in the 1890s bolstered Fairview's ability to import equipment and export its surplus goods, immensely benefitting the town's economic strength as it did for other Sanpete communities. Fairview's fortunes rose and fell with the cycles of the regional economy after the railroad-enhanced boom and its population high-water mark in 1900, however.

The twentieth century brought diversified businesses and industries, including dairies, roller mills, coal mines, and fur ranches. The Fairview State Bank was organized in 1914, reflecting the optimism of the local economy. Yet as Fairview approaches the threshold of the twenty-first century, agriculture and livestock raising remain the dominant ways of making a living. Unlike other parts of the county where cattle and turkey raising are the leading cash producers, sheep continue to outpace all other economies in Fairview, accounting for 46 percent of the farm and ranch operations in northeast Sanpete County.

Like most of the other towns in the county, Fairview has a rich architectural legacy. The many remaining historic structures not only inform us of the varied types of materials, crafts, and styles employed by Fairview's forebears, they also remind us of the many kinds of activities that gave the town its past and present nature. The two 1920s-30s masonry meetinghouses, replacing simpler, earlier edifices, speak of the continuing Mormon presence, while the two-story rock school (now the Fairview Museum) and brick town hall suggest something of the town's bygone stature. The Fairview Roller Mills, one of the most picturesque industrial buildings in the county, is a monument to the agrarian foundation of Fairview's existence. Impressive business buildings remain clustered along Main Street, while houses and outbuildings of every type, style, and material dot the blocks to the east and west. Long gone are the log meetinghouse, store fort, tall rows of poplars, and the Sanpete Infirmary (or "Poor House"), but remnants of the rural landscape remain which identify key elements of Fairview's history and present character.

Fayette

Although it is located only about five miles north of Gunnison, Fayette was settled out of Springville in Utah County. Fayette's founders did not know the place prior to seeing it for the first time. In the spring of 1861, the families of James Mellor and Joseph Bartholomew packed their belongings into ox-drawn wagons and headed south looking for a new place to live. In a few days, after traveling into Juab Valley and then into the northwest reach of Sevier Valley along the west edge of the Sanpitch Mountains, they arrived at a small stream. Because of its high temperature, they called it Warm Creek. They bridged the creek, then moved on to Hog Wallow (Gunnison). Finding it too crowded for their liking, they turned around and headed back to Warm Creek and its nearby abundance for grass, water, fish, and game.

The Springville presence was increased in 1864 when Brigham

Fayette Meetinghouse. (Utah State Historical Society)

Young called John E. Metcalf to move to Warm Creek and build a flour mill along the never-frozen stream. He arrived in 1866. Following the advice of Apostle Orson Hyde, they changed the name to Fayette, in honor of Fayette, New York, where the Church of Jesus Christ of Latter-day Saints was organized in 1830. Another apostle, George A. Smith, encouraged the families to survey lots, obtain a grant for their townsite, and divide the land and water among themselves. Eventually six blocks, all in a row, were developed in the low-density form that exists today.

Abandoned during the Black Hawk War, the colony was reoccupied in 1868. Mrs. Palmer taught the first school; James Mellor operated the first post office; and Joseph Bartholomew ran the first store, later the Fayette Co-op. Fayette grew as irrigation water was brought to town, the first canal being dug by John James and sons who used Warm Creek water to grow crops on the bench north of town. More land was brought under cultivation after a group of Fayette citizens built an extension to the Kearns and Robbins Canal in 1893–94. Fayette's expansion was halted and then reversed during 1910–16 when Millard County irrigation companies, needing to store water, dammed the Sevier River about twenty miles north of town. The new reservoir backed its water over the crop land of many Fayette farmers who felt compelled to sell out and move away. Others stayed and took advantage of the extension of the Paiute Canal on the West Bench. Local citizens created there own irrigation enterprise, the Fayette Canal Company, in 1896.

The hills surrounding town have furnished pasture and range for sheep and cattle and livestock raising, an important local industry. Poultry was raised by the Fayette Turkey Growers who built a plant in the late 1940s. Major local crops were sugar beets, peas, corn, grain, and hay. Milk and eggs have been common products. Although Fayette has never been on a railroad line, it has been within shipping distance of the RGW to the east and the Oregon Short Line to the west. The stone meetinghouse erected in 1875 was razed about a hundred years later and a modern brick meetinghouse stands above the town to the east. It is being expanded in 1998–99. Many of the historic structures remain, including Palmer's Store or the Fayette Mercantile—the town's only commercial building—and some early houses built of red sandstone, brick, and wood-frame construction. Fayette's population today is about 200.

Fountain Green

The area known as Fountain Green, located six miles south of the northwestern county line, was the first potential settlement site seen by the vanguard of Mormon pioneers entering Sanpete Valley in late 1849. Fountain Green was the site of an early-day fracas with Indians in 1853. Four wagons enroute from Manti to Salt Lake City were ambushed by the Utes, and all four drivers were killed. The area before settlement was know as Uintah Springs. Settled in 1859, the town was christened Fountain Green by George W. Johnson because of the water running out of the abundant springs nearby that spread over a beautiful meadow. In later years Fountain Green became an important wool-producing town.

The place called Uintah Springs had been a favorite camping spot for the pioneers traveling into Sanpete County from Salt Lake City via Nephi and Salt Creek Canyon. In fact, virtually all of the 2,000 or so pioneers who had entered the county had seen the springs and the other desirable characteristics of the area. It was not until 1859, how-

ever, that George W. Johnson of Santaquin was called to start a colony
at the springs. He and his son, Amos P., scouted the location in July
and commissioned Albert Petty and his son Heber to plat a survey.
Named Fountain Green by Johnson, the townsite had twenty blocks
of about 4.5 acres each. Johnson returned to Santaquin, packed up
his wife and children, and made the final trip back to Fountain Green
in August. From a grove of quaking aspens, he cut down trees and
built the hamlet's first log house. The Johnsons were soon joined by J.
S. Holman, who built the second cabin, and several others. A log
meeting house was erected in 1860, and in the same year, an irrigation ditch was dug, a post office created and Roberts L. Johnson was
appointed as presiding elder. An LDS ward was created the next year
with Johnson as the first bishop. He also opened the first store and
hotel in town.

Fountain Green remains a fitting description for the lush, green
hillside village abundantly watered by what is now called Big Springs
and Silver Creek which emanates from it. Artesian wells and later
pumped water supplemented the water supply, allowing the development of agriculture and stock raising, the town's economic staples
from 1860 to the present. In 1865 a sawmill was constructed, followed in 1866 by an adobe meetinghouse, and in 1867 a flour mill.
Due to hostilities and one death during the Black Hawk War, the
town was abandoned briefly and a rock fort was erected in 1866.
After peace was made with the Sanpitch and other Ute Indians,
growth and progress continued unhindered, and significant crops of
wheat, oats, and potatoes were harvested.

Although Fountain Green was the first Sanpete community to
receive the railroad in the 1880s, it did not take full advantage of this
opportunity, being the only major town in the region to drop in population between 1880 and 1890. Locals did use the railroad to export
some of their flour, brick, lumber, and food products. Experiencing
less fluctuation in size than most other Sanpete villages, Fountain
Green reached its zenith of about 1,150 people in 1920, about twice
its 1990 size of nearly 600. The town's flourishing in the early twentieth century, during which it was considered to be "the richest town"
in the country, was due mostly to its wool growing industry.
Expanding from a cooperatively owned herd of Spanish Merino

Residents of Fountain Green gather in front of the church house for a celebration. (Utah State Historical Society)

sheep in the 1880s, sheep growers greatly enhanced their profits after upgrading their herds with high wool producing Rambouillet stock. In 1902, 40,850 sheep were owned by twenty-six growers, for an average of 1,571 head each, although some owned far more than others. The Fountain Green Woolgrowers Association was founded in 1908 and became the dominant group in town, with the possible exception of the LDS church, whose members they shared in common. The association crated the nationally famous Jericho Pool of 100,000 sheep, giving Fountain Green its nickname, "Wool City." A celebration called the "City of Lambs Day" is still held annually, although the sheep industry has diminished in importance over the years. In 1987, 47 percent of the farms in northwestern Sanpete County raised turkeys, while only 26 percent still produced sheep, revealing an economic shift from Fountain Green to Moroni, the new center of the county's turkey industry.

From 1869 when a ZCMI store was established along the main highway, a small string of general stores, shops, public and religious buildings has gradually filled in the modest business district. The

ZCMI was initially a profitable venture, delivering a 68 percent dividend in 1870, its first full year of operation. In time, other private co-ops and general mercantiles were founded to give some competition. A general store built of rock in 1880, with an 1884 dance hall and theater addition, was the most impressive of the private commercial structures in the early days. By 1885 Fountain Green formally organized its city government, electing Reese R. Llewllyn as the first town president.

A substantial Mormon meetinghouse, built over a thirty-year period beginning in 1880, was the most prominent religious structure in nineteenth-century Fountain Green. A tithing office built in 1906 and a church-built theater and dance hall erected in 1917 allowed for expanded economic and social activity. The influence of the Mormon church was pervasive, as it remains today, with its Sunday school, Relief Society, choir, children's organizations, and overall concern for the community's welfare and progress. Members of other religious faiths have lived in Fountain Green during much of its history, although no group has managed to establish a permanent foothold. A varied ethnic makeup also helped to shape the town's early nature, with 65.3 percent of its adult married population being foreign-born in 1880.

The twentieth century brought incorporation as a city in 1910, plus several new improvements for Fountain Green including a large elementary school in 1907, an improved water system in 1913 (updated in 1935), a high school in 1920, a city park in 1935, and a state fish hatchery in 1939–40. In recent decades new religious, educational, and business facilities, together with the restoration and new construction of residences, mark the town's continued vitality.

A drive down Fountain Green's Main Street and up its hilly lanes of square blocks to the west helps one understand the community's story. An outstanding collection of historic red brick homes stands witness to the town's once-thriving brick industry and the presence of one of Sanpete's first architects, William Huggins. The two-story elementary school and the fine, restored brick tithing office and theater on Main Street also remain, along with important residence such as the Hans Peter Olsen house (on the National Register of Historic Places). Many of the log, adobe and brick houses are vacant now, but their varied architecture testifies to the ingenuity and talent of their builders. Although there may be more buildings than people in Fountain Green today—evidence of years of gradual out-migration, a trend that seems to have reversed itself in the last decade—the town remains a vital part of Sanpete County.

Freedom

Freedom is located along the road from Fountain Green to Wales, about four miles northwest of Moroni and four miles north of Wales. In 1870 the five sons of William Draper and their families established farms along Current Creek east of the West Mountains. Originally called Draper after the founding polygamist families, the place became a precinct in 1875, formed an LDS ward, and changed its name to Freedom in 1877. The little ward was disbanded in 1881 but reestablished in 1897 after the arrival of the polygamous families of Martin Van Buren Taylor and other families from nearby Moroni. The settlers planted and successfully cultivated orchards—some say the best in the county—and established the Meadow View Creamery. Still, from 1880 through 1950, the population never reached 180 and the ward was discontinued for the final time in 1926. Freedom is most seen now by visitors headed west to beautiful Maple Canyon.

Gunnison

Gunnison is a town settled from both inside and outside of Sanpete County, and, like Mayfield, it was first settled in pieces by different groups. Years before its colonization, the upper Sevier Valley was used as grazing land by the older villages to the north. It was initially settled in 1859 at Brigham Young's behest by a group mostly from Manti. They were joined that fall by a group from Springville. At first, the groups settled in different locations, but they eventually merged into a unified community. The earliest group occupied the south bank of the Sanpitch River at Chalk Hill, about two miles east of the present town. The later-comers formed a camp about three miles west of the first group. Apostle Orson Hyde advised in the spring of 1861 that the two groups join and form a new community. They decide on a place on the north bank of the river on the lowland south and west of the present town. There they created a ward with

H. H. Kearns of Springville as bishop, and called the place Kearns Camp.

Present-day Gunnison began to take its form in 1862 during a resettlement and merging of two fledgling communities starting in 1859. During a visit to the area, Brigham Young counseled the earlier settlers to move out of their smaller, swampy area, "too muddy for a hog's wallow," to the higher and more expansive bench. Following Young's advice, in late 1862 James Mellet and others moved their cabins to the new townsite surveyed into regular eight-acre blocks by Edward Fox. They named the place Gunnison in honor of government explorer and surveyor John W. Gunnison who was killed with six of his men by Pahvant Indians on the Sevier River in Millard County in 1853.

In their new location, the pioneers were now a long distance from water, so the first public task was to dig a ditch from the river to their bench-top village. Early settlement efforts were hampered by difficulties with Indians during the Black Hawk War. Although a few colonists died in skirmishes, an unexpected benefit occurred in April 1868 when some of the people evacuated from the Sevier County settlements relocated permanently to Gunnison.

Building construction was facilitated after 1863 with a sawmill featuring a vertical "pit saw," followed soon after by a horse-powered circular sawmill. A blacksmith shop was started in 1867 by Lorentz Dastrup. Early structures were erected by stonemason Christ Tollestrup, adobe craftsmen Eric Larsen and Harmon Christensen, and carpenter William Christensen.

Concurrent with town building was the commencement of farming. A committee divided up the land, drew up rules, and distributed the land to settlers. The first irrigation system was improved and expanded throughout the valley. Irrigation companies were founded and dams, reservoirs, and canals were built.

Gunnison settlers were coalesced into a more cohesive group by Joseph S. Horne who was sent from Salt Lake City to serve as bishop in 1868. Young and progressive, he directed the creation of a cooperative store, the opening of a rock-salt mine, and the formation of the Farmers,' Gardeners' and Foresters' Club. In 1876 Horne was acknowledged for his role in managing "the building of schools,

Gunnison Main Street, 29 May 1917. (Utah State Historical Society)

meeting and mercantile and private houses, grist and sawmills, salt boilers, in improvements of roads, enlargement of farming lands, extension of planting of trees and other laudable pursuits of home industry."

As in other Sanpete villages, Gunnison's survival has depended on sustaining an agrarian economy. In the nineteenth century, irrigation brought vegetable crops and sugar beets. The success of sugar as an export crop led to the construction of a sugar beet processing factory in the valley. Grain crops, alfalfa and truck farming, together with dairy products, turkeys (for which there is a local processing plant), sheep, and especially beef cattle, have kept the city viable in the twentieth century.

With the coming of the railroad, Gunnison's fortunes prospered and the city's population more than doubled in the decade ending in 1900. As it grew, the town developed as the commercial center of the valley, featuring flour and feed mills, a co-op store, general and specialty stores, and the Gunnison Valley Bank. Religious, civic, and educational facilities were built as the city expanded, including several impressive Mormon and Presbyterian structures in the mid-1880s, a dance hall in 1896, and a new city hall and the stone Washington School in 1899. The telegraph had arrived in 1882, and Gunnison officially became a town in 1893. The turn of the century brought the first telephone to town, and in 1910 a new water system was installed and the first power plant was built.

By 1921 Gunnison and the surrounding environs had grown sufficiently to build a separate high school, a one-story brick facility erected on the east side of Main Street between the south of town and nearby Centerfield. The second half of the century ushered in similar improvements, including a new state corrections facility built north of town. The prison is one of the county largest employers. Gunnison's population has increased gradually since 1970, reaching 1,198 in 1990.

Many of Gunnison's historic sites and buildings are gone, but several important ones remain, including the 1899 city hall, 1909 bank (with a compatible addition), the 1921–23 high school, Hermansen's Roller Mills, the rare, Beaux-Arts style Star Theater, and many impressive residences. Considered together with the newer buildings, the town's architecture conveys a strong sense of the community's past and present. The local talk of the "Big Three" cities in Sanpete County is now sometimes modified to include Gunnison, the center of southern Sanpete, among the "Big Four," although the city actually ranks fifth in size behind Moroni.

Indianola

Indianola, the northernmost community of Sanpete County, was formerly known as Thistle Valley, because of the abundance of thistles which grew there. The general area in which the present community is situated is still sometimes referred to by that name. The elevation is over 7,000 feet, a geographic fact which is reflected in climatic statistics. It is probably the coldest valley in Sanpete. Settled in 1871, Indianola is one of the smallest occupied communities in the county, and it remains entirely agricultural. The community's name is derived from the historic fact that at one time it was a favorite dwelling place for large numbers of Ute Indians. The valley is bowl-like, surrounded by rims of mountains, and is not far from Spanish Fork Canyon, which provides access to both the Utah Valley and the route to Colorado. The mountain peak nearby to the east is still known as Black Hawk Peak, a high point used by the Utes for smoke-signaling. In the Red Cliffs area is an old Indian burial ground. Indianola was also a Ute reservation at one time.

As was the case with several Sanpete settlements, Indianola was first used as a pasture land for pioneer livestock before being permanently established as a town. Colonists from Fairview and Mount Pleasant maintained portable herd houses here similar to the sheepherders' wagons still in use today. Originally called Thistle Valley, the area had been a home for a local Sanpitch band which occupied "Indian Hollow," a protected cove in the southeast part of the valley. An area in the Red Cliffs east of the peak of Black Hawk Mountain was an important Indian burial site. The valley was also a staging ground for a major militia military encampment during the Black Hawk War. Following the killing of the Givens family here in 1865, Captain Albert P. Dewey and his troops were engaged in a day-long battle with Black Hawk and his forces in 1866. It may have been because of these many Indian associations that Thistle Valley (renamed Indianola in 1880 by apostle Erastus Snow) was chosen by Brigham Young as a "perpetual home" for the Indians. But in 1873, the year following the end of hostilities, it became a Mormon town.

Among the area's first settlers were stock raisers Hyrum and William H. Seeley. Others soon followed, built homesteads, and began farming and raising stock. Often church leaders in Salt Lake would send newcomers from outside the county to Sanpete to provide leadership when it was not considered available locally. Thus John Spencer of Payson was sent to Indianola in 1874 to be a missionary and interpreter to the Indians, as well as to organize a ward and serve as its bishop. Due to the sparse population, some pioneers found themselves serving in multiple capacities. Mormon V. Selman, for example, was at one time the Indian interpreter, justice of the peace, road superintendent, school trustee, and presiding elder.

An agricultural, stock raising, and wool growing village, Indianola also developed a few related businesses such as David D. Tanner's dairy and cheese factory. Richard H. Spencer, a merchant and implement dealer, also operated a store, as did Hyrum Seeley, and several men joined together to found a co-op store. A few other shops and stores followed but they are gone now as the remote hamlet never developed a significant commercial center despite the arrival of the Denver and Rio Grande Western railroad nearby. As in other Mormon communities, the church and its various organizations were established and staffed over the years, first meeting in a multi-purpose log meetinghouse and later in the still-extant but vacant brick meetinghouse erected in 1883. Reaching a population of nearly 200 by 1900, with fifty-four students in the area, a new school was built in the same year. It was abandoned in 1934 after which pupils were transported to Fairview.

After the end of the two Mormon-Indian wars, a place was needed to house the surviving local Indians who did not go to the reservation in the Uintah Basin. Indianola became that place in Sanpete County. In 1880, of the village's population of 100, half were Indians. Brigham Young hoped that by establishing an Indian farm, educating and converting the natives, and giving them land for homesteads, they would succeed in assimilating into the Mormon way of life. It was reported near the turn-of-the-century that the "Indians are quiet, peaceable and industrious, pursuing their daily avocations in the same manner as their white neighbors." Young tried to buy the white-owned property and give it to the Indians, but many Mormon settlers would not sell either their land or their water rights. Eventually the Sanpete Utes moved away or died, unable to replenish their numbers with children. As they did, the whites took over the Indian lands although their numbers also dwindled after 1920 for similar reasons. The ward was disbanded in 1926 and church members attended first in Milburn and then in Fairview.

As the county's economy changed in the early twentieth century, so it changed in Indianola. Beginning in 1923, Ray S. Tanner started what would become a major, modern turkey business which flourished for decades. His complex of facilities was enhanced with the arrival of electricity which entered the town in 1946. Many of Indianola's inhabitants now live in newer homes dispersed throughout the valley, especially in the southern end. Mobile homes also are common as the new dwellings are beginning to outnumber the old as the town becomes a bedroom community.

Manasseh

Genesis 48 tells of Joseph adopting his father's sons, Mannaseh and Ephraim, and including them among the Twelve Tribes of Israel. Although the oldest of the two sons, Ephraim was more favored and blessed. Fittingly, the town of Ephraim prospered over the settlement of Manasseh, located four miles due west near the Sanpitch River. Manasseh, in this instance, was the younger of the two, established about 1875 as a satellite of Ephraim. Between them, Manasseh and its neighbor, West Point, were home to about a dozen families in 1880. They built a schoolhouse and hoped to prosper agriculturally from the waters of Excel and Dry creeks. But they were too dry too often and the population found insufficient resources to grow a community. Today one can still find some scattered homesteads with houses, outbuildings, and long-unused hay derricks.

Manti

In 1849, two years after the first Mormon pioneers arrived in Utah, Brigham Young responded to a request from Ute Indian chief Walker, and directed that a settlement be established in the Sanpete Valley.

Young sent men to the valley to explore for water, timber, and a desirable location that could be used as a base for further settlement of southern Utah. The explorers recommended the present site of Manti, and on 19 November 1849 a company of fifty young families comprised of 224 men, women, and children arrived to establish a town.

Isaac Morley, Seth Taft, and Charles Shumway were the ecclestical and civil leaders, and Nelson Higgins represented the military authority. People had been carefully chosen for their skills and were equipped with food, seeds, milling equipment, and tools required to create a successful agricultural community.

Unfortunately, as soon as the settlers arrived, they began to experience severe winter snows which reached three feet in depth. Some settlers huddled in dugouts on the south side of Temple Hill and some protected themselves under wagon boxes. Food began to run out and in January 1850 riders were dispatched to Salt Lake City to secure additional supplies.

The returning wagons became stalled in Salt Creek Canyon where the snow was ten feet deep on the level and twenty to thirty feet in drifts. Supplies were hauled to the settlement on hand sleighs, and in March the snow crusted enough to hold the weight of the wagons which were then brought to the settlement.

Of the 240 head of cattle brought into the valley, only 113 were still alive by spring. The others had starved to death in spite of efforts to clear snow from the grass. With the coming of spring, hundreds of rattlesnakes came out and the settlers overcame another daunting challenge.

Brigham Young agreed with the name "Manti" which Isaac Morley suggested for the new settlement. Territorial surveyor Jesse Fox laid out the town site in 1850, and soon log, adobe, and limestone homes and buildings were being erected.

Manti was incorporated on 6 February 1851, the third community incorporated in the Utah Territory. Earlier Manti was designated the county seat of Sanpete County when the county was created by the territorial legislature on 31 January 1850. Manti had the attention and support of Mormon leaders in matters of religious organization, politics, economic survival, and Indian relations. It was designated the hub for other colonization endeavors in the valley and for other settlements to the south and east.

In April 1851 the first election was held and all "free white male inhabitants of the age of eighteen years" were allowed to vote. Among the elected city officials was Dan Jones, the "Welsh Prophet" and LDS missionary extraordinare, who was voted in as the first mayor. Manti's initial form of government consisted of the mayor, four alderman, and nine council members. By 1853 a post office had been established, and in that year Manti's ranks were swelled by a large group of Danish converts to Mormonism, the "second largest ethnic group to settle central Utah." With many of the first settlers hailing from Great Britain or the eastern states, and others coming later from Norway, Sweden, Denmark, and Switzerland, Manti became an ethnic melting pot.

Manti residents gather on 3 June 1902 to go and fight grasshoppers. (Utah State Historical Society)

To gain protection from Indian attacks during the Walker War, three forts were built in Manti, causing it to be sometimes called Manti Forts. The first was the Little Stone Fort, expanded by the Log Fort and, in 1854, the Big Fort which enclosed nine square blocks. During the war years, the settlers lived in the forts but walked or rode to their outlying fields to farm. Indian raids during the Walker War slowed town development, as did years of devastating grasshopper infestations which greatly reduced harvests. In spite of these privations, by October 1853 the first city census showed that Manti had 647 men, women, and children, nearly three times the number of settlers who had come less than four years earlier.

Among the early improvements were the Log Fort on Block 77 (the first Little Stone Fort occupied the northwest corner of Block 64) and the Big Fort, enclosing nine blocks and erected in 1854. Veteran millwright Phineas W. Cook built the first grist mill, and a sawmill was put into operation by Charles Shumway. During the day irrigation ditches were dug to the Old, Middle, Brigham, Cane, Quarry, and Danish fields, while at night weary settlers still had energy to enjoy Esther Smith's "Amateur Thespians." When not too busy, a few settlers attended the school taught by Mary Whiting. With the construction of the first major public building, the council house, a multiple-use, two-story stone edifice erected in 1855–56, Manti's position as the county seat was made even more secure.

The arrival of the telegraph in 1866 vastly improved communications with the outside world and probably hastened the end of the Black Hawk War as the telegraph improved communications for military operations by the militia. The pioneers were glad for the end of hostilities in 1872 and thereafter moved out from the forts to explore and settle new town sites, expand farming operations, and use the bench and mountain rangelands for feeding livestock—especially cattle and sheep. Because the climate is semi-arid, irrigation was developed beginning in the earliest years. Eventually technology allowed the replacement of the primitive ditch-and-furrow method with modern pressurized piping and sprinkling.

Water presented a different problem starting about 1889 as floods rushed out of the mountain canyons and ravaged the town, causing extensive damage. Overgrazing of the higher rangelands, together with heavy spring run off and storms, resulted in floods during most years through 1905. Despite the creation of the Manti National Forest (now the Manti-LaSal National Forest)—an action specifically requested by the leaders in Manti—and conservation measures over three-quarters of a century, the floods of 1983 washed through the city waterways wiping out the railroad line west of Manti and destroying roads and bridges.

Manti's economy benefitted significantly in 1880 from the arrival of the narrow gauge Sanpete Valley Railway and from the standard gauge Denver and Rio Grande Western Railroad in 1891. The railroad facilitated transportation of people as well as the import and export of manufactured goods and agricultural products. Between 1890 and 1920, Manti reached its population peak of more than 2,500 residents. Its commercial district expanded during the same period.

As Manti grew, it diversified farming and livestock industry production. Starting in the 1920s, poultry became a major enterprise. The early twentieth century brought the Rocky Mountain Packing Corporation's Pea Factory in 1923, the Manti Cheesery in the same year, and the Apex and Peerless hatcheries. An industry developed out of war need was the Reliance Manufacturing Company, a major employer during the 1940s. In recent decades the economy has continued to diversify, as evidenced by the new businesses along Main Street and the modern farming and ranching methods being practiced, which includes several turkey operations.

Still extant are the LDS tabernacle, a stately limestone edifice built between 1879 and 1904, the old city hall and Presbyterian church from the 1880s, the 1910 Carnegie library, and the 1921–22 high school. Long gone are the original forts, the bowery and early churches, the council hall of 1855–56, the original courthouse, the Victorian "Red" school and "White" high school, and the North Ward Chapel. The two-story limestone Manti Grocery Store (co-operative) has been dismantled and rebuilt in Old Deseret Village in Salt Lake City's This is the Place State Park. Also gone is the 1908–1909 Manti Theatre which fell into disrepair in the 1980s.

Without doubt, the finest building erected in the county is the Manti temple. Building was commenced in 1877, the year Brigham Young died, and the same year he created the Sanpete Stake (4 July 1877). The Manti temple looms cathedral-like over the city and is visible for miles in every direction. Designed by architect William Folsom, the temple has been an important religious structure for Mormons throughout central, eastern, and southern Utah since its completion in 1888.

Manti's growth as a municipality was enhanced by several public improvements. The city started a waterworks in 1889 and installed piped water in 1892. The Manti Telephone Company brought in the first telephones in 1907, while Manti Power and Light illuminated the city's homes, businesses, and streets starting in 1910. During the Great Depression of the 1930s, the Sanpete County Courthouse and the former armory, both modern stone buildings, were erected and still remain in service. Manti also hosts the county fair each year, as well as the Mormon Miracle Pageant which attracts over 100,000 visitors annually.

Mayfield

At the mouth of scenic Twelve Mile Canyon, almost in the center of the state, nestles the community of Mayfield at an elevation of 5,575 feet and with a population of 498 in 1999. To the south and east is Musinea, a mountain peak named by Chief Arapeen. If the city fathers had used Indian names, the town would be called "Aw Wan Ah Voo" in Arapeen Valley. Instead they chose Mayfield because of the beauty nature lavishly displays in the month of May.

Long before the arrival of Mormon settlers, the well-watered and sheltered valley was a traditional settlement for Arapeen's band of Utes. Because this was so, Mormon newcomers chose to establish an Indian farm here in an effort to teach the Indians the domesticated skills that made village living successful for whites. The creating of this farm in 1851 may have been a direct response to Chief Walker's request that the Mormons teach his people white ways. Attempts to teach Indians to farm must have born some fruit as the San Pete Indian Farm, the county's first, was converted to reservation-farm status in 1856. Due to a lack of funding and opposition from territorial governor Alfred Cummings, along with crop failures and difficulties in keeping the nomadic Indians on the farm, it was doomed to failure. However, the land is still called "The Indian Farm."

The early settlers encountered considerable trouble with the Ute Indians. Many horses and other livestock were stolen and some lives were lost. Chief Arapeen and many Indian families spent their summers camping on the hill where the chapel now stands, farming and pasturing their horses in the level field on the south side of Twelve Mile Creek on the Indian farm. After the Black Hawk War began in the spring of 1865, Indian families no longer came to Arapeen Valley to live.

The first white settlers came from Gunnison, eight miles to the west, in 1873 and settled on the north side of Twelve Mile Creek which runs through the valley. These early families agreed to live by the rules of the United Order, having all things in common. This practice continued until 1877.

Early in the spring of 1875, twenty-one families moved from Ephraim and settled on the south side of the creek. They called this

The Mayfield Roller Mill, erected in 1882. (Courtesy Ruth D. Scow)

settlement "New London." They built small log homes, rough lumber shanties, corrals, and fences. They dug ditches and canals through almost impregnable rocky crags to carry water to the fields and gardens and for drinking water.

The two settlements combined under the name of Mayfield when an LDS ward was organized 4 July 1877. The LDS church has been the town's most important organization. At first religious meetings were held in homes and Sunday services were held under a bowery.

The north side and south side each had its own schools. A rock school and meeting house built on the north side in 1884 still stands and has been converted into family living quarters. It is one of Sanpete's oldest remaining meeting houses. When the Relief Society Hall was completed in 1885 on the south side, Sunday meetings, weddings, dances, socials, theatricals, and other entertainments were held there. This building has been preserved and remodeled into a home. In 1900 a two-story, four- room brick school was constructed on the site of Arapeen's summer home to serve all the children from beginners to the eighth grade.

The division made by Twelve Mile Creek was more than physical and was encouraged and maintained with vigor. Separate schools and church functions were provided. Each side sponsored a well-practiced ball team, and regular competitive games were played with much excitement, enthusiasm and occasional arguments. There was a time when one hundred families had an average of eight members each. Eight, ten, and even sixteen children to a household were not unusual in the early days.

The first store, a tent stocked with $75 worth of merchandise, grew in proportion with the settlement. Although agriculture was the main industry, the settlers built sawmills from which they freighted ties and timber to mines in Utah and Nevada. Blacksmith shops were busy. A water-powered burr flour mill (later converted into a roller mill) served the entire Gunnison Valley.

After Mayfield was incorporated in 1909, it installed an electrical system in 1911 and its first piped and pressurized water system in 1912. Mayfield is not a small isolated community but an important segment in church, county, state, and national government. Opportunities for education and financial security have taken many of the young people to other locations but they love to come home to visit or retire. A modern school building was erected in 1921 and used until 1956 when all students, first through twelfth grades, were transported to school in Gunnison. The school house has been converted into the Mayfield Community Care Center Nursing Home.

On 10 September 1944 a new LDS Mayfield Ward chapel was dedicated. Ward members were delighted to have their own meeting place after attending church in the schoolhouse for over twenty years. The chapel was remodeled and updated in 1996. Residents of Christianburg attend church in Mayfield and are an important part of community life.

Stores have come and gone, but a new modern store, the Mayfield Merc, serves the community. Mayfield has a beautiful park and a well-kept cemetery. The old post office is now the city hall where council meetings and election meetings are held. A new post office is adjacent.

A well was drilled in 1977 to supplement the city water and in 1984 a new culinary system was installed. That same year a pressurized irrigation system for the city and the fields has added to the economy of the community. A television booster was installed on the white hills west of town to improve reception. Gunnison Telephone gives residents direct dialing service, Utah Power and Light provides electricity, and Questar provides gas for heating furnaces. Mayfield residents use the Gunnison Valley Hospital and the services of eight highly trained doctors and several specialists.

Because of the coal mining in Sevier and Emery counties, some of the young men are able to live in Mayfield and work in the mines. Several of the residents are employed by the Central Utah Correctional Facility in Gunnison. There are also twenty-nine educators teaching in the public schools. A few residents are still involved in agricultural activities as dairy men, stock raisers, and farmers.

Mayfield residents enjoy an abundant life today and owe a debt of gratitude to those who came before. The town's ancestors built well to establish a rich heritage. The people of Mayfield accept their challenge to make their town a better place for those who will follow after them.

Milburn

Situated east of the upper Sanpitch River six miles directly north of Fairview, Milburn occupies one of Sanpete's most pastoral and picturesque valleys. Originally used as herding grounds for the people of Fairview, who built a herd house there in 1865, the narrow, four-mile-long valley was first permanently settled as Dry Creek in 1875 by Richard Graham, his brothers George and John, Thomas Housekeeper and his mother, and Orson M. and Alvin D. Terry. In the following two decades, several others arrived, building along Dry Creek, Milburn's first townsite.

The LDS church was established quickly with Peter C. Jensen serving as presiding elder after moving there in 1879. During the same year, Swen O. and Lars Neilson built the area's first sawmill on Dry Creek Canyon. In the mid-1880s, a two-story cooperative mercantile and social hall was built of limestone by Swen Neilson and Francis Stewart on the east side of the main road. Due to the smallness of the town, the store went out of business by the late 1890s, but its four walls make an impressive architectural ruin today. Never incorporated as a city, Milburn's only public officer in the nineteenth century was Ezra B. Jones, appointed justice of the peace. Despite its small size, a line of the Marysvale branch of the Rio Grande Western Railroad was completed to Milburn in 1890 largely to export timber harvested from the mountain forests to the north and east. Its flag station also made it possible to receive daily mail. In 1894 a red brick schoolhouse was built with separate entries for girls and boys. No longer extant, the school served the district's 88 students. In 1890 Milburn's first Mormon ward was formed with James W. Stewart as bishop, and the village received its first postmaster, Richard Graham.

A pivotal event in Milburn's history was the huge flood of late summer 1902. The flood surged out of Dry Creek Canyon, sweeping through the townsite and destroying its houses and property. Discouraged but not defeated, the people moved away from the townsite and onto individual farms spread throughout the valley, although many had already chosen to establish farmsteads outside of the little town. Talk of building a reservoir to control floods and store water never got beyond the planning stages. From the beginning to the present, farming and livestock raising have been the economic mainstays. Milburn is located at an elevation of 6,350 feet above sea level. Both irrigated and dry farmed grain and hay have been raised. Wool growing and dairy farming also have been successful.

The conveniences of modernity reached Milburn a little later than most places. The first telephone line was extended from Fairview in 1903. Electrical power did not arrive, however, until Christmas Eve 1943, when it was turned on in the LDS chapel finished in May of that year. The church was dedicated 12 February 1944 while Loyal Graham was bishop. The building survives as a residence. Freeman Stewart brought the first automobile to town in 1915. Whenever it has had a ward or a branch, Milburn has maintained a full complement of Mormon organizations, auxiliaries and activities. During World War I, the Milburn Relief Society sold 20,706 pounds of wheat for $547.79 and later built its own hall. In 1932 it was decided to transport the area's students to Fairview rather than hold classes in the brick school. Over the years many of the town's younger generations have moved away, keeping the population small. In 1961 after the number of LDS church members had declined to thirty-three, the ward was dissolved and the members were asked to attend the Fairview Ward.

Moroni

In the spring of 1859, a party from Nephi, consisting of George Washington Bradley, J. W. Wolf, Isaac Morley, H. Gustin, Neil Cummins, and N. O. Christensen, selected a location for a colony in the lowlands along the Sanpitch River. This was later moved into the hills in the center of the location and was eventually named Moroni. Originally, it was called Sanpitch, for the local chief of the Utes, and then Mego, for another Indian. In its history the site has also been called Duck Springs and Little Rome (because of its settlement on seven or more hills). The name "Moroni" has always been its "official" name, however, derived from the name of a major figure in the Book of Mormon.

Because the area was fairly flat and more convenient for digging irrigation ditches, the pioneers first developed a townsite southwest of their first camp along the river. The plan was to divide a one-square-mile plat into five-acre blocks of four lots per block. After building dugouts in the river banks and log cabins on the flat, a dam was built and a three-mile-long irrigation canal was dug to convey water to the farm land. By 1862 a log bridge had been erected, a road graded, and a flour mill and meetinghouse built. As progress became evident, settlers from more populated Sanpete colonies moved to newly renamed Moroni.

Within a year of settlement, Moroni colonists built a one-room, multi-purpose structure of adobe, but it collapsed during a heavy snow storm in 1862. The improvements made at great effort would come to naught, however. In 1862 the friendly river which had attracted and fed the settlers, overflowed its banks, flooding the town, its fields, canals, and ditches. It reduced to a pile of mud the multi-purpose meetinghouse, itself made of sun-baked adobe mud. It was a matter of good common sense for Brigham Young to instruct the Moroni Saints to give up their river bottom site for a new one on the low hills to the north and northeast. The tedious and redundant work of relocating and reconstructing their town commenced at once.

Millwright Charles Kemp erected a flour mill in 1861–62 and a new log meetinghouse was built for worship, school, town meetings, and socials. In 1863 a salt refinery was built as one of Moroni's first export industries. In the same year, progressive Moroni became the new county seat and George Bradley was appointed Sanpete County's probate judge. After only ten months, however, the seat was moved back to Manti. Early farming efforts were successful, and by 1864 Moroni was selling flour to Salt Lake City for $20 per hundred pounds. At the same time, crops failed in some of the lower land due to frost and "saleratus," necessitating the development of new fields to the west and north. During the Black Hawk War, Moroni erected a stockade with a stone bastion and observation tower. The people of Wales and Fountain Green moved into the fort due to hostilities in the spring of 1866. Following the war, the colonists moved out of the fort and began building houses and businesses in the platted townsite. A cooperative store was started in a 13-by-20-foot building. It grew into the Moroni Co-operative which operated out of two large buildings, one of which still stands on the north side of Main Street where other businesses sprang up starting in 1862. A brick industry was started in the late 1860s, and the 1867–68 Jabez Faux house on the west side of town is one of the county's first brick structures.

When the North Sanpete Railroad brought a line into Moroni in 1885, the town became the distribution point for goods, exported products, and mail for the rest of the county. This brought a period of prolonged prosperity as reflected by the many impressive new residential, public, and commercial structures built over the next thirty years. Outgrowing the old log meetinghouse, a new adobe edifice, 45-by-75-feet, was erected and used until it was replaced by the tabernacle in 1889. Designed by Manti temple architect William Folsom, the tabernacle was a magnificent stone masonry structure with a tall, central tower and steeple. A labor of love, it took eleven years to complete. It is no longer extant, falling victim to fire. To satisfy the recreational desires of those with new-found leisure time, a dance hall was constructed by a group of men in 1890. In 1891 Mons Monson and T. J. Morley erected the "best-equipped opera house in the county," a 35-by-85-foot structure with a 35-by-25-foot stage, a balcony, and a seating capacity said to be 1,000. This Monson House and the later

Armada Theater were popular play and movie houses until they closed in 1915 after William Call built the Kozy.

Improvements and growth in Moroni continued after the turn of the century. Irrigation companies were formed, electric power was brought to town in 1902, and the Bank of Moroni was founded in 1905. A telephone system was installed in 1912 and an improved water system was constructed the following year. A boon to the local economy was the sugar refinery erected in Moroni in 1916–17. It lasted only until 1937, but by then the poultry business was growing rapidly and taking up the financial slack. The Moroni Feed Corporation built a large turkey processing plant south of town in 1935 and has expanded its operations ever since. The plant is one of the largest producers in the United States and is one of Sanpete's major employers. It has also brought a new ethnic flavor to the area as it has attracted a sizable number of Hispanic workers. In late 1920 Moroni was divided into two LDS wards, the East and West. The former built a new, Colonial-style chapel in 1926–27, now in use as the city hall. Continued growth brought the formation of the Moroni Stake in 1929. The LDS church and all of its programs remain active in Moroni, now the fourth largest city in Sanpete County with a population of 2,092 in 1990.

Morrison

Located two to three miles east of Sterling, Morrison was a small mining town in the 1890s. A narrow-gauge branch line of the Rio Grande railroad was extended into the camp in 1894–95 for the purpose of extracting coal from the Morrison Mines first established in 1888. Coal was first discovered in the Sterling area in 1887 by several experienced miners from Wales on the other side of the county. The Edmunds Mine, named after Wales resident Edmund Edmunds, was worked first. In 1894 the Sterling Coke and Coal Company was organized by persons connected with the Sanpete Valley Railroad. The railroad was built from Nephi to the mines, including the Edmunds which the company purchased.

During the twenty years of mining activity, several substantial homes and mining structures were built at Morrison as families lived there year-round. In more typical mining camp style, frame homes were scattered along narrow canyon roads, unlike the orderly Mormon villages in the flatter valley floors below. Other buildings were constructed to service the mines and miners. Eventually water flooded the mine and it became too expensive to remove it. Because of this problem and the fact that coal could be less expensively obtained elsewhere, the town was abandoned and the spur was removed in 1907. Other local men spent considerable time and money to resurrect the mine but to no avail.

Mount Pleasant

During the winter of 1851–52, Madison D. Hambleton and Gardner Potter left Manti to build a lumber mill on Pleasant Creek. The next spring a half-dozen families under their direction also left Manti to found a new colony.

They located on both sides of Pleasant Creek below, or northwest, of where the present town lies. They called the place Hambleton and cleared land a mile north of where the railroad depot later stood on 500 West Main. On 28 June 1852 a precinct was created by the Sanpete County Court. Moving quickly to establish an orderly, well-governed community, two school districts were formed and elections were held in August 1852.

More settlers arrived in 1853, and that summer the first serious Indian troubles erupted, starting with raids on livestock. The sawmill was attacked on 9 July, and on 19 July two Indians were killed in another skirmish. On 23 July a battle at the mill claimed the lives of six Indians killed by militiamen from Provo. The settlers packed up their belongings and moved to the Allred Settlement six miles south. The fifteen families there had built only a crude fort, but it was better than having no fort at all. While they were evacuating, the Indians burned the mill and the lumber left behind. Soon after, the residents of both settlements moved to the superior protection of the Manti Forts. Under guard, some came back to their fields to care for and harvest their crops.

Nothing more was done to occupy the area until mid-August 1858. After the "Big Move Caravan" traveled from Manti to Ephraim, an exploring party was sent north from Ephraim to select a new site for settlement. They picked Pleasant Creek near the former

Hambleton settlement. James Allred and James R. Ivie, Sr., were chosen to go to Salt Lake City to meet with Brigham Young and present a petition asking permission to start a settlement there. Young approved, and upon their return, a colonizing team was assembled. Albert Petty of Manti surveyed a town site 1.5 miles east of old Hambleton, plus 1,300 acres which were divided into twenty-acre farm lots. Planning carefully and deliberately, a group of men met in Ephraim in mid-October to draw lots for the land.

In another Ephraim meeting held in January 1859, James R. Ivie, Sr., was chosen as president of the new settlement. In mid-February a colonizing party—consisting mostly of young Scandinavians moved to a location west of the townsite and pitched camp. Hilda Madsen Longsdorf, in her history *Mount Pleasant: 1859–1939*, lists those comprising this group as Mads Madsen, Peter Madsen, Andrew Madsen, Niels Madsen, Christian Madsen, George Frandsen, Rasmus Frandsen, Christian Jensen lst, Mortin Rasmussen, Peter Mogensen [Monsen], James Larsen Sr., Niels Johansen lst, Alma Allred, Peter Johansen, Niels Widergren Anderson, Christian Widergren Anderson, Mickel Christensen, Soren Jacobsen, James C. Meiling, and Hans Y. Simpson.

After cutting cedar posts and constructing more adequate living quarters than the tents, wagon beds, and dugouts in which they had been living, they sent for their families to join them. The first colonizing party was continually increased, primarily with the addition at the end of April and first part of May of newcomers from Battle Creek (now Pleasant Grove)who included William Stewart Seeley, John Carter, Moroni Seeley, Jesse W. Seeley, Justus Wellington Seeley, Orange Seeley, John Tidwell, George Farnsworth, Harvey Tidwell, Jefferson Tidwell, Nelson Tidwell, George Meyrick, Joseph Coats, and others. In addition, new arrivals included other members of the Allred Family.

The plat was extended by 1,200 acres, and in April James Ivie sent Brigham Young a progress report to which Young responded favorably. In mid-May a meeting was called at which building a fort was discussed, then implemented. The fort was built in a very organized manner, and full records of the time, teams, wagons and men used are still extant. Four supervisors—Jahu Cox, Thomas Woolsey, Sr., W.

S. Seeley, and John Tidwell, Sr.—were in charge of the project with each responsible for one wall. Each leader had three captains under his command, and each captain directed the work of a team or "line" of men. Work on the twelve-foot-high rock walls started in mid-May, and the massive project was finished by 18 July. Inside its walls were 5.5 acres of land with cabins each measuring sixteen feet square, plus platforms for guards at the corners, two big gates, and a stream from Pleasant Creek running through the center. It had the distinction of being the finest fort in Sanpete County.

While some were building the fort, others were working the land. In the first month alone, 1,000 acres were cleared, planted, and watered from several ditches. Grist and sawmills were started at about the same time, and the population burgeoned to 800, then 1,000, as citizens of Mount Pleasant were determined that their town would become a town of importance.

By the time the final peace treaty bringing an end to the Black Hawk War was signed in Bishop Seeley's house on State Street in 1872, many settlers had already erected homesteads outside the fort. Among them were Andrew Madsen and James Hansen. Although the townsite is large in scale, the density is relatively low due to the original layout which allowed for only four lots per block.

The townsite is situated 100 miles south of Salt Lake City and 22 miles northeast of Manti in almost the geographical center of the state. Among the founding settlers were Mormon converts from Scandinavia, the British Isles, eastern Canada, and the eastern United States. By 1880 Mount Pleasant was the county's largest city with a population of 2,000. More than 72 percent of its married adults were foreign-born. This ethnic diversity had an important impact on village life during the nineteenth and early twentieth centuries. For decades, five languages were commonly spoken in town, creating confusing and sometimes amusing communication problems.

Mormon influence was felt in all religious, political, economic, educational, and social aspects of life in early Mount Pleasant. Self-sufficiency was a virtue, and home-grown and home-manufactured food, clothing, and furnishings were far more available than rarely found imported items. Some of the first industries included leather tanning, shoemaking, blacksmithing, basket making, and freighting.

Eventual modernization brought such improvements as the Deseret Telegraph in 1869, *The Pyramid* newspaper in 1890—still the county's largest—and a telephone system in 1891.

Sawmills and flour mills were built, irrigation systems were dug, and a municipal government was created to oversee public laws and improvements. The city was incorporated in 1868, a year after the first cooperative store was founded, starting what became a flourishing commercial district.

From its inception, Mount Pleasant has been a progressive community in terms of providing educational and cultural advantages for its residents. Often the two have been combined. As early as 1860 a small school was convened inside the fort. This soon gave way to more permanent log and adobe buildings which were constructed in each of the four wards of town. One of the first was a red brick building erected on the corner of First West and First North, near where one of the earlier schools had been. This was later remodeled and used as City Hall. Currently it serves as a mortuary.

Eventually a Territorial Superintendent of Public Instruction was named. He was assisted by a county superintendent and, locally, by a board of trustees. Hamilton Elementary School was completed in 1896 at the corner of First East and Main and remained in continuous use until it was replaced by a new elementary school in 1962. One highlight of the academic year at Hamilton was the annual school operetta in which every child in the school had a role to play.

In 1911 the North Sanpete High School District, comprised of the "Common School Districts" of the northern part of the county, was created. By 1912 the first high school—North Sanpete—had been put into use, though some of the rooms were yet to be completed. The county had been divided into two school districts. Although several attempts at consolidating the two into one district have been made, these efforts have consistently failed, though education remains a high priority in both North and South Sanpete districts. In 1957 North Sanpete High School was incorporated with Moroni High School, upper-class students attending school in Mount Pleasant and junior high students in Moroni. Some years later, new buildings for both schools were constructed.

Mount Pleasant has long been considered the most diverse city in the county, in part because of the liberal Mormons and Protestant groups which challenged the dominant Mormon population in the late nineteenth century. Liberal Hall, built on Main Street in 1875 and still existing, and Wasatch Academy, Utah's oldest private boarding school, established by Presbyterians the same year, remain as visible and functional testaments of the city's historic and ongoing diversity. Mount Pleasant has been culturally varied as well, with numerous musical, theatrical, and artistic groups, secret societies and saloons, several businesses, and one of Utah's largest historical societies, founded in 1909 and still active.

Upon the arrival of the Denver and Rio Grande Western Railroad in 1890, both the local population and the city's prosperity increased dramatically. By 1900 Mount Pleasant had grown to nearly 3,000 persons, the largest size reached by any Sanpete city to that time, earning the town one of its nicknames—Hub City.

The city's new-found wealth became immediately apparent— with the help of a major fire on 25 July 1898—in a building boom which saw the replacement of its small wood-frame commercial buildings with much more impressive, architect-designed stone and brick structures such as the 1888 Sanpete County Co-op, the gentile store which competed with ZCMI, the Mormon store. The resulting Main Street district is today so architecturally distinctive that the two-block-long area has been listed on the National Register of Historic Places. Equally striking were the Victorian churches, schools, and residences which replaced the simpler adobe and log buildings of the pioneer period.

The twentieth century brought continued changes and improvements to the face of the "Queen City," its most popular nickname. The commercial and residential districts continued to fill with fine buildings, bespeaking the prosperity of the community.

The year 1912 brought construction of Armory Hall. Elite Theater was constructed as a fireproof building in 1913; it burned down seven decades later. In 1917 a fine Carnegie library was built in the then-popular Prairie Style. Marie Hotel (later renamed Overland) was erected in 1920, and a large cheese factory came on the scene in 1930, the same year that long-distance bus service came to town. The completion of U.S. Highway 89 in 1936 was a boon which softened the impact of the Great Depression. A new City Hall built in 1939 and a hospital in 1945, together with new schools and church buildings, gave Mount Pleasant a full complement of public buildings. Growth has increased in recent decades, as is evidenced by the small new shopping center on the south edge of town.

The northernmost of Sanpete's "big three" cities, Mount Pleasant was well situated near forested mountains, vast, fertile fields, and a good, albeit occasionally temperamental, supply of water. While several commercial and small industrial enterprises have flourished in or near the city since the nineteenth century, agriculture and stock raising have always been the area's economic staples. Currently, nearly half of all the farms and ranches are involved in wool growing, while 30 percent raise cattle. Dairy farming, turkeys, grain, and hay are other significant contributors to the local economy. Rambouilett sheep and shorthorn cattle were prominent at the turn of the twentieth century, while modern livestock breeds and food strains dominate today.

In the late 1990s, Mount Pleasant continues to be a thriving, steadily growing city. New buildings exist side-by-side with many remaining historic structure such as the library, Liberal Hall, Sanpete County Co-op, Jensen, Rasmussen, Madsen, Hansen, and Seeley homes, and the campus of Wasatch Academy. In addition, the commercial district has recently undergone a sensitive facelift. Queen City continues to be a fitting nickname for this delightful town.

Mountainville

Not on today's maps and little known by county residents living outside the northeast section of Sanpete, Mountainville, situated on the little rise between Fairview and Mount Pleasant, was settled by Mormon Battalion veteran Caratat Rowe and others. In the mid-1880s, after obtaining land through the Homestead Act, several families drew water from Birch and North creeks and began irrigating and building a scattered agricultural community. The first log meetinghouse was erected in 1886, followed by a larger one in 1890. A more modern multi-purpose structure was built of brick in 1917–18. The Mountainville Branch of the Mount Pleasant LDS North Ward was established on 11 April 1920. A month later a Relief Society was

formally organized. The Sunday school, Primary, and Young Men and
Women's Mutual Improvement Associations were also active. An LDS
ward was created in 1947 but was disbanded in 1966 after which
members were required to travel to Mount Pleasant for church meetings. Beginning in 1920, students were transported to Mount
Pleasant by covered wagon and, later, a covered truck. So many members of the Shelley Family lived in the place that some called it
Shelleyville.

Mountainville never had a large, gridded townsite but instead
was built up along both sides of the long road going south from
Fairview. Unlike other little villages like Dover and Clarion, however,
Mountainville's buildings and cultivated fields remain. Several interesting houses and large barns dot the landscape as sure signs of the
area's vitality a century ago. Newer structures include vacation homes
and a resort tucked away on brush-covered slopes.

Always an agricultural village, Mountainville's principal crops
were alfalfa, wheat, oats, and barley. Mountainville also developed
dairies and fruit orchards producing apples, peaches, pears, plums,
raspberries, and strawberries. A poultry business was active for many
years, and most people sustained their families with gardens and a
little livestock. A dairy was still operating in the area in the late 1980s.

New Jerusalem

New Jerusalem, or just Jerusalem, is apparently on offshoot of
Freedom, a mile or two to the south. It may also have received some
of its small population from Moroni. Located at the end of a short
road about four miles south and a little west of Fountain Green, New
Jerusalem and its neighboring village, Freedom, are perhaps the most
mysterious places in Sanpete County. They are rarely if ever mentioned in all previous county and town histories. Judging by the age
of the oldest buildings, the hamlet of New Jerusalem seems to date
from about 1915, or the time the Jewish colony was living in Clarion.
Like Freedom, the LDS members have been absorbed into the
Moroni Ward. Most of its farm and range land have been bought up
by interests from Moroni except for a few families who hold on to
their properties along the spring-fed eastern foothills of West
Mountain.

Oak Creek

After the colonization of Fairview and Milburn, farmers began to settle on the land along the road between the two earlier communities. The meadows and rangeland along the Sanpitch River and Oak Creek were used to graze stock removed from the newly created Manti National Forest after 1902. Here Oak Creek was founded and gained most of its population after 1912. Never a typical platted Mormon townsite, the scattered populace was nevertheless sufficiently large in 1916 to merit the formation of an LDS ward. Members met in a building erected as a schoolhouse along the Fairview-Milburn Road. The ward survived only until 1928 when it was annexed into the Fairview. Many of the early twentieth-century homes and outbuildings remain and the area is still farmed.

Pettyville

As Manti's resources dwindled due to growth and overcrowding, some of its citizens looked elsewhere for improved living conditions. In 1873 a group of fifteen families from Manti relocated to a site on the Sanpitch River about six miles southwest of Manti and 1.2 miles west of present Sterling. They were led by George Petty and called the place Pettyville, although it was also known as Buncetown and Leesbury. Pettyville was sited by a reddish foothill of the Sanpitch or West Mountains on Indian reservation land. The settlers occupied the place as squatters, but the Black Hawk War had ended the previous year and there was no serious challenge to their presence. Church meetings were at first held in homes. Although a store and amusement hall were built early on, the settlement was short-lived. It lost most of its occupants, including Petty, its leader, to Sterling after it was formally founded in 1881. Pettyville's houses and other buildings were either moved or dismantled for salvage. Today not even the foundations are apparent as the most of the area has been assimilated into Olsen's cattle ranch west of the old wagon and railroad route and the Highland Canal.

Spring City

The town of Spring City was first settled in 22 March 1852 by James Allred and Elizabeth Warren Allred, their son James T. S.

(Tillman Sanford) and his wife Eliza Bridget, their two daughters, Eliza Marie and Ellen; a son, Andrew Jackson Allred, grandsons George M. Allred, Charles Whitlock, and James F. Allred, and two adopted Indian children. The original group was later joined by Wiley Payne Allred, Reuben Warren Allred, Andrew Whitlock, Eleaser King, a widow Parker and son Frank, Henry Oviatt, and others.

When James Allred and his family arrived in Utah in the fall of 1851, from Council Bluffs, they first proceeded to Manti where their son lived. They considered Manti "overcrowded" even though it had been in existence for less than two years. The Allreds stopped over there for only a few months, just long enough to be protected that winter and to gather provisions. As soon as weather permitted, they moved north, exploring the Canal Creek area in early 1852.

Immediately upon arrival, the settlers began clearing land, planting crops, bringing irrigation ditches to their fields from Canal Creek, and erecting log shelters. Their logs were sawn in a mill by pioneers at Hambleton's Camp, settled just a little later and six miles to the north.

During the summer of 1852 James T. S. Allred made a 100-acre townsite survey which he divided into five-acre lots. That first year 90 acres were fenced in, while 39 acres were cleared of brush and sowed in wheat, corn, oats, potatoes and vegetables. While they were busy building and planting, the local Sanpitch Indians began visiting and complaining about the taking of their land.

Several homes were built during the summer of 1852 including two of adobe. James T. S. had brought his cabin with him from Manti by ox team, although it was probably constructed from Canal Canyon logs in 1851. His cabin was sixteen feet square and could be easily assembled.

Indian problems began for the pioneers nearly as soon as they arrived. This area, blessed by several creeks and springs, was one of their homelands. On one occasion about 300 Sanpitch warriors threatened the settlers as they were tending crops. James T. S. Allred, who spoke their language, pacified them and a temporary truce was established. There were no attacks that first year, though the settlers lived in constant fear.

Wherever the location, surviving the first winter seemed to be the first major test of a colony's survival fitness. The winter of 1852–53 proved to be a severe test for the Allred Settlement due to extreme temperatures and weather, food deficiencies, and crowded living conditions in the few small dwellings. They made it through to spring and, a year after arriving, organized the first Mormon ward, with Reuben W. Allred, one of the six sons, ordained bishop by Brigham Young. The planting cycle began anew, this time on more acreage, but their unstable peace with the Indians deteriorated that summer after the Walker War erupted in Manti in July. Some raids and deaths that month caused settlers in Hambleton to retreat to the Allred Settlement for safety. There the reinforced villagers moved their cabins together and placed rocks between them to craft a hastily completed, makeshift fort.

Previously, in May 1852, President Young had strongly advised the Allreds to maintain a strong fort "for the purpose of securing themselves against attacks from the Indians which council was subsequently found to be very timely. . . ." However, it does not appear that his advice was heeded since the fort was not in place when attacks erupted.

Upon hearing the news in Manti, a relief party was sent to the Allred Settlement where the people were found frightened, poorer, but alive. Seeing the relative defenselessness of their situation, the settlers abandoned their fort and retreated to the greater safety of Manti. Under the protection of the local militia, some of the colonists returned periodically to water and harvest their crops, some of which were salvaged.

Although the Indians returned later and burned down the fort, their attacks resulted in an eventual benefit to the settlement. Two months after the first raid, James Allred and his son, the new bishop, Reuben W. Allred, traveled to Salt Lake City to attend the fall general conference. There they asked church leaders to reinforce their fledgling colony by sending as many new settlers as possible. This request was granted, and that same October a large group of newly arrived Danish converts was called to go to the Allred Settlement. James and Reuben helped organize and equip the party, and on 14 October 1853, 297 immigrants who had been in Utah only two weeks headed for Sanpete. On their way, they were shocked to see the site near

Uintah Springs (Fountain Green) where four men from Manti had just been killed by Indians.

Strengthened by the new Danish contingent, the settlement was repopulated in October 1853 by those who had fled to Manti. Together the hybrid group enlarged the fort, cut hay for the animals, and started a meetinghouse. With the fifty Danish families to bolster the community, the Allred Settlement came to be known as Little Denmark. It also was called Canal Creek and Spring Town. Despite the colony's size, however, it was still no match against another major Indian attack. Forewarned of such an impending raid, Captain James T. S. Allred of the militia was ordered to vacate the town and again move the people to Manti. The order came in mid-December, and the unhappy residents endured the evacuation "in the midst of (a) heavy snow storm and a fierce and intense cold weather." With the settlers gone, the Indians came on 6 January 1854 and burned the fort and any remaining belongings. Thus reduced to ashes, Little Denmark would not be settled again for more than half a decade.

The resettlement of Little Denmark in mid-July 1859 was initiated by William Y. Black, an Irish convert, who received Brigham Young's written permission to make the move there from Fort Ephraim. Black was joined by his wife, Jane, two sons George and Joseph S. and their wives, along with Joseph T. Ellis and his wife. A new townsite of 640 acres was laid out by county surveyor Albert Petty in orderly Mormon fashion, and a new town was born. Soon after the arrival of the first settlers, John Lemmond and William Major arrived, and subsequently Reddick N. Allred, William Hudson, John Neild, Barnery Stevens, Henry Stevens, Isaac Morley Allred, Joseph Allred, Sidney R. Allred, and others joined them. Black wrote President Young in August 1859 that he expected thirty more families to arrive in the fall. He underestimated the response to his persuasive promptings, however. Reddick N. Allred and Joseph T. Ellis reportedly built the first homes in the village. The 1860 census recorded 220 persons living in what by then was being called Spring Town. As before, in the 1860s the pioneers attended to the basics of clearing land, planting, irrigating, raising stock, building homes, and growing families. Spring Towners enjoyed only a few years of relative peace before bracing themselves again for encounters with increasingly angry Indians.

The Black Hawk War had broken out in April 1865 in part due a conflict in Manti. By the time hostilities reached Spring Town, the residents had built a rock fort and were better prepared than previously. This afforded the settlement better protection than it had in the mid-1850s, but again, seeing evidence of a future attack, Brigham Young advised retreating rather than fighting. The third evacuation, the "Big Move," occurred in May 1866 as the town's colonists packed off to Ephraim because there weren't enough men in Spring Town to fight off the Indians. They would go back every couple of weeks to take care of things there. While there, we would sleep on the floor of the old meetinghouse. This time the residents did not stay away long. They returned on Pioneer Day 24 July 1866, and thereafter stayed in town under constant guard until the end of the war. Women and young people helped stand guard and prepare food for the militia. One of these women, Sarah S. Justesen, made crackers of flour, water, and lard—pounding them before rolling and baking. The crackers were vital supplies for the militia while away from home.

On 13 August 1867 a band of Indian warriors swept into the valley stampeding the animals being herded in the hayfields below the stone quarry. Men herding cows and hauling hay included Sanford Allred, Samuel Allred, Reuben Allred, Nephi Jack, Niels Benson, and Charles Kofford. James Meek and Martin Andrew Johansen were killed by Indians in the hayfields by the stone quarry. Both men were buried in the pioneer cemetery. Others in the group survived and escaped, but some were wounded in the encounter. The last casualty of the war—really a series of skirmishes and raids—was Daniel Morgan Miller from Nephi. He was killed near Spring Town on 26 September 1872 while he and his son Dan were hauling lumber from the Snow Sawmill at the mouth of Oak Creek Canyon, east of Spring City. Miller and his son Dan loaded their wagon on the night of 25 September and spent the night in the sleeping quarters near the sawmill. The Millers rose early on the 26th, hitching their mules to their wagon to begin their journey down the canyon, and on to Nephi. Not far down the canyon Miller stopped his wagon to adjust something. The Indians attacked. Miller was hit through one arm and

Main Street in Spring City with the 1893 city hall. (Utah State Historical Society)

in the side under the arm, while another bullet passed through his bowels, breaking his back. His son Dan was shot through one thigh and through one wrist. Dan was able to run down the road toward Spring City where he met some men looking for stock. Miller passed away shortly after his rescuers loaded him into the wagon. His twelve-year-old son was taken to the home of Reddick Allred, where he was cared for until he was able to return to Nephi. Just a week earlier, what was hoped to be the final peace treaty had been signed in Mount Pleasant. By this time, the militia's forces had tightened their grip and there were no more deaths on either side. Each group could now move on to the futures destiny had in store for them. For the residents of Spring Town, newly called Spring City, there would be the growth and maturity of a Mormon village.

Following the resolution of Indian troubles in 1867, Spring City grew gradually but steadily, reaching a population of 850 in 1880 and a peak of about 1,230 in 1900.

Like other Sanpete Valley communities, Spring City has always depended primarily on agriculture and animal raising for its economic base. After the seven-by-ten-block townsite had been laid out, land was distributed, cooperative irrigation ditches were dug, a common stock herd was created, and farming commenced in earnest. The town's earliest commercial enterprise was a cooperative store, initially operating out of a home. The store owner purchased grain and produce and sold merchandise and farm equipment. Many residents engaged in stock raising, wool growing, and lumbering. Upon the arrival of the Rio Grande Western Railroad in the early 1890s, Spring City's economic fortunes prospered. It exported local products, including native oolite stone, which was shipped to larger northern cities for use in the construction of fine buildings.

Predominantly a Mormon community throughout its existence, Spring City also has been home to Presbyterians, Methodists, and other denomination at various times. As the town grew, its residents built meetinghouses, schools, an amusement hall, an opera house, a small group of business buildings along Main Street, and more than 200 residences in both Scandinavian and several American architectural styles.

If, as many claim, Sanpete County possesses Utah's greatest treasury of architecturally significant buildings from the pioneer and early twentieth-century eras, then Spring City is its crown jewel. The town's wealth of impressive structures is due to its talented early designers and builders, as well as to the fact that the population decreased every decade from 1900 to 1970, reducing the need to destroy older structures. Spring City's remarkable LDS meetinghouse, or tabernacle, and city hall—both limestone edifices—and its spectacular Victorian elementary school and bishop's storehouse—both of brick—are among its most important public buildings. The unique Greek Revival John Frank Allred School, Baxter/Schofield Store, Orson Hyde house, Behunin, Monson, Johnson, and Ericksen residences—all of masonry construction—also are outstanding, but probably the most impressive is the Jens Peter Carlson House built in 1896. The one-and-a-half story Victorian house is noteworthy for its finely polished stone masonry. No other residence in Sanpete County exhibits the high level of masonry which Carlson, himself the mason, lavished on this house. He dressed the rocks on his house with a chisel and then rubbed them smooth to give them an almost marble-like character. In addition, Spring City possess a good collection of early log, adobe, and frame structures, including several "urban" barns and other agricultural and livestock outbuildings—many of which sit within a few hundred feet of Main Street.

Spring City's twentieth-century history has followed the socio-economic patterns established earlier; its relatively pristine visual environment has resulted in the town being listed as an historic district on the National Register of Historic Places. In the nineteenth century, the key road through the county, now U.S. Highway 89, bypassed Spring City a mile west of town. This economic disadvantage has been partly compensated for by the lack of newer structures replacing historic sites. As a result, since the mid-1970s, many architectural gems have been restored, both by local residents and by interested newcomers. Some of the vacant buildings have been converted to new commercial, cultural, or residential uses, in part accounting for the city's population growth each decade since 1970. Some 715 persons lived in town in 1990. Accommodating economic and social growth while retaining its historical character will be a continuing challenge for Spring City as it approaches the twenty- first century.

Sterling

Located six miles southwest of Manti along Highway 89, the area of Sterling was first settled in 1873 when George Petty and fifteen families from Manti settled on a site just west of the present community. The first settlement was known as Pettyville. The land originally settled was actually part of the Indian reservation that also included Gunnison and Mayfield. In 1881 James C. Snow secured rights to the present location of Sterling, which he surveyed and laid out.

A few families had already begun to homestead the area by 1877. After Snow had the town surveyed into its present four-block townsite, settlers came in greater numbers. A one-room adobe meeting-house and school was soon built. One of the earliest houses was erected by George Petty, founder of now-abandoned Pettyville. He was also chosen as the first bishop, with the new town's founder, J. C. Snow, as Sunday school superintendent, ward clerk, and the first post master.

Sterling's name was selected from a contest won by Gus Clark, a teacher, who was paid the $5.00 raised for the idea. The hamlet sits on a high bank along Six Mile Creek with its source in a canyon of the same name. To the south is Nine Mile Reservoir, Palisade Lake, a popular recreation center, lies upstream to the northeast. With water in abundance and fertile valley land, Sterling has enjoyed agricultural success. The early crops were wheat, oats, potatoes, corn, and alfalfa hay. In time fruit and sugar beet growing proved successful. The latter were replaced with peas after the Rocky Mountain Canning Company was established in Manti. Poultry and cattle were raised, the latter grazing on the mountain ranges to the east. To control the water that irrigated the land south of Six Mile Creek, the Sterling Irrigation Company was organized in 1888. The next year the North Six Mile Creek Irrigation Company was formed.

The discovery of coal near Sterling by men from Wales (Sanpete County) in 1887 invigorated Sterling's economy by providing employment for local men. The Sterling Coke and Coal Company was founded in 1894 by men of the Sanpete Valley Railroad. They arranged for the railroad from Nephi into the county to be extended to Morrison, the camp town near the Edmunds mine (see Morrison above). With the coming of the D&RG line to Sterling in 1891 came regular mail delivery, the ability to import and export, and daily contact with the outside world.

School was first held in a one-room adobe structure. Built by Walter Morminster and adobe-makers Warren and Joseph H. Snow, it was a multi-purpose building. A recreational structure known as the Old Bowery was erected about 1890. Another one-room school was built above the first one at about the same time. The old school was given to the Relief Society, while the new edifice was also used for town meetings, elections, and showing silent movies. The most substantial schoolhouse was the one erected in 1898–99 of brick and stone in eclectic Victorian styling. Like its predecessors, it was used for most school, social, and civic purposes. Beginning in 1919, Sterling's students were transported to Manti where educational facilities and programs were of a higher quality. In 1924 a stone and brick church meetinghouse was built in the same style under the leadership of Bishop Olsen, who died before the building's completion. It lasted until the 1984 when it was replaced by the present modern brick church.

Early businesses were a sawmill up the canyon and John Edmonston's blacksmith shop. George Petty was the first bishop, while the first Relief Society president was Jane Snow. Sterling's first store was operated out of a house by Bunts and Dixon. It was followed by a store on the state road where Erickson's Grocery was built later. It was a co-operative run by Walter K. Barton. In 1945 Evan T. Thomas built a new store known as the Evans Grocery. The diminutive but colorful place still operates, now as the Thomas Grocery, one of only two stores in town. In the mid-twentieth century, a major employer was the Azom Mining Company. Its twenty employees in the 1940s made cement block and mineralizer. Hode Harman, Jefferson Bradley, and Will Musig ran sawmills upstream in the early decades, while Bishop Oscar Peterson, August Otten, and Lafe Ludvigson ran one in the 1940s. In town clothing was manufactured on local looms and spinning wheels.

As Sterling grew, civic improvements were made. After an electric plant was built in 1910, the town's homes and few businesses was furnished with electric lights. Street lights were introduced in 1945. Unable to provide power for Sterling, Mayfield, and Gunnison Valley, the plant was merged with the Telluride Power Company of Beaver in 1914. The village was first incorporated in 1935 with W. H. Baily, the town president, elected the first mayor. The same year a municipal water system was commenced and completed the next year. It depended on the springs improved by the Larsen family in 1898.

Despite its advantages of water, power, and favorable location, the town is limited in size due to its geography, and it has remained small and overshadowed by Manti. During its existence, Sterling's population has fluctuated between 150 and 350. In 1990 it was 191, down slightly from 199 in 1980.

Wales

Wales is located four miles west of Chester and about five miles southwest of Moroni at the foot of the Sanpitch or West Mountains. Wales was started in 1854 by Mormon converts from Wales, Great

The Wales schoolhouse in 1912. (Courtesy of Jane Thomas)

Britain, some of whom had already been living in the county. In that year the Indian Tabiona, one of the four brothers of Chief Walker and claimant to the valley and canyons in the Wales area, showed Brigham Young a black rock which burned. It was coal to whites, a solid form of "black gold," a highly useful resource for industrial development. Young asked Welshmen John Rees of Ephraim and John Price of Manti to locate the coal and determine its potential for mining. They did, and Tabiona "sold" his coal-rich canyon for "a few head of cattle and some sheep." Soon after the Rees and Price started to surface mine. When not mining, they built dugouts west of the present site of Wales and brought their daughters, Betsy Rees and Ann Price, to cook for them. Soon the families joined them, constructed more dugouts, and called the place "Coalbed."

In the first settlement group were Richard Price, Thomas Campbell, Daniel Lewis, George Muir, Richard Babbitt, Daniel Washburn David Hutcheson, and Moses Gifford. Their dugouts were built near a stream half a mile east of the first two dugouts. The group was strengthened in 1856 and 1859 by large parties of Welsh immigrants. The Coalbedders of the 1860s devised an alternative way of surviving the Indian difficulties which tormented them. Instead of spending their valuable time (they were, after all, primarily miners), materials, and money building a large fort (as had been done at great cost in Manti and Ephraim), they erected a small adobe fort which contained only enough room for a meetinghouse and places to sleep at night. During the day they lived in their houses outside of the fort. Here again their town building was unorthodox by Mormon standards. They erected more than a dozen log houses in a single row rather than on lots in blocks. Across the road from each house was a corral for the animals belonging to each family. This pattern of houses and corrals closely spaced along a road was no doubt the way they had built mining towns in their homeland of Wales.

This anomalous Welsh-Mormon town was not to last, however. With the houses and animals outside the little fort, they were vulnerable to Indian raids. In 1866 the people of Coalbed felt compelled to dismantle their cabins and move the entire community to the fort in Moroni for protection. There they stayed until 1868 when they returned to their abandoned townsite. In rebuilding Coalbed the second time, they followed traditional Mormon town planning precepts, copying what had seen in Moroni. The community was renamed Wales in 1869 when it received a post office. In 1873, after a patent was granted to the Wales Township, a townsite of twenty-six blocks (five north-south and four east-west) was laid out. As in Moroni, each block had five acres and four lots. Family leaders drew for lots, each receiving an irrigated lot and a dry lot. With town growth now proceeding with typical Mormon orderliness, the colonists were no longer satisfied with log cabin homes. Peter Christensen built a brick kiln south of town, resulting in the many fine red brick dwellings in Wales. Peter C. "Miller" Anderson built a grist mill and a boarding house and hotel for newcomers.

As Utah Territory's need for coal increased, mining activity intensified in Wales. The original miners sold the mines to a mining company which constructed twelve coke ovens, crushing, and washing machines. Thanks to funding raised in England by Simon Bamberger, a new mining company was capitalized about 1875. It arranged for the first railroad to be brought into the county from Nephi to the old mines, as well as a new mine in Pete's Canyon. At one time, 200 men were employed in the mines, and Wales reached its all-time, though short-lived population peak of more than 600.

Eventually the mines proved unprofitable, however, as better quality coal was found and purchased in other locations. Finally the mines were closed and the families of the original settlers were left to farm. Two irrigation companies were formed in 1889 and many improvements were made, including the digging of a reservoir in 1898. After reaching a population of more than 400 in 1900 and 1910, the hamlet slowly declined in size each decade thereafter until a modest growth spurt corresponding to a countywide resurgence started in the 1970s.

Like Sanpete's other Mormon town, the LDS church and its various organizations were developed as the population increased. In 1868 Wales created a branch of the church. A ward was formed in Wales in conjunction with the creation of the county's first stake. John E. Rees was the first bishop. Since the 1860s, a Sunday school and Relief Society had been active, with "Mutuals" coming in the mid-1870s. A new brick chapel was erected at a cost of $20,000 in 1946. It replaced a brick church built in 1892. A 28-by-70-foot Primary building was added to the church grounds in 1982, at which time the ward had 230 members. School was held first in the Common House and then in the town hall and homes. Soon a lumber schoolhouse was constructed, and in 1908 a fine, three-room schoolhouse was built of brick. It was used until 1956 when students where transported to Moroni. In about 1891, townspeople combined their funds and invested in a combined town and social hall, enlarged in 1904. An open-air dance hall was erected in 1939 thanks partially to the federal Works Progress Administration. The people of Wales were noticeably happy to have their road oiled for the first time in 1950.

Due to its size and location, Wales has never been a commercial center. Still, it has maintained a few stores, the best remembered being the co-op started in 1871. It operated until 1968. The present vacant store, a one-story brick structure, dates from about 1894 when the Wales Co-op was enlarged and incorporated. The leaders of the cooperative established a creamery in 1900 which operated for many years before closing. More than fifty years after its initial settlement,

Wales was incorporated as a town in 1908. A water system was installed in 1912, and electricity arrived in 1918 from the Big Springs Power Company in Fountain Green. To celebrate their heritage, Wales has sponsored Welsh Days occasionally since about 1983. A town history was written and sold to raise funds for the inaugural event. The population in 1990 was 189. For the last several decades, ranching has been the economic mainstay in Wales. Hereford cattle have been popular, and earlier sheep were important. Others are employed at the turkey plant in Moroni. The town is also proud of the number of professionals it has produced.

Other Places

As one travels Sanpete's backroads, one occasionally notices little clusters of vacant cabins, houses, and outbuildings, usually near a stand of ancient trees. Some of these places, now nameless and unnoted by the historian's pen, were remote family complexes and others were started as would-be villages that never developed their intended potential. A few places, like Pigeon Hollow, on the unpaved road halfway between Spring City and Ephraim, and Shumway Springs, a picnic and lovers spot three miles southwest of Ephraim, have retained a name and a few buildings. The names of Spearmint, Hardscrabble or Crowleyville, and Buckinburg are known only to locals, while the other places await further research and rediscovery—a mission for a future book.

Selected Bibliography

Alexander, Thomas G. *Utah: The Right Place, The Official Centennial History*. Salt Lake City: Gibbs Smith Publisher, 1995.

Antrei, Albert C.T., editor. *The Other Forty-Niners: A Topical History of Sanpete County, Utah, 1849–1983*. Salt Lake City: Western Epics, 1982.

Antrei, Albert C.T. *View from the Red Point*. Manti: Manti Messenger Printing and Publishing Co., 1976.

Arrington, Leonard J. *Great Basin Kingdom: Economic History of the Latter-day Saints of Utah, 1847–69*. Boston: Harvard University Press. 1958.

Barron, Howard H. *Orson Hyde, Missionary, Apostle, Colonizer*. Bountiful: Horizon Publishers, 1977.

Campbell, Eugene. *Establishing Zion:The Mormon Church in the American West, 1847–1869*. Salt Lake City: Signature Books, 1988.

Centennial Committee of Manti, Utah. *Song of a Century*. Manti: Centennial Committee of Manti, 1949.

Daughters of Utah Pioneers, Sanpete County. *These Our Fathers, A Centennial History of Sanpete County, 1849–1947*. Springville: Art City Publishing Co., 1947.

Godfredson, Peter. *Indian Depredations in Utah*, 2nd ed. Salt Lake City: Merlin G. Christensen, 1969.

Lever, W. H. *History of Sanpete and Emery Counties.* Ogden, Utah: Published by the author, 1898.

Manti Temple Centennial Committee. *The Manti Temple.* Manti: Manti Temple Centennial Committee, 1988.

Merkel, Henry M. *History of Methodism in Utah.* Colorado Springs: The Dentan Printing Co., 1938.

Mulder, William. *Homeward to Zion: The Mormon Migration from Scandinavia.* Minneapolis: University of Minnesota Press, 1957.

Nelson, G. Lowry. *The Mormon Village.* Salt Lake City: University of Utah Press, 1952.

Our Yesterdays: A History of Ephraim, Utah, 1854–1979. Ephraim: Ephraim City Corp., 1981.

Papanikolas, Helen Z. *The Peoples of Utah.* Salt Lake City: Utah State Historical Society, 1976.

Peterson, Gary B. and Lowell C. Bennion. *Sanpete Scenes, A Guide to Utah's Heart.* Eureka, Utah: Basin/Plateau Press, 1987.

Peterson, John Alton. *Utah's Black Hawk War.* Salt Lake City: University of Utah Press, 1998.

Rice, Cynthia. "A Geographic Appraisal of the Acculturation Process of Scandinavians in the Sanpete Valley, Utah, 1850–1900." M.A. Thesis, University of Utah, 1973.

Stokes, William Lee. *Geology of Utah.* Salt Lake City: Utah Museum of Natural History, 1986.

Warrum, Nobel. *Utah in the World War.* Salt Lake City: Utah State Council of Defense, 1924.

Index